Shojo Beat

Story & Art by
MITSUBA TAKANASHI

CONTENTS

Game 27
Soul Days
3

Game 28
The Rumored Couple
45

Game 29
Straight Toward You
87

Game 30
Turmoil
127

STORY THUS FAR

Nobara Sumiyoshi is a first-year student in high school who lives for her one passion, volleyball. She's the successor to Seiryu, the high-class ryotei restaurant her family runs, but she enrolls in Crimson Field High School expressly to play volleyball.

Nobara begins living and working in Crimson Dorm, the dorm for the boys' volleyball recruits. There she meets and falls in love with Yushin, only to be rejected by him. It is then that Coach Shima arrives and begins to whip the mentally unprepared girls' team into shape. The goal: the Spring Tournament!

Nobara's dedication stirs something in Yushin's heart, and the two promise each other to become a couple after they've both made it to the Spring Tournament. In the meantime, Nobara has to deal with harassment from her classmate, Kaz, and figure out how to be open in her friendship with boys'-team ace Haibuki, who also likes her. Yushin comes clean with Haibuki on the very day that their team's victory in the Newcomers' Tournament qualifies them for the next level of competition. Stunned, Haibuki runs out of Crimson Dorm and stops attending school. Can Nobara and Yushin achieve their dreams without him?!

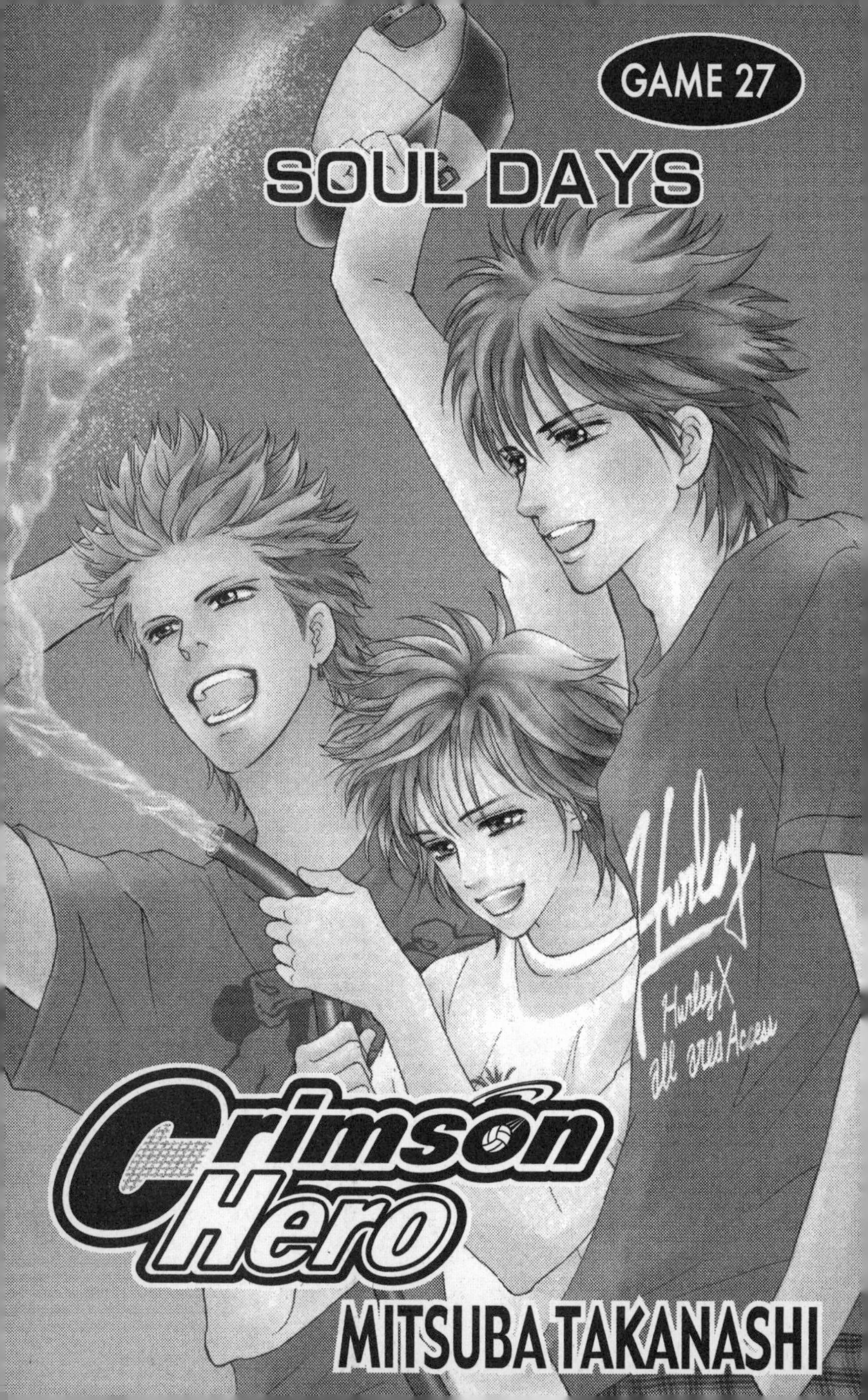
GAME 27
SOUL DAYS
Crimson Hero
MITSUBA TAKANASHI

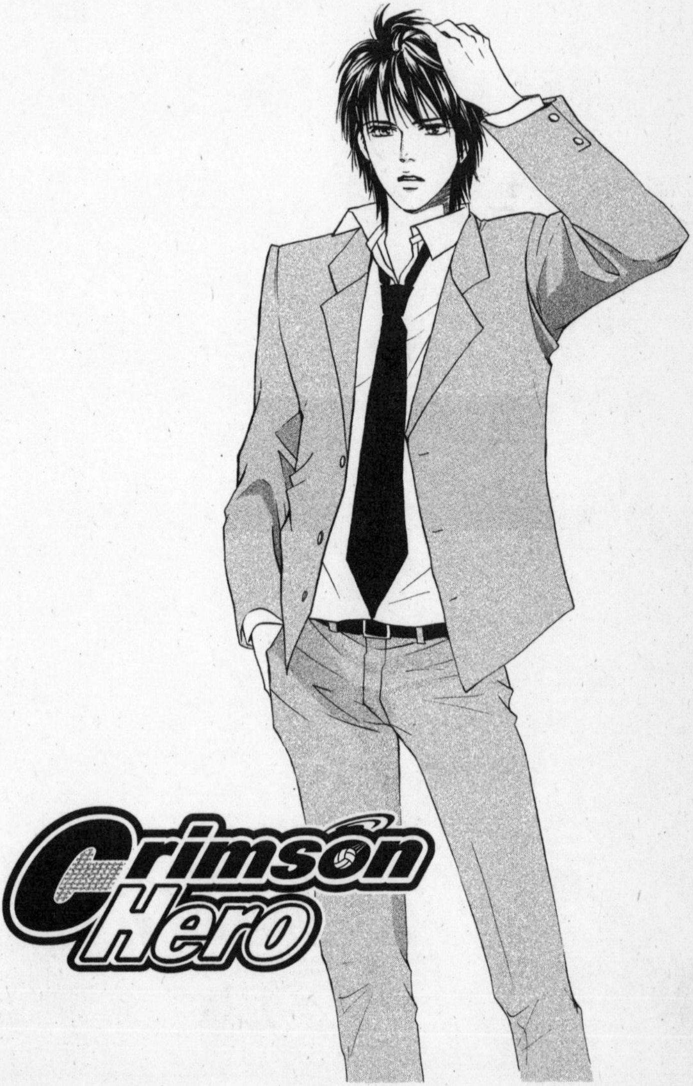
Crimson
Hero

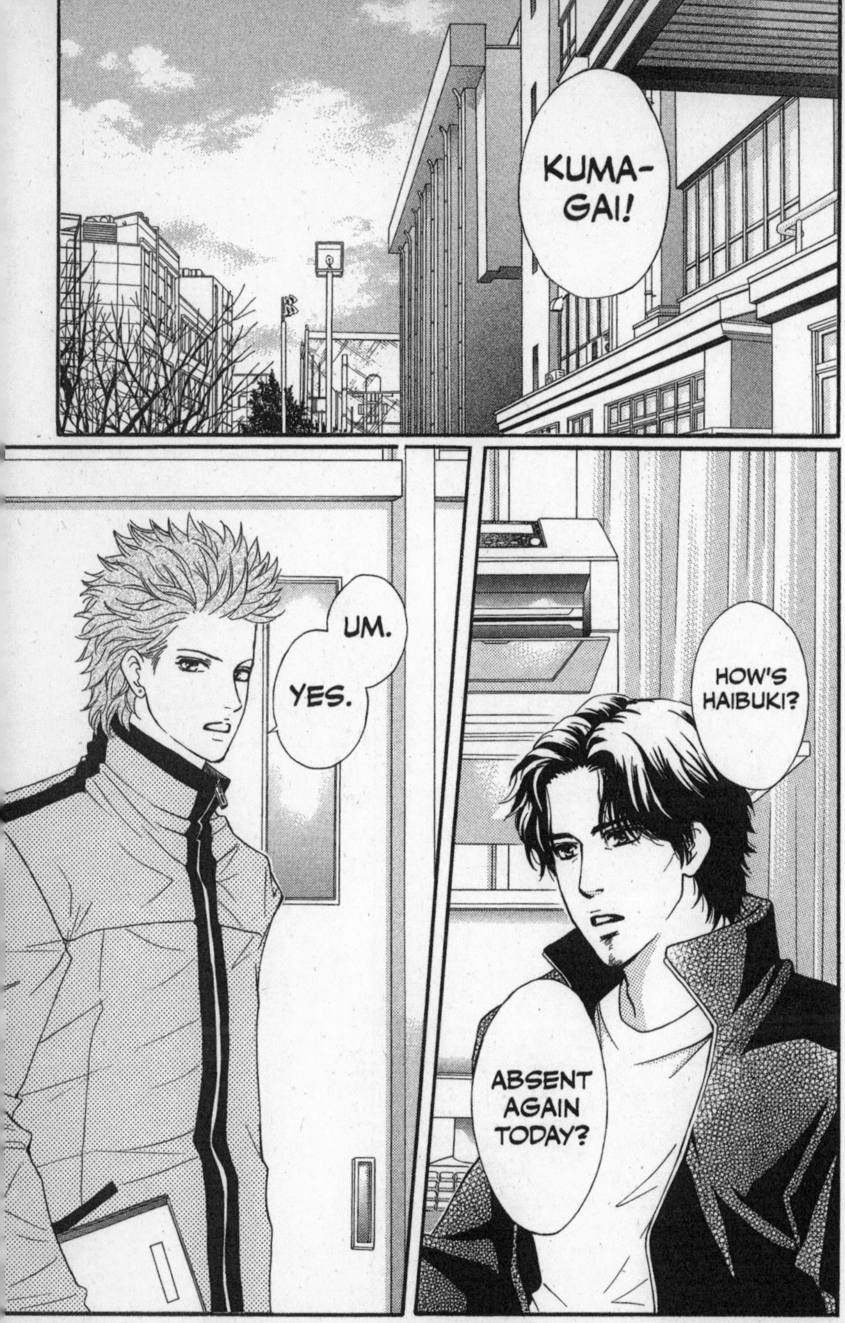
KUMA-GAI!
HOW'S HAIBUKI?
ABSENT AGAIN TODAY?
UM.
YES.

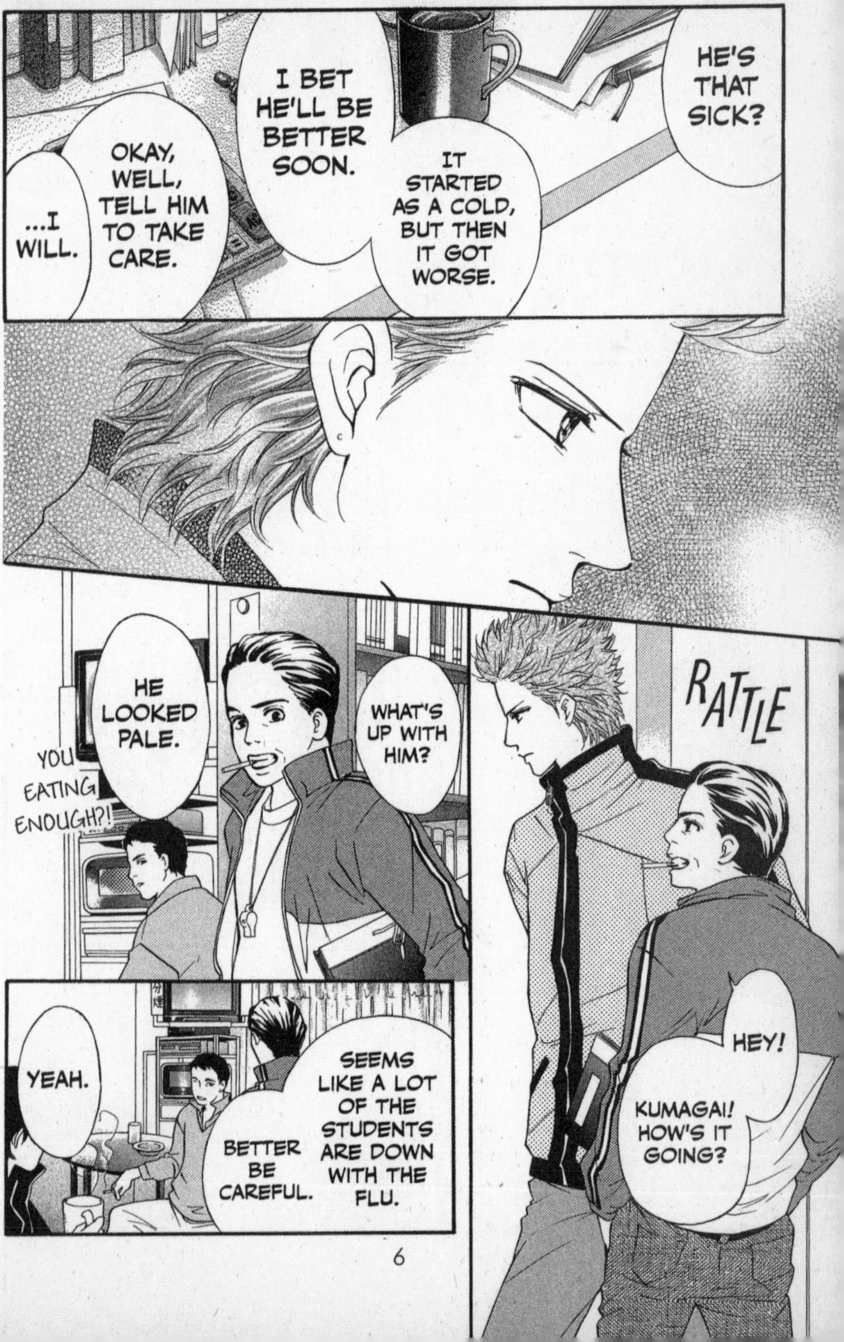
HE'S THAT SICK?
IT STARTED AS A COLD, BUT THEN IT GOT WORSE.
I BET HE'LL BE BETTER SOON.
OKAY, WELL, TELL HIM TO TAKE CARE.
...I WILL.
RATTLE
HEY!
KUMAGAI! HOW'S IT GOING?
WHAT'S UP WITH HIM?
HE LOOKED PALE.
YOU EATING ENOUGH?!
SEEMS LIKE A LOT OF THE STUDENTS ARE DOWN WITH THE FLU.
BETTER BE CAREFUL.
YEAH.

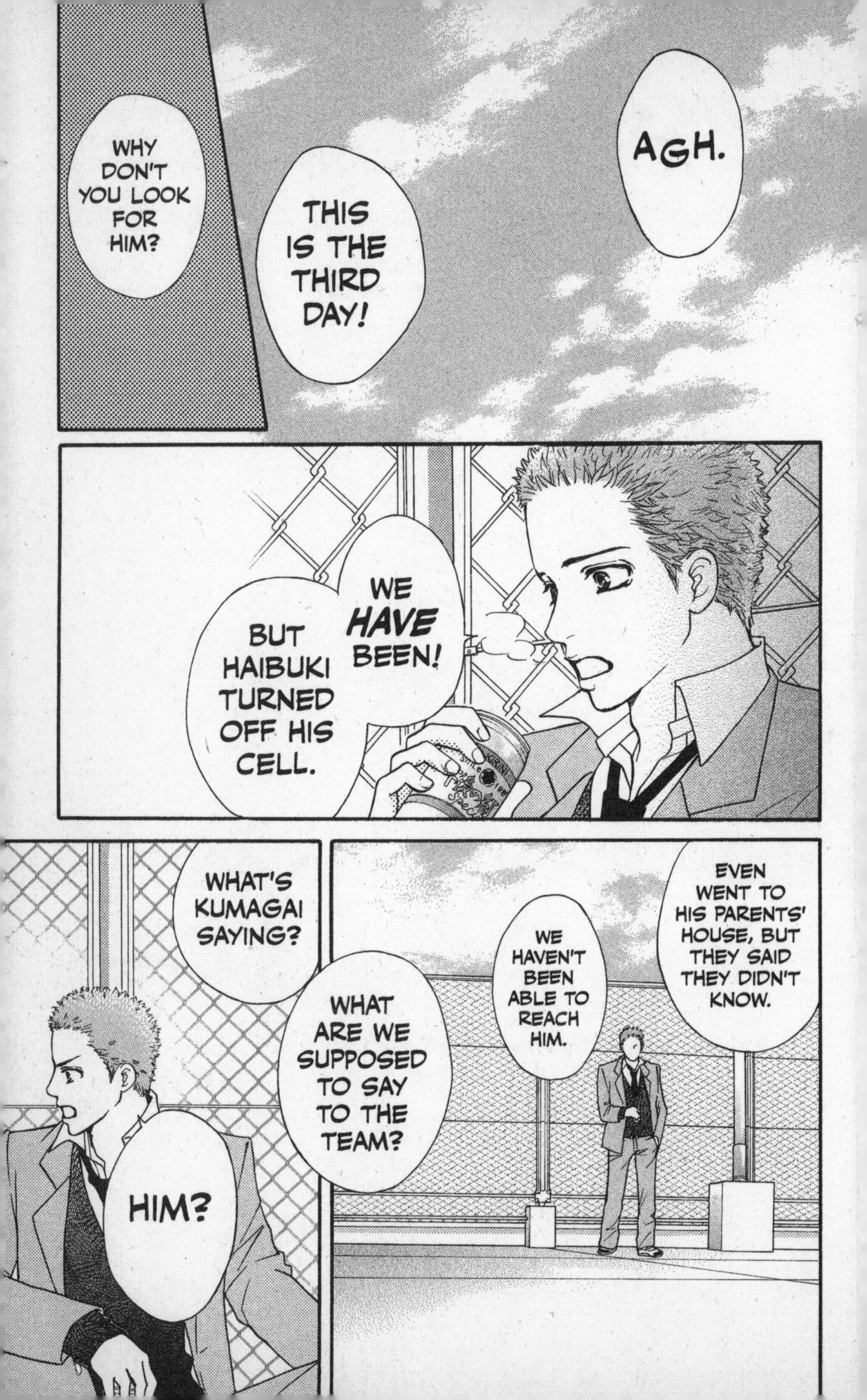
AGH.
THIS IS THE THIRD DAY!
WHY DON'T YOU LOOK FOR HIM?
WE *HAVE* BEEN!
BUT HAIBUKI TURNED OFF HIS CELL.
EVEN WENT TO HIS PARENTS' HOUSE, BUT THEY SAID THEY DIDN'T KNOW.
WE HAVEN'T BEEN ABLE TO REACH HIM.
WHAT'S KUMAGAI SAYING?
WHAT ARE WE SUPPOSED TO SAY TO THE TEAM?
HIM?

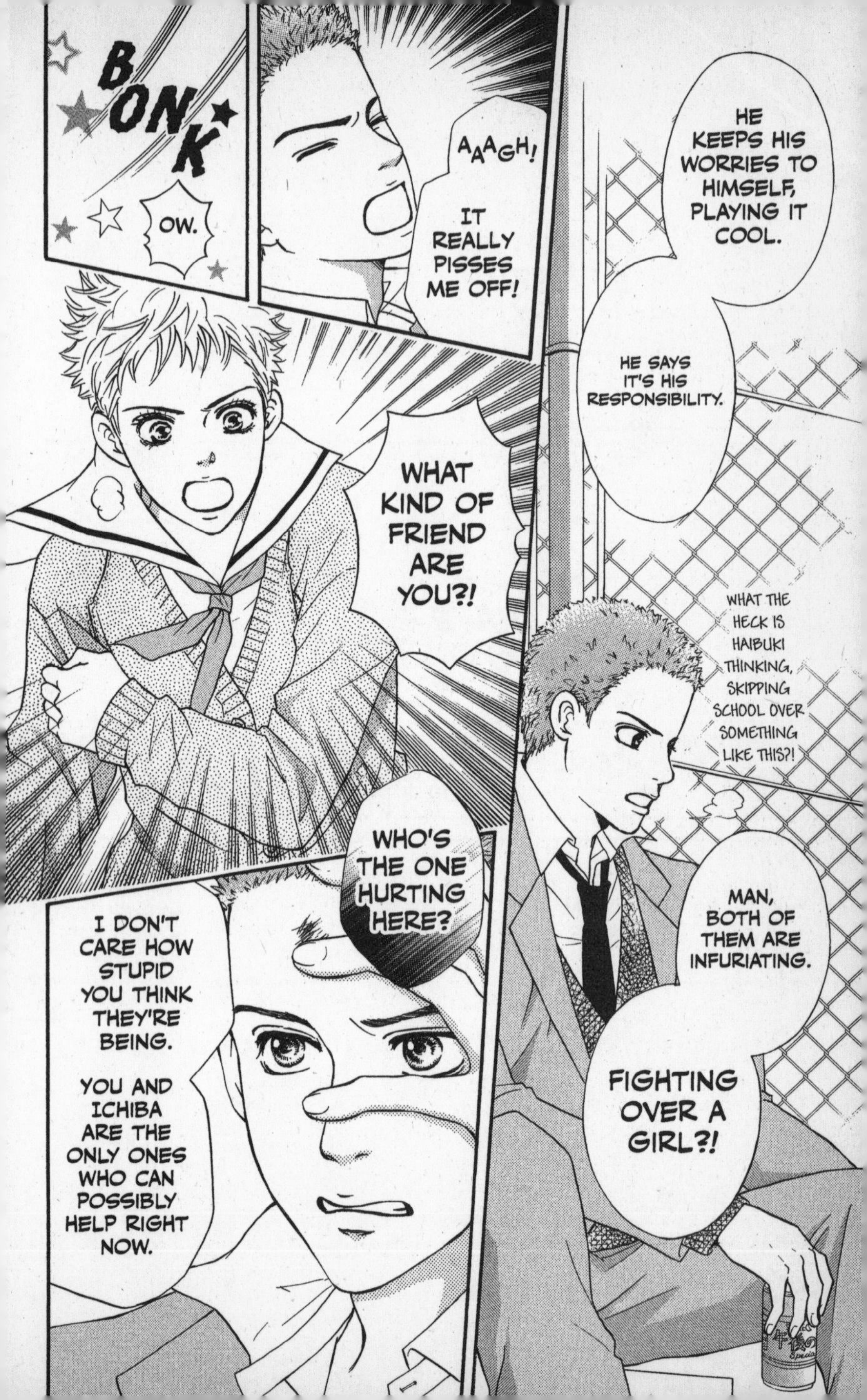
HE KEEPS HIS WORRIES TO HIMSELF, PLAYING IT COOL.
HE SAYS IT'S HIS RESPONSIBILITY.
WHAT THE HECK IS HAIBUKI THINKING, SKIPPING SCHOOL OVER SOMETHING LIKE THIS?!
MAN, BOTH OF THEM ARE INFURIATING.
FIGHTING OVER A GIRL?!
AAAGH!
IT REALLY PISSES ME OFF!
BONK
OW.
WHAT KIND OF FRIEND ARE YOU?!
WHO'S THE ONE HURTING HERE?
I DON'T CARE HOW STUPID YOU THINK THEY'RE BEING.
YOU AND ICHIBA ARE THE ONLY ONES WHO CAN POSSIBLY HELP RIGHT NOW.

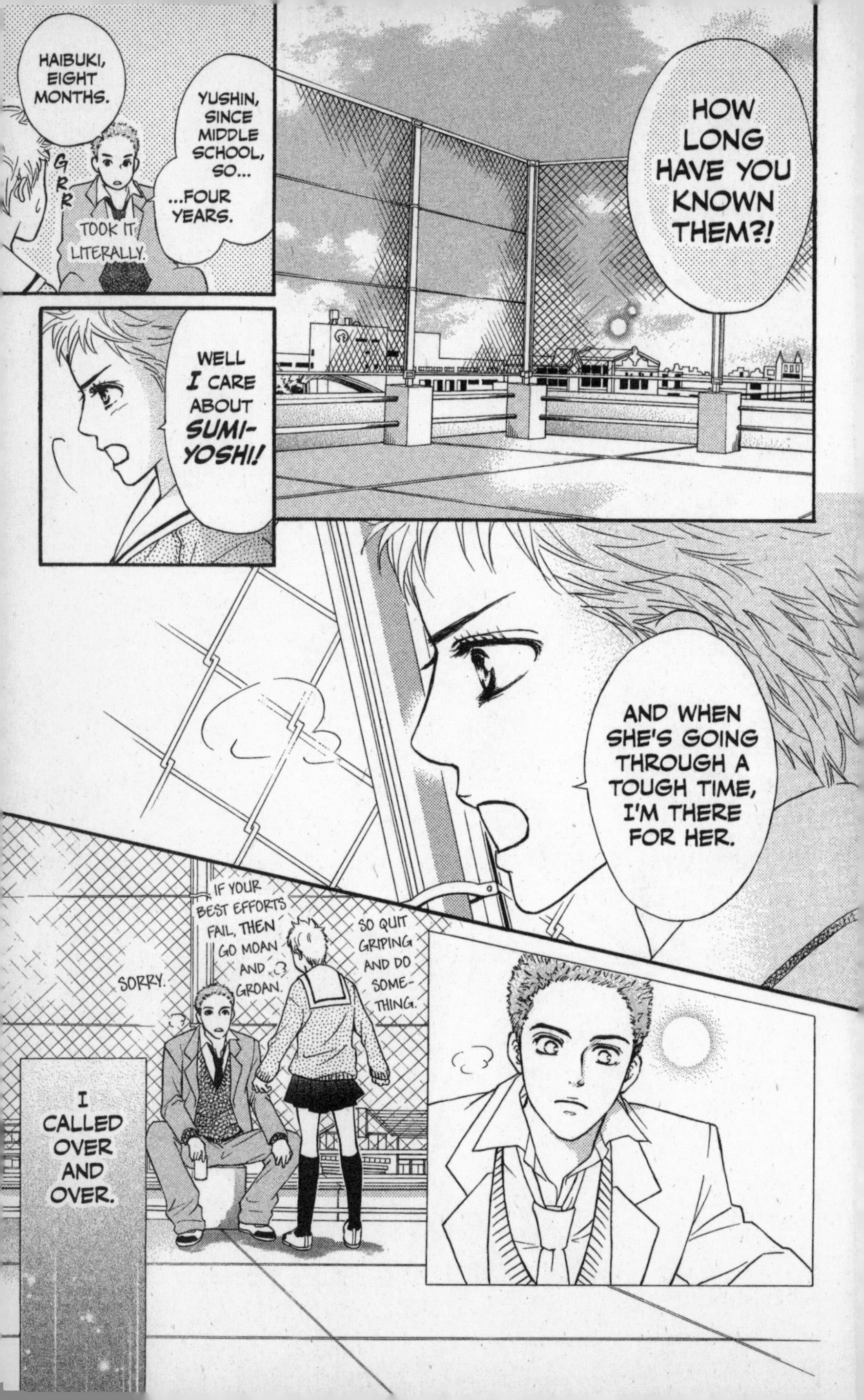
HOW LONG HAVE YOU KNOWN THEM?!
HAIBUKI, EIGHT MONTHS.
YUSHIN, SINCE MIDDLE SCHOOL, SO...
...FOUR YEARS.
GRR
TOOK IT LITERALLY.
WELL I CARE ABOUT SUMI-YOSHI!
AND WHEN SHE'S GOING THROUGH A TOUGH TIME, I'M THERE FOR HER.
SO QUIT GRIPING AND DO SOME-THING.
IF YOUR BEST EFFORTS FAIL, THEN GO MOAN AND GROAN.
SORRY.
I CALLED OVER AND OVER.

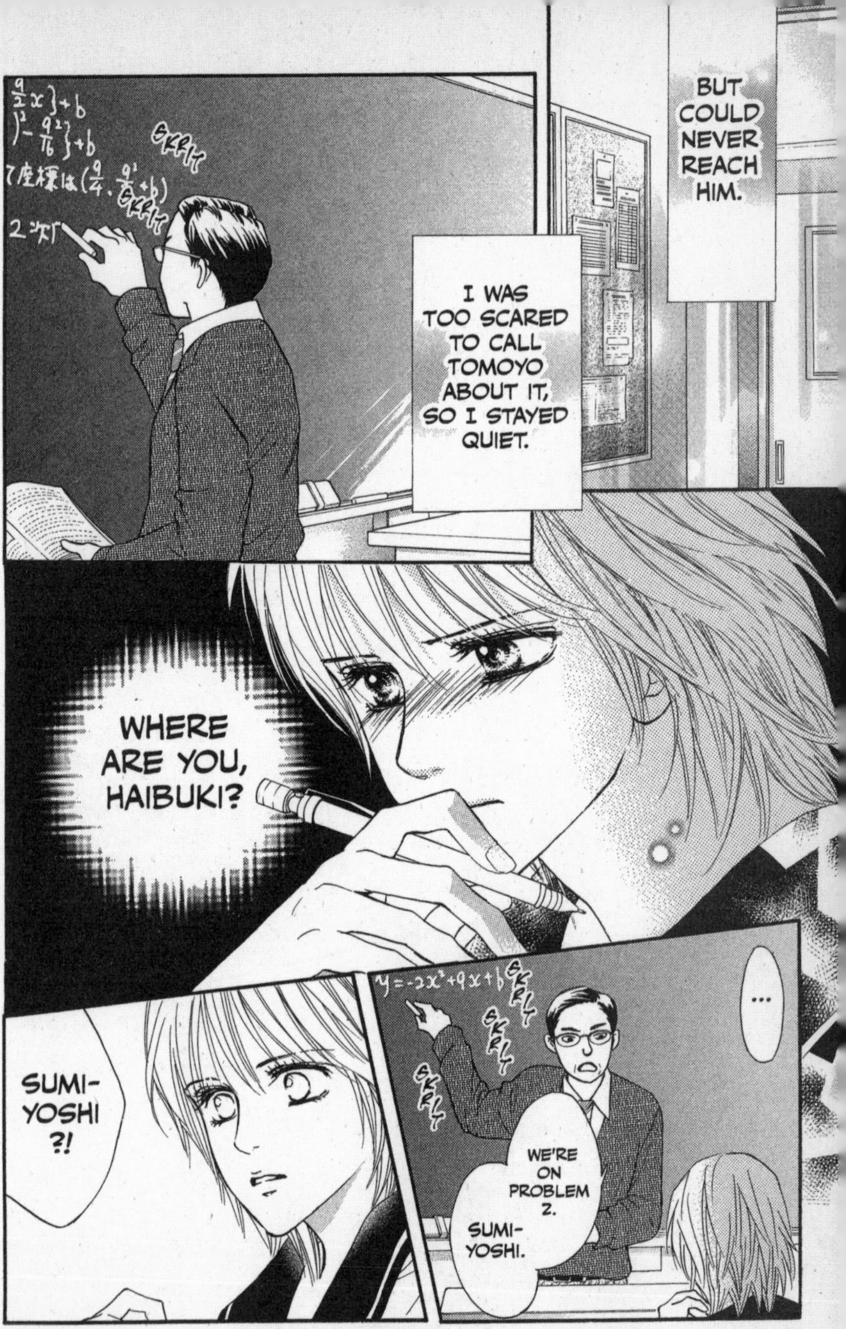
BUT COULD NEVER REACH HIM.
I WAS TOO SCARED TO CALL TOMOYO ABOUT IT, SO I STAYED QUIET.
WHERE ARE YOU, HAIBUKI?
...
WE'RE ON PROBLEM 2.
SUMI-YOSHI.
SUMI-YOSHI ?!

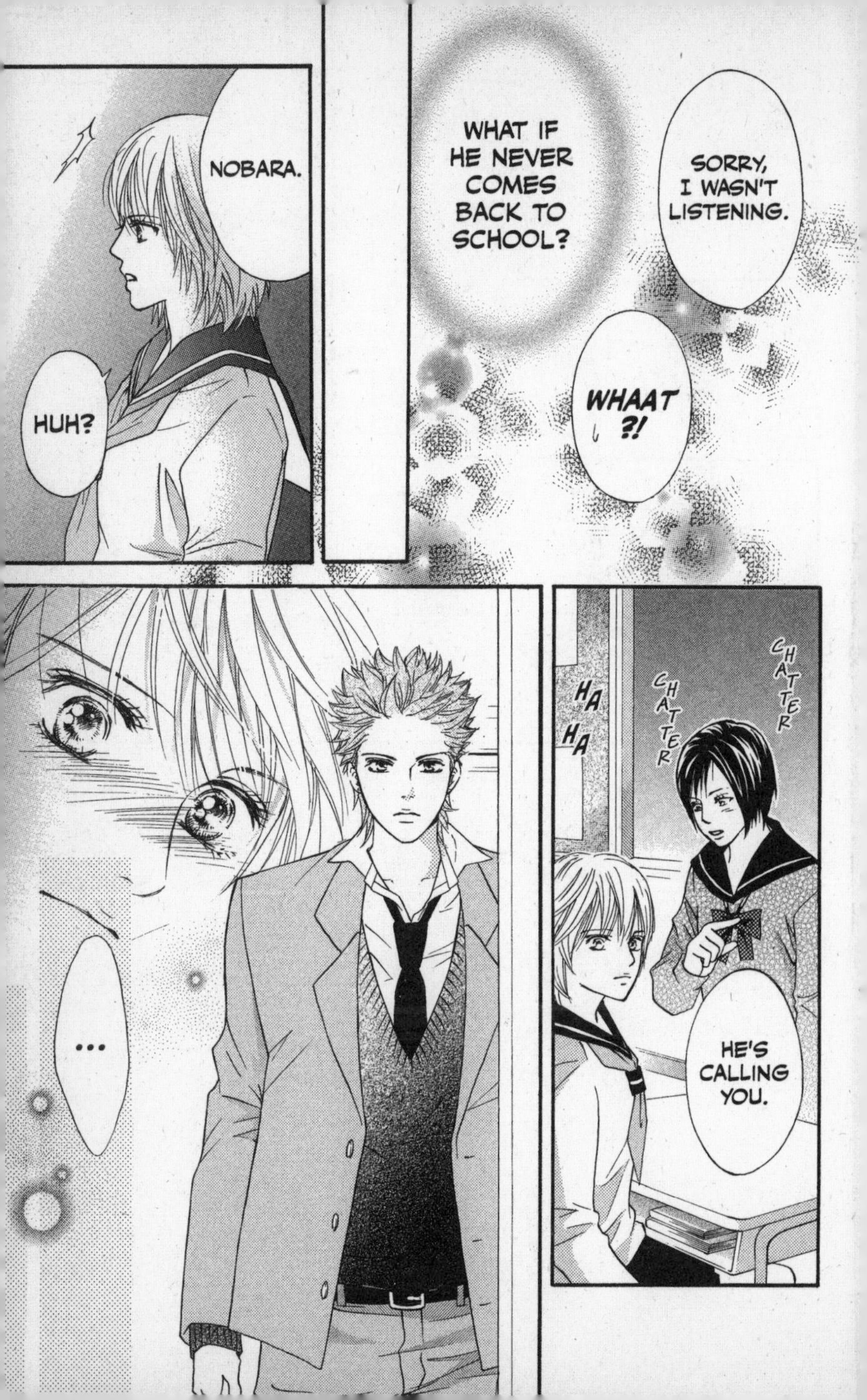
SORRY, I WASN'T LISTENING.
WHAT IF HE NEVER COMES BACK TO SCHOOL?
WHAAT ?!
NOBARA.
HUH?
CHATTER
CHATTER
HA HA
HE'S CALLING YOU.
...

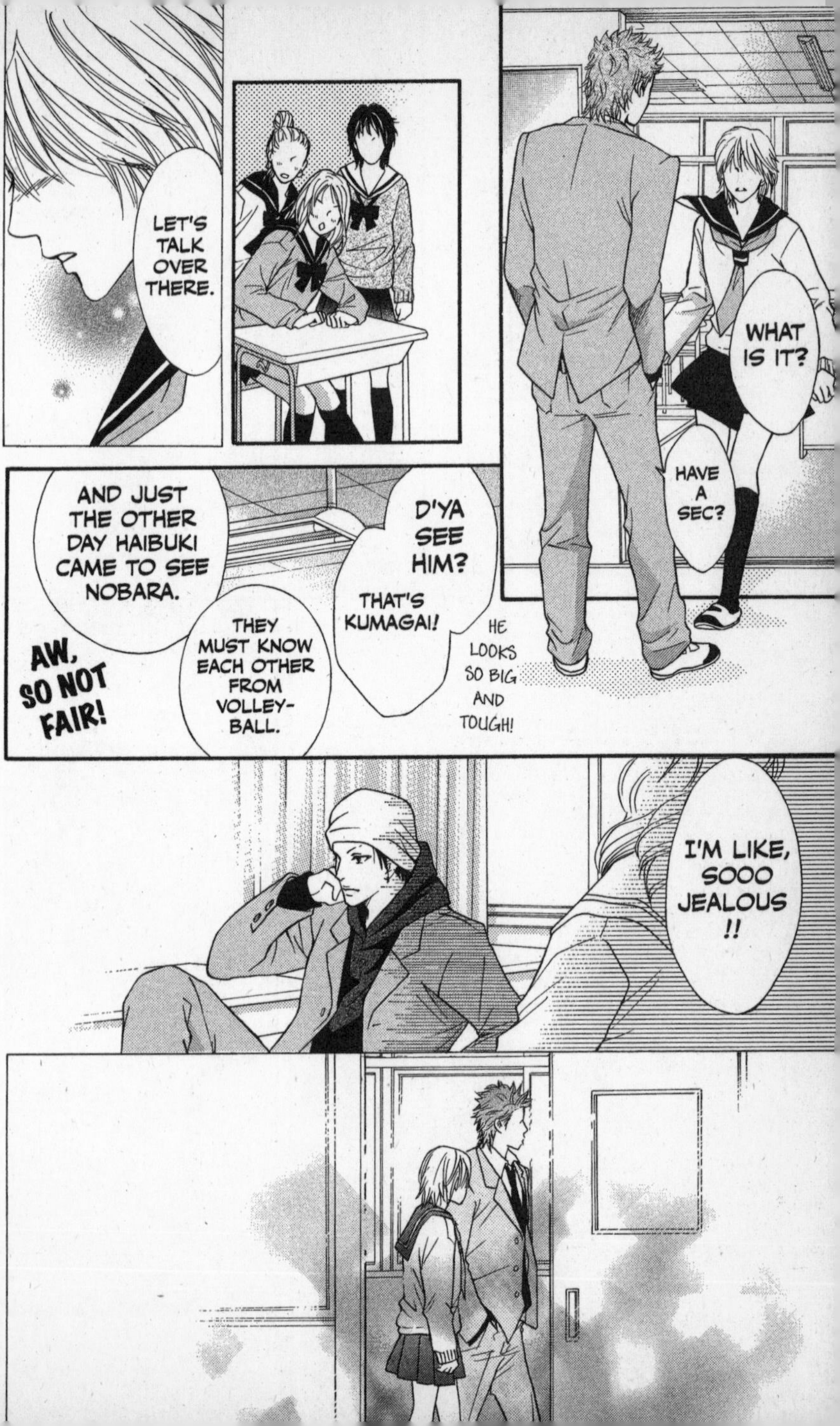
WHAT IS IT?
HAVE A SEC?
LET'S TALK OVER THERE.
D'YA SEE HIM?
THAT'S KUMAGAI!
HE LOOKS SO BIG AND TOUGH!
AND JUST THE OTHER DAY HAIBUKI CAME TO SEE NOBARA.
THEY MUST KNOW EACH OTHER FROM VOLLEY-BALL.
AW, SO NOT FAIR!
I'M LIKE, SOOO JEALOUS!!

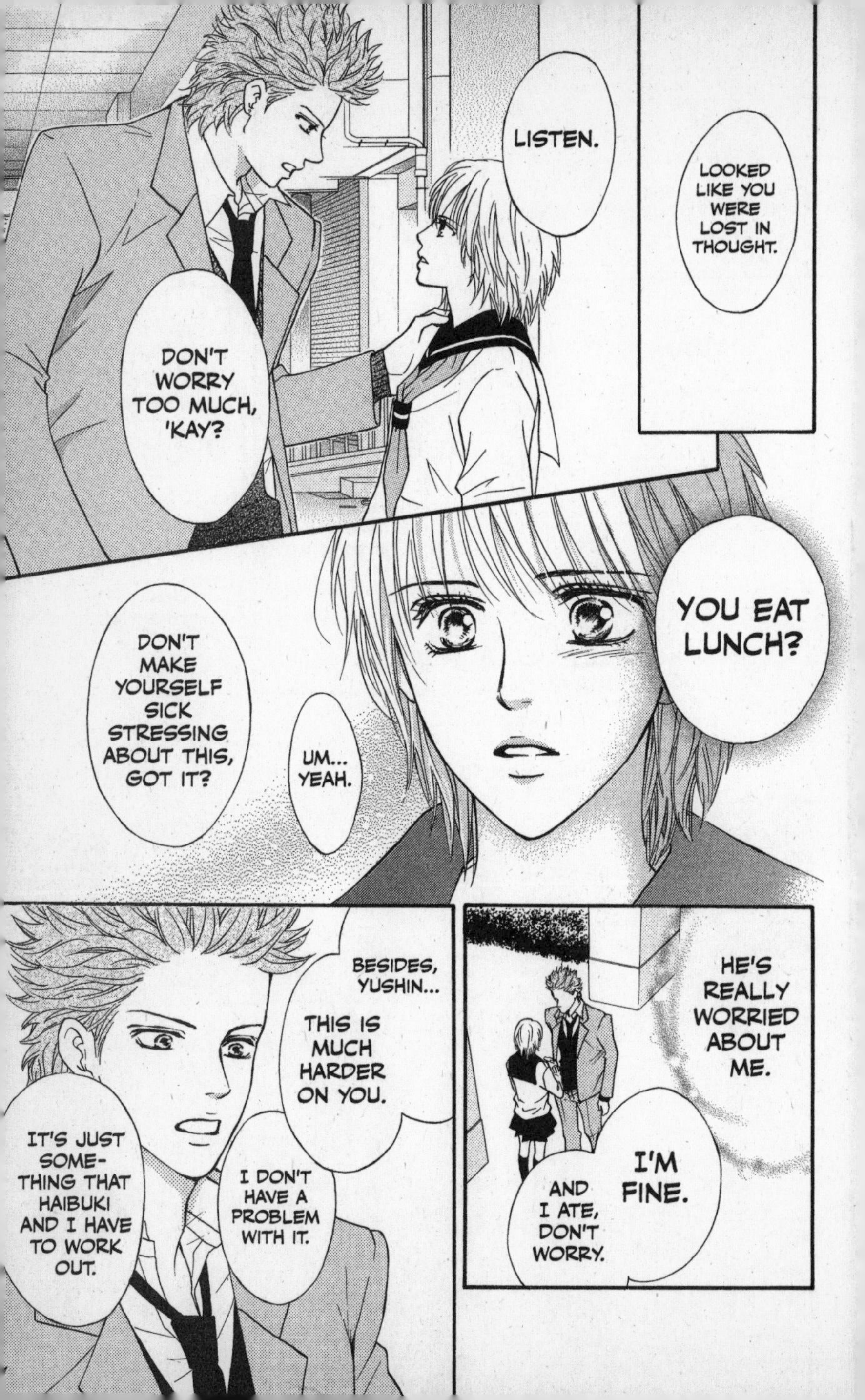
LOOKED LIKE YOU WERE LOST IN THOUGHT.
LISTEN.
DON'T WORRY TOO MUCH, 'KAY?
YOU EAT LUNCH?
UM... YEAH.
DON'T MAKE YOURSELF SICK STRESSING ABOUT THIS, GOT IT?
HE'S REALLY WORRIED ABOUT ME.
I'M FINE.
AND I ATE, DON'T WORRY.
BESIDES, YUSHIN...
THIS IS MUCH HARDER ON YOU.
I DON'T HAVE A PROBLEM WITH IT.
IT'S JUST SOME-THING THAT HAIBUKI AND I HAVE TO WORK OUT.

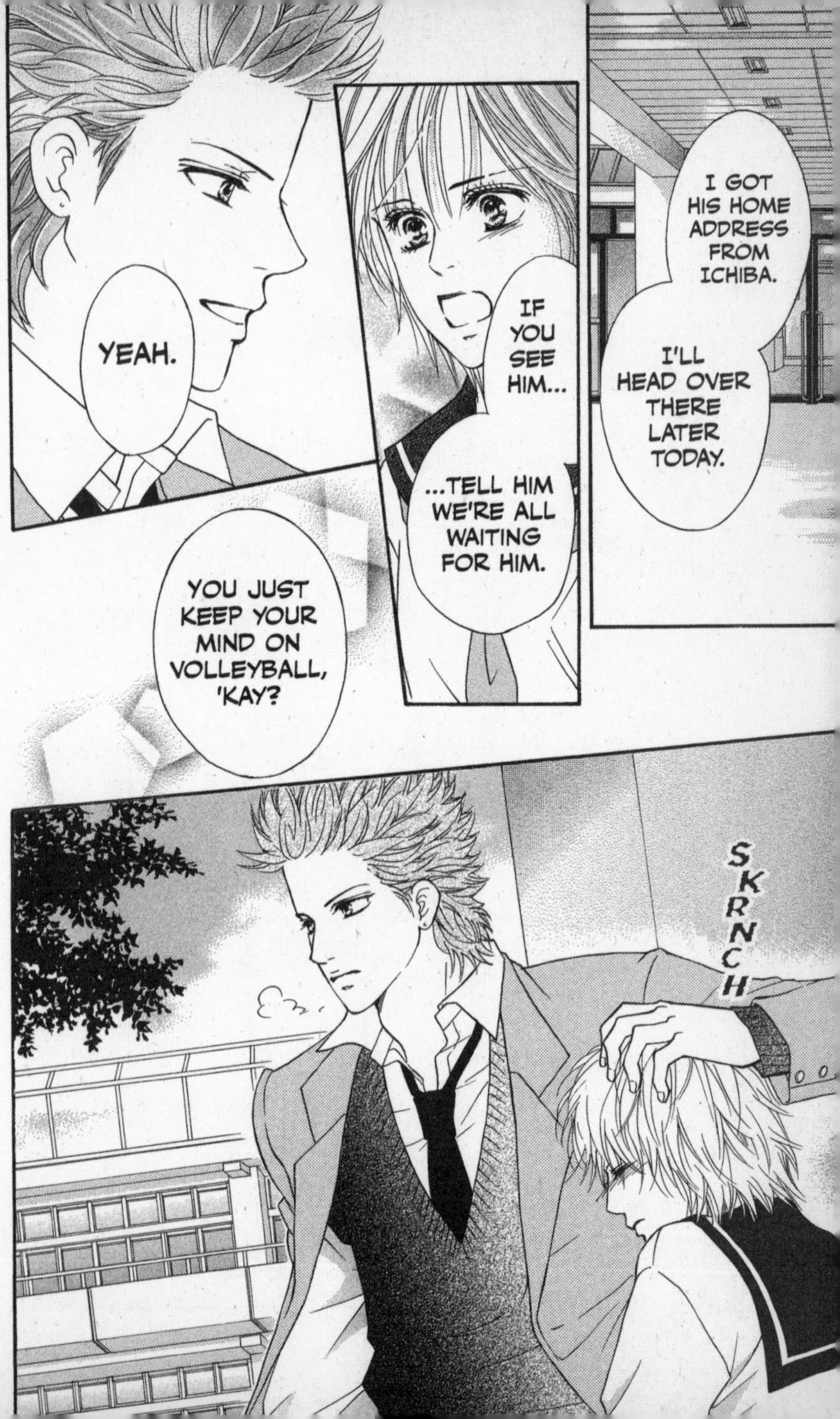
I GOT HIS HOME ADDRESS FROM ICHIBA.
I'LL HEAD OVER THERE LATER TODAY.
IF YOU SEE HIM...
...TELL HIM WE'RE ALL WAITING FOR HIM.
YEAH.
YOU JUST KEEP YOUR MIND ON VOLLEYBALL, 'KAY?
SKRNCH

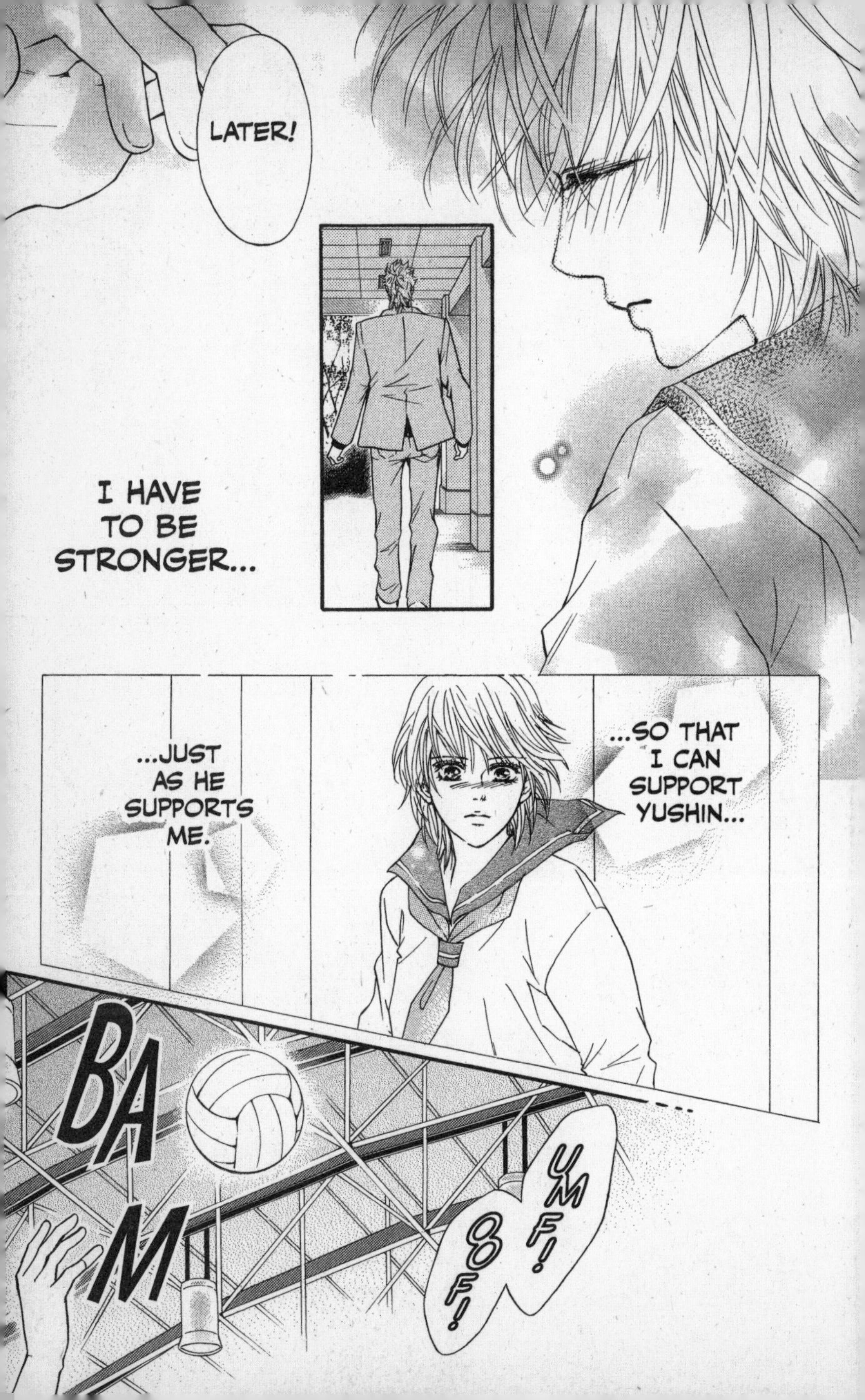
LATER!
I HAVE TO BE STRONGER...
...SO THAT I CAN SUPPORT YUSHIN...
...JUST AS HE SUPPORTS ME.
BAM
UMF! OOF!

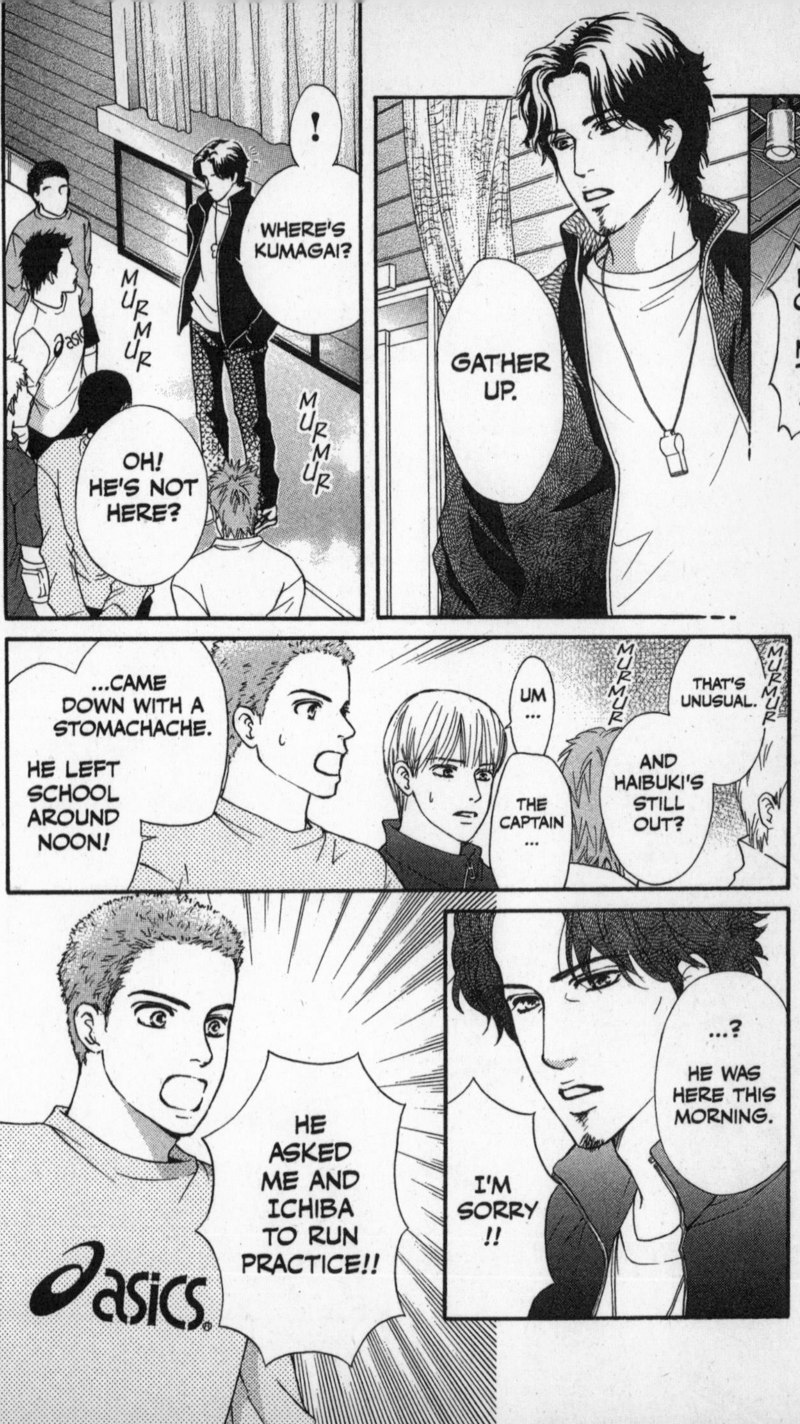

POINT!
GATHER UP.
!
WHERE'S KUMAGAI?
MURMUR
MURMUR
OH! HE'S NOT HERE?
MURMUR
THAT'S UNUSUAL.
MURMUR
AND HAIBUKI'S STILL OUT?
UM ...
THE CAPTAIN ...
...CAME DOWN WITH A STOMACHACHE.
HE LEFT SCHOOL AROUND NOON!
...?
HE WAS HERE THIS MORNING.
I'M SORRY !!
HE ASKED ME AND ICHIBA TO RUN PRACTICE!!

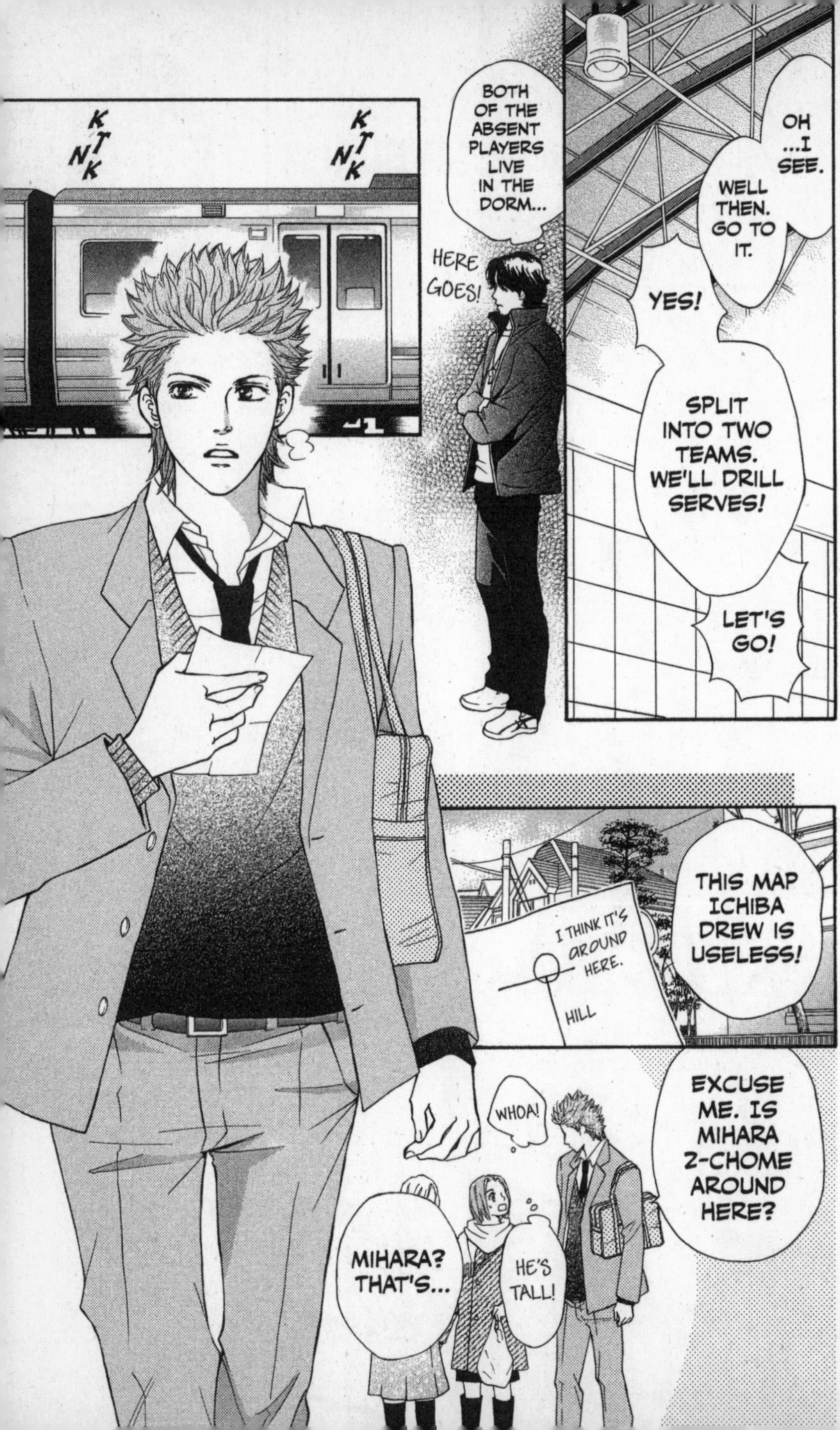
OH ...I SEE.
WELL THEN. GO TO IT.
YES!
SPLIT INTO TWO TEAMS. WE'LL DRILL SERVES!
LET'S GO!
BOTH OF THE ABSENT PLAYERS LIVE IN THE DORM...
HERE GOES!
KTNK
KTNK
THIS MAP ICHIBA DREW IS USELESS!
I THINK IT'S AROUND HERE.
HILL
EXCUSE ME. IS MIHARA 2-CHOME AROUND HERE?
WHOA!
HE'S TALL!
MIHARA? THAT'S...

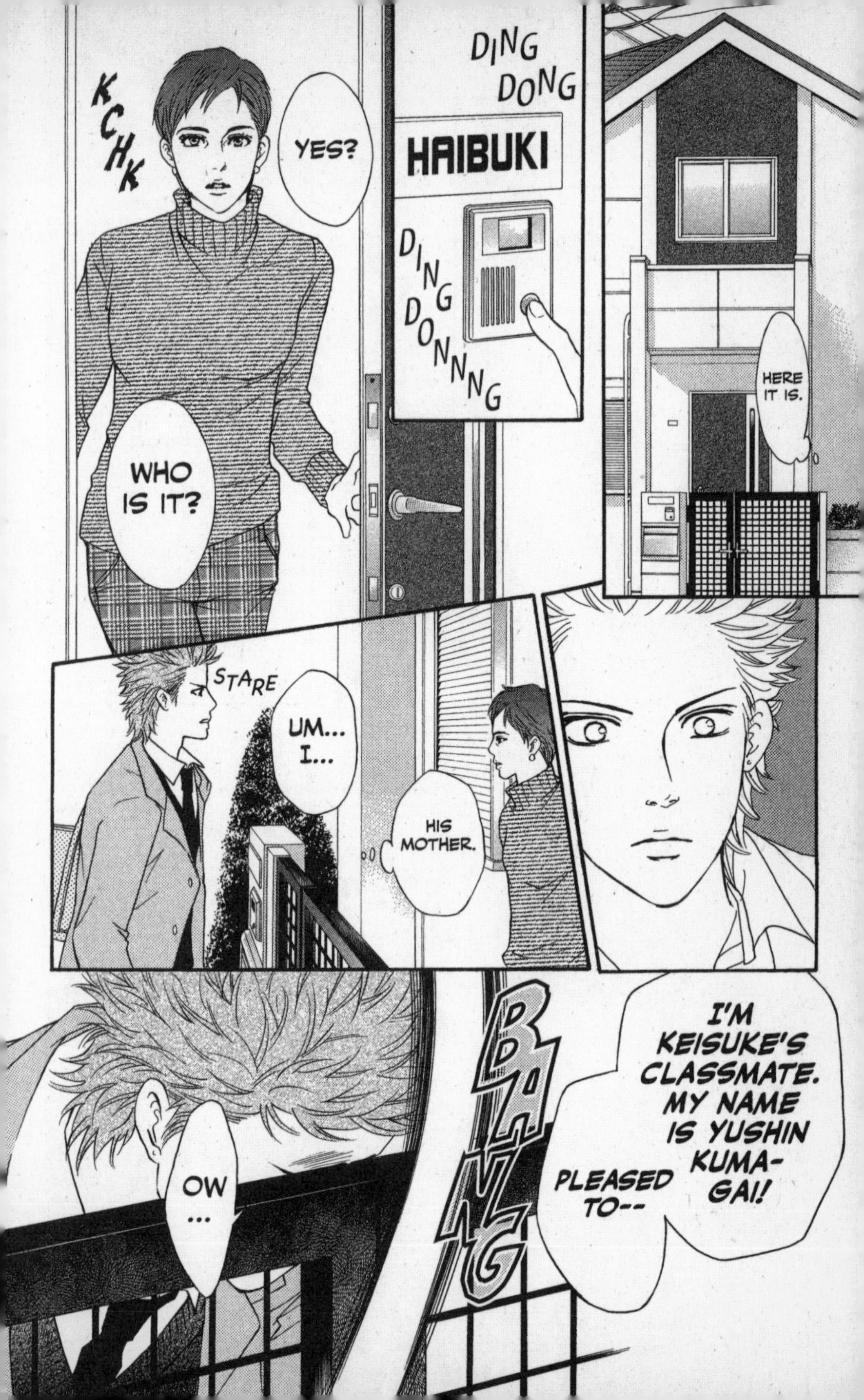
HERE IT IS.
DING DONG
HAIBUKI
DING DONNNG
KCHK
YES?
WHO IS IT?
HIS MOTHER.
STARE
UM... I...
I'M KEISUKE'S CLASSMATE. MY NAME IS YUSHIN KUMA-GAI!
PLEASED TO--
BLANG
OW ...

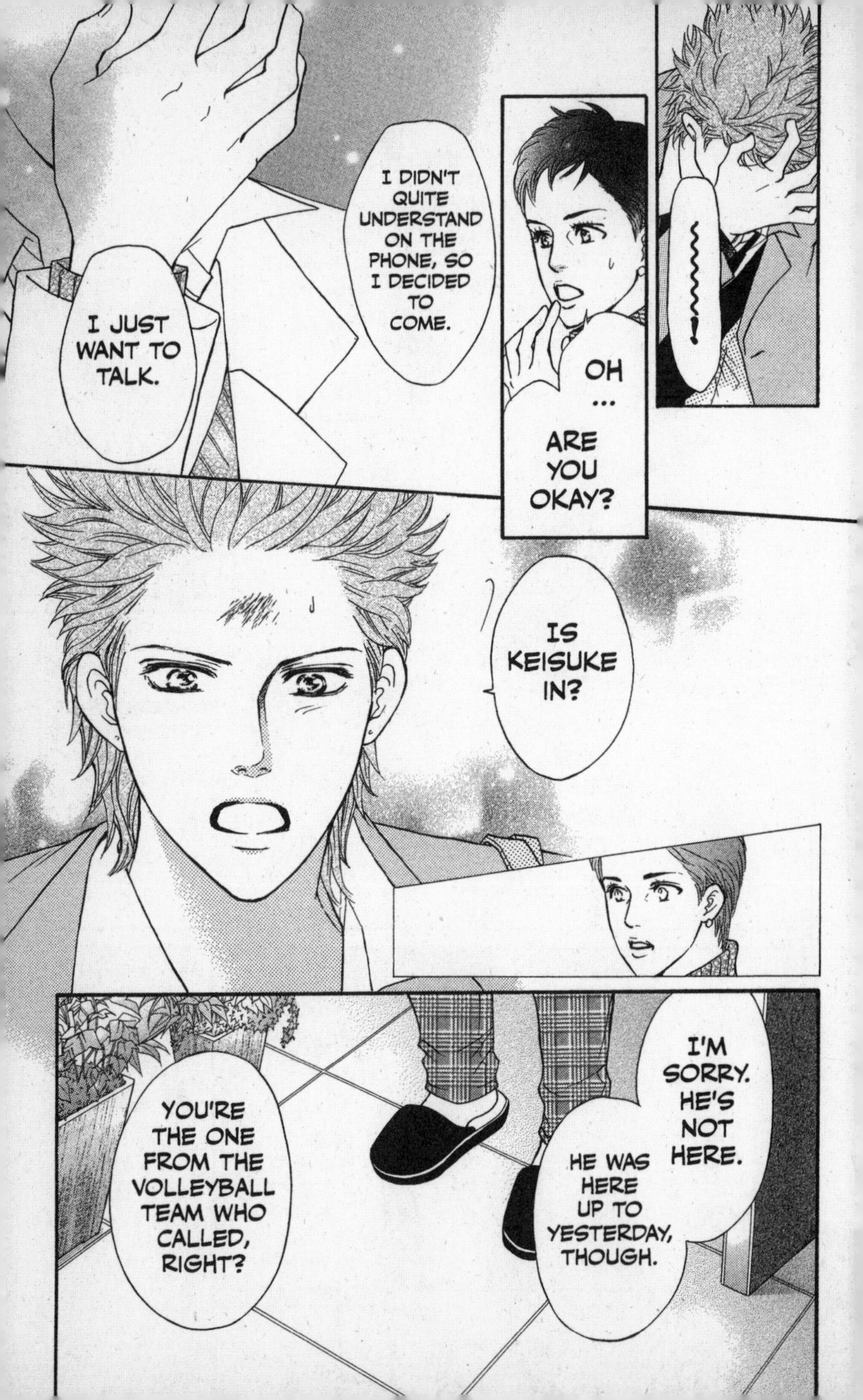
......!
OH ... ARE YOU OKAY?
I DIDN'T QUITE UNDERSTAND ON THE PHONE, SO I DECIDED TO COME.
I JUST WANT TO TALK.
IS KEISUKE IN?
I'M SORRY. HE'S NOT HERE.
HE WAS HERE UP TO YESTERDAY, THOUGH.
YOU'RE THE ONE FROM THE VOLLEYBALL TEAM WHO CALLED, RIGHT?

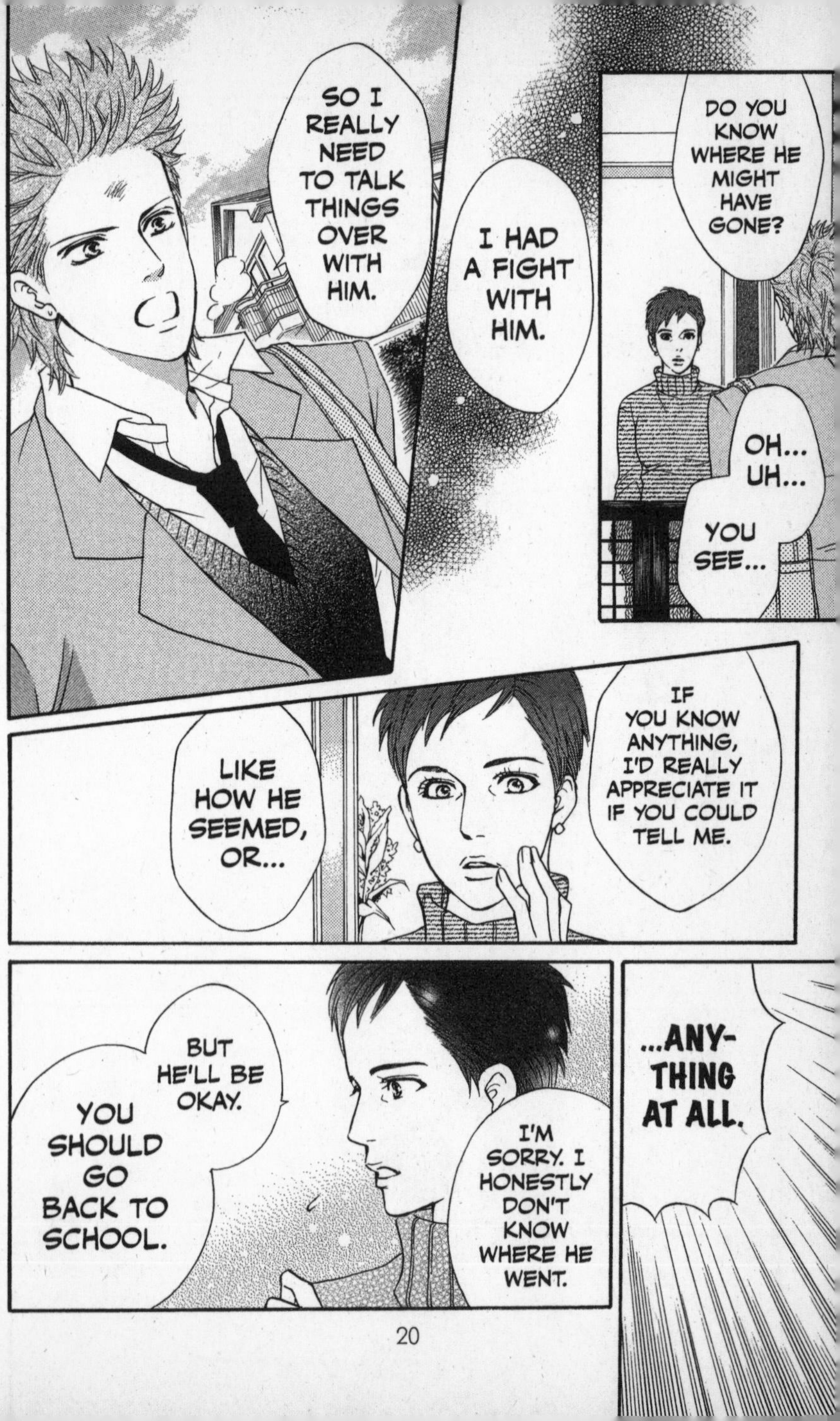
DO YOU KNOW WHERE HE MIGHT HAVE GONE?
OH... UH...
YOU SEE...
I HAD A FIGHT WITH HIM.
SO I REALLY NEED TO TALK THINGS OVER WITH HIM.
IF YOU KNOW ANYTHING, I'D REALLY APPRECIATE IT IF YOU COULD TELL ME.
LIKE HOW HE SEEMED, OR...
...ANYTHING AT ALL.
I'M SORRY. I HONESTLY DON'T KNOW WHERE HE WENT.
BUT HE'LL BE OKAY.
YOU SHOULD GO BACK TO SCHOOL.

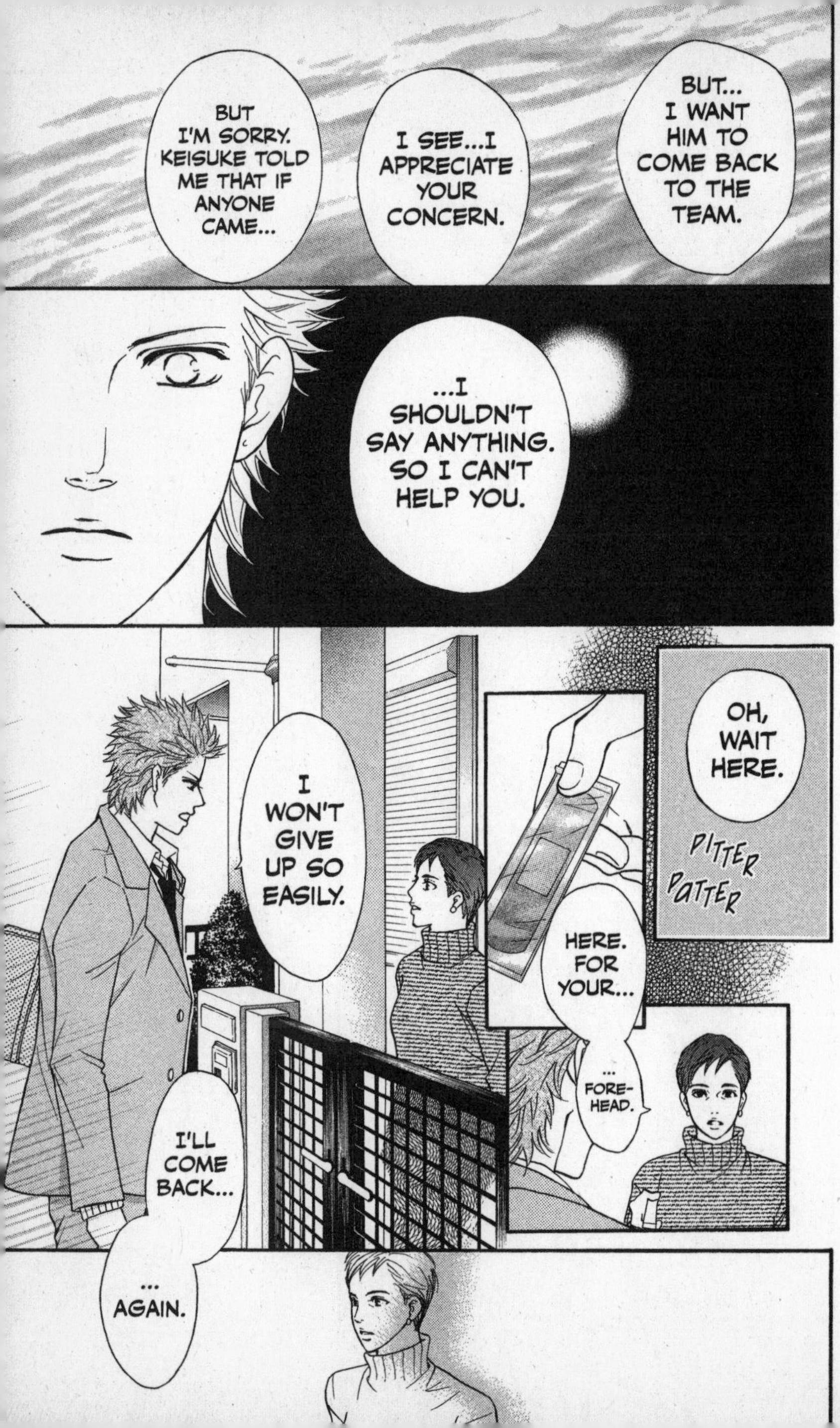
BUT... I WANT HIM TO COME BACK TO THE TEAM.
I SEE...I APPRECIATE YOUR CONCERN.
BUT I'M SORRY. KEISUKE TOLD ME THAT IF ANYONE CAME...
...I SHOULDN'T SAY ANYTHING. SO I CAN'T HELP YOU.
OH, WAIT HERE.
PITTER PATTER
HERE. FOR YOUR...
...FOREHEAD.
I WON'T GIVE UP SO EASILY.
I'LL COME BACK...
...AGAIN.

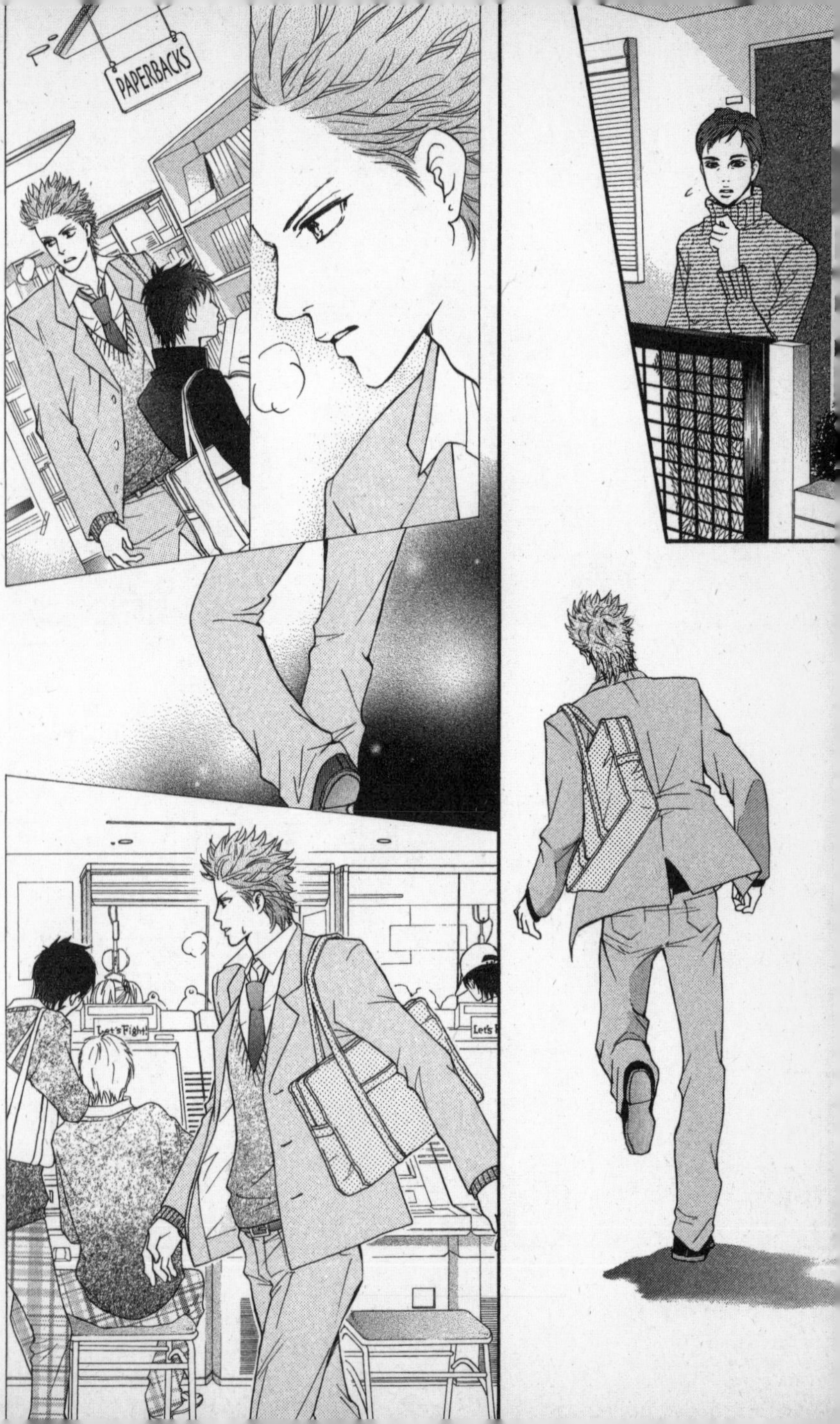
PAPERBACKS
Let's Fight!

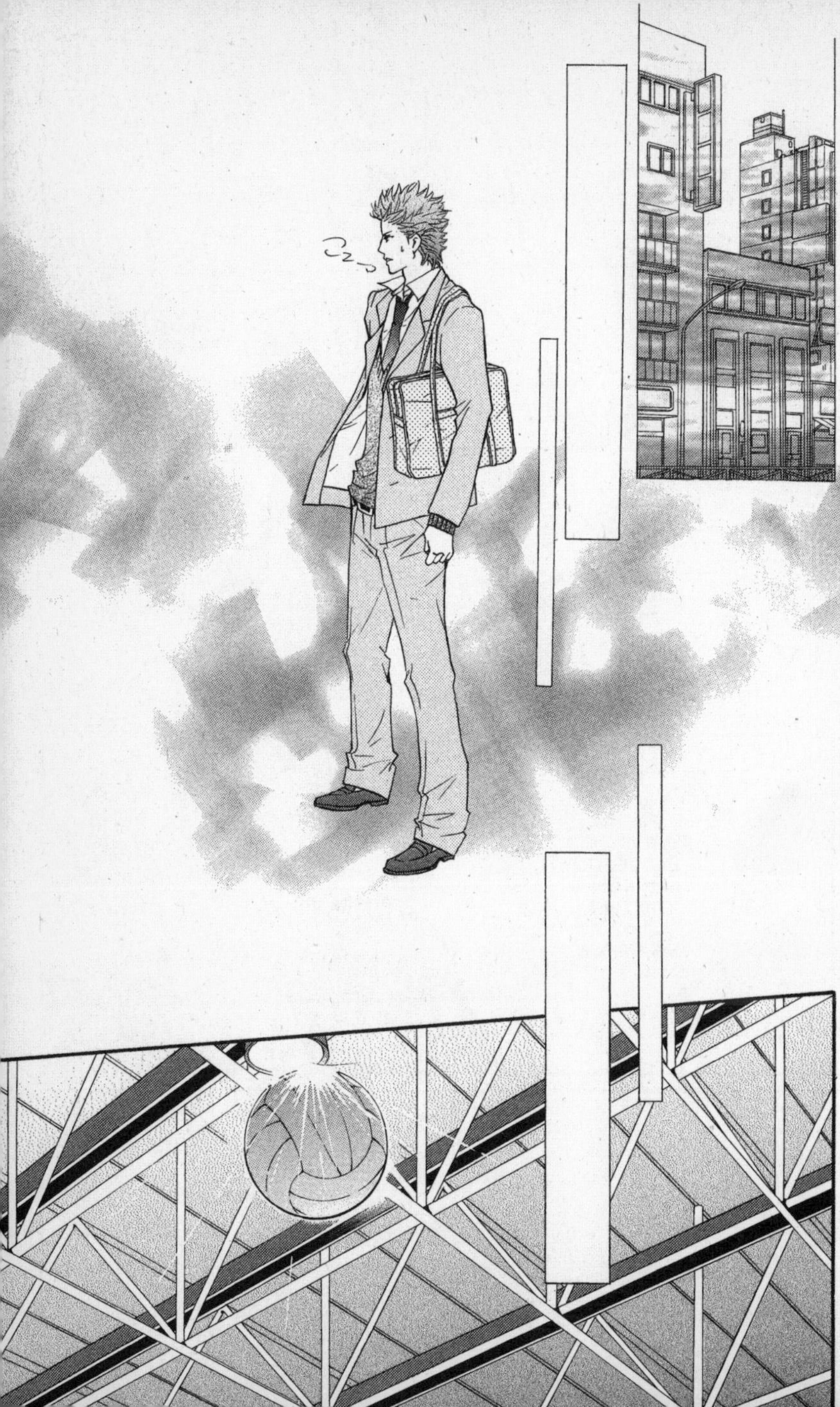

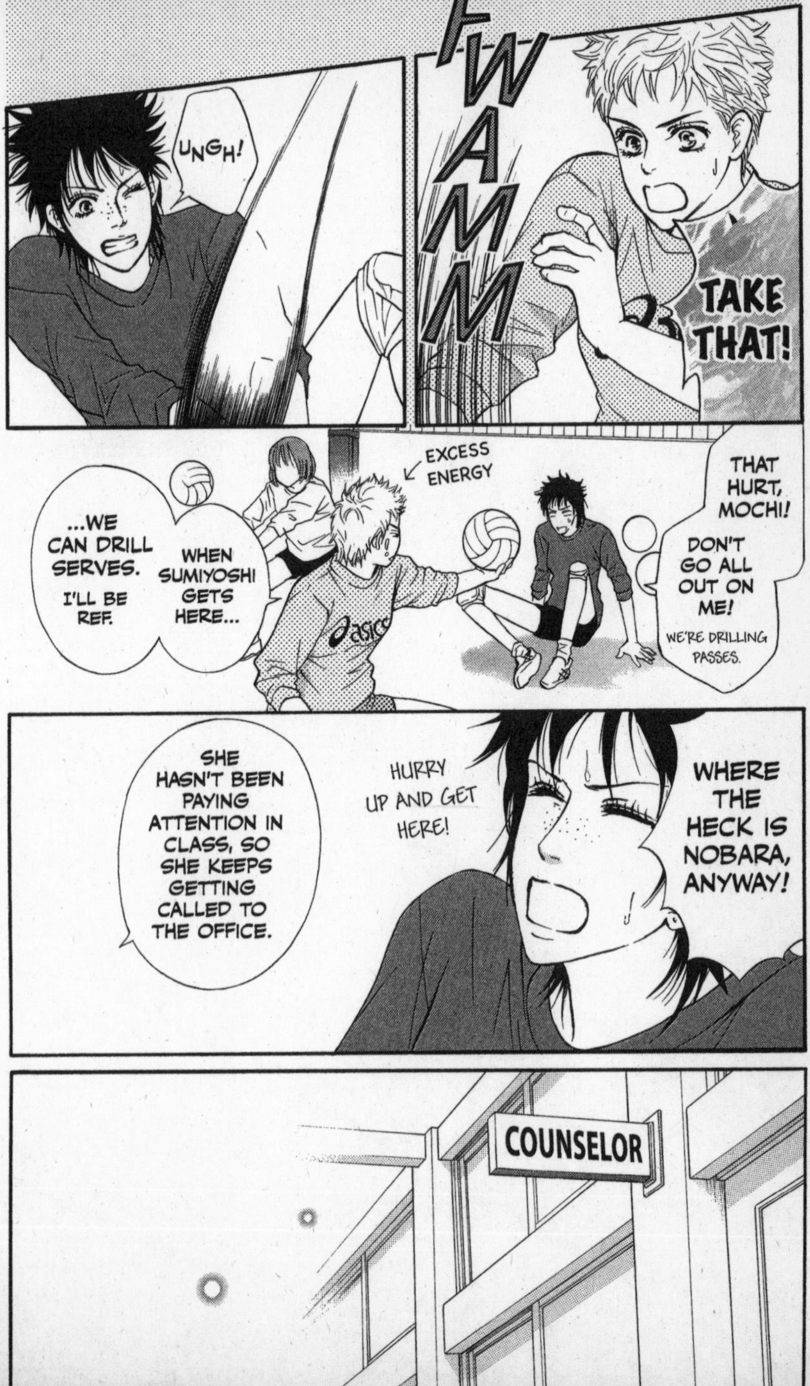
FWAMM
TAKE THAT!
UNGH!
THAT HURT, MOCHI!
DON'T GO ALL OUT ON ME!
WE'RE DRILLING PASSES.
EXCESS ENERGY
WHEN SUMIYOSHI GETS HERE...
...WE CAN DRILL SERVES.
I'LL BE REF.
WHERE THE HECK IS NOBARA, ANYWAY!
HURRY UP AND GET HERE!
SHE HASN'T BEEN PAYING ATTENTION IN CLASS, SO SHE KEEPS GETTING CALLED TO THE OFFICE.
COUNSELOR

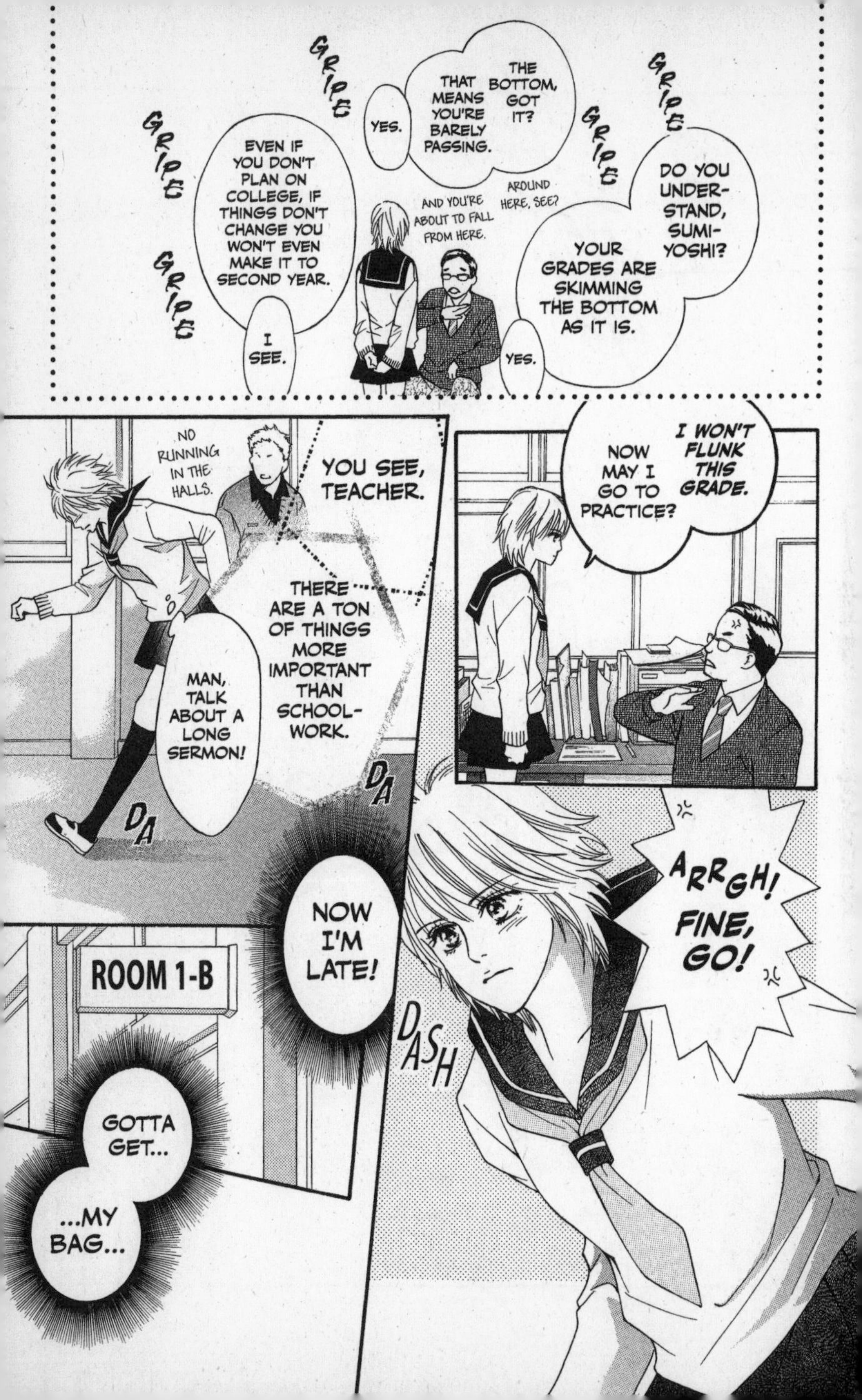
GRIPE
GRIPE
DO YOU UNDERSTAND, SUMI-YOSHI?
YOUR GRADES ARE SKIMMING THE BOTTOM AS IT IS.
YES.
AROUND HERE, SEE?
AND YOU'RE ABOUT TO FALL FROM HERE.
THE BOTTOM, GOT IT?
THAT MEANS YOU'RE BARELY PASSING.
YES.
GRIPE
GRIPE
EVEN IF YOU DON'T PLAN ON COLLEGE, IF THINGS DON'T CHANGE YOU WON'T EVEN MAKE IT TO SECOND YEAR.
I SEE.
I WON'T FLUNK THIS GRADE.
NOW MAY I GO TO PRACTICE?
ARRGH! FINE, GO!
DASH
YOU SEE, TEACHER.
THERE ARE A TON OF THINGS MORE IMPORTANT THAN SCHOOL-WORK.
NO RUNNING IN THE HALLS.
MAN, TALK ABOUT A LONG SERMON!
DA
DA
NOW I'M LATE!
ROOM 1-B
GOTTA GET...
...MY BAG...

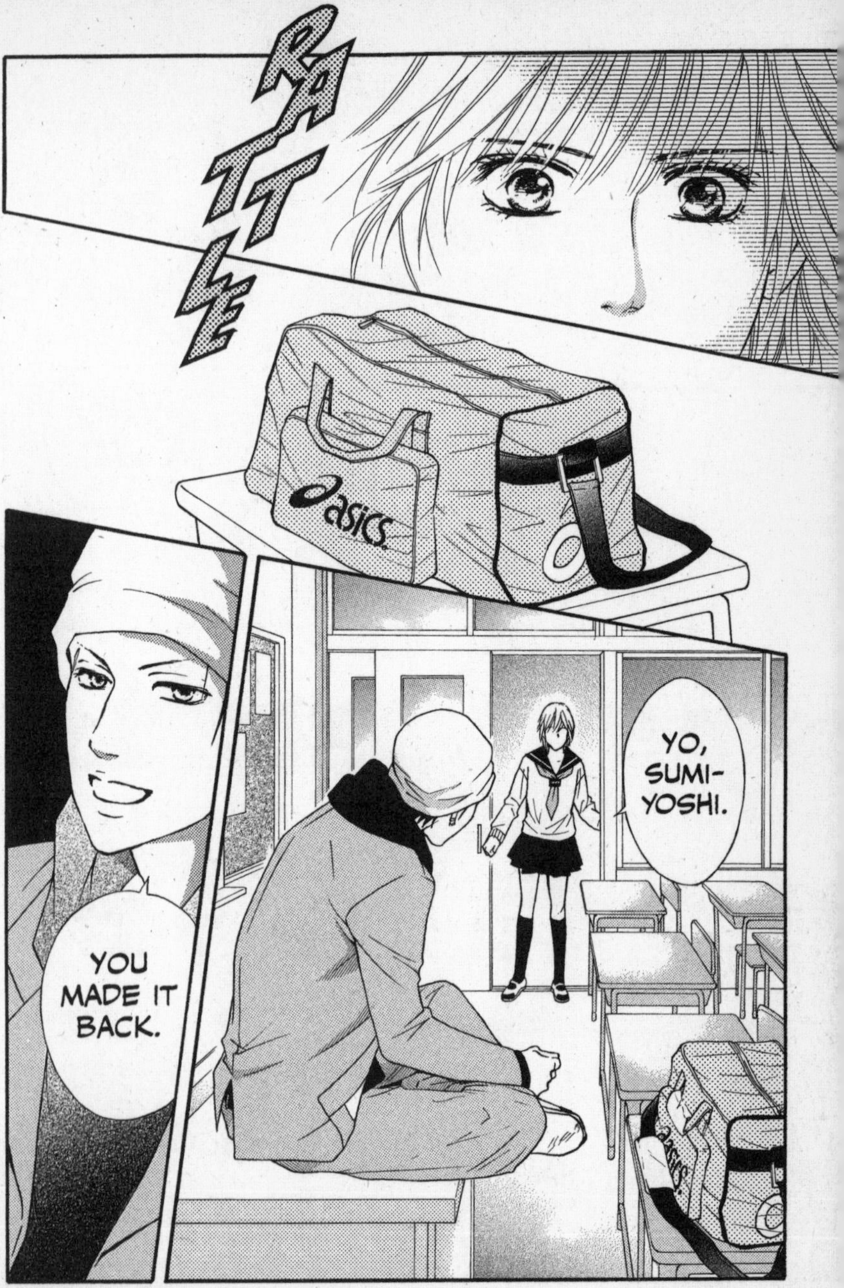
RATTLE
YO, SUMI-YOSHI.
YOU MADE IT BACK.

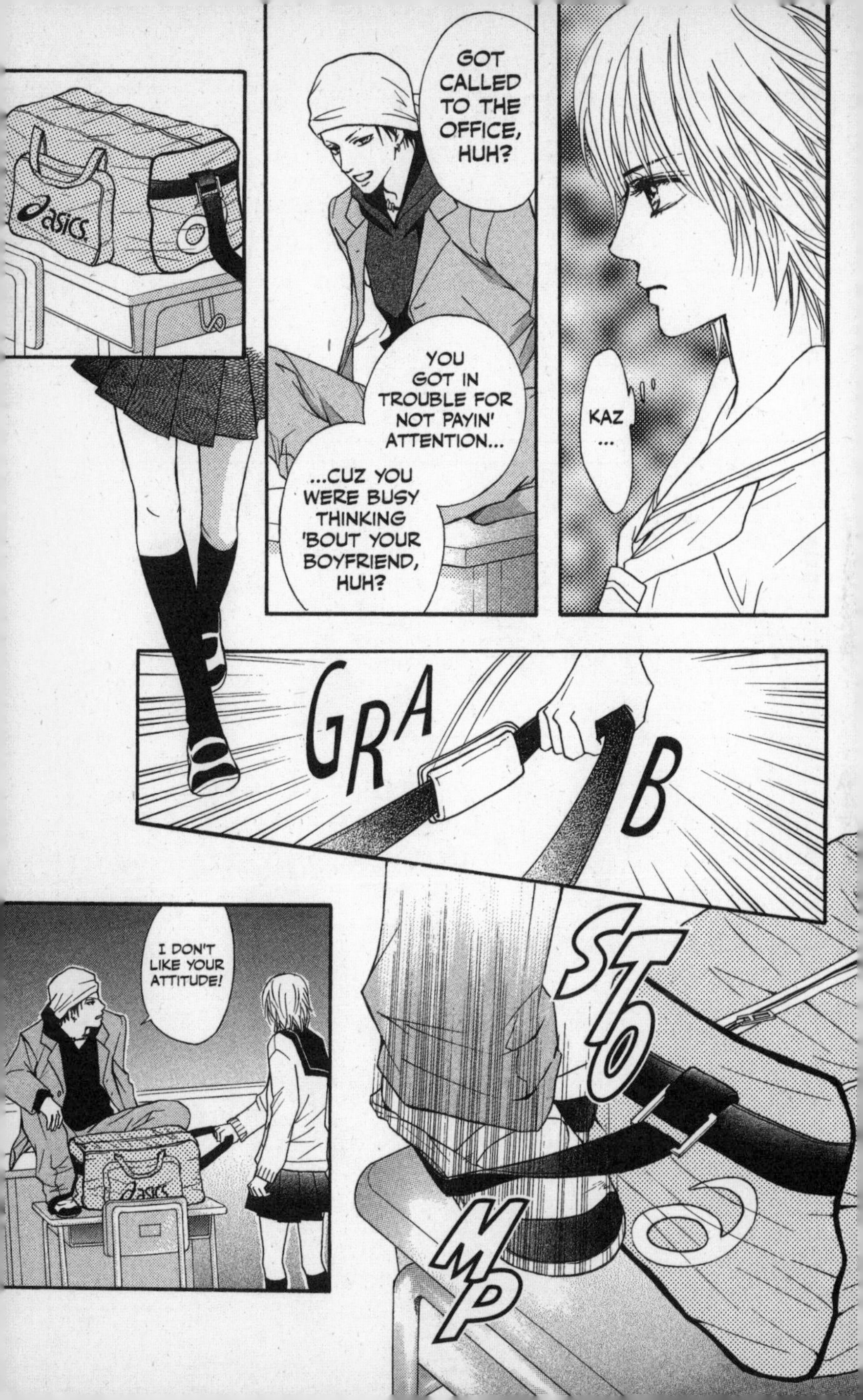

GOT CALLED TO THE OFFICE, HUH?
KAZ ...
YOU GOT IN TROUBLE FOR NOT PAYIN' ATTENTION...
...CUZ YOU WERE BUSY THINKING 'BOUT YOUR BOYFRIEND, HUH?
GRAB
STOMMP
I DON'T LIKE YOUR ATTITUDE!

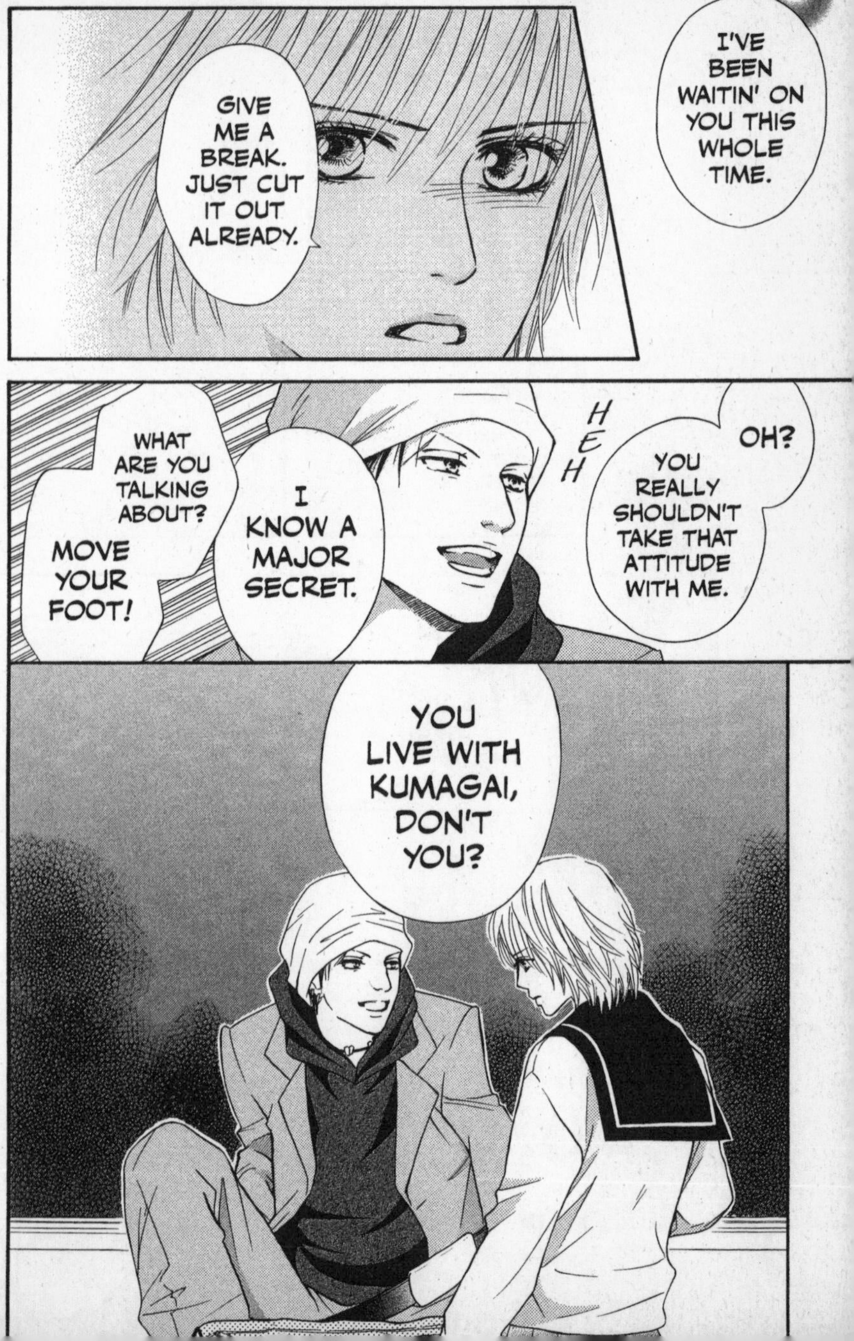
I'VE BEEN WAITIN' ON YOU THIS WHOLE TIME.
GIVE ME A BREAK. JUST CUT IT OUT ALREADY.
OH?
YOU REALLY SHOULDN'T TAKE THAT ATTITUDE WITH ME.
HEH
I KNOW A MAJOR SECRET.
WHAT ARE YOU TALKING ABOUT?
MOVE YOUR FOOT!
YOU LIVE WITH KUMAGAI, DON'T YOU?

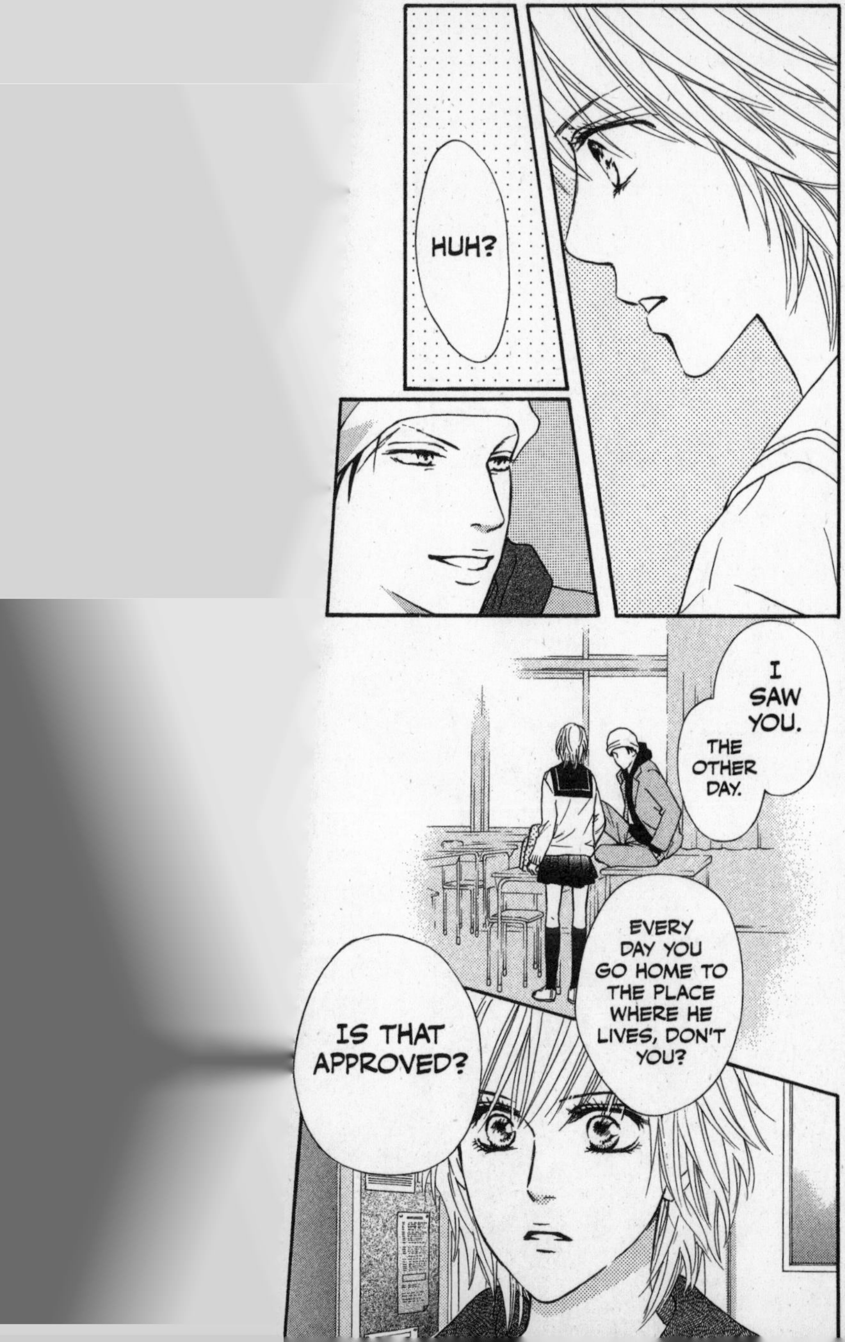
HUH?
I SAW YOU.
THE OTHER DAY.
EVERY DAY YOU GO HOME TO THE PLACE WHERE HE LIVES, DON'T YOU?
IS THAT APPROVED?

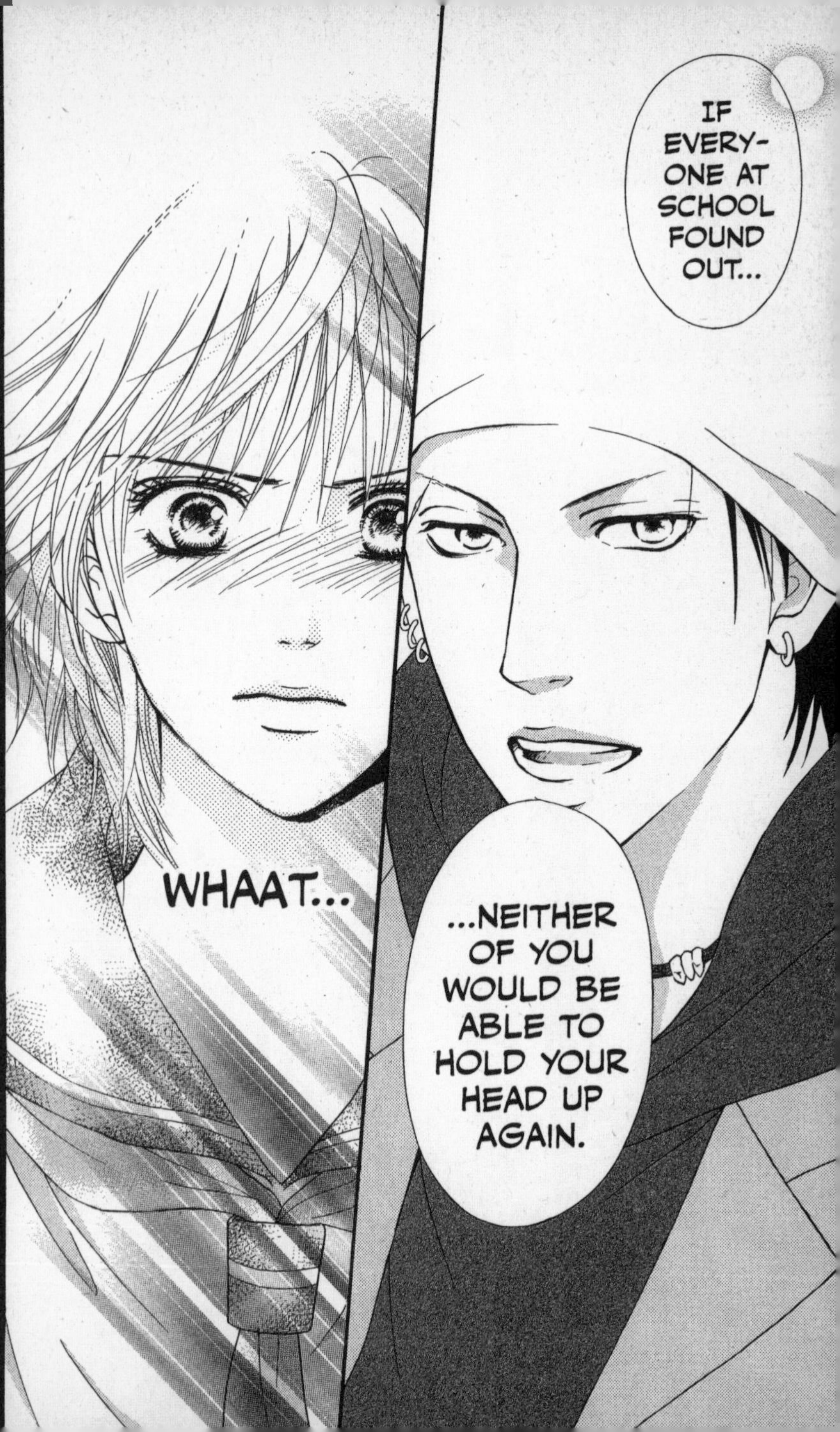
IF EVERY-ONE AT SCHOOL FOUND OUT...
...NEITHER OF YOU WOULD BE ABLE TO HOLD YOUR HEAD UP AGAIN.
WHAAT...

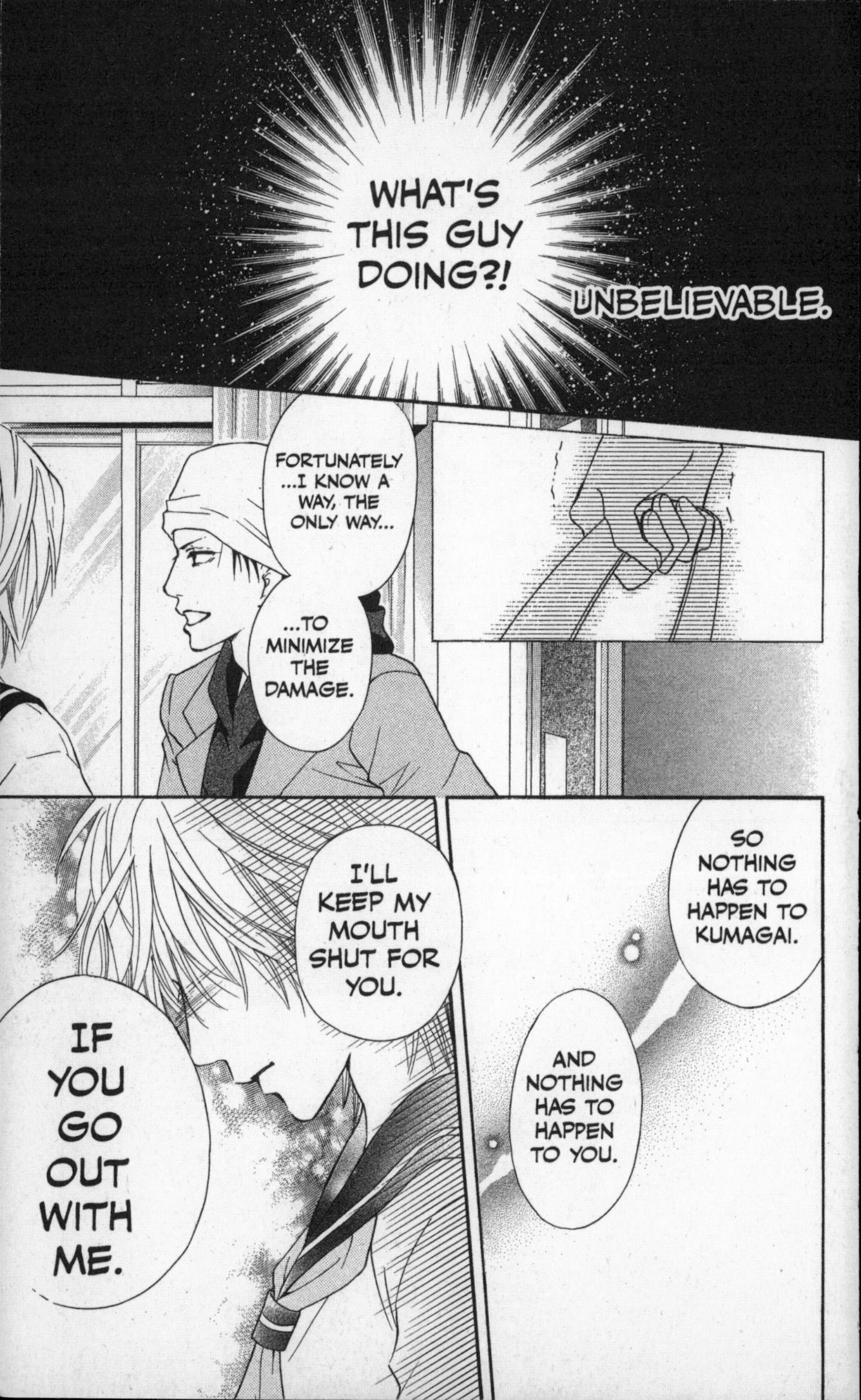
WHAT'S THIS GUY DOING?!
UNBELIEVABLE.
FORTUNATELY ...I KNOW A WAY, THE ONLY WAY...
...TO MINIMIZE THE DAMAGE.
SO NOTHING HAS TO HAPPEN TO KUMAGAI.
AND NOTHING HAS TO HAPPEN TO YOU.
I'LL KEEP MY MOUTH SHUT FOR YOU.
IF YOU GO OUT WITH ME.

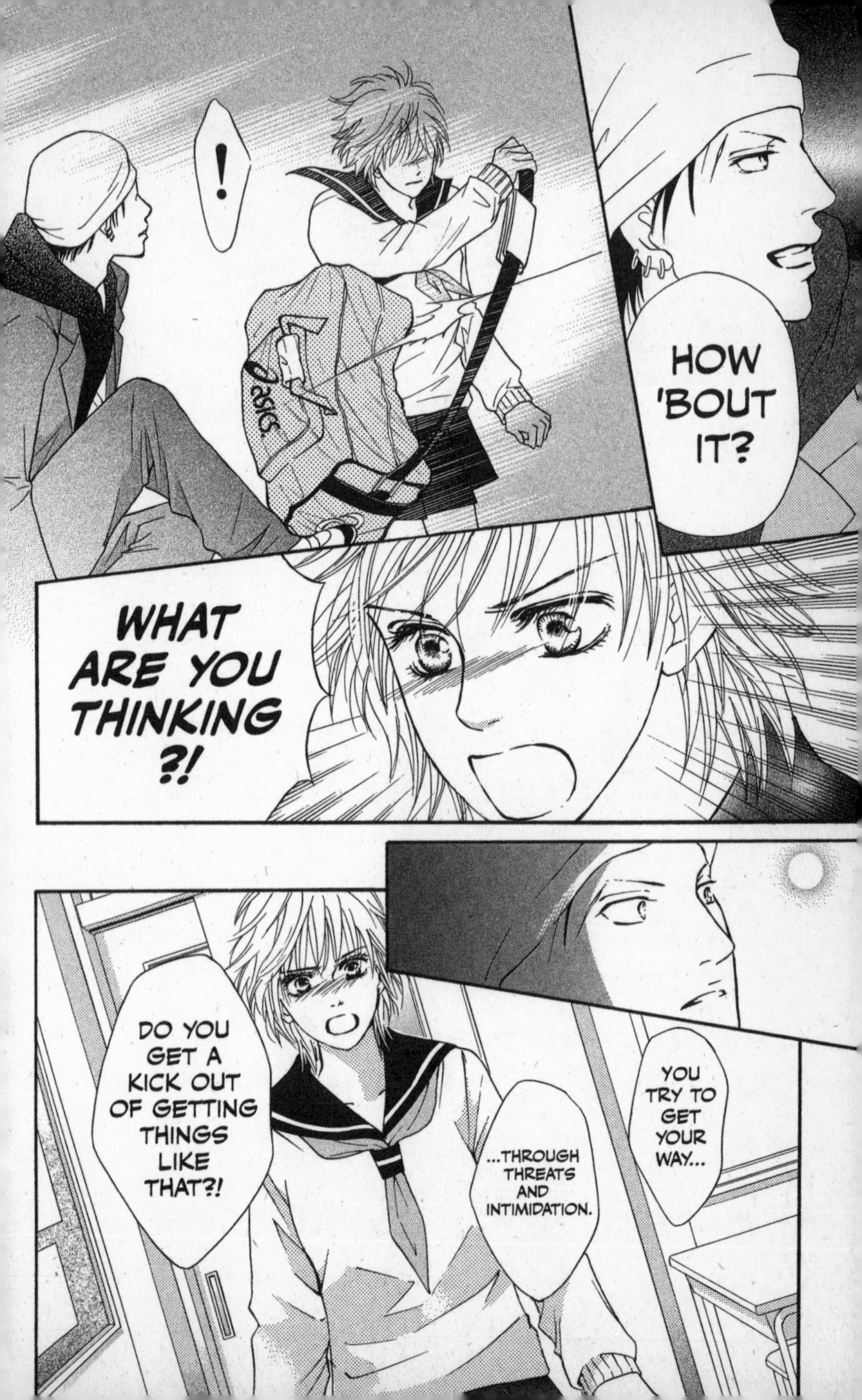
HOW 'BOUT IT?
!
WHAT ARE YOU THINKING ?!
YOU TRY TO GET YOUR WAY...
...THROUGH THREATS AND INTIMIDATION.
DO YOU GET A KICK OUT OF GETTING THINGS LIKE THAT?!

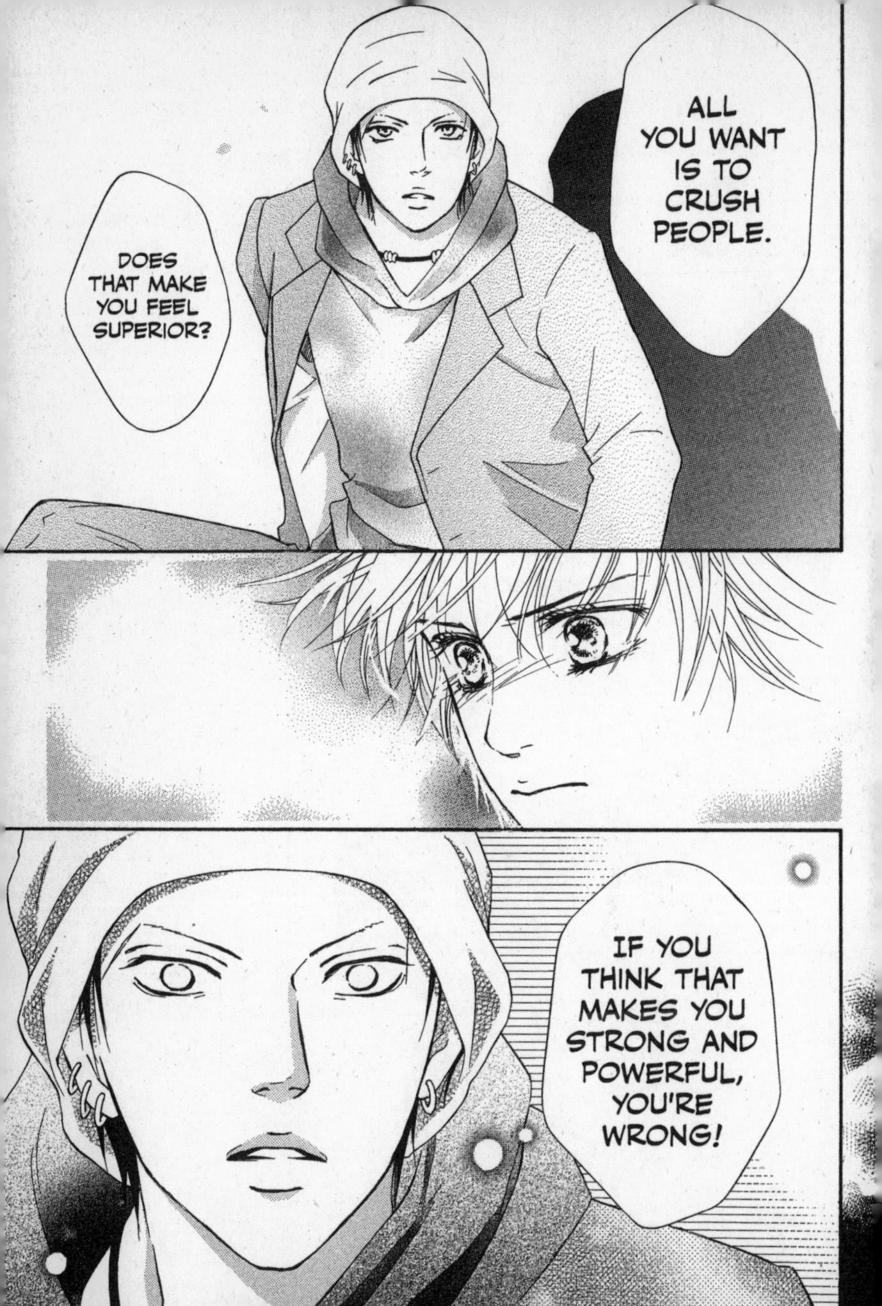
ALL YOU WANT IS TO CRUSH PEOPLE.
DOES THAT MAKE YOU FEEL SUPERIOR?
IF YOU THINK THAT MAKES YOU STRONG AND POWERFUL, YOU'RE WRONG!

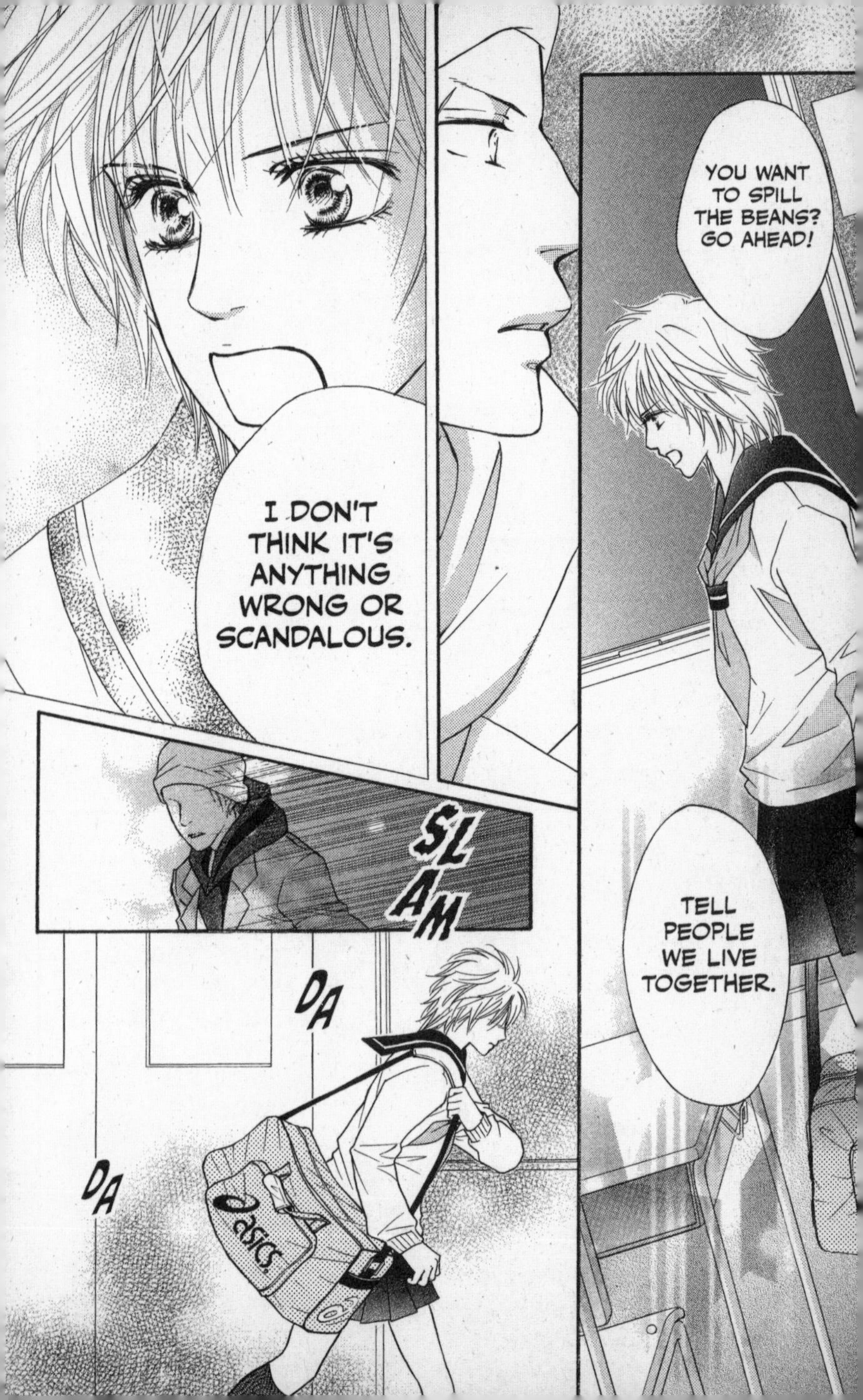
YOU WANT TO SPILL THE BEANS? GO AHEAD!
TELL PEOPLE WE LIVE TOGETHER.
I DON'T THINK IT'S ANYTHING WRONG OR SCANDALOUS.
SLAM
DA
DA

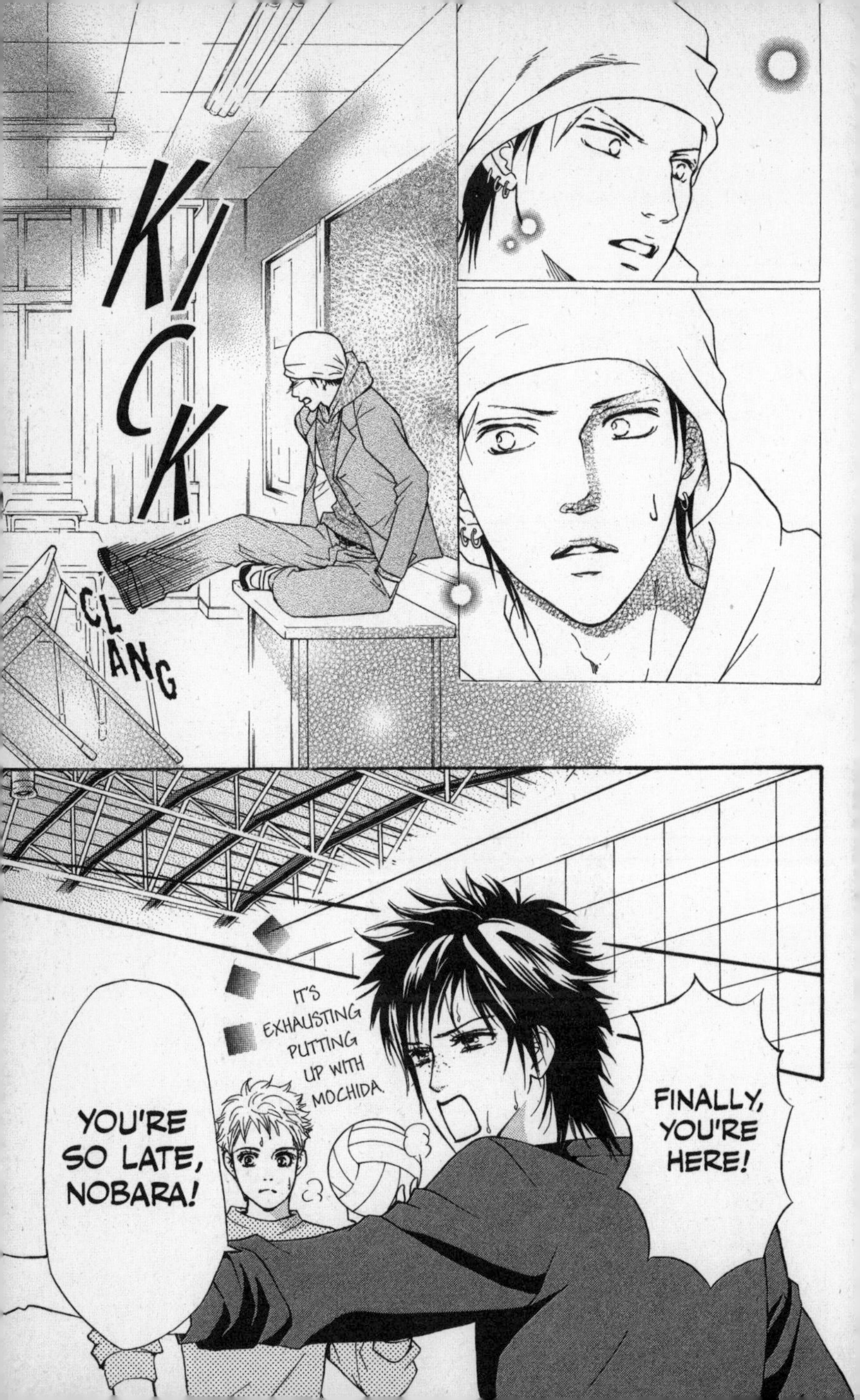
KICK
CLANG
FINALLY, YOU'RE HERE!
IT'S EXHAUSTING PUTTING UP WITH MOCHIDA.
YOU'RE SO LATE, NOBARA!

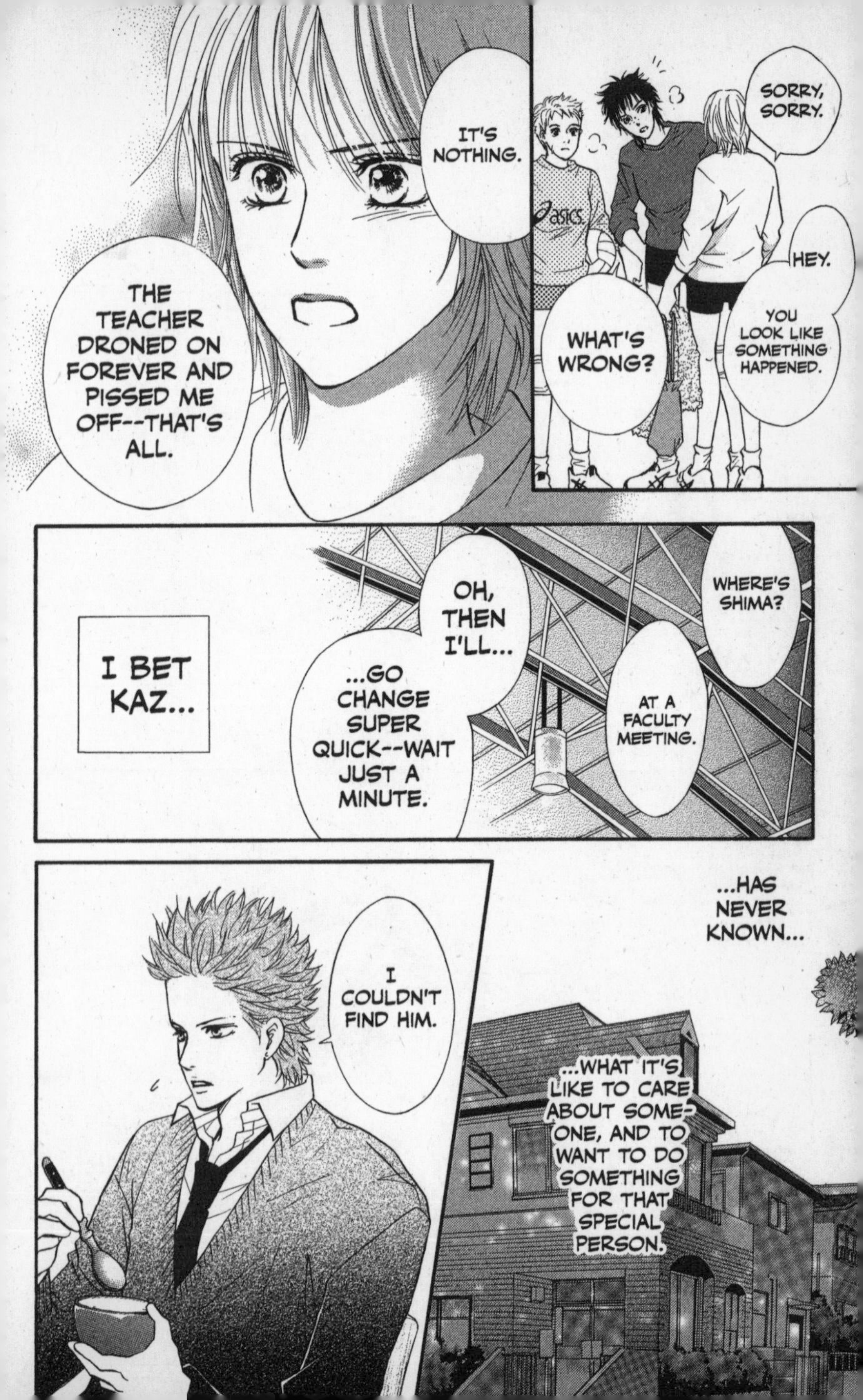
SORRY, SORRY.
HEY.
YOU LOOK LIKE SOMETHING HAPPENED.
WHAT'S WRONG?
IT'S NOTHING.
THE TEACHER DRONED ON FOREVER AND PISSED ME OFF--THAT'S ALL.
WHERE'S SHIMA?
AT A FACULTY MEETING.
OH, THEN I'LL...
...GO CHANGE SUPER QUICK--WAIT JUST A MINUTE.
I BET KAZ...
...HAS NEVER KNOWN...
...WHAT IT'S LIKE TO CARE ABOUT SOME-ONE, AND TO WANT TO DO SOMETHING FOR THAT SPECIAL PERSON.
I COULDN'T FIND HIM.

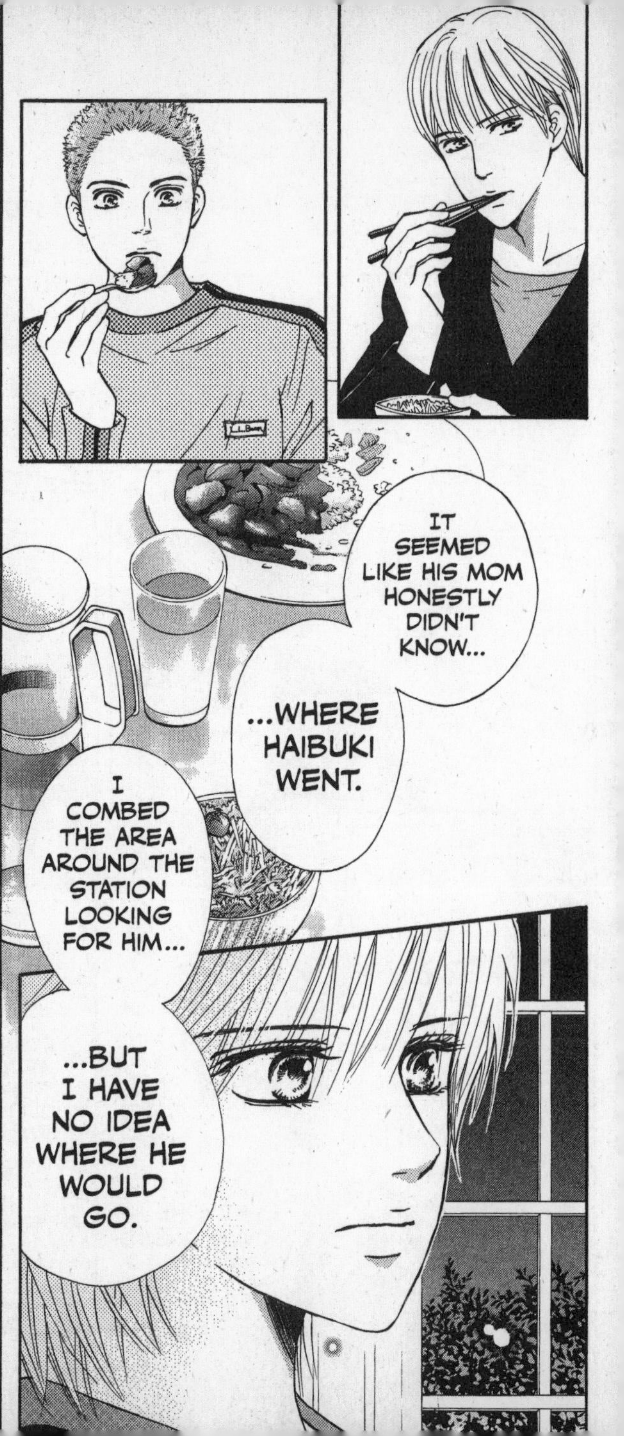
IT SEEMED LIKE HIS MOM HONESTLY DIDN'T KNOW...
...WHERE HAIBUKI WENT.
I COMBED THE AREA AROUND THE STATION LOOKING FOR HIM...
...BUT I HAVE NO IDEA WHERE HE WOULD GO.

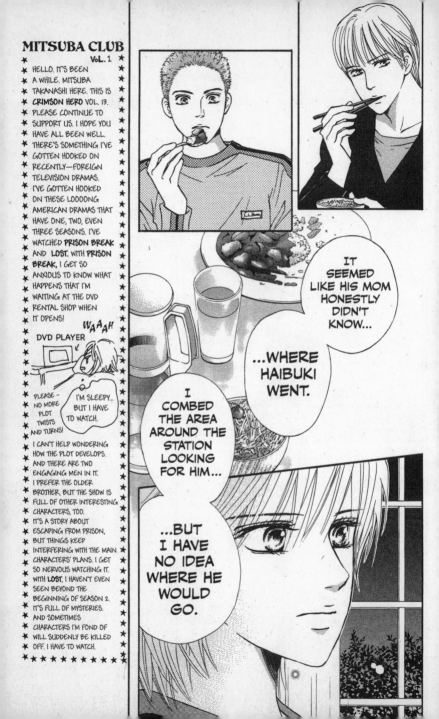

MITSUBA CLUB

VoL. 1

HELLO. IT'S BEEN A WHILE. MITSUBA TAKANASHI HERE. THIS IS **CRIMSON HERO** VOL. 13. PLEASE CONTINUE TO SUPPORT US. I HOPE YOU HAVE ALL BEEN WELL. THERE'S SOMETHING I'VE GOTTEN HOOKED ON RECENTLY—FOREIGN TELEVISION DRAMAS. I'VE GOTTEN HOOKED ON THESE LOOOONG AMERICAN DRAMAS THAT HAVE ONE, TWO, EVEN THREE SEASONS. I'VE WATCHED **PRISON BREAK** AND **LOST**. WITH **PRISON BREAK**, I GET SO ANXIOUS TO KNOW WHAT HAPPENS THAT I'M WAITING AT THE DVD RENTAL SHOP WHEN IT OPENS!

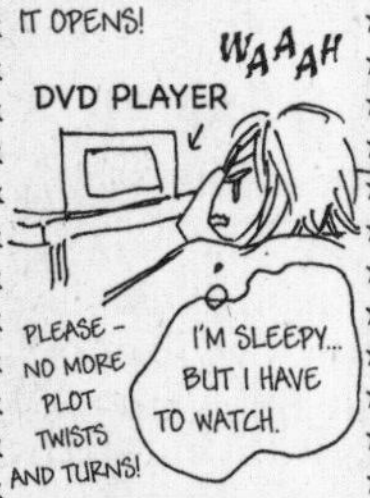
WAAAAH
DVD PLAYER
PLEASE - NO MORE PLOT TWISTS AND TURNS!
I'M SLEEPY... BUT I HAVE TO WATCH.

I CAN'T HELP WONDERING HOW THE PLOT DEVELOPS. AND THERE ARE TWO ENGAGING MEN IN IT. I PREFER THE OLDER BROTHER, BUT THE SHOW IS FULL OF OTHER INTERESTING CHARACTERS, TOO. IT'S A STORY ABOUT ESCAPING FROM PRISON, BUT THINGS KEEP INTERFERING WITH THE MAIN CHARACTERS' PLANS. I GET SO NERVOUS WATCHING IT. WITH **LOST**, I HAVEN'T EVEN SEEN BEYOND THE BEGINNING OF SEASON 2. IT'S FULL OF MYSTERIES. AND SOMETIMES CHARACTERS I'M FOND OF WILL SUDDENLY BE KILLED OFF. I HAVE TO WATCH.

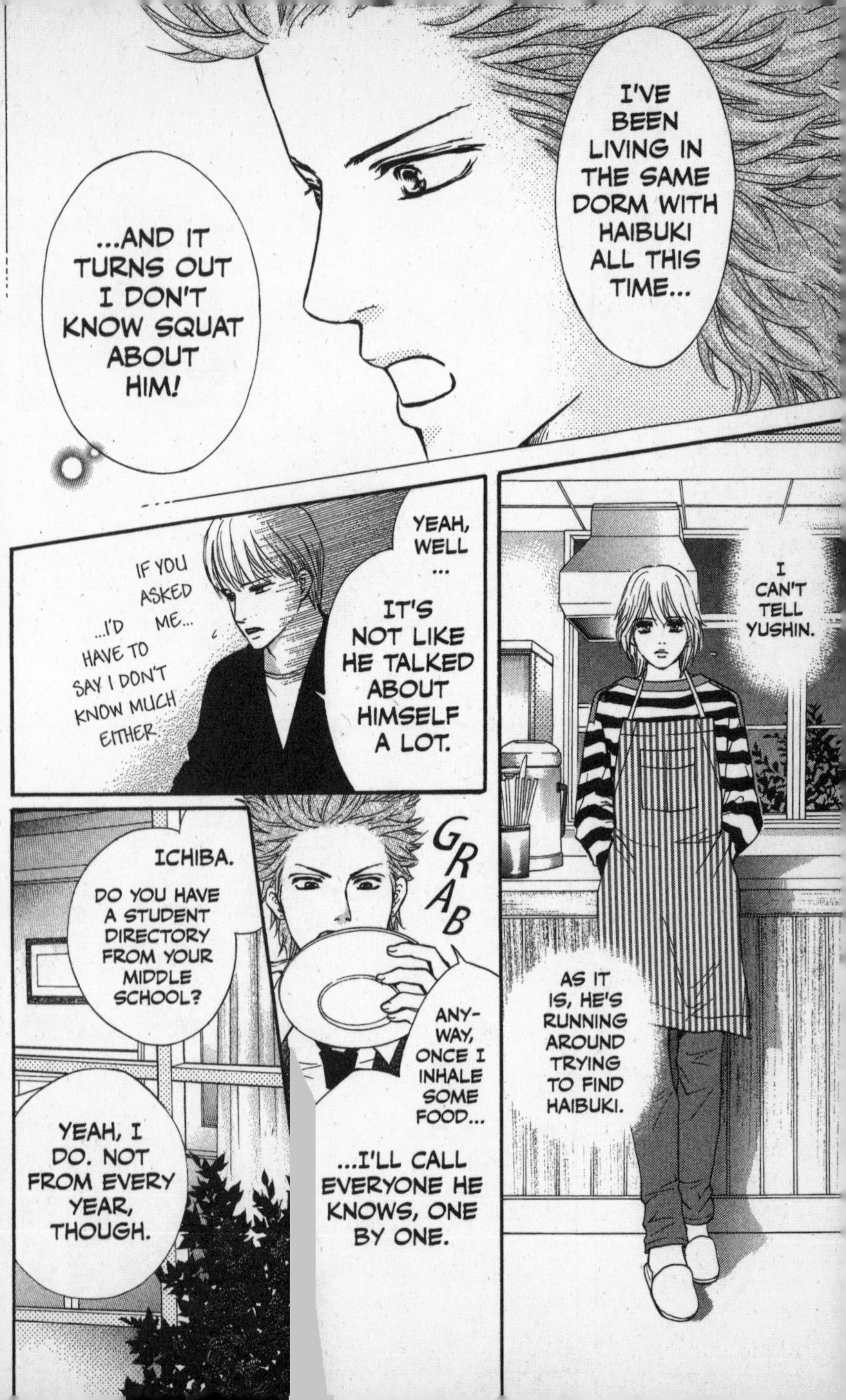
I'VE BEEN LIVING IN THE SAME DORM WITH HAIBUKI ALL THIS TIME...
...AND IT TURNS OUT I DON'T KNOW SQUAT ABOUT HIM!
I CAN'T TELL YUSHIN.
AS IT IS, HE'S RUNNING AROUND TRYING TO FIND HAIBUKI.
YEAH, WELL ...
IT'S NOT LIKE HE TALKED ABOUT HIMSELF A LOT.
IF YOU ASKED ME... ...I'D HAVE TO SAY I DON'T KNOW MUCH EITHER.
ICHIBA.
DO YOU HAVE A STUDENT DIRECTORY FROM YOUR MIDDLE SCHOOL?
GRAB
ANY-WAY, ONCE I INHALE SOME FOOD...
...I'LL CALL EVERYONE HE KNOWS, ONE BY ONE.
YEAH, I DO. NOT FROM EVERY YEAR, THOUGH.

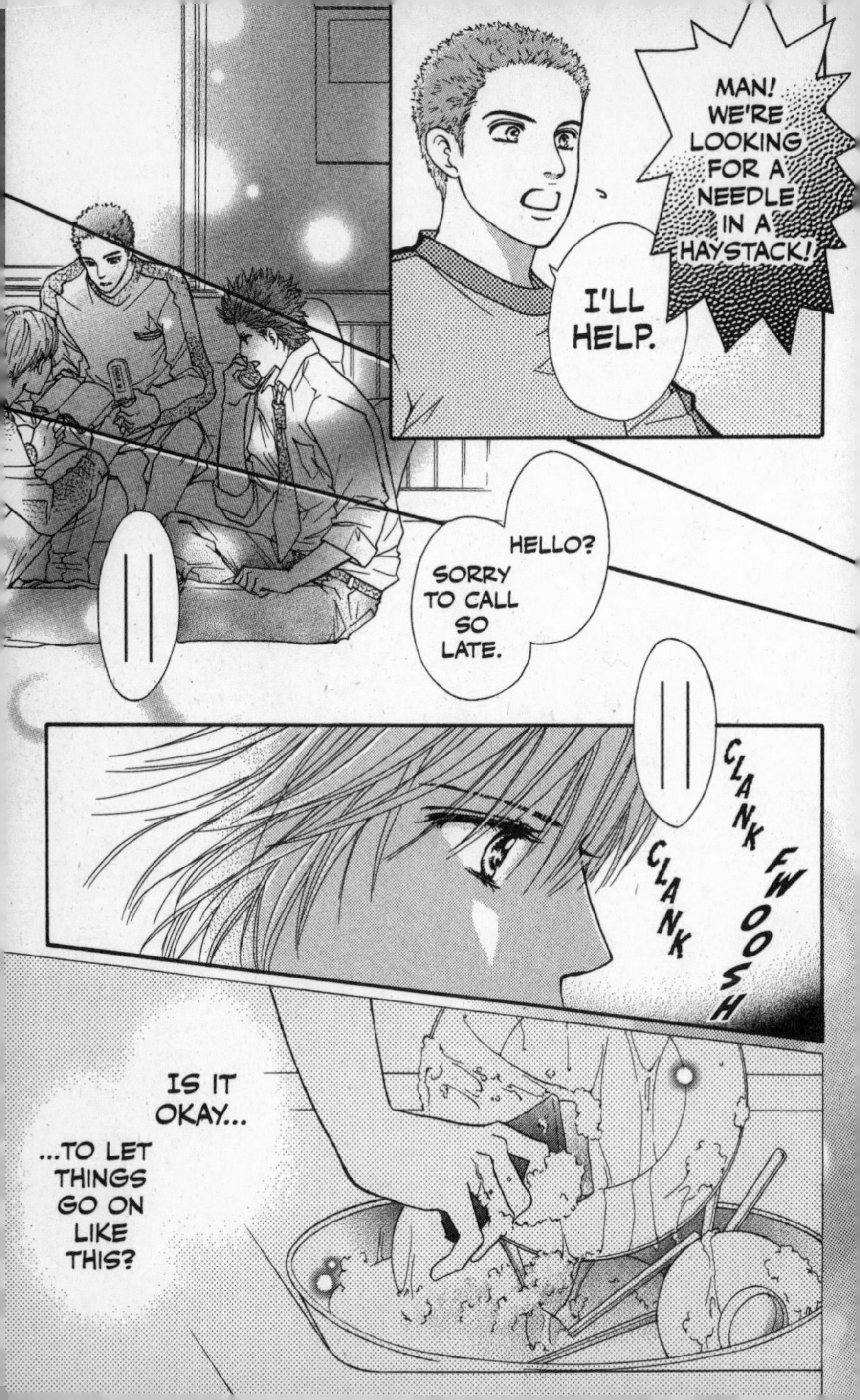

MAN! WE'RE LOOKING FOR A NEEDLE IN A HAYSTACK!
I'LL HELP.
HELLO? SORRY TO CALL SO LATE.
—
—
CLANK
FWOOSH
CLANK
IS IT OKAY...
...TO LET THINGS GO ON LIKE THIS?

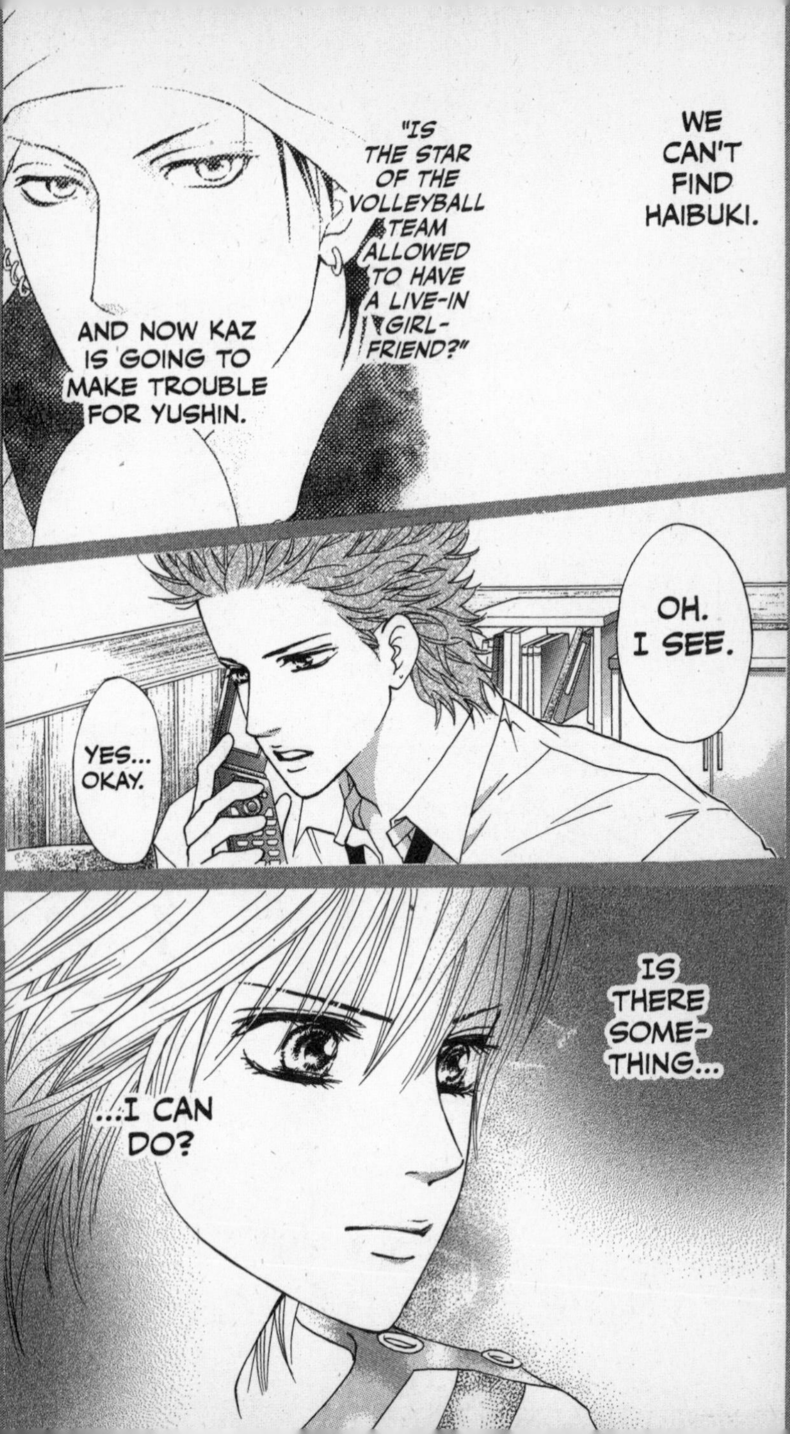
WE CAN'T FIND HAIBUKI.
"IS THE STAR OF THE VOLLEYBALL TEAM ALLOWED TO HAVE A LIVE-IN GIRL-FRIEND?"
AND NOW KAZ IS GOING TO MAKE TROUBLE FOR YUSHIN.
OH. I SEE.
YES... OKAY.
IS THERE SOME-THING...
...I CAN DO?

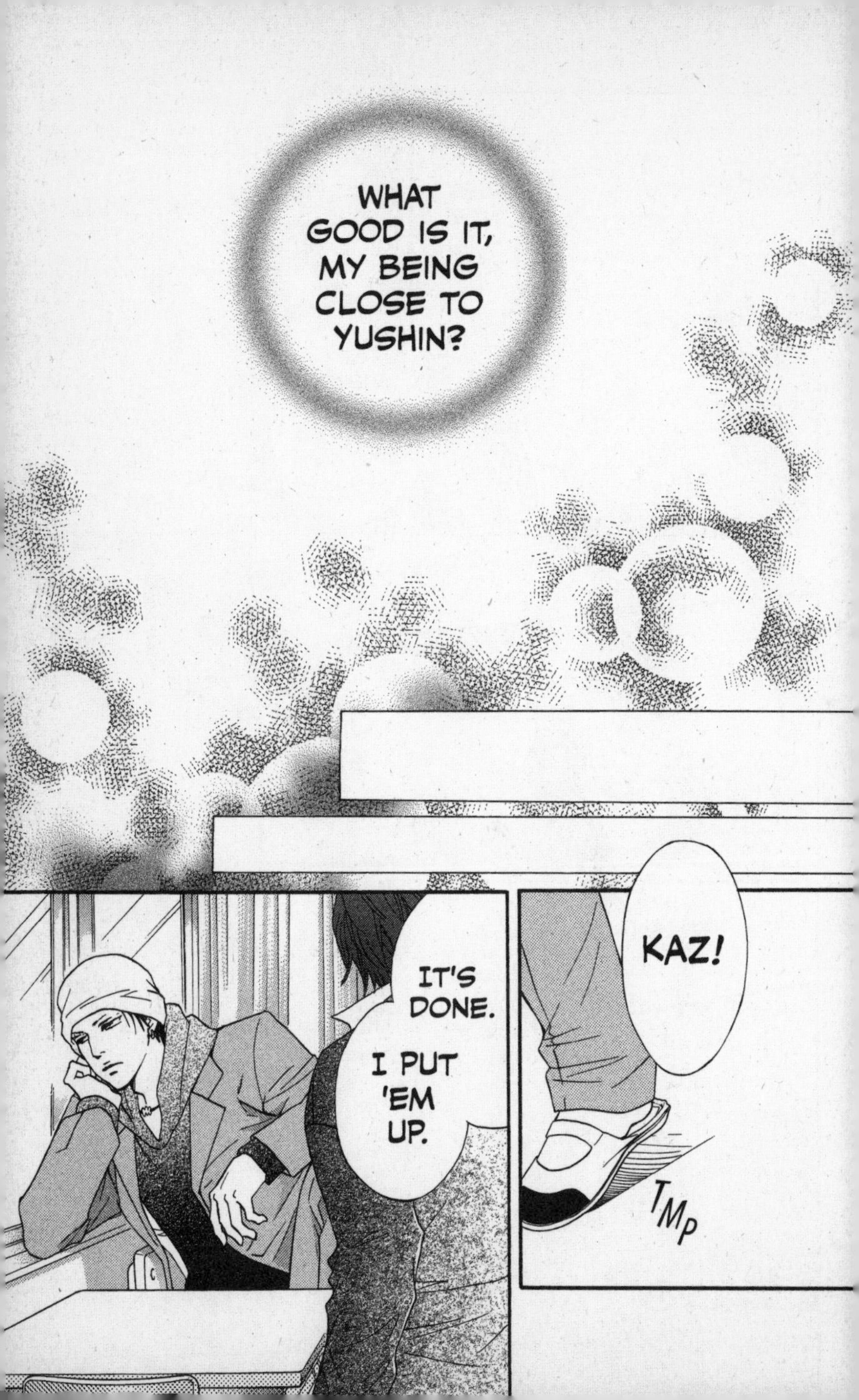
WHAT GOOD IS IT, MY BEING CLOSE TO YUSHIN?
KAZ!
TMP
IT'S DONE.
I PUT 'EM UP.

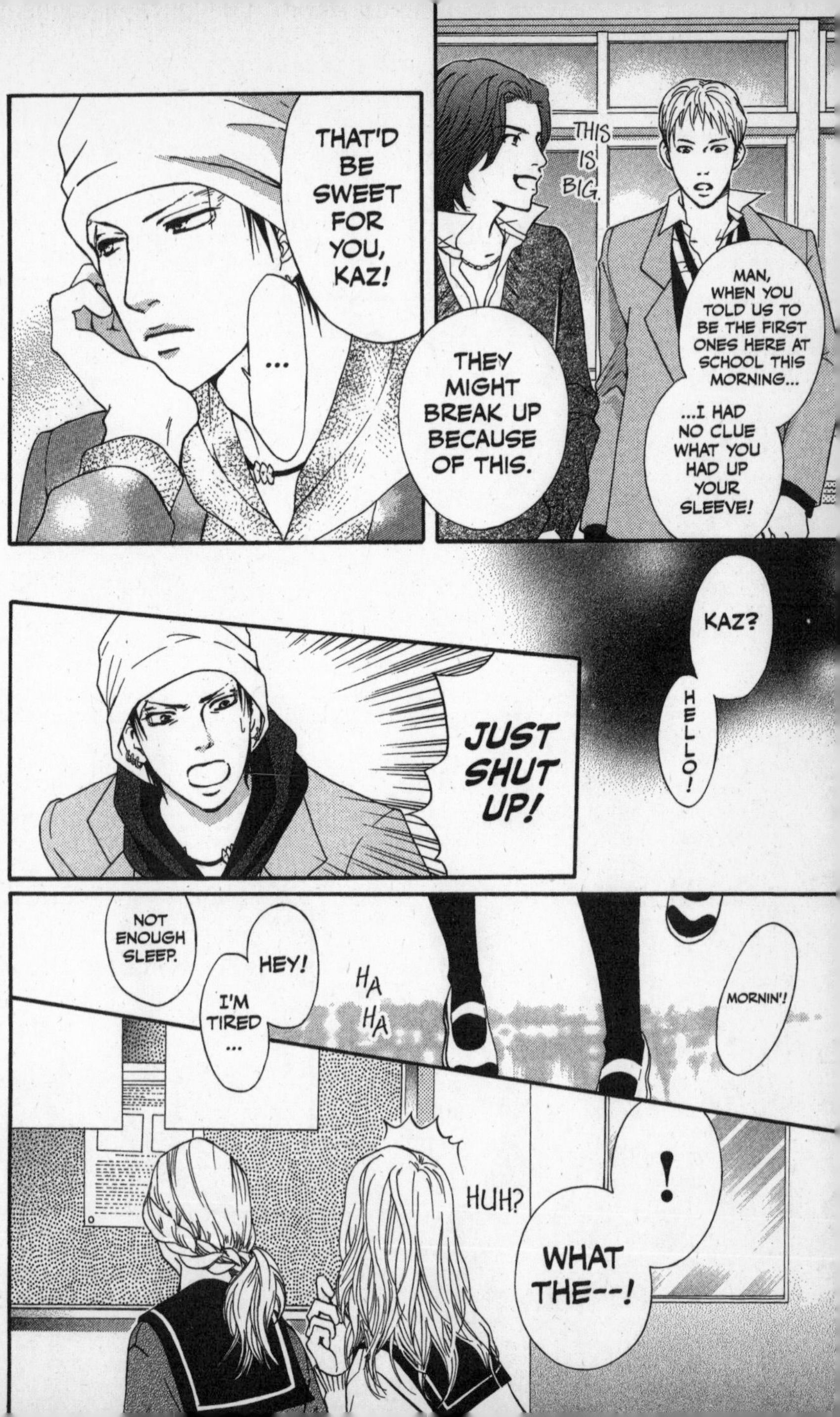
THIS IS BIG.
MAN, WHEN YOU TOLD US TO BE THE FIRST ONES HERE AT SCHOOL THIS MORNING...
...I HAD NO CLUE WHAT YOU HAD UP YOUR SLEEVE!
THEY MIGHT BREAK UP BECAUSE OF THIS.
THAT'D BE SWEET FOR YOU, KAZ!
...
KAZ?
HELLO!
JUST SHUT UP!
MORNIN'!
HA HA
HEY!
I'M TIRED...
NOT ENOUGH SLEEP.
!
WHAT THE--!
HUH?

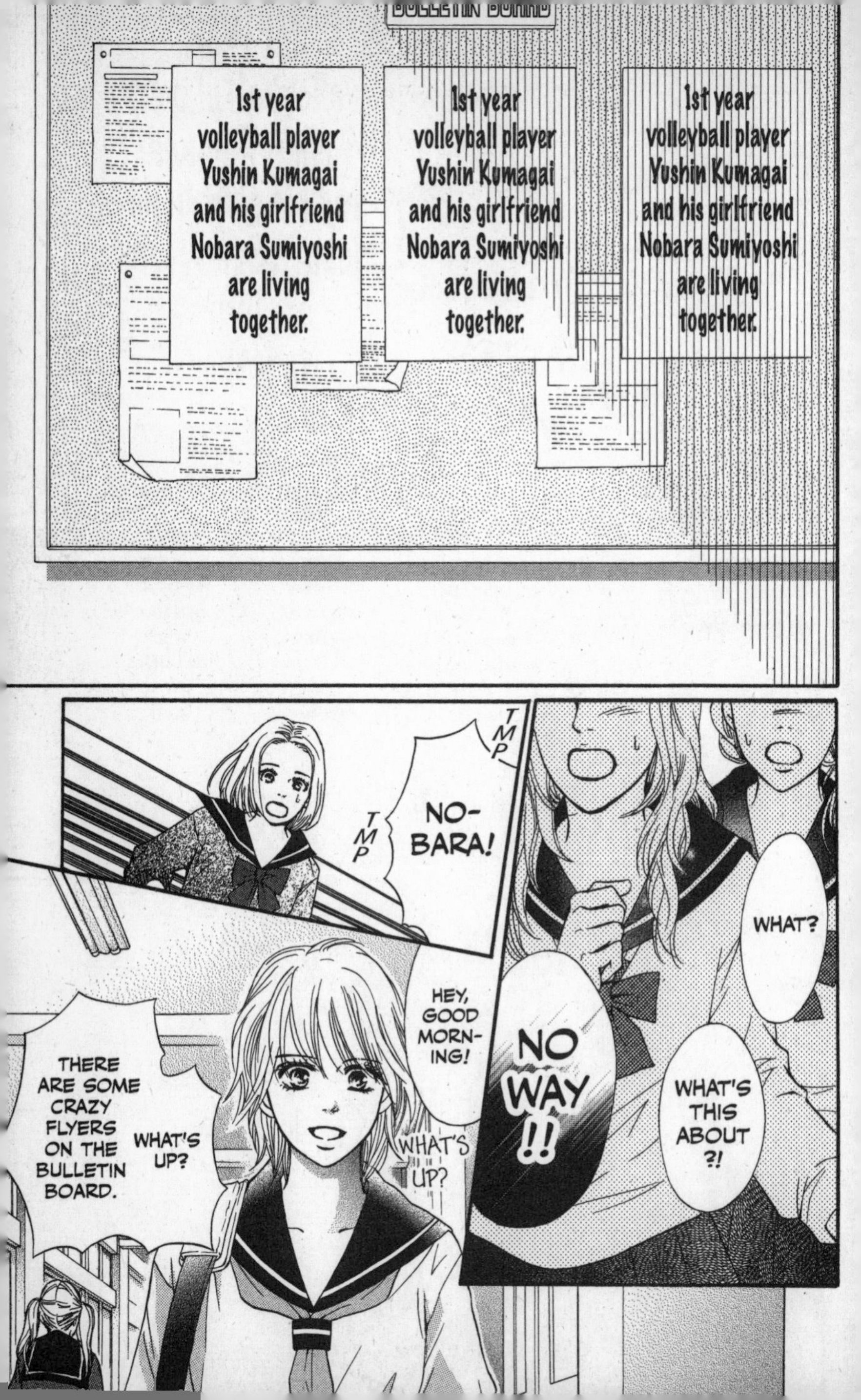
1st year volleyball player Yushin Kumagai and his girlfriend Nobara Sumiyoshi are living together.
1st year volleyball player Yushin Kumagai and his girlfriend Nobara Sumiyoshi are living together.
1st year volleyball player Yushin Kumagai and his girlfriend Nobara Sumiyoshi are living together.
WHAT?
WHAT'S THIS ABOUT ?!
NO WAY !!
TMP
TMP
NO-BARA!
HEY, GOOD MORNING!
WHAT'S UP?
WHAT'S UP?
THERE ARE SOME CRAZY FLYERS ON THE BULLETIN BOARD.

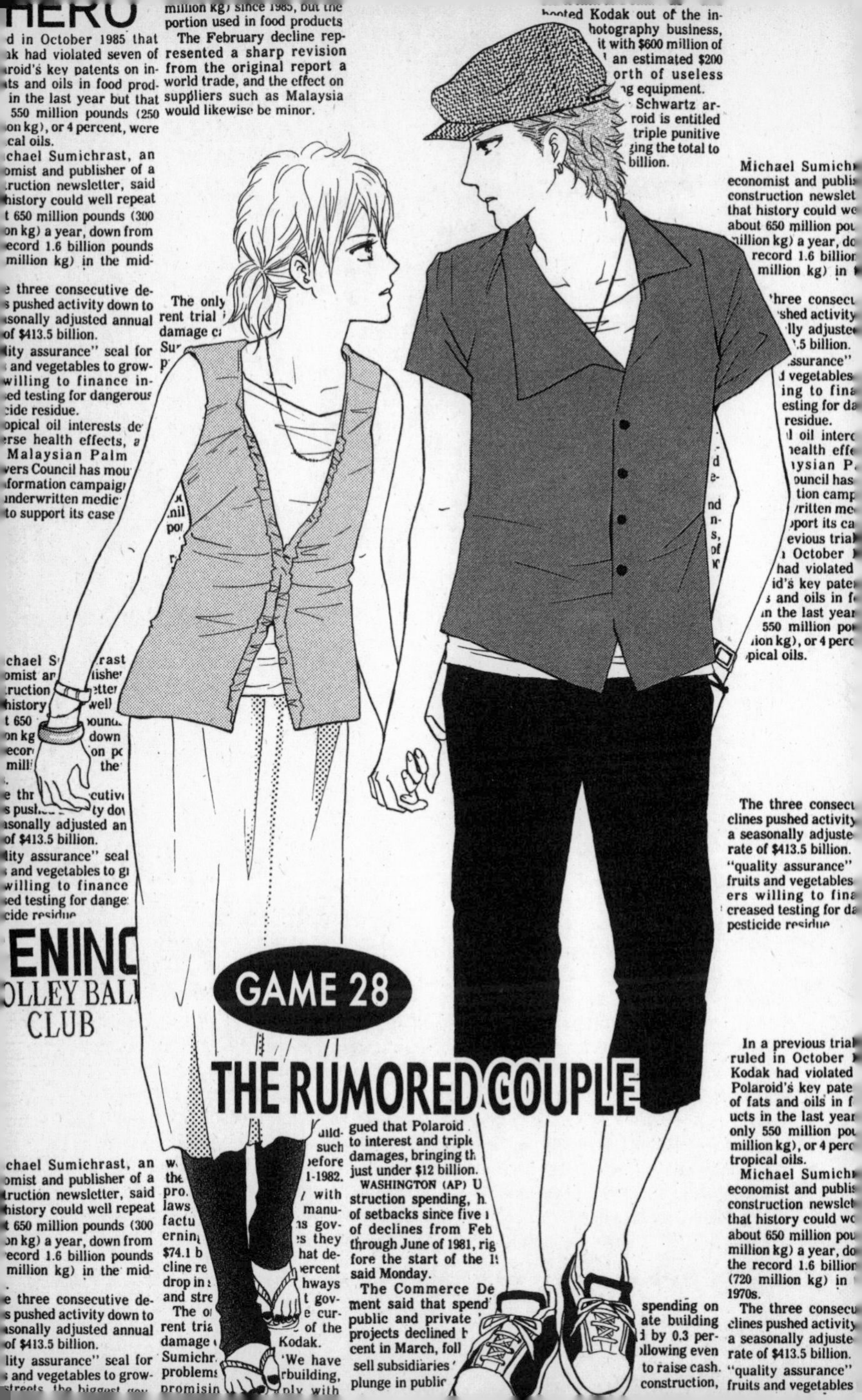
GAME 28
THE RUMORED COUPLE
ENING
OLLEY BAL
CLUB

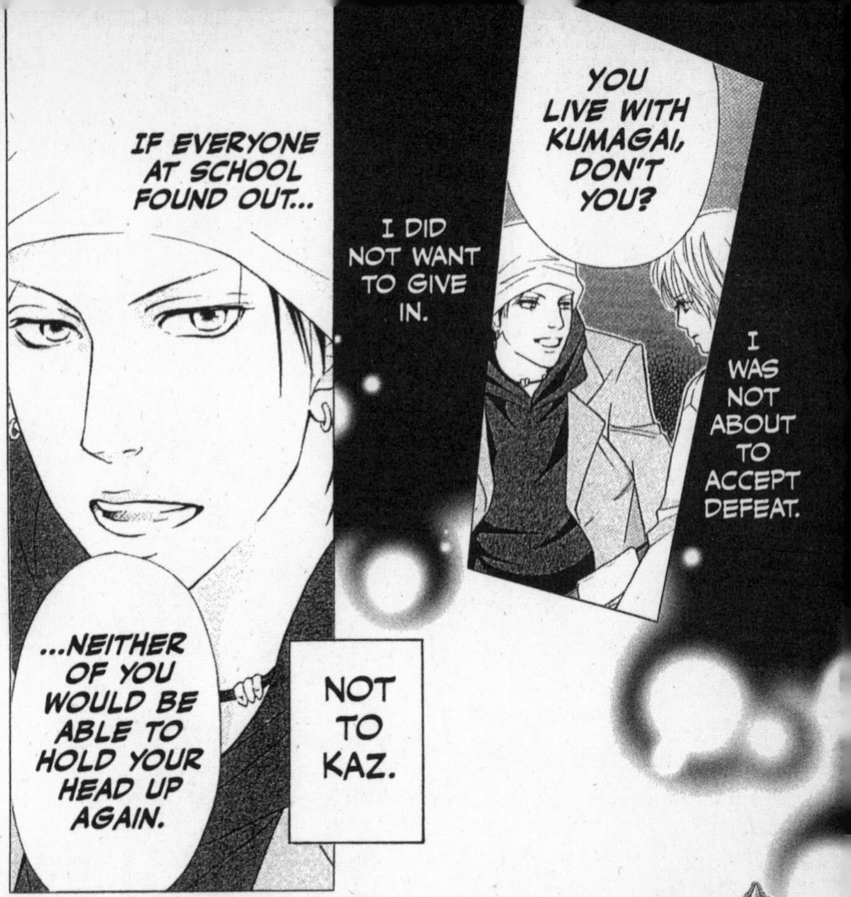
YOU LIVE WITH KUMAGAI, DON'T YOU?
I WAS NOT ABOUT TO ACCEPT DEFEAT.
I DID NOT WANT TO GIVE IN.
IF EVERYONE AT SCHOOL FOUND OUT...
...NEITHER OF YOU WOULD BE ABLE TO HOLD YOUR HEAD UP AGAIN.
NOT TO KAZ.

THE MAKING OF Crimson Hero

"KAZ."

MOST OF YOU READERS PROBABLY DETEST KAZ. AS I KEEP DRAWING HIM, I'VE ACTUALLY DEVELOPED A LIKING FOR HIM. I KNOW HE'S HOPELESS AND AWKWARD. I KNOW SOMEONE WHO WAS HOPELESS, AND THAT PERSON IS TRYING TO CHANGE, BUT IT'S NOT EASY TO CHANGE YOUR CORE. MAYBE THAT'S TOO PESSIMISTIC. I MEAN, THIS IS MANGA. BUT I FEEL SOME FONDNESS TOWARD HIM. HMM...I'M JUST TALKING TO MYSELF. MAYBE I STILL HAVEN'T FOUND WITHIN MYSELF THE REASON I CREATED KAZ. I RATHER LIKE ANTAGONISTS. I THINK ACTORS THAT PLAY THE BAD GUYS ARE SUPER VALUABLE. FOR ME,THE KING OF ACTORS WHO PLAY BAD GUYS IS KAZUKI KITAMURA. HE'S BEEN ON SHOWS LIKE *JUYON SAI NO HAHA* (14-YEAR-OLD MOTHER). OH, THE WAY HE LAUGHS!! WHENEVER HE APPEARS I FEEL LIKE SOMETHING BAD'S GOING TO HAPPEN AND I GET SCARED. I THINK HE'S AN AMAZING ACTOR. ON ANOTHER NOTE, I REALLY ENJOYED THE NOVEL I READ RECENTLY—*AKUNIN* (BAD PERSON) BY SHUICHI YOSHIDA. I CRIED. AT THE END I FELT LIKE THE NOVEL WAS ASKING, WHO IS THE BAD PERSON, REALLY? IT WAS EASY TO READ—IF YOU'RE INTERESTED, PLEASE READ IT.

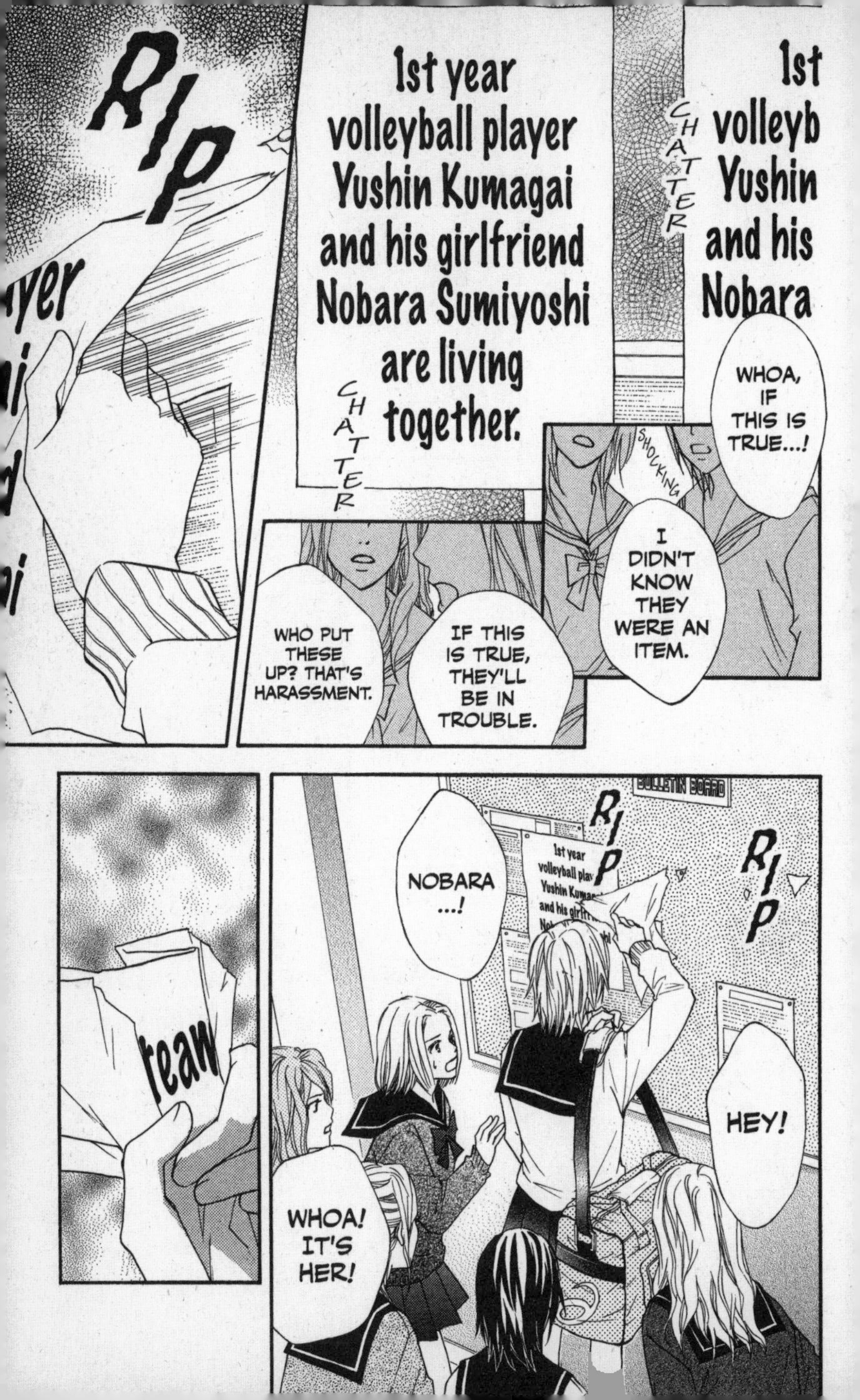
1st
volleyb
Yushin
and his
Nobara
CHATTER
WHOA, IF THIS IS TRUE...!
1st year
volleyball player
Yushin Kumagai
and his girlfriend
Nobara Sumiyoshi
are living
together.
CHATTER
SHOCKING
I DIDN'T KNOW THEY WERE AN ITEM.
IF THIS IS TRUE, THEY'LL BE IN TROUBLE.
WHO PUT THESE UP? THAT'S HARASSMENT.
RIP
BULLETIN BOARD
RIP
RIP
HEY!
NOBARA ...!
WHOA! IT'S HER!
team

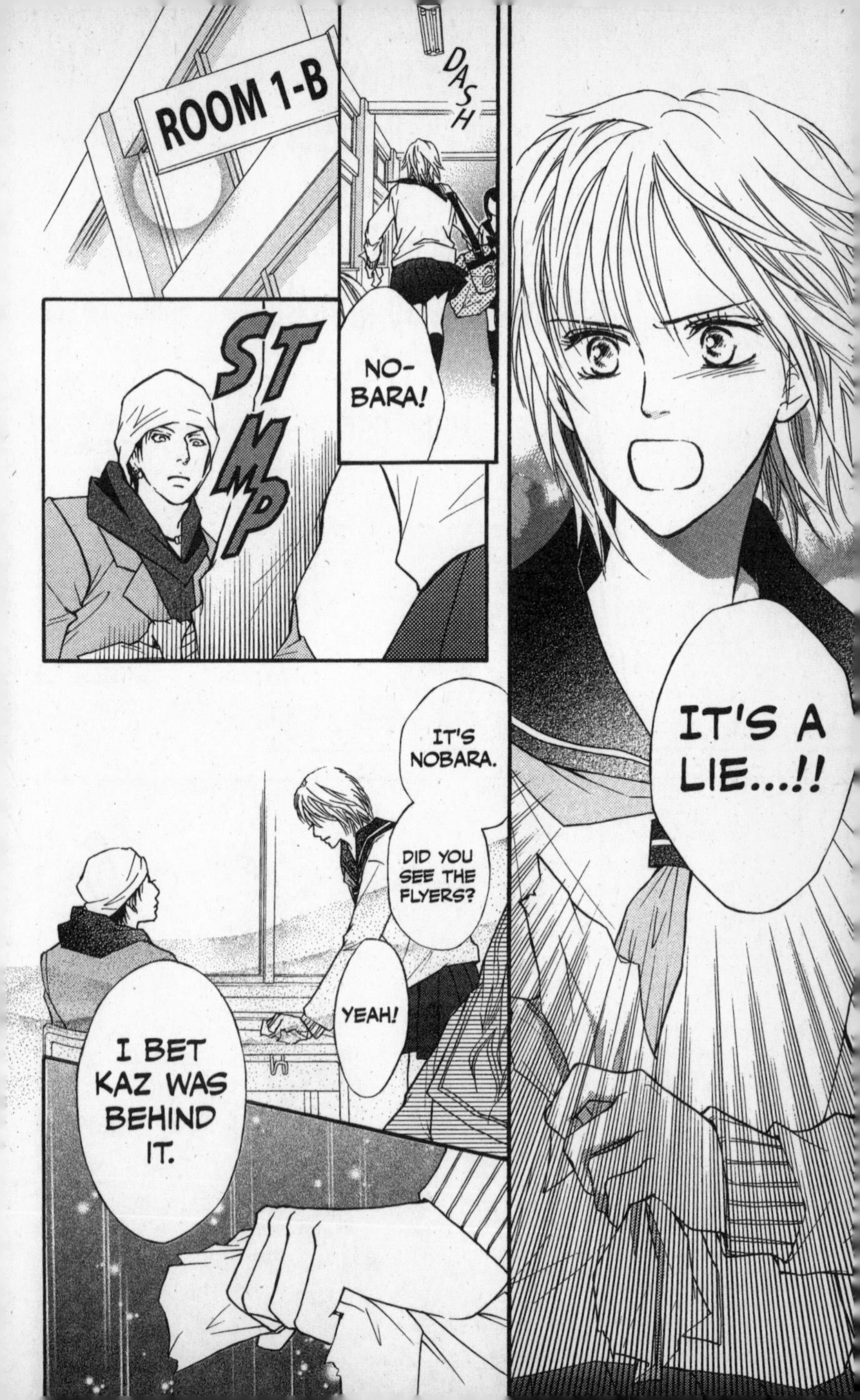
IT'S A LIE...!!
ROOM 1-B
DASH
NO-BARA!
STMP
IT'S NOBARA.
DID YOU SEE THE FLYERS?
YEAH!
I BET KAZ WAS BEHIND IT.

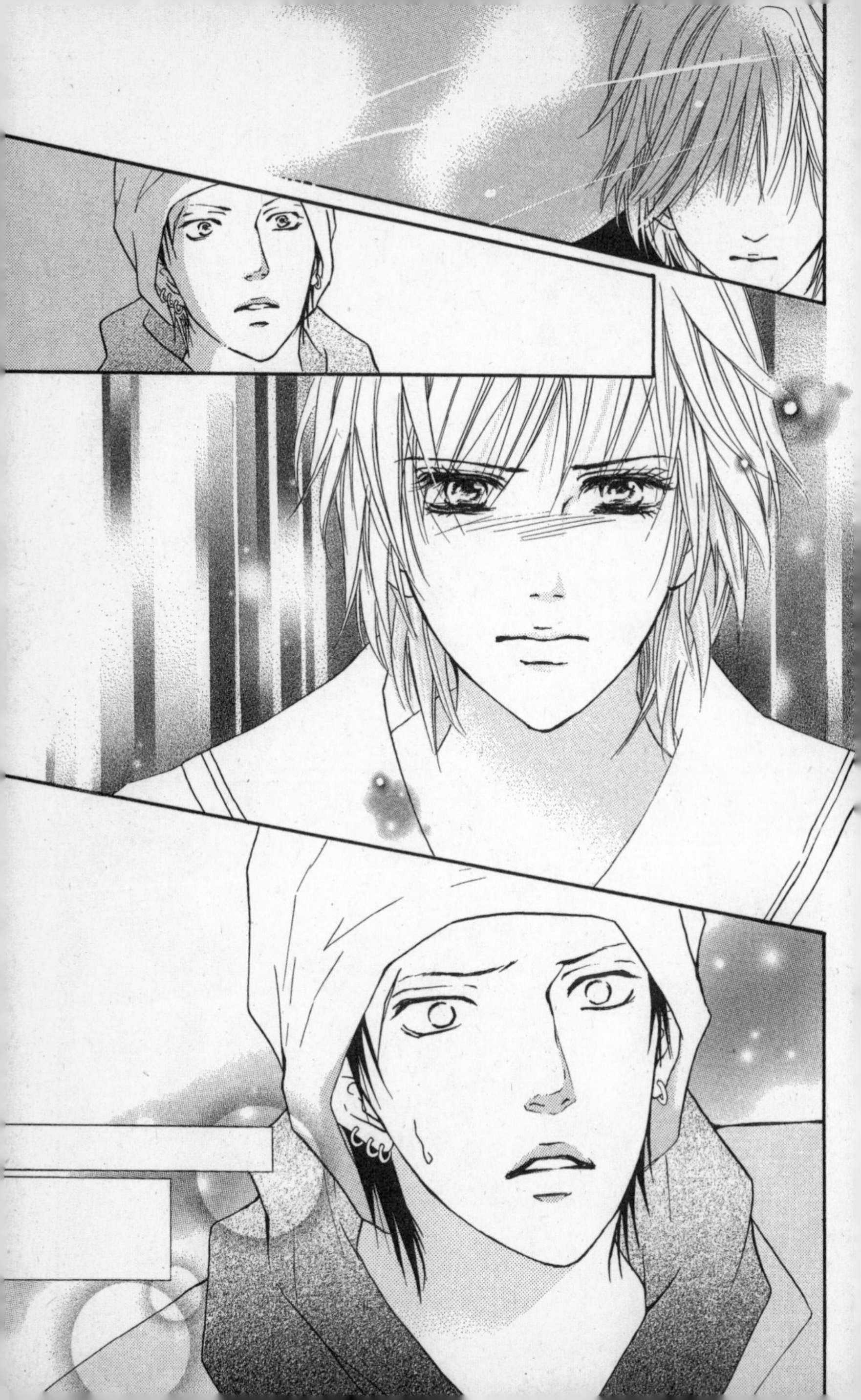

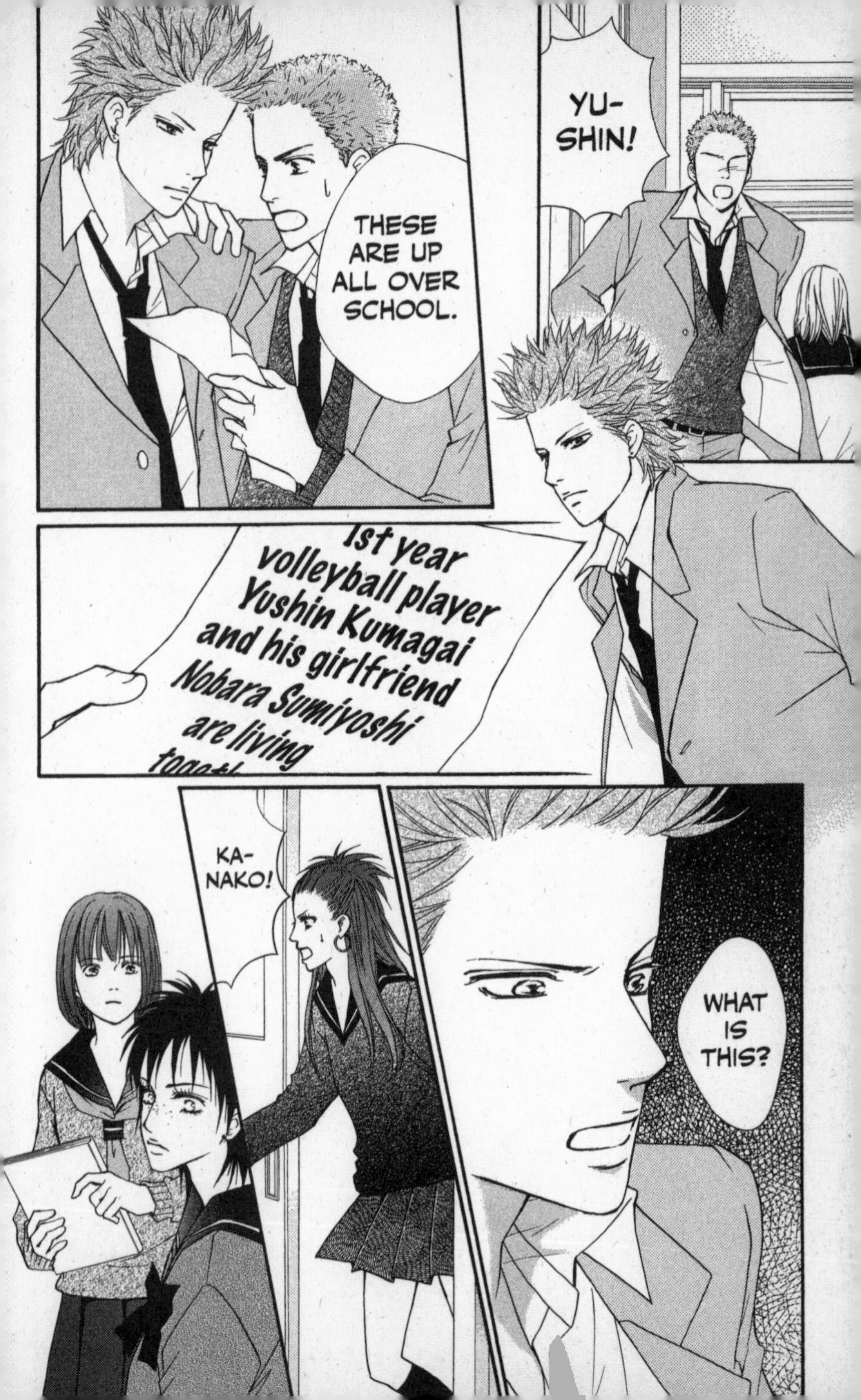
YU-SHIN!
THESE ARE UP ALL OVER SCHOOL.
1st year volleyball player Yushin Kumagai and his girlfriend Nobara Sumiyoshi are living
WHAT IS THIS?
KA-NAKO!

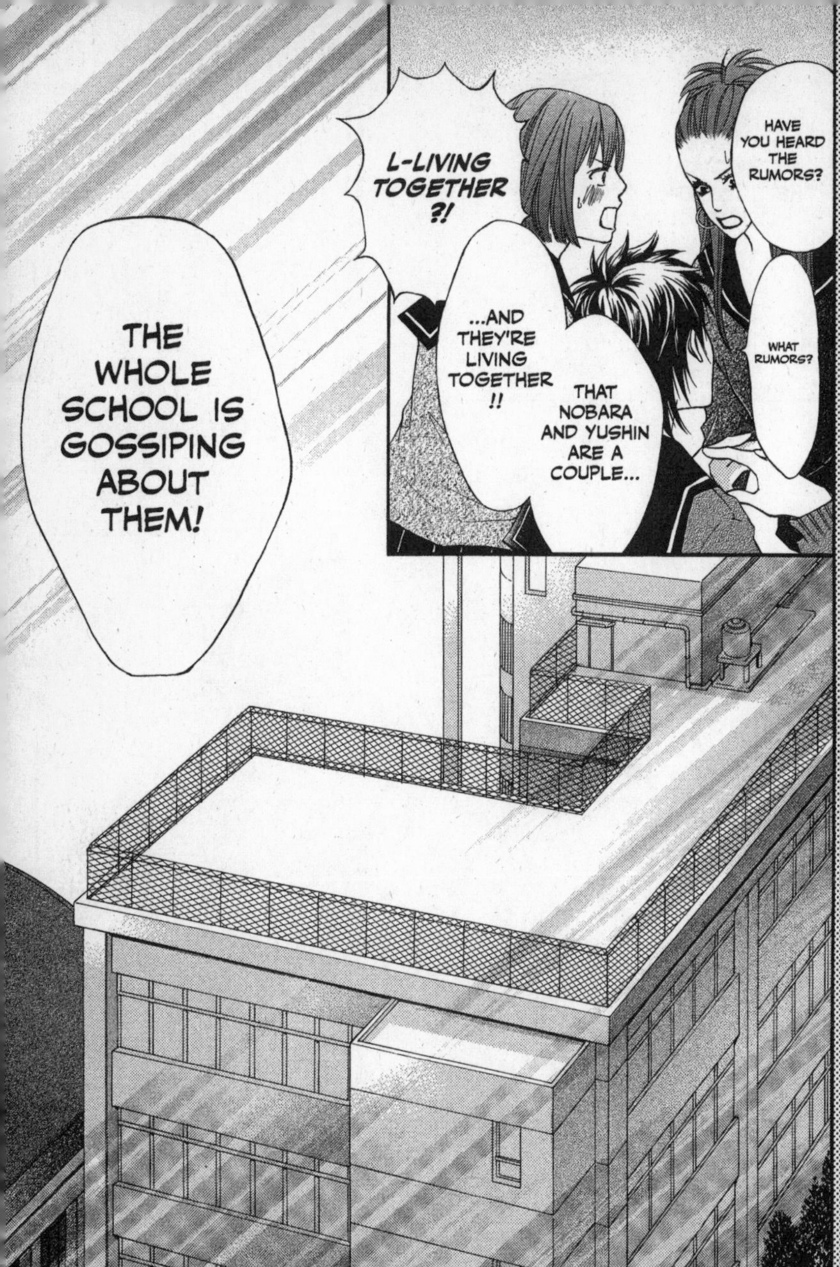
HAVE YOU HEARD THE RUMORS?
WHAT RUMORS?
THAT NOBARA AND YUSHIN ARE A COUPLE...
...AND THEY'RE LIVING TOGETHER!!
L-LIVING TOGETHER?!
THE WHOLE SCHOOL IS GOSSIPING ABOUT THEM!

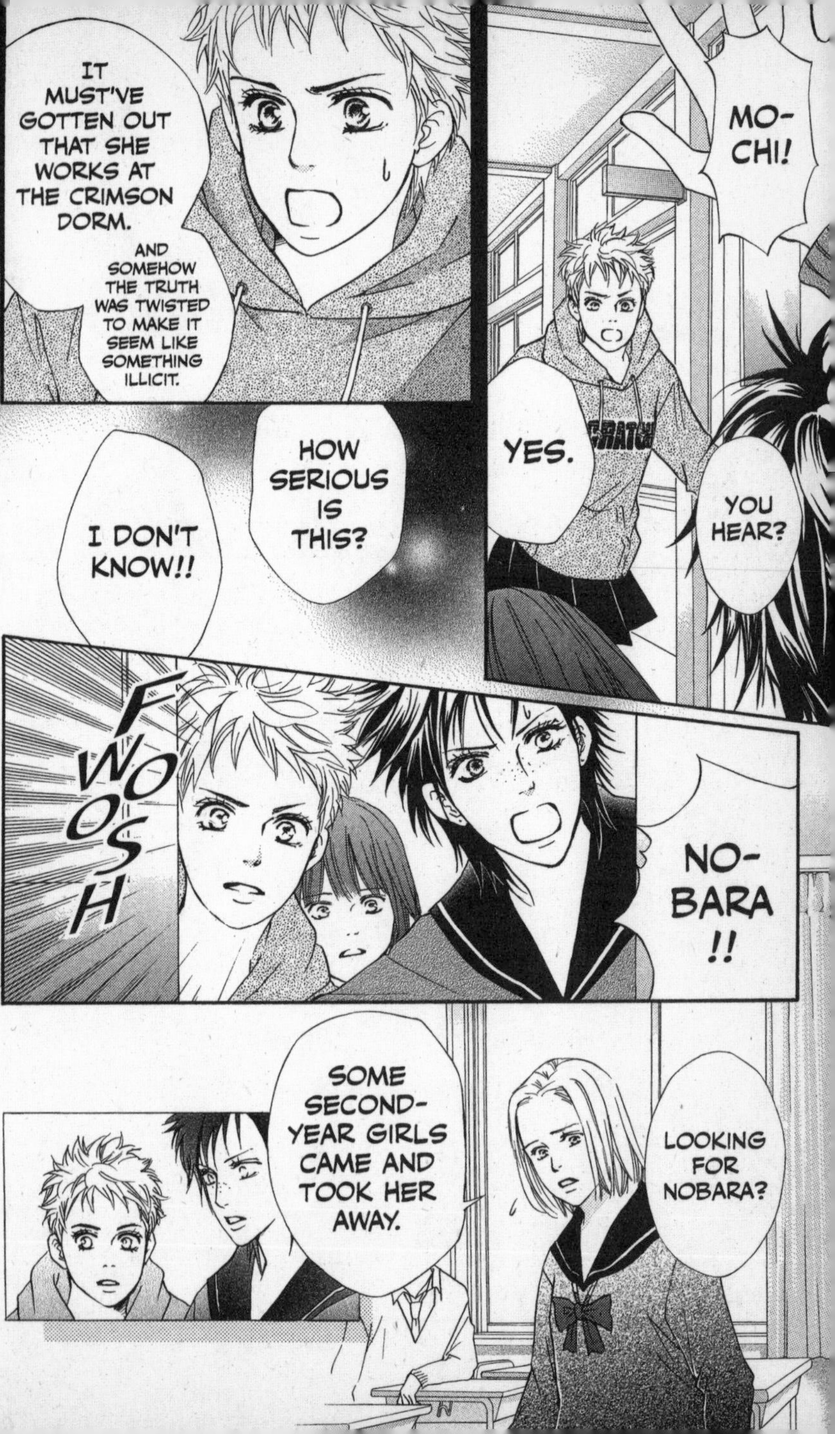
MO-CHI!
YOU HEAR?
YES.
IT MUST'VE GOTTEN OUT THAT SHE WORKS AT THE CRIMSON DORM.
AND SOMEHOW THE TRUTH WAS TWISTED TO MAKE IT SEEM LIKE SOMETHING ILLICIT.
HOW SERIOUS IS THIS?
I DON'T KNOW!!
NO-BARA!!
FWOOSH
LOOKING FOR NOBARA?
SOME SECOND-YEAR GIRLS CAME AND TOOK HER AWAY.

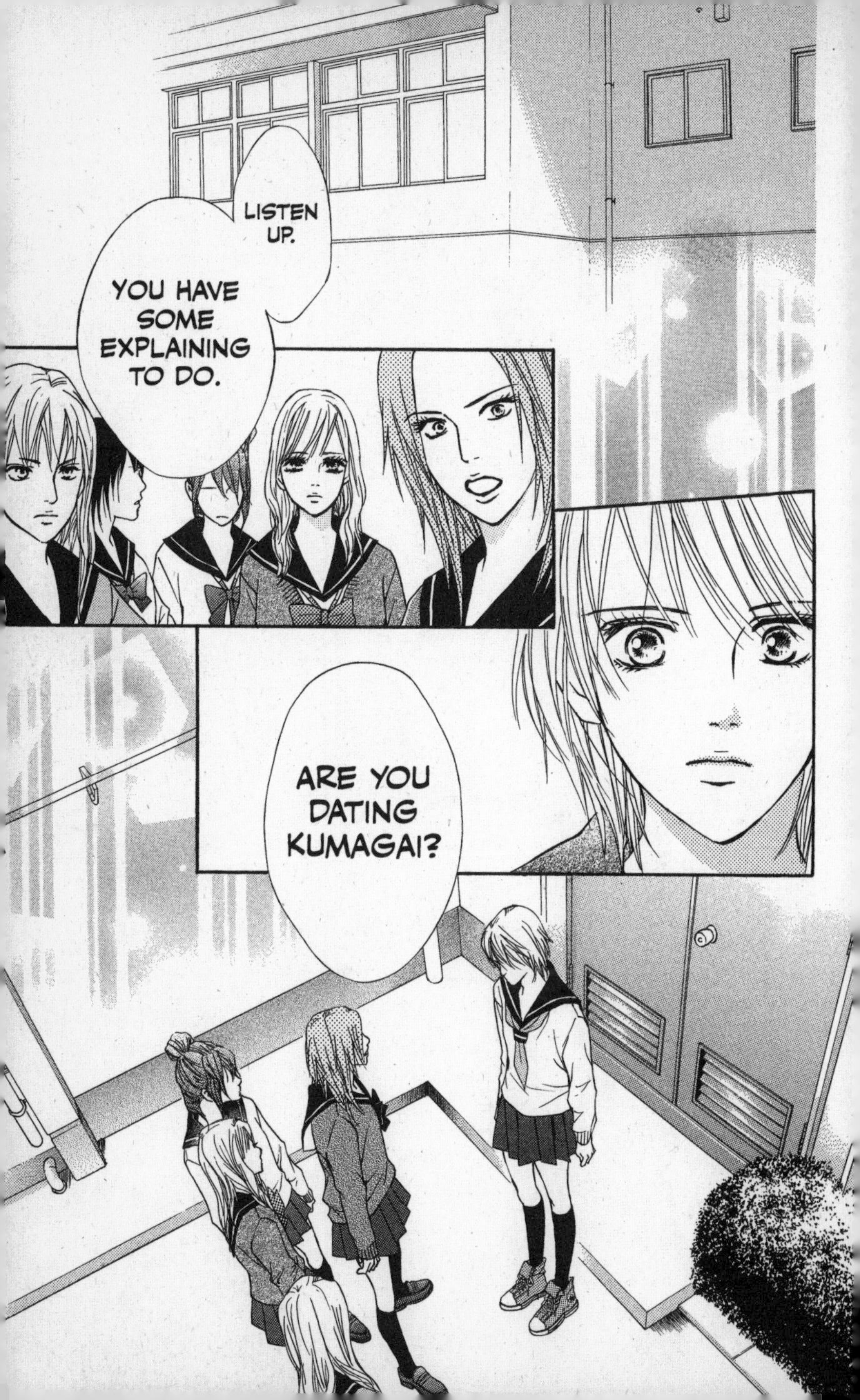
LISTEN UP.
YOU HAVE SOME EXPLAINING TO DO.
ARE YOU DATING KUMAGAI?

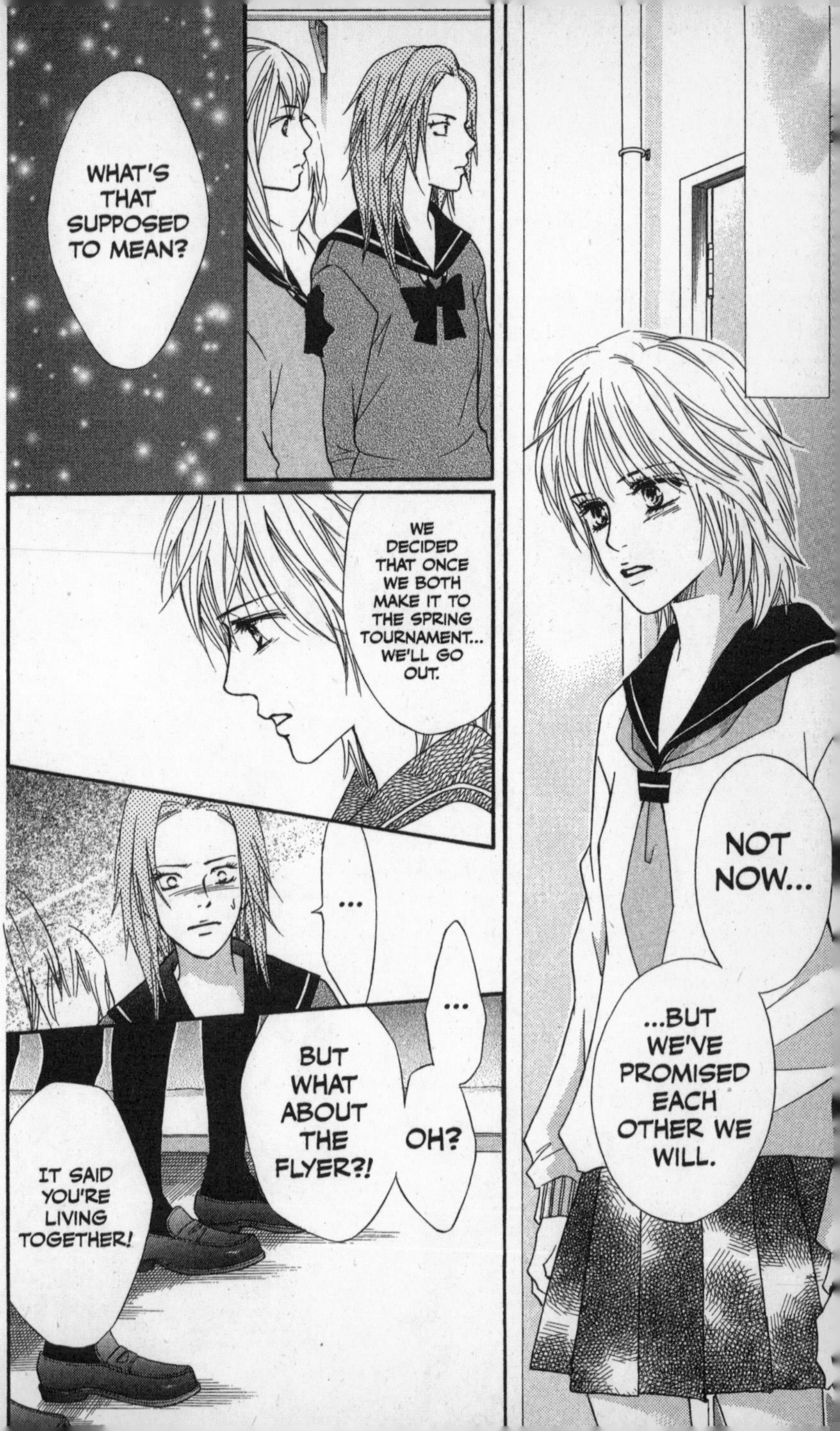
NOT NOW...
...BUT WE'VE PROMISED EACH OTHER WE WILL.
WHAT'S THAT SUPPOSED TO MEAN?
WE DECIDED THAT ONCE WE BOTH MAKE IT TO THE SPRING TOURNAMENT... WE'LL GO OUT.
...
...
OH?
BUT WHAT ABOUT THE FLYER?!
IT SAID YOU'RE LIVING TOGETHER!

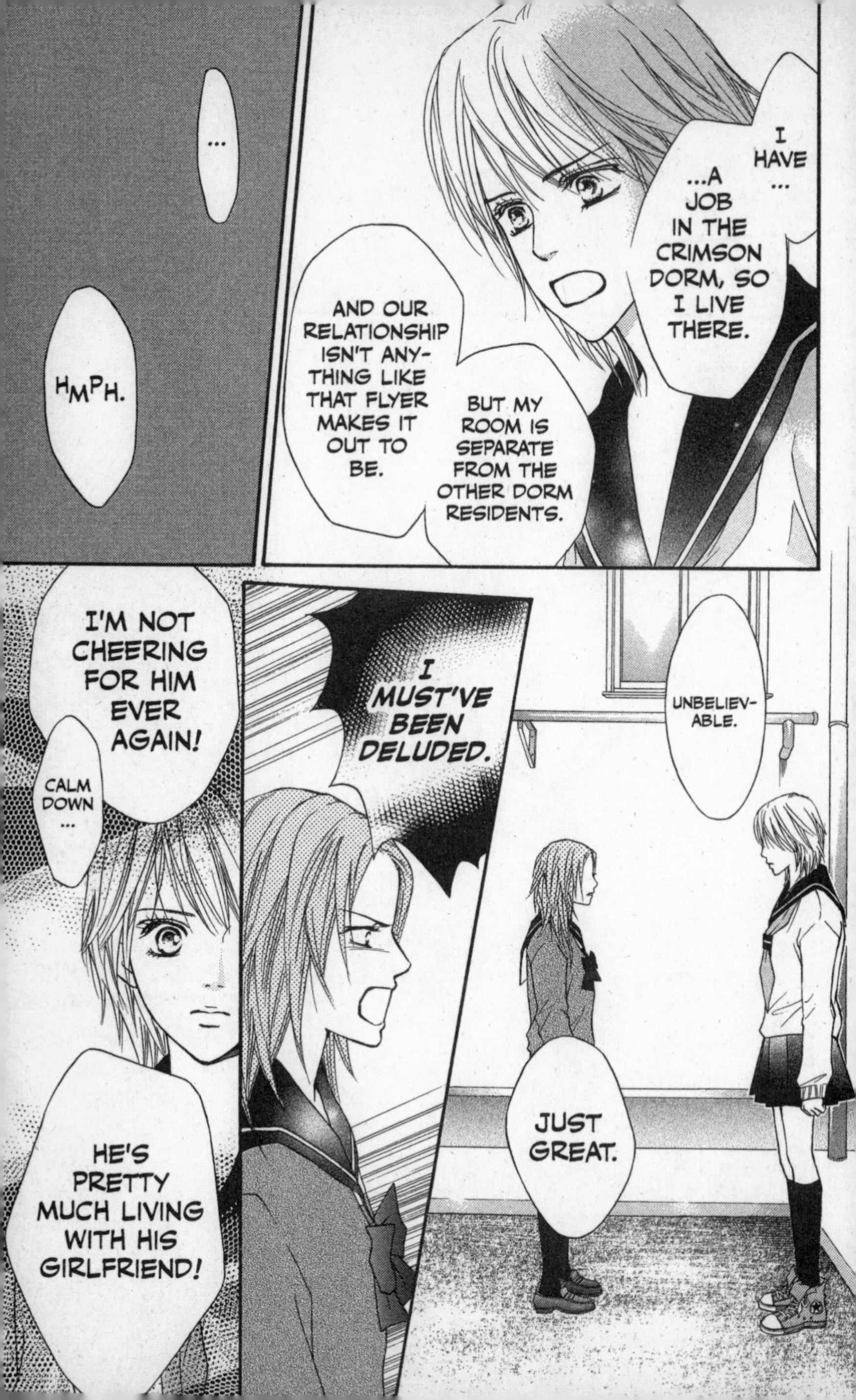
I HAVE ...
...A JOB IN THE CRIMSON DORM, SO I LIVE THERE.
BUT MY ROOM IS SEPARATE FROM THE OTHER DORM RESIDENTS.
AND OUR RELATIONSHIP ISN'T ANYTHING LIKE THAT FLYER MAKES IT OUT TO BE.
...
HMPH.
UNBELIEVABLE.
JUST GREAT.
I MUST'VE BEEN DELUDED.
I'M NOT CHEERING FOR HIM EVER AGAIN!
CALM DOWN ...
HE'S PRETTY MUCH LIVING WITH HIS GIRLFRIEND!

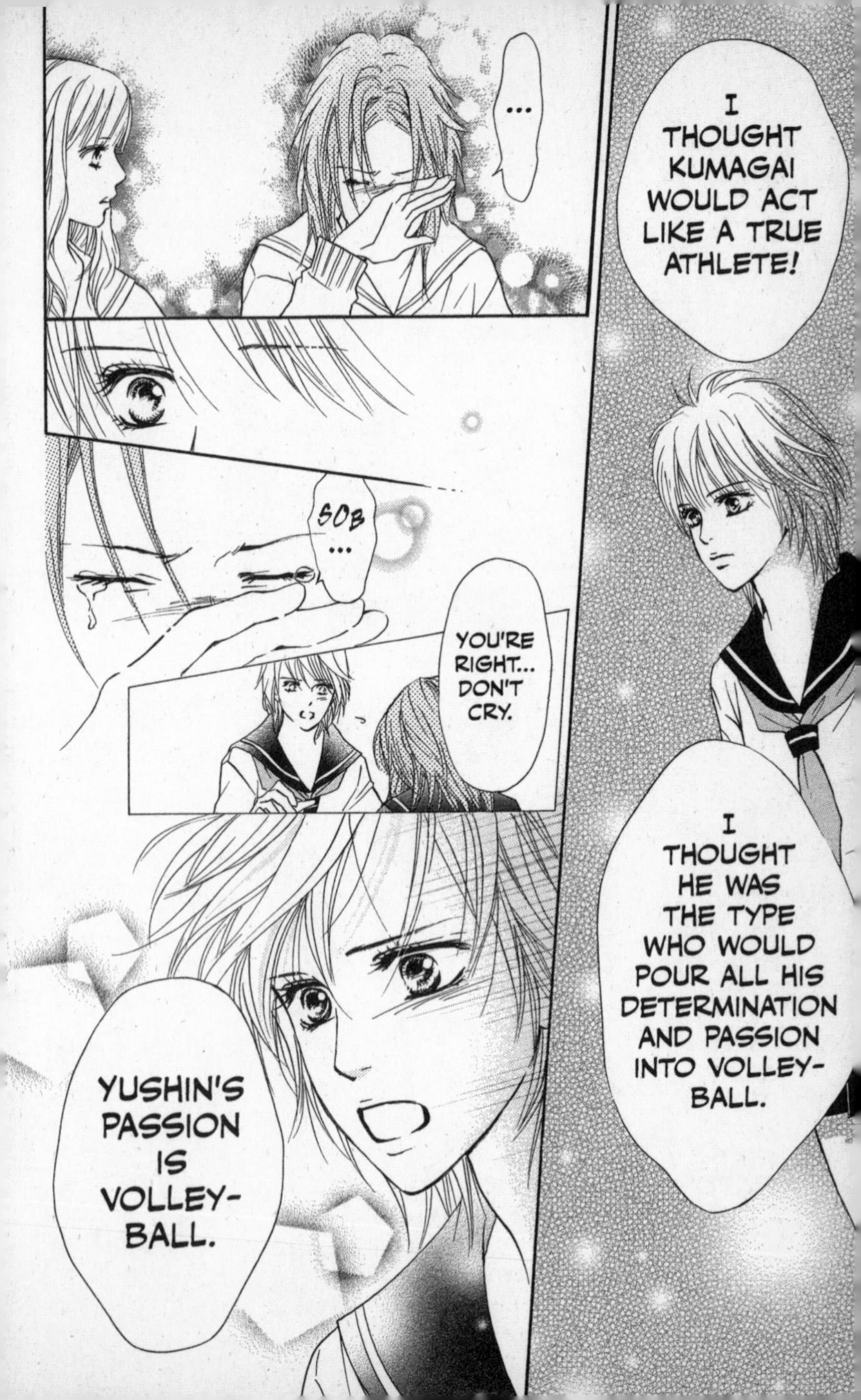
I THOUGHT KUMAGAI WOULD ACT LIKE A TRUE ATHLETE!
I THOUGHT HE WAS THE TYPE WHO WOULD POUR ALL HIS DETERMINATION AND PASSION INTO VOLLEY-BALL.
...
SOB...
YOU'RE RIGHT... DON'T CRY.
YUSHIN'S PASSION IS VOLLEY-BALL.

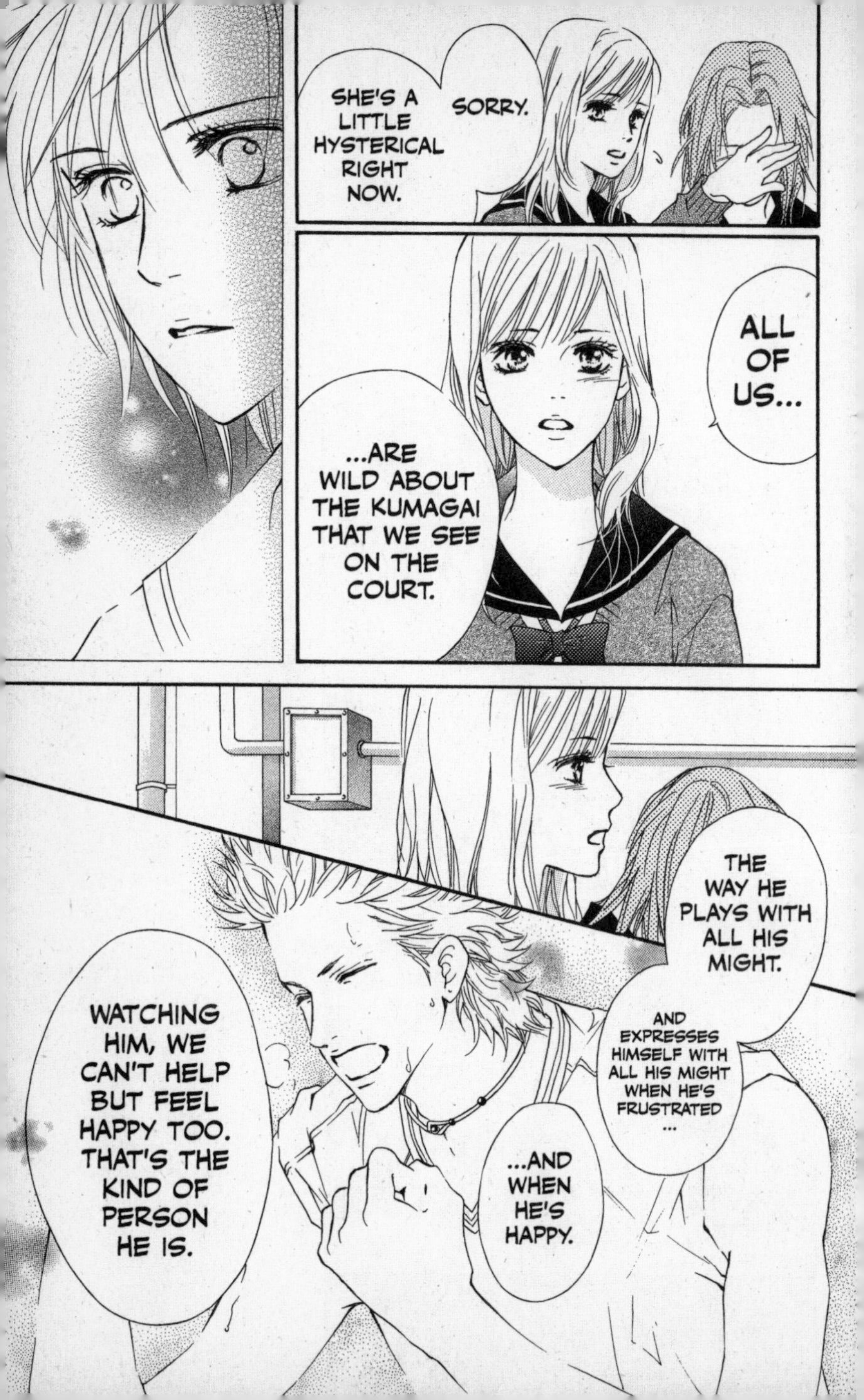
SORRY.
SHE'S A LITTLE HYSTERICAL RIGHT NOW.
ALL OF US...
...ARE WILD ABOUT THE KUMAGAI THAT WE SEE ON THE COURT.
THE WAY HE PLAYS WITH ALL HIS MIGHT.
AND EXPRESSES HIMSELF WITH ALL HIS MIGHT WHEN HE'S FRUSTRATED...
...AND WHEN HE'S HAPPY.
WATCHING HIM, WE CAN'T HELP BUT FEEL HAPPY TOO. THAT'S THE KIND OF PERSON HE IS.

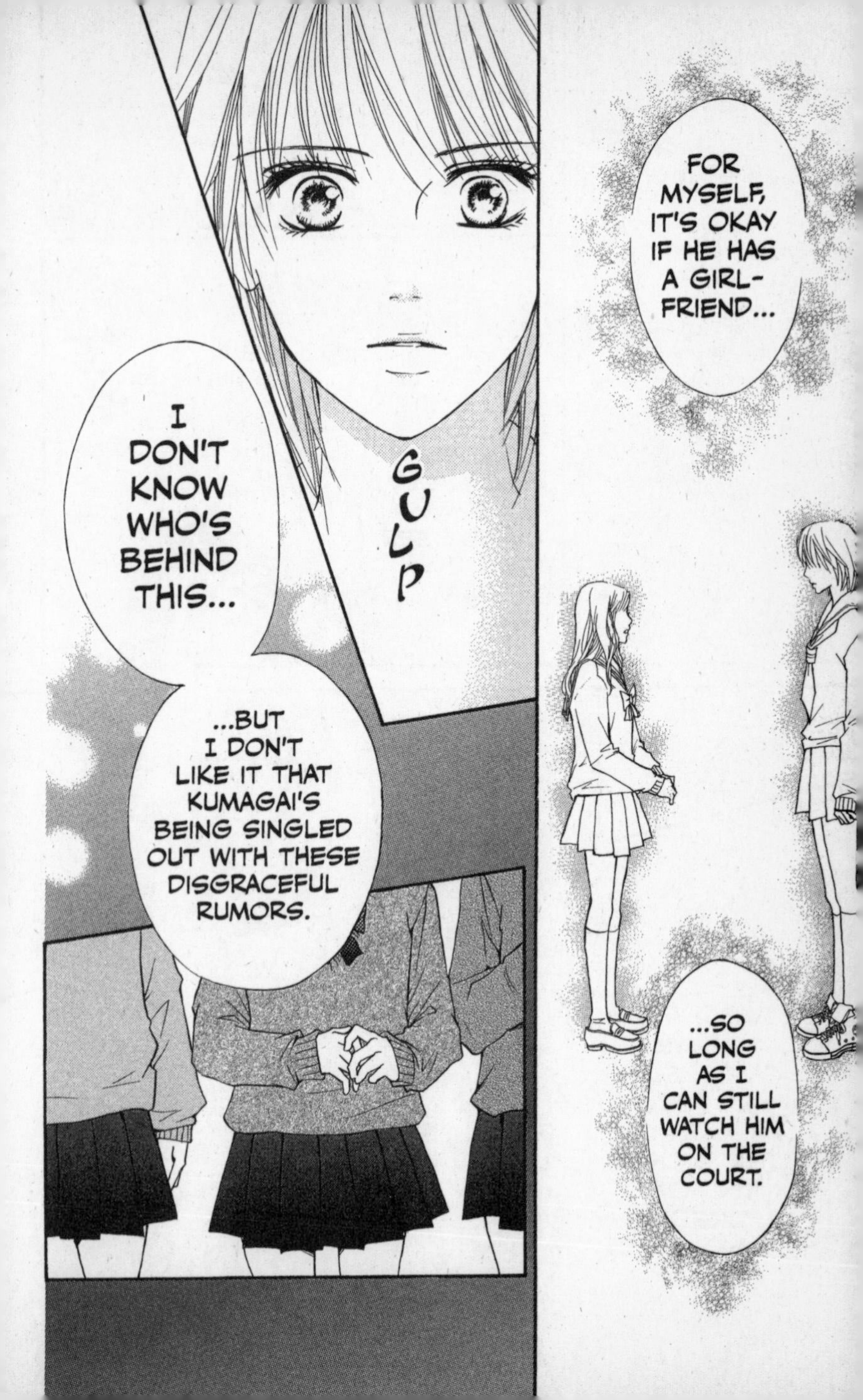
FOR MYSELF, IT'S OKAY IF HE HAS A GIRL-FRIEND...
...SO LONG AS I CAN STILL WATCH HIM ON THE COURT.
GULP
I DON'T KNOW WHO'S BEHIND THIS...
...BUT I DON'T LIKE IT THAT KUMAGAI'S BEING SINGLED OUT WITH THESE DISGRACEFUL RUMORS.

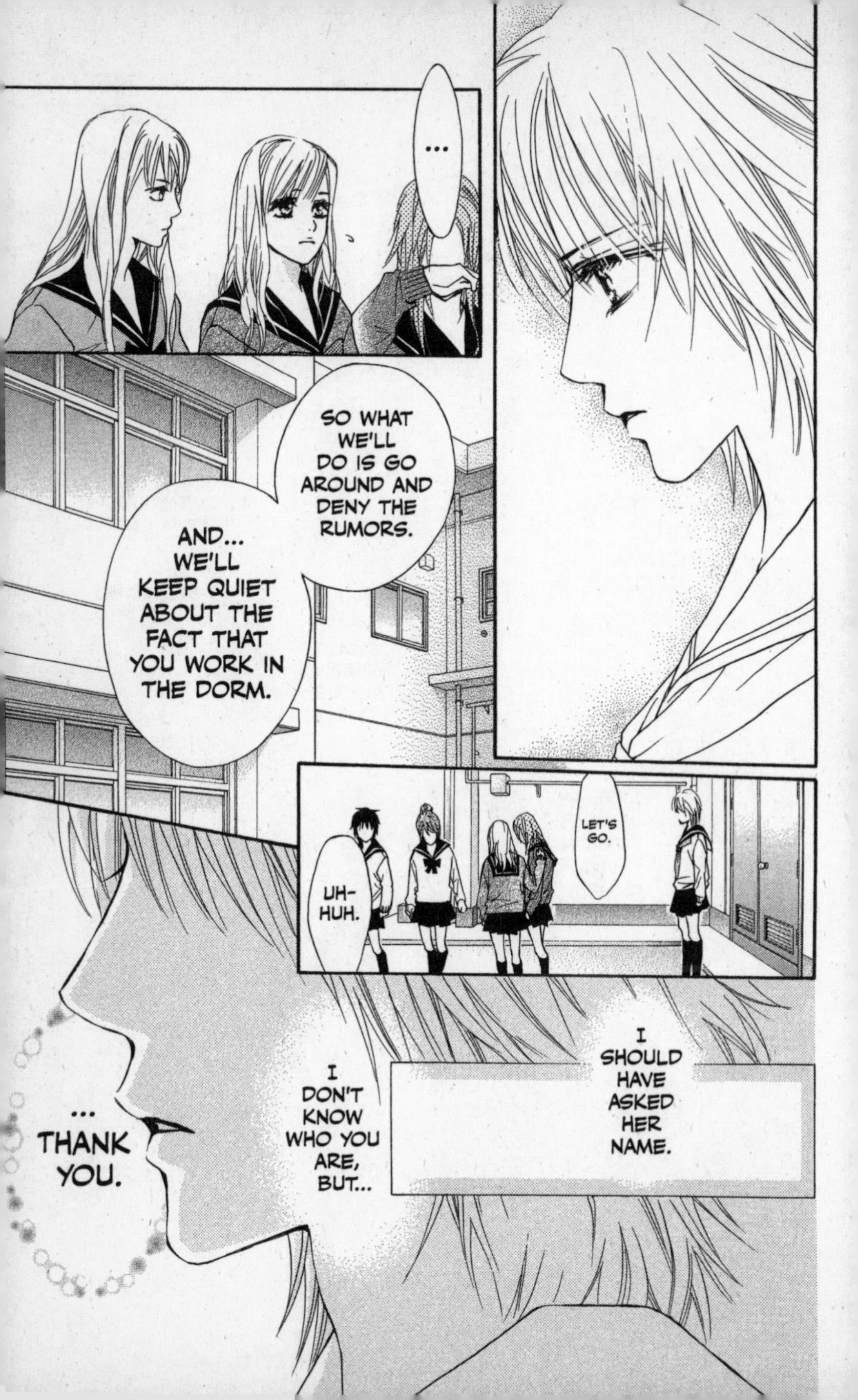
...
SO WHAT WE'LL DO IS GO AROUND AND DENY THE RUMORS.
AND... WE'LL KEEP QUIET ABOUT THE FACT THAT YOU WORK IN THE DORM.
LET'S GO.
UH-HUH.
I SHOULD HAVE ASKED HER NAME.
I DON'T KNOW WHO YOU ARE, BUT...
...THANK YOU.

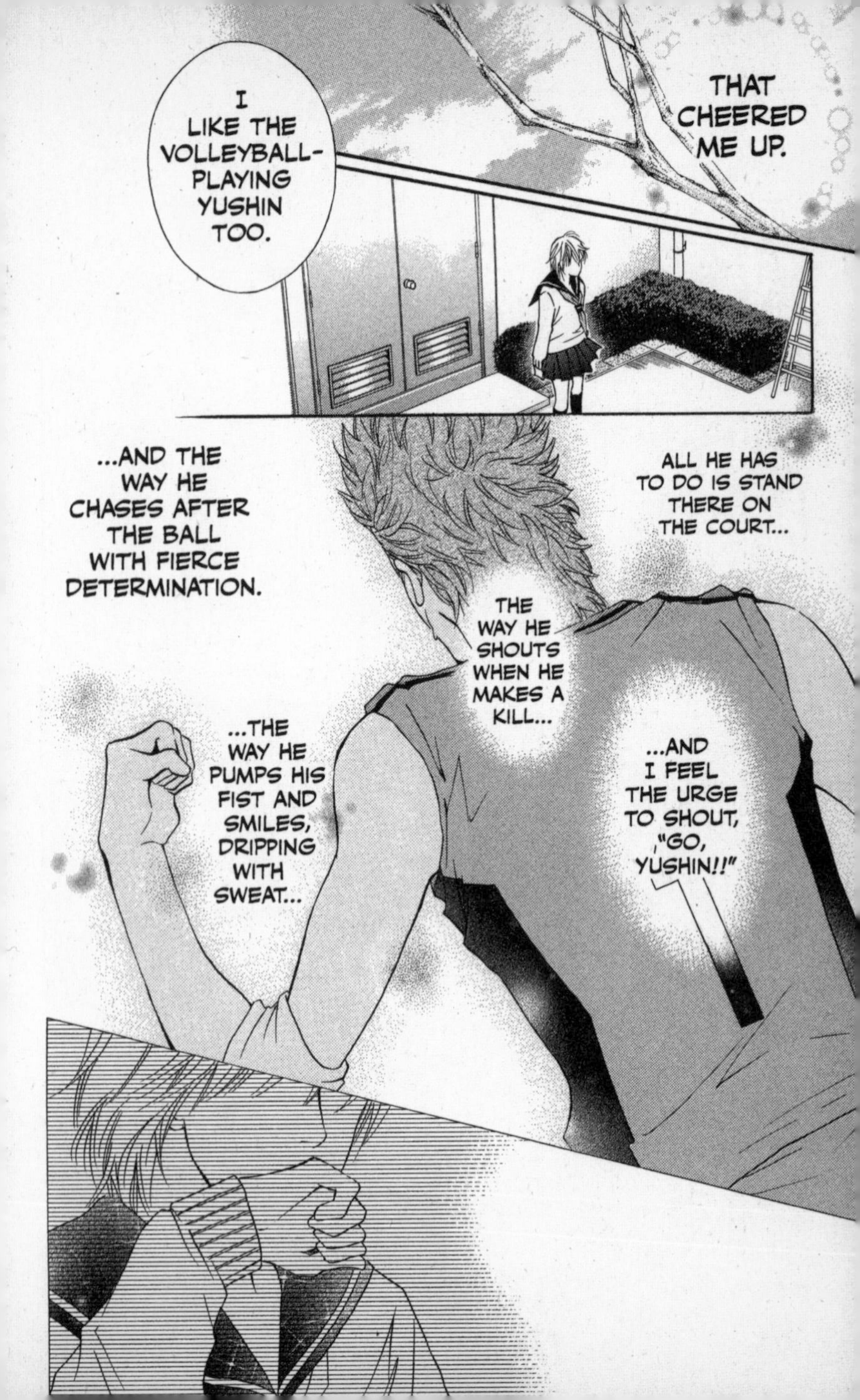
THAT CHEERED ME UP.
I LIKE THE VOLLEYBALL-PLAYING YUSHIN TOO.
ALL HE HAS TO DO IS STAND THERE ON THE COURT...
...AND I FEEL THE URGE TO SHOUT, "GO, YUSHIN!!"
THE WAY HE SHOUTS WHEN HE MAKES A KILL...
...THE WAY HE PUMPS HIS FIST AND SMILES, DRIPPING WITH SWEAT...
...AND THE WAY HE CHASES AFTER THE BALL WITH FIERCE DETERMINATION.

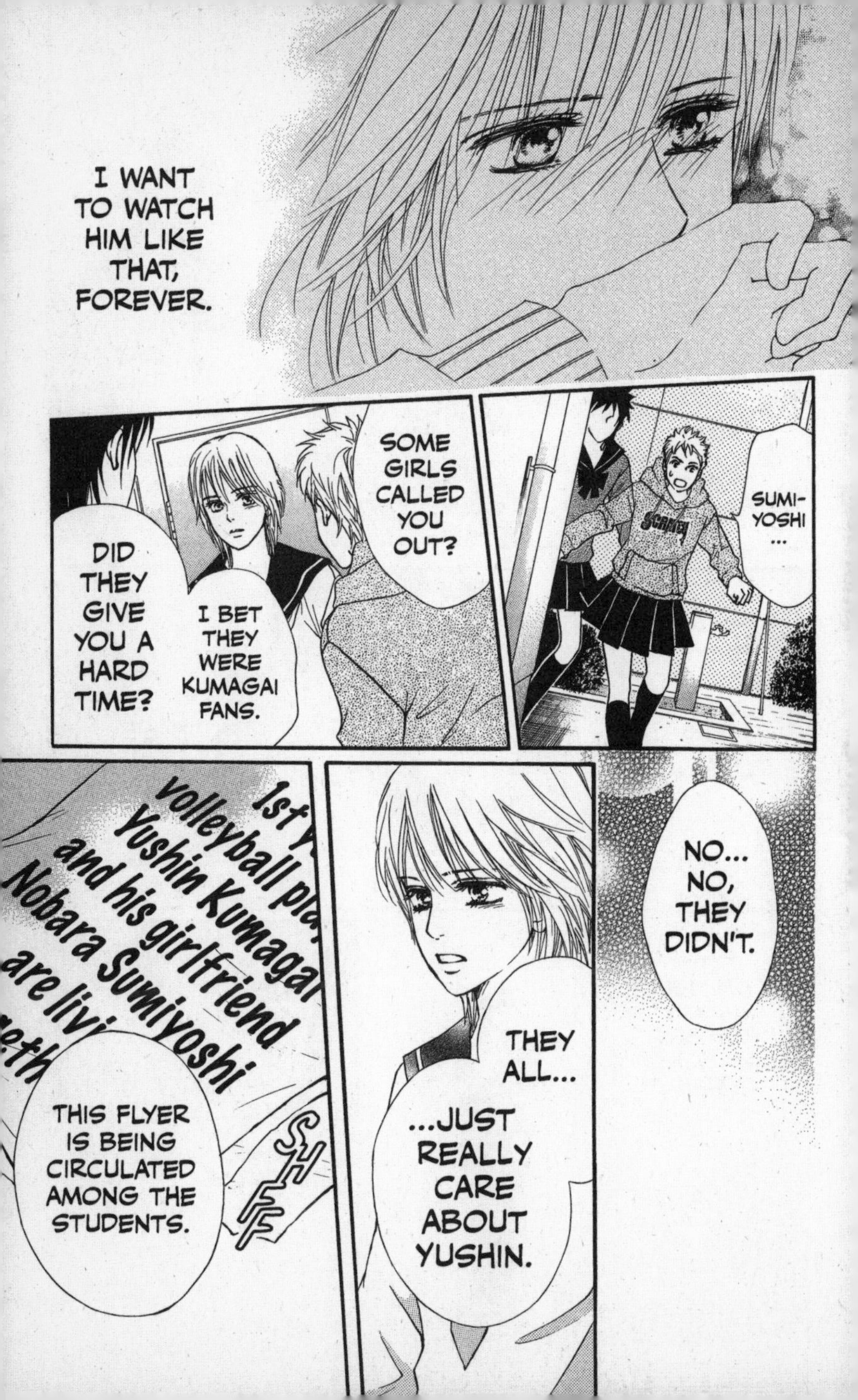
I WANT TO WATCH HIM LIKE THAT, FOREVER.
SUMI-YOSHI...
SOME GIRLS CALLED YOU OUT?
I BET THEY WERE KUMAGAI FANS.
DID THEY GIVE YOU A HARD TIME?
NO... NO, THEY DIDN'T.
THEY ALL...
...JUST REALLY CARE ABOUT YUSHIN.
Yushin Kumagai
and his girlfriend
Nobara Sumiyoshi
THIS FLYER IS BEING CIRCULATED AMONG THE STUDENTS.

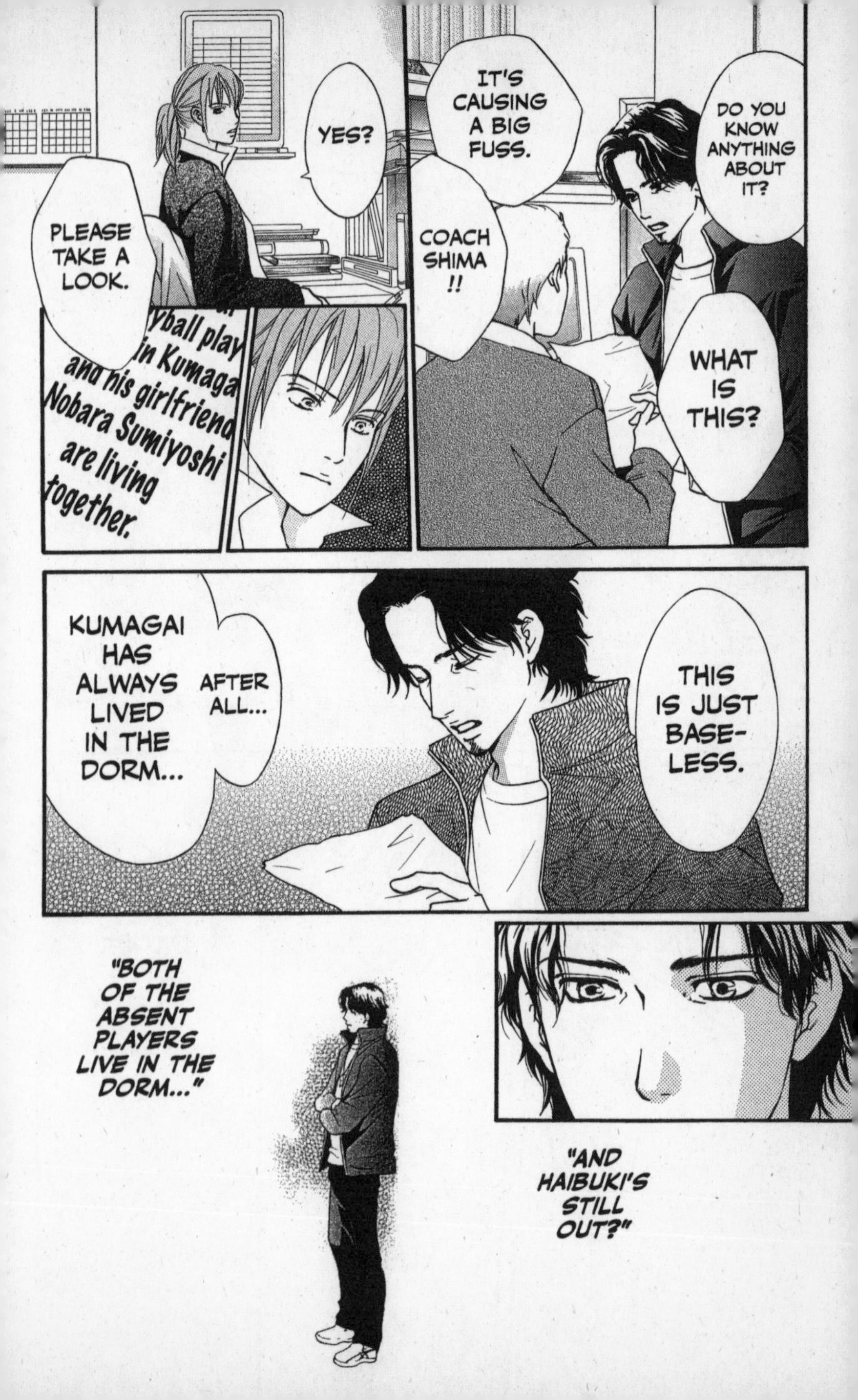
DO YOU KNOW ANYTHING ABOUT IT?
IT'S CAUSING A BIG FUSS.
COACH SHIMA !!
WHAT IS THIS?
YES?
PLEASE TAKE A LOOK.
yball play
in Kumaga
and his girlfriend
Nobara Sumiyoshi
are living
together.
THIS IS JUST BASE-LESS.
KUMAGAI HAS ALWAYS LIVED IN THE DORM... AFTER ALL...
"AND HAIBUKI'S STILL OUT?"
"BOTH OF THE ABSENT PLAYERS LIVE IN THE DORM..."

MITSUBA CLUB

"I'M SHAROTAN." VoL. 2

WE HAVE TWO CATS AT HOME, AND THEIR PERSONALITIES ARE SO DIFFERENT YOU WOULDN'T BELIEVE IT. SHARON OFTEN WATCHES ME FROM THE SHADOWS.

QUIET...

OUR OWN ETSUKO ICHIHARA?

WE CALL THIS SITUATION "SHAROTAN SAW IT." IF I SAY, "WHAT'S THE MATTER?" SHE CRIES "BIAAAAA," AND WHEN I GET CLOSER SHE'LL GO DOWN THE STAIRS AHEAD OF ME, LEADING ME TO THE LIVING ROOM. THAT'S WHERE THE FOOD IS, AND SINCE I SIT ON THE FLOOR I'M CLOSER TO HER LEVEL, AND I SUSPECT SHE THINKS I'LL PET HER.

BLEH

SHARON SEEMS TO LIKE HAVING HER BACK RUBBED. WHENEVER I RUB HER BACK IT MUST FEEL SO GOOD TO HER, CUZ HER TONGUE COMES OUT. IT'S NOT VERY LADYLIKE OF HER, BUT SHE STICKS HER TONGUE OUT AND GOES, "BLEH, BLEEEEH."

CHIRO THROWS HER CAT PUNCHES. CHIRO WAS HERE FIRST AND DOESN'T LIKE HER. BUT SHARON'S JUST LIKE...

I WON'T LOSE.

DON'T OVERDO THE EXERCISE.

I'M A LITTLE FAT AND IN THE WINTER MY HAIR IS TOO LONG AND GETS TANGLED, BUT I WON'T LOSE!

ETSUKO ICHIHARA IS A JAPANESE ACTRESS. AMONG OTHER THINGS, SHE STARRED IN A TELEVISION MYSTERY DRAMA CALLED KASEIFU WA MITA (THE HOUSEKEEPER SAW IT). –ED.

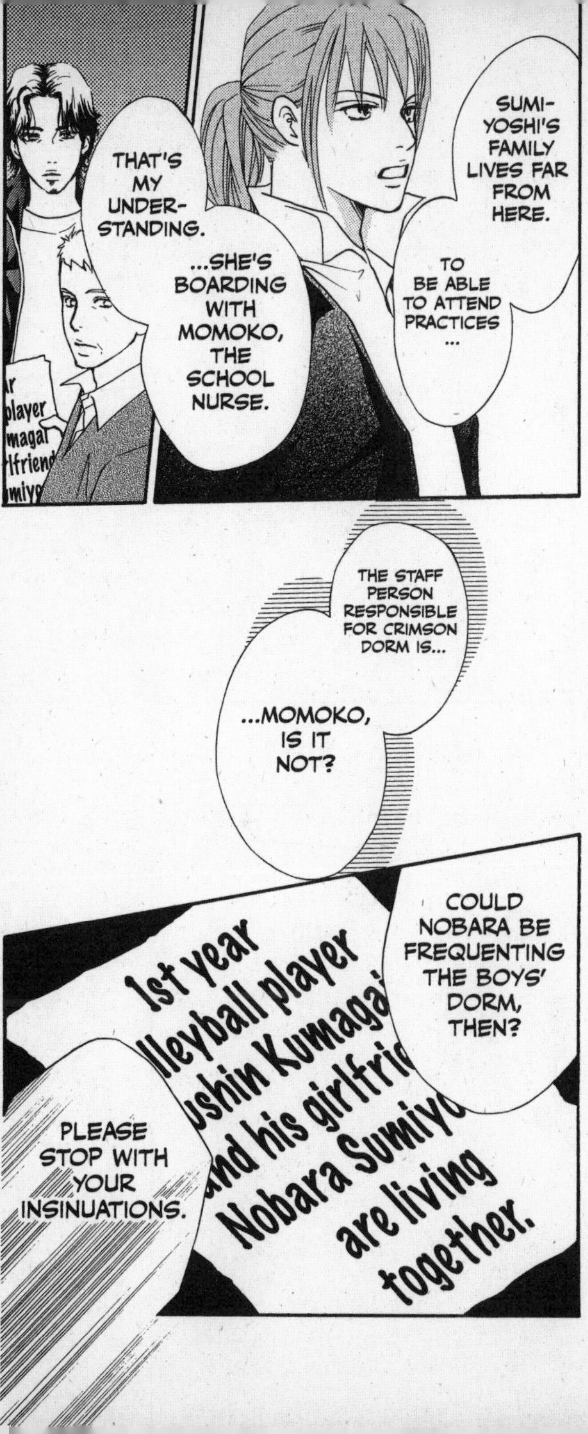

SUMI-YOSHI'S FAMILY LIVES FAR FROM HERE.
TO BE ABLE TO ATTEND PRACTICES...
THAT'S MY UNDER-STANDING.
...SHE'S BOARDING WITH MOMOKO, THE SCHOOL NURSE.
THE STAFF PERSON RESPONSIBLE FOR CRIMSON DORM IS...
...MOMOKO, IS IT NOT?
COULD NOBARA BE FREQUENTING THE BOYS' DORM, THEN?
1st year
lleyball player
ushin Kumaga
and his girlfrie
Nobara Sumiyo
are living
together.
PLEASE STOP WITH YOUR INSINUATIONS.

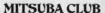

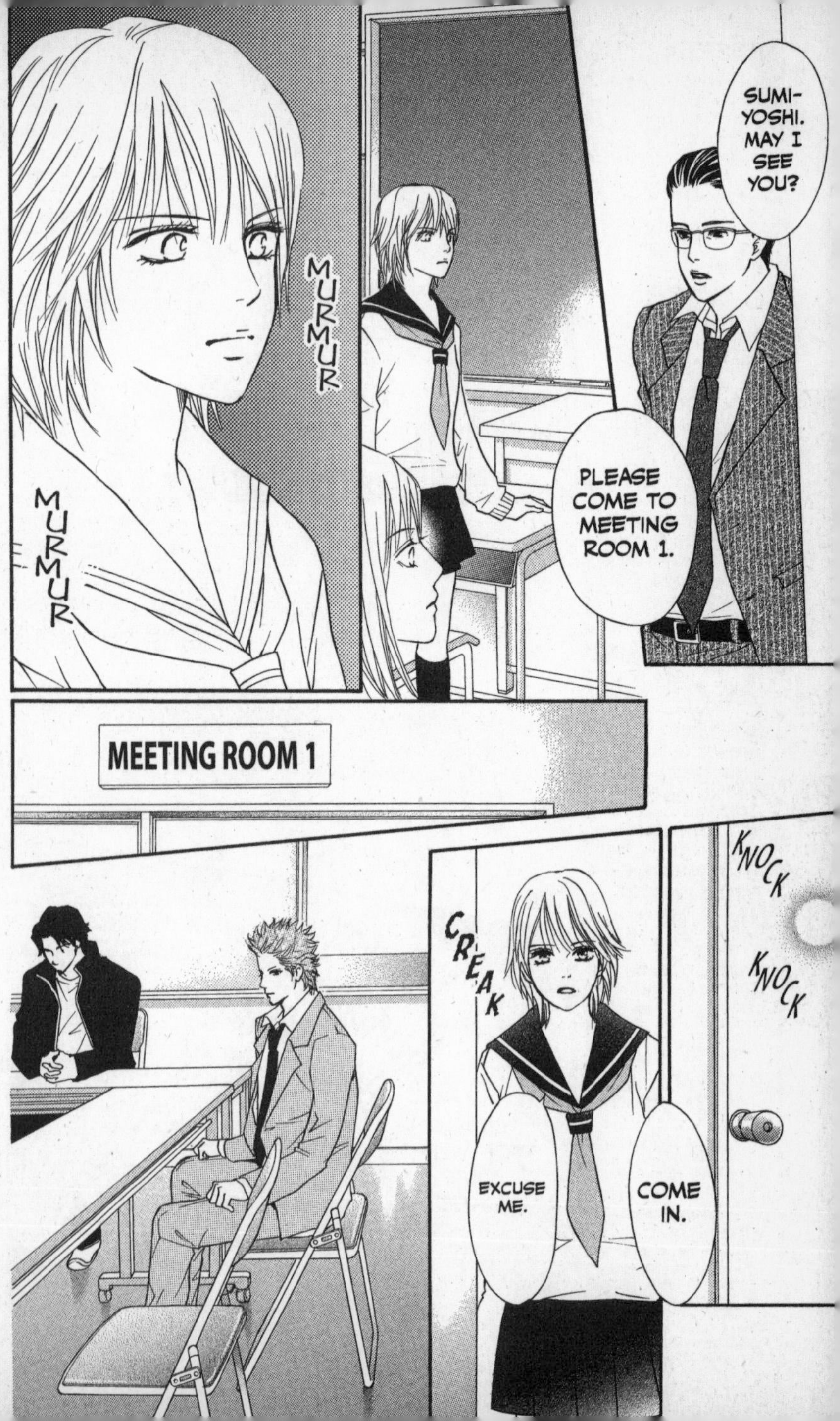
SUMI-YOSHI. MAY I SEE YOU?
PLEASE COME TO MEETING ROOM 1.
MURMUR
MURMUR
MEETING ROOM 1
KNOCK
KNOCK
CREAK
COME IN.
EXCUSE ME.

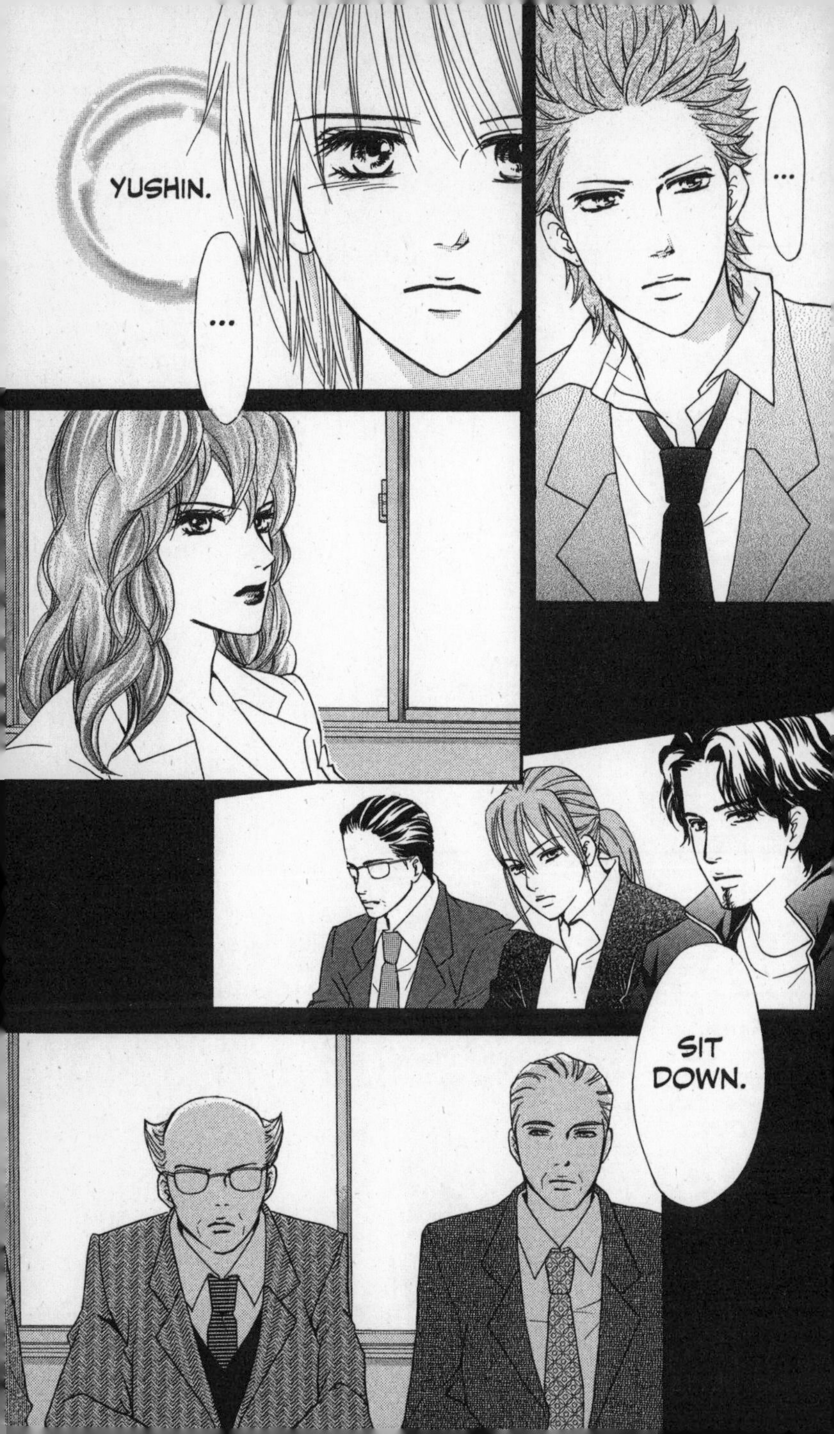
...
YUSHIN.
...
SIT DOWN.

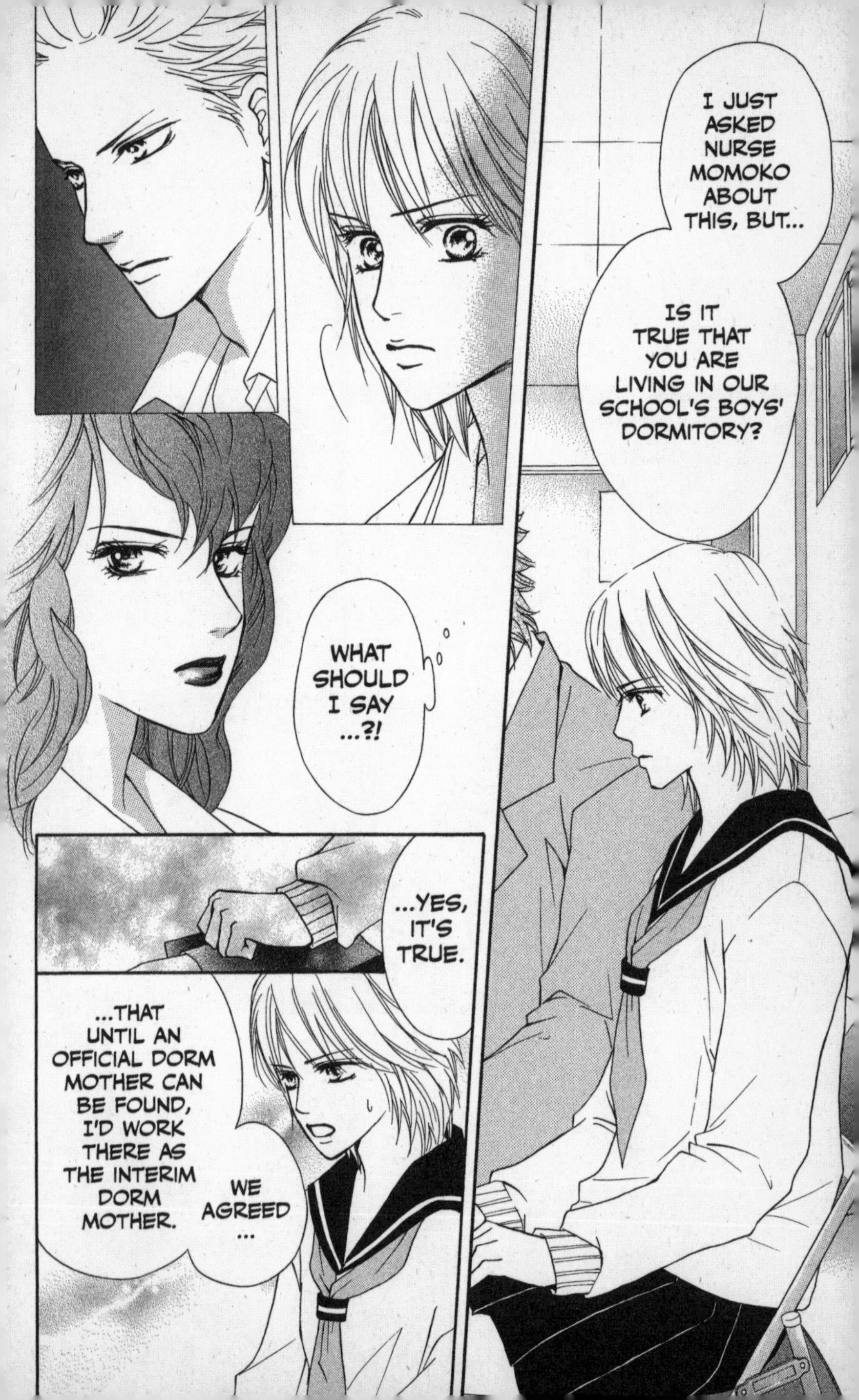
I JUST ASKED NURSE MOMOKO ABOUT THIS, BUT...
IS IT TRUE THAT YOU ARE LIVING IN OUR SCHOOL'S BOYS' DORMITORY?
WHAT SHOULD I SAY ...?!
...YES, IT'S TRUE.
WE AGREED ...
...THAT UNTIL AN OFFICIAL DORM MOTHER CAN BE FOUND, I'D WORK THERE AS THE INTERIM DORM MOTHER.

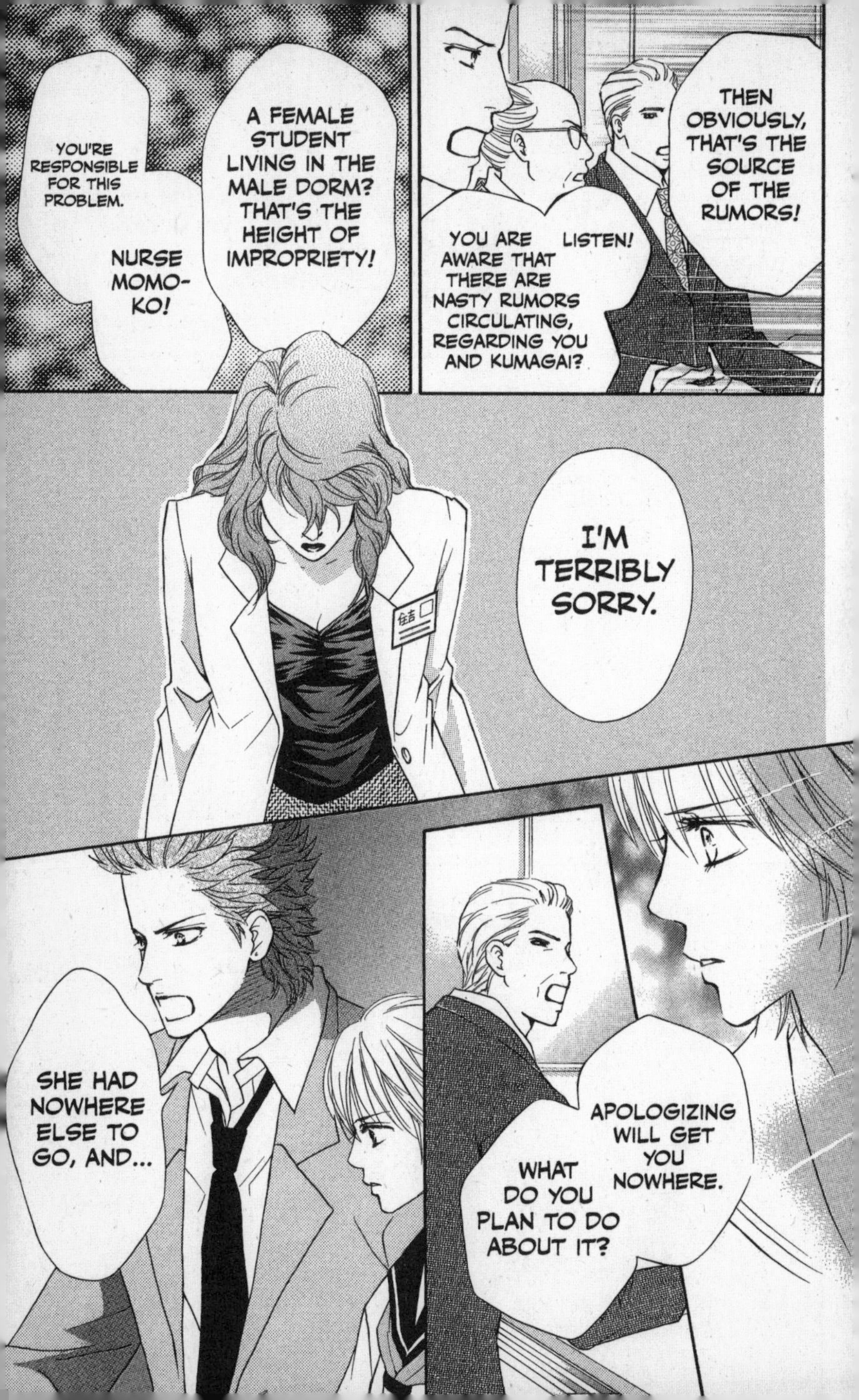
THEN OBVIOUSLY, THAT'S THE SOURCE OF THE RUMORS!
LISTEN! YOU ARE AWARE THAT THERE ARE NASTY RUMORS CIRCULATING, REGARDING YOU AND KUMAGAI?
A FEMALE STUDENT LIVING IN THE MALE DORM? THAT'S THE HEIGHT OF IMPROPRIETY!
NURSE MOMOKO! YOU'RE RESPONSIBLE FOR THIS PROBLEM.
I'M TERRIBLY SORRY.
APOLOGIZING WILL GET YOU NOWHERE. WHAT DO YOU PLAN TO DO ABOUT IT?
SHE HAD NOWHERE ELSE TO GO, AND...

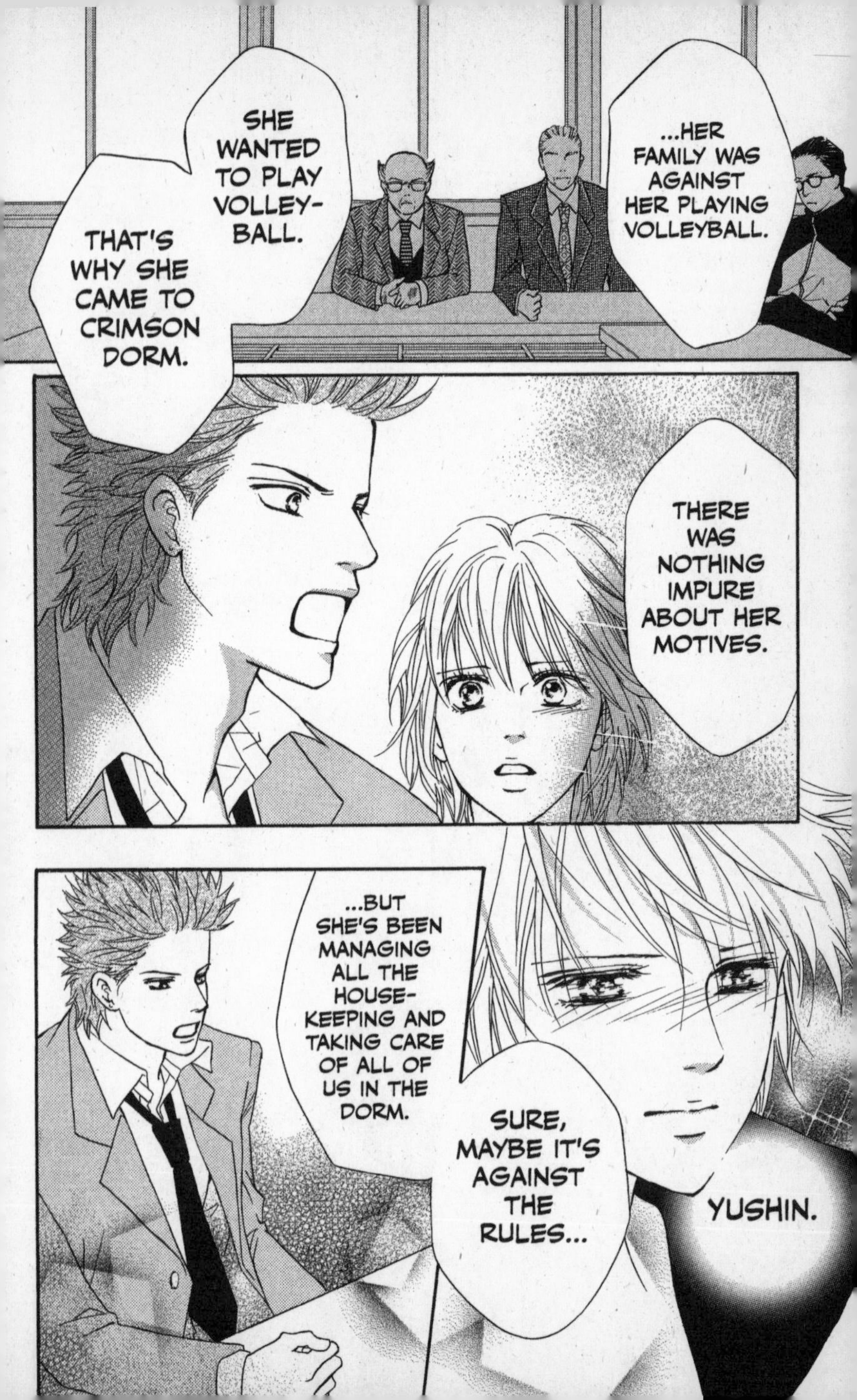
...HER FAMILY WAS AGAINST HER PLAYING VOLLEYBALL.
SHE WANTED TO PLAY VOLLEY-BALL.
THAT'S WHY SHE CAME TO CRIMSON DORM.
THERE WAS NOTHING IMPURE ABOUT HER MOTIVES.
YUSHIN.
SURE, MAYBE IT'S AGAINST THE RULES...
...BUT SHE'S BEEN MANAGING ALL THE HOUSE-KEEPING AND TAKING CARE OF ALL OF US IN THE DORM.

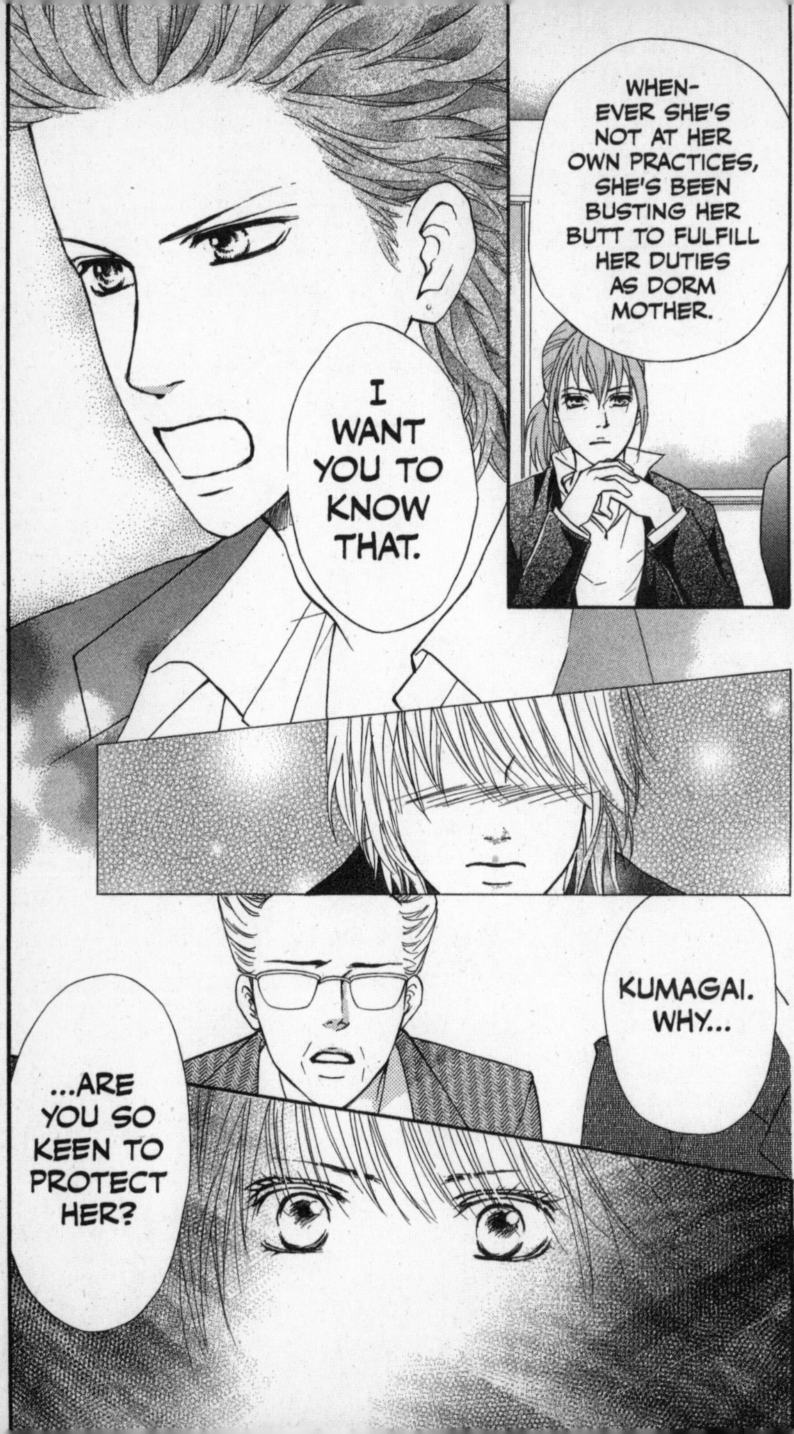
WHEN-EVER SHE'S NOT AT HER OWN PRACTICES, SHE'S BEEN BUSTING HER BUTT TO FULFILL HER DUTIES AS DORM MOTHER.
I WANT YOU TO KNOW THAT.
KUMAGAI. WHY...
...ARE YOU SO KEEN TO PROTECT HER?

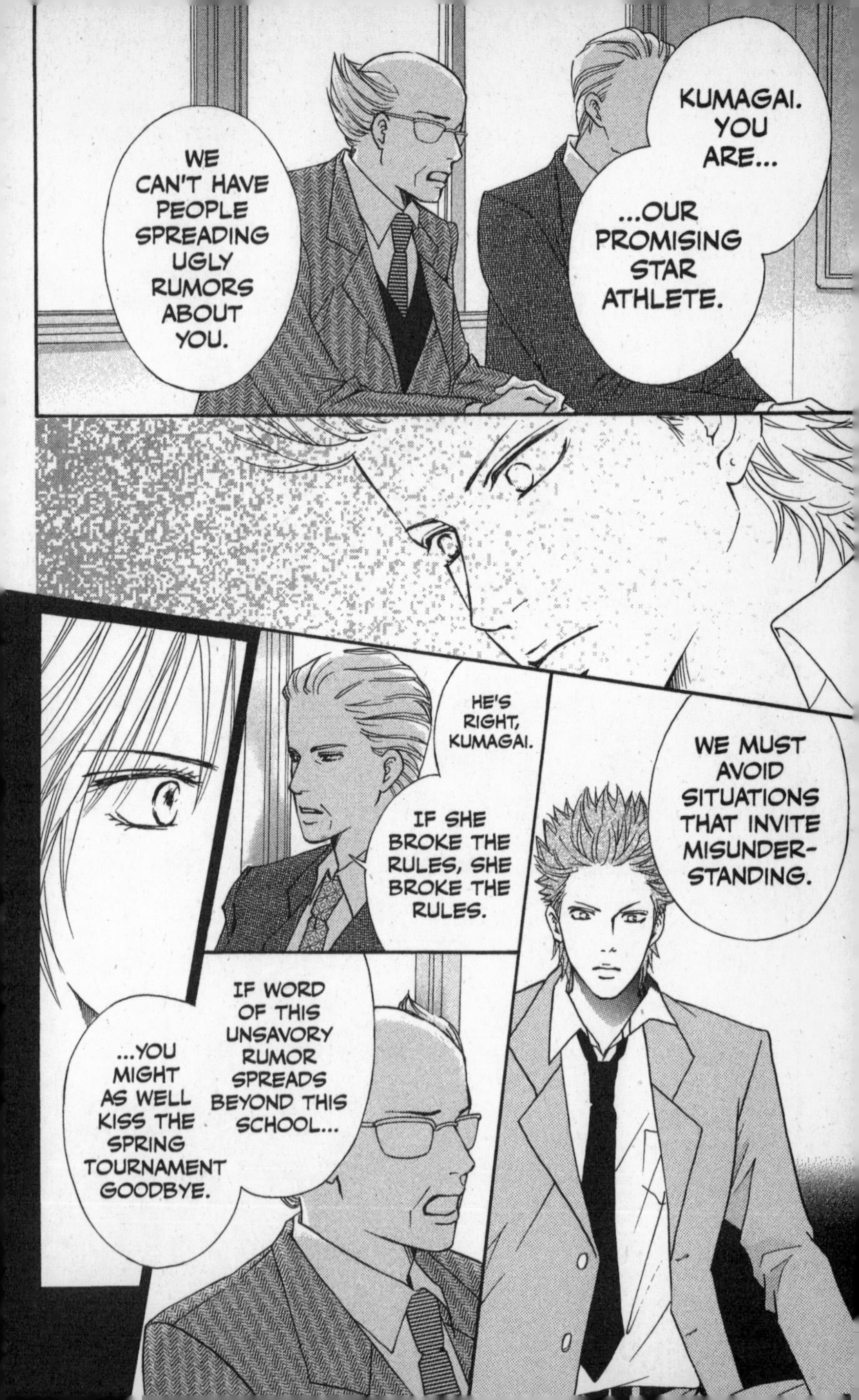
KUMAGAI. YOU ARE...
...OUR PROMISING STAR ATHLETE.
WE CAN'T HAVE PEOPLE SPREADING UGLY RUMORS ABOUT YOU.
WE MUST AVOID SITUATIONS THAT INVITE MISUNDER-STANDING.
HE'S RIGHT, KUMAGAI.
IF SHE BROKE THE RULES, SHE BROKE THE RULES.
IF WORD OF THIS UNSAVORY RUMOR SPREADS BEYOND THIS SCHOOL...
...YOU MIGHT AS WELL KISS THE SPRING TOURNAMENT GOODBYE.

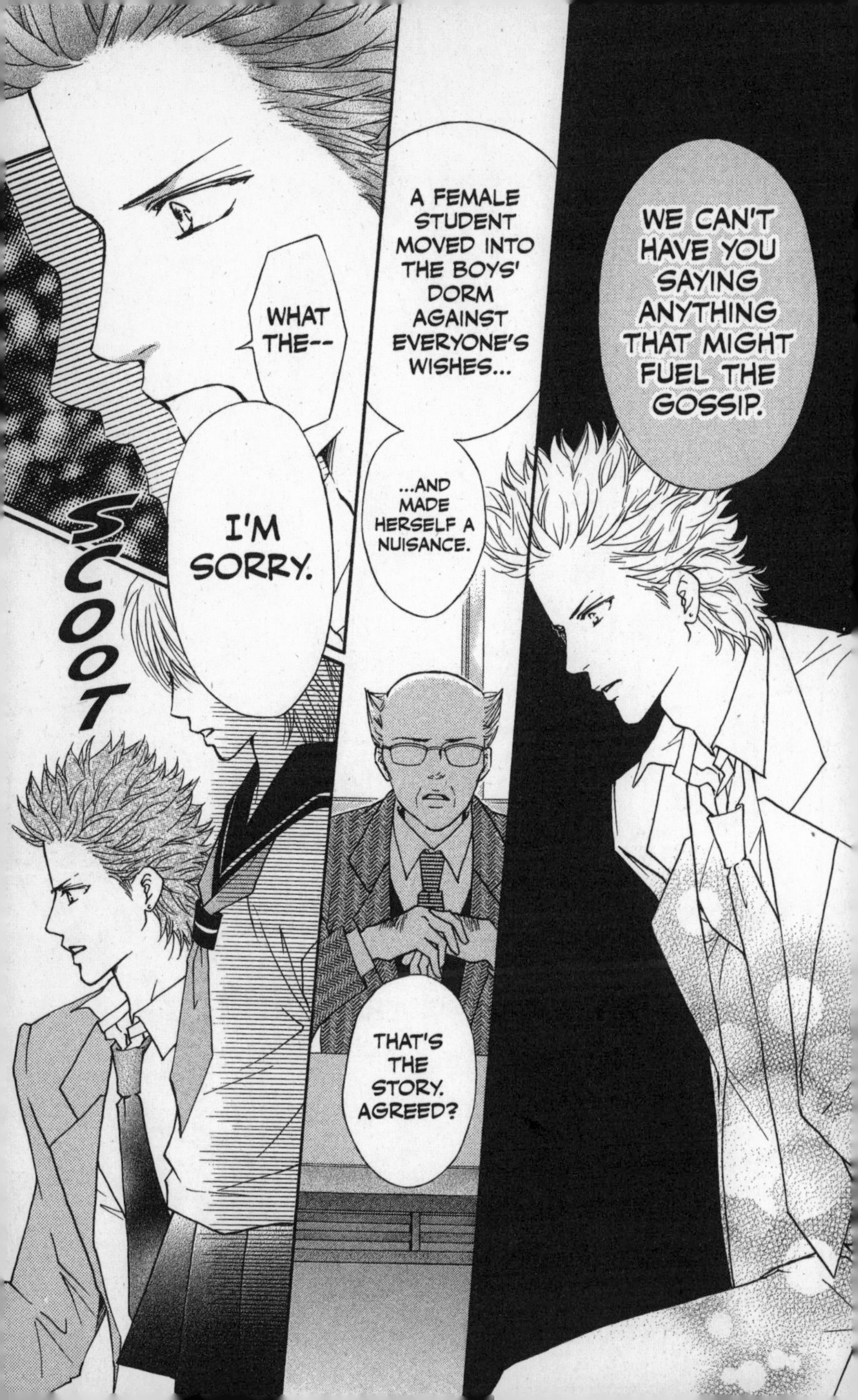
WE CAN'T HAVE YOU SAYING ANYTHING THAT MIGHT FUEL THE GOSSIP.
A FEMALE STUDENT MOVED INTO THE BOYS' DORM AGAINST EVERYONE'S WISHES...
...AND MADE HERSELF A NUISANCE.
THAT'S THE STORY. AGREED?
WHAT THE--
I'M SORRY.
SCOOT

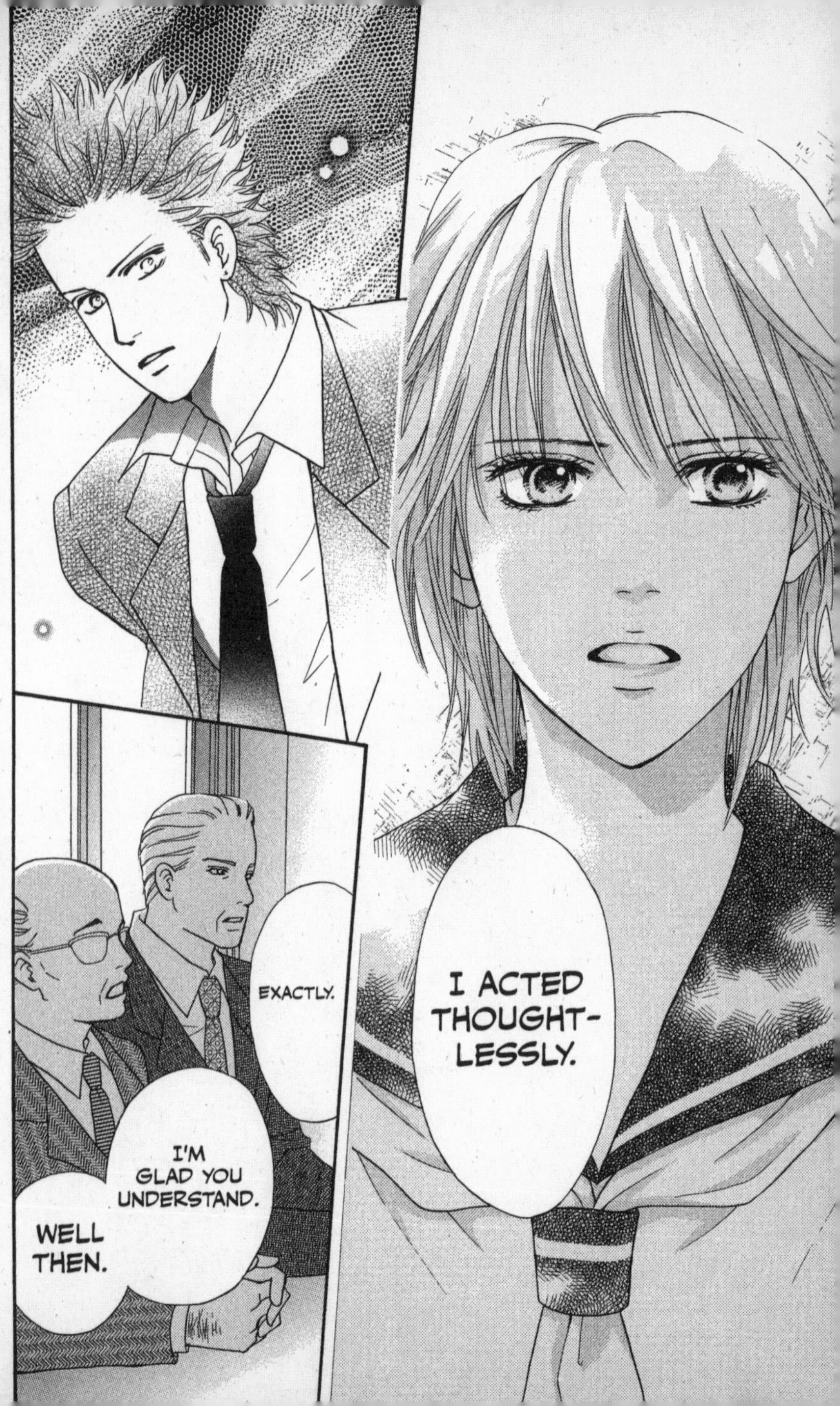
I ACTED THOUGHT-LESSLY.
EXACTLY.
I'M GLAD YOU UNDERSTAND.
WELL THEN.

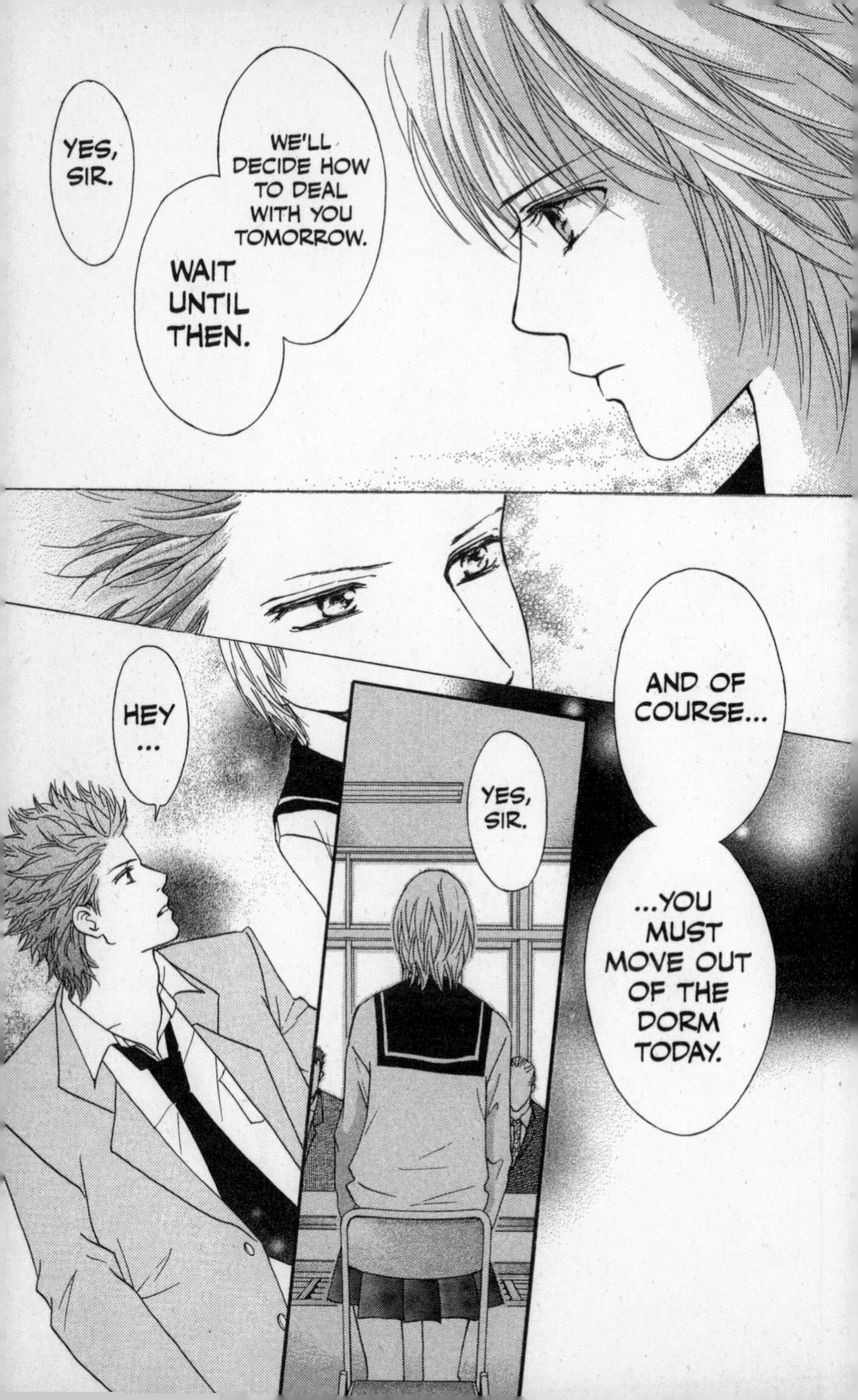
WE'LL DECIDE HOW TO DEAL WITH YOU TOMORROW.
WAIT UNTIL THEN.
YES, SIR.
AND OF COURSE...
...YOU MUST MOVE OUT OF THE DORM TODAY.
YES, SIR.
HEY ...

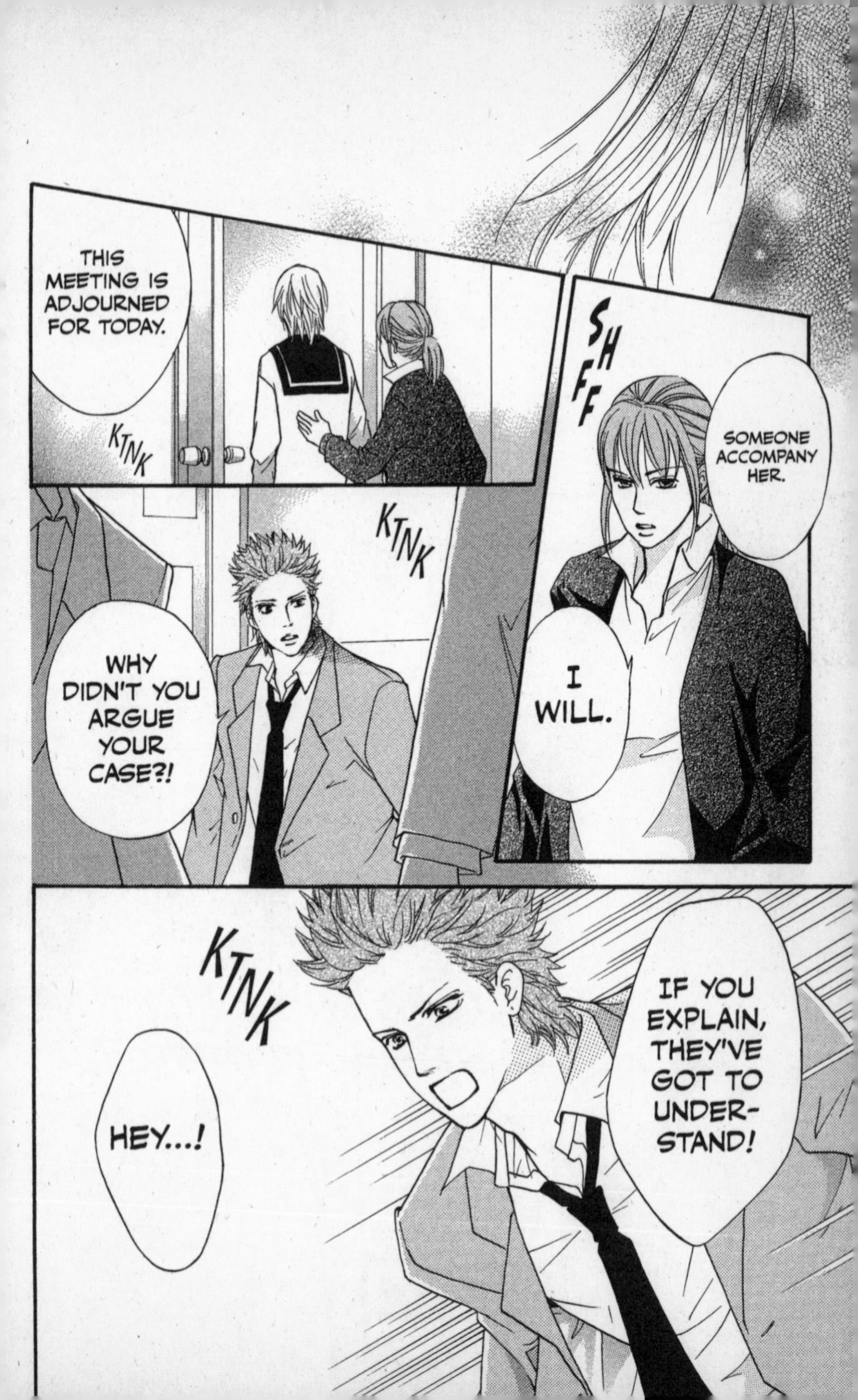
THIS MEETING IS ADJOURNED FOR TODAY.
KTNK
SHFF
SOMEONE ACCOMPANY HER.
I WILL.
KTNK
WHY DIDN'T YOU ARGUE YOUR CASE?!
KTNK
IF YOU EXPLAIN, THEY'VE GOT TO UNDER-STAND!
HEY...!

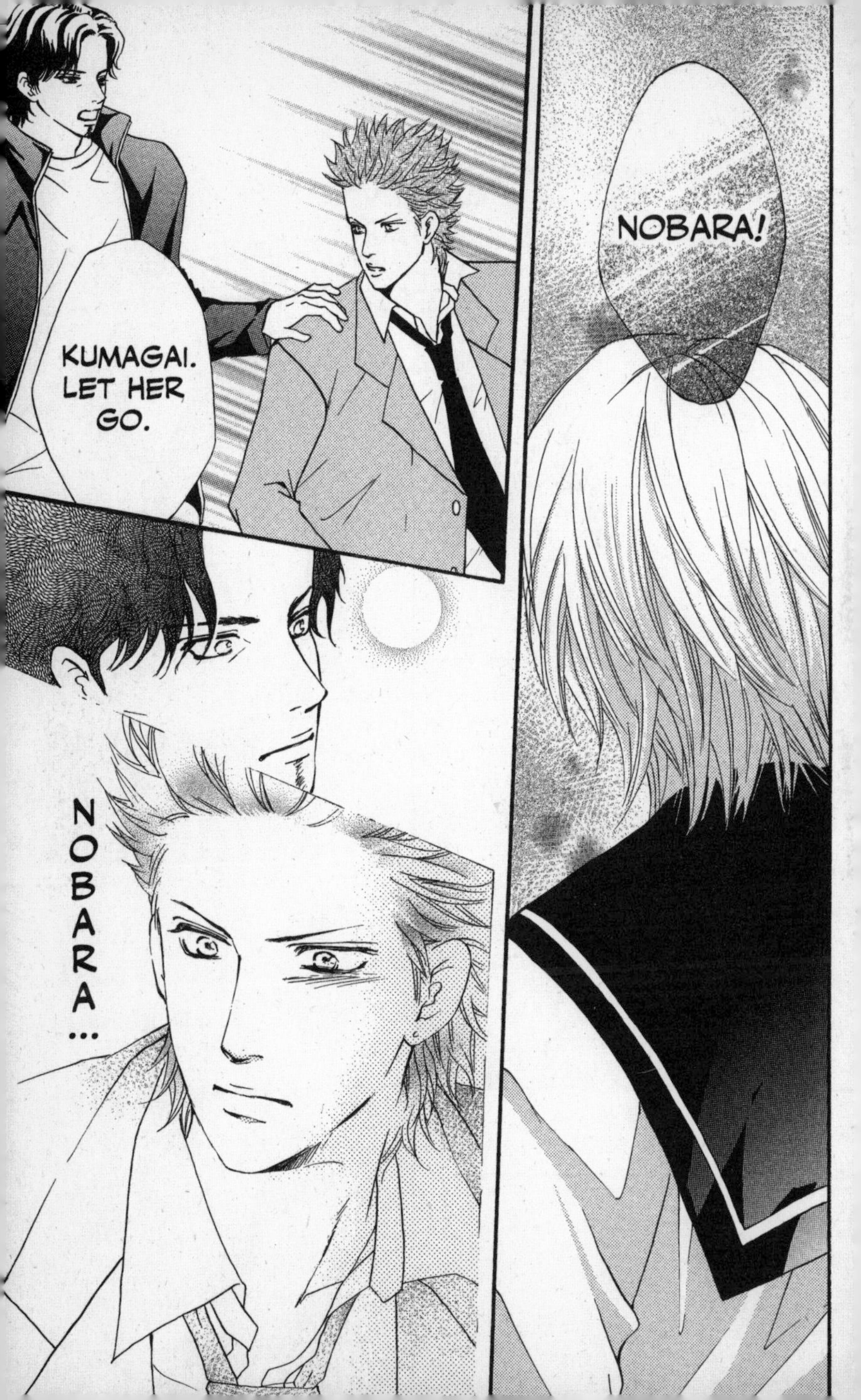
NOBARA!
KUMAGAI. LET HER GO.
NOBARA...

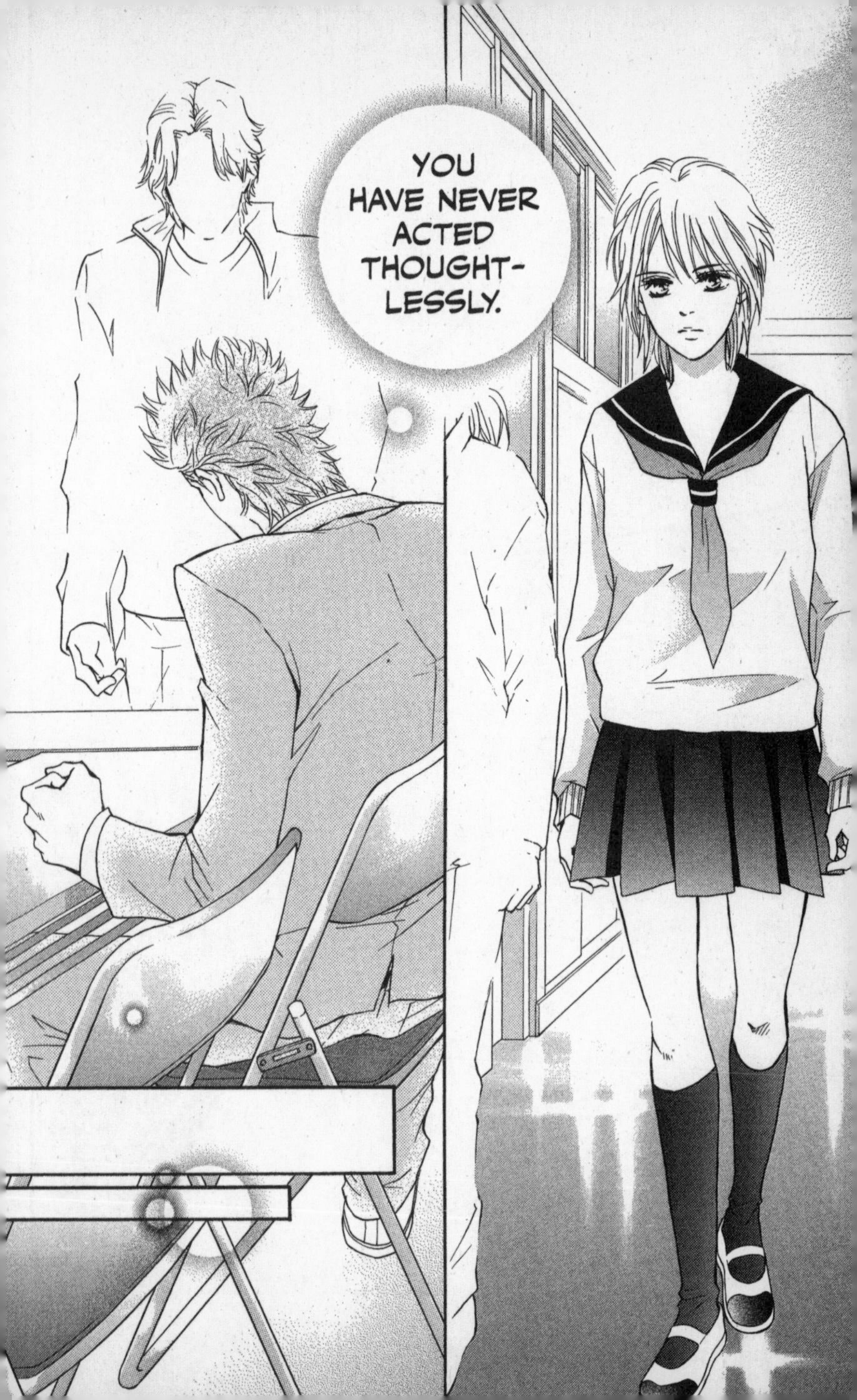
YOU HAVE NEVER ACTED THOUGHT-LESSLY.

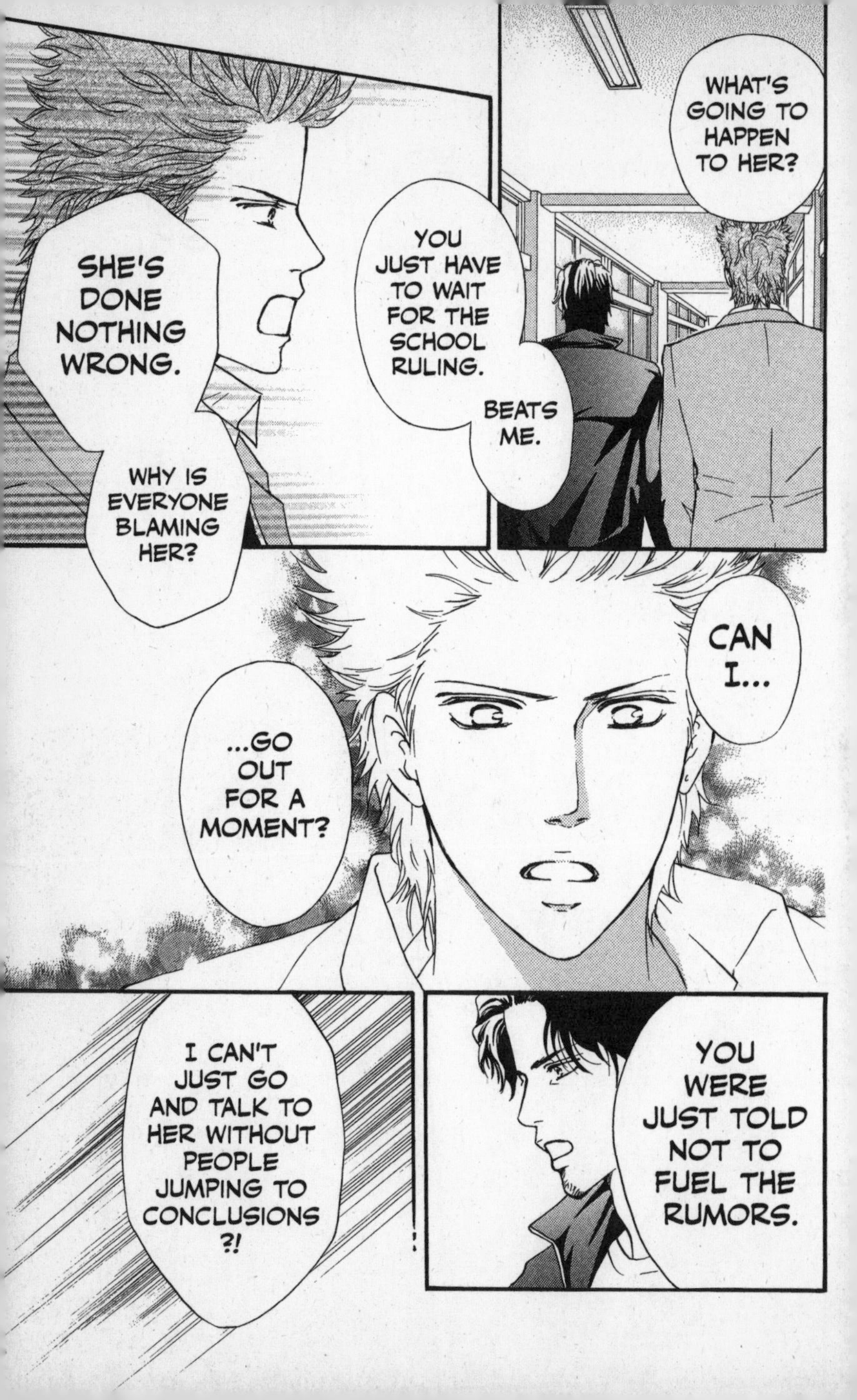

WHAT'S GOING TO HAPPEN TO HER?
BEATS ME.
YOU JUST HAVE TO WAIT FOR THE SCHOOL RULING.
SHE'S DONE NOTHING WRONG.
WHY IS EVERYONE BLAMING HER?
CAN I...
...GO OUT FOR A MOMENT?
YOU WERE JUST TOLD NOT TO FUEL THE RUMORS.
I CAN'T JUST GO AND TALK TO HER WITHOUT PEOPLE JUMPING TO CONCLUSIONS?!

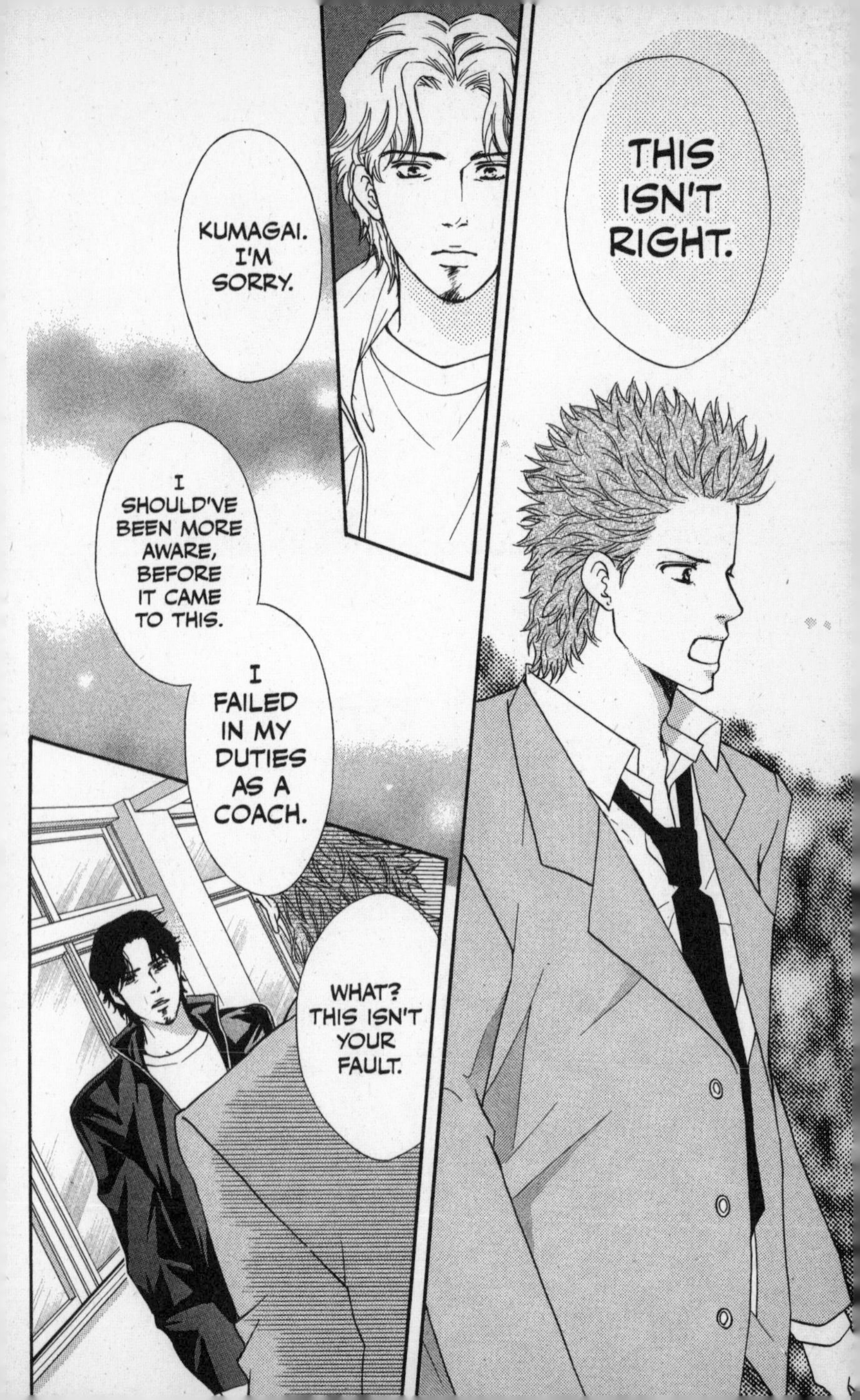
THIS ISN'T RIGHT.
KUMAGAI. I'M SORRY.
I SHOULD'VE BEEN MORE AWARE, BEFORE IT CAME TO THIS.
I FAILED IN MY DUTIES AS A COACH.
WHAT? THIS ISN'T YOUR FAULT.

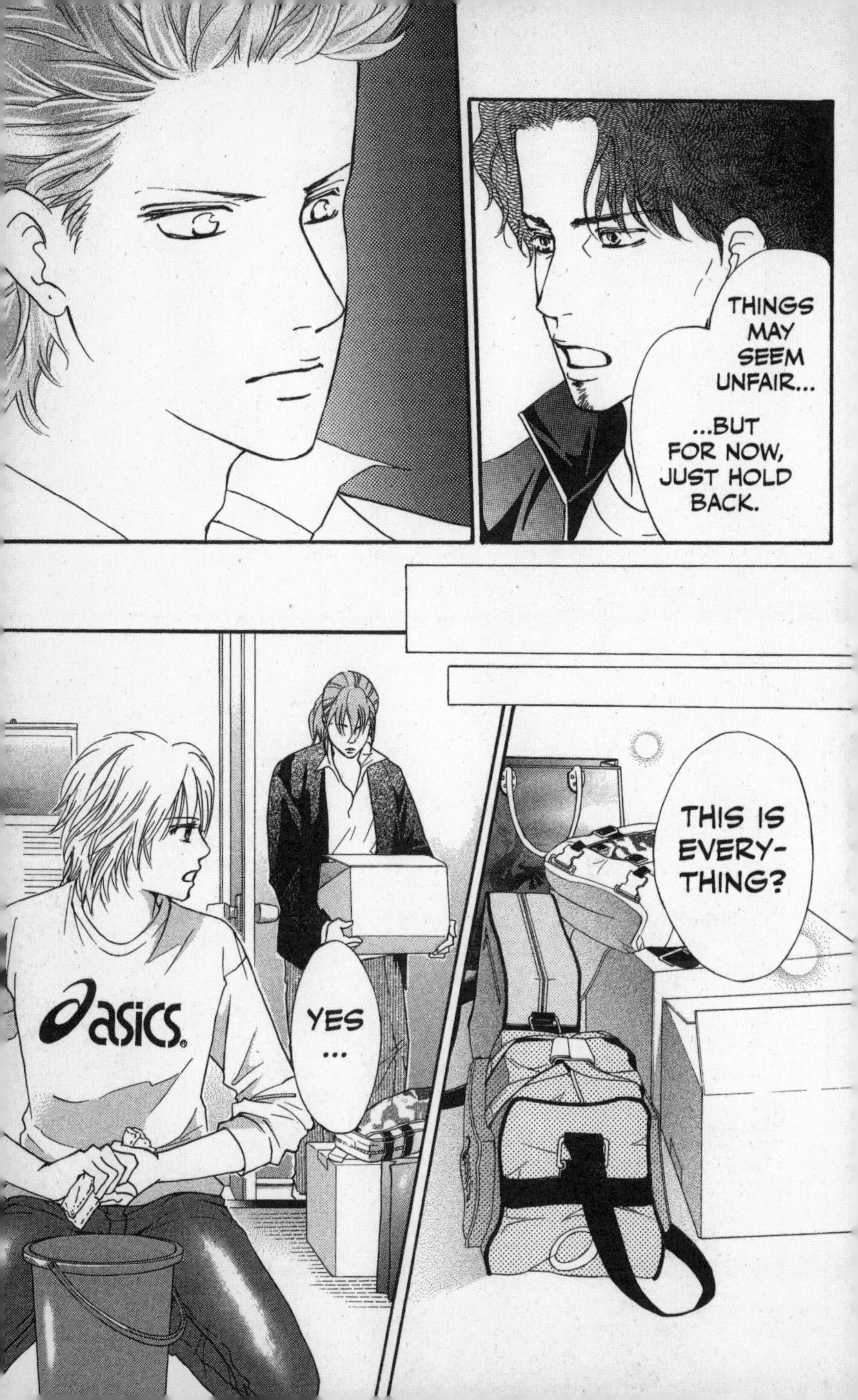
THINGS MAY SEEM UNFAIR...
...BUT FOR NOW, JUST HOLD BACK.
THIS IS EVERY-THING?
YES...
asics

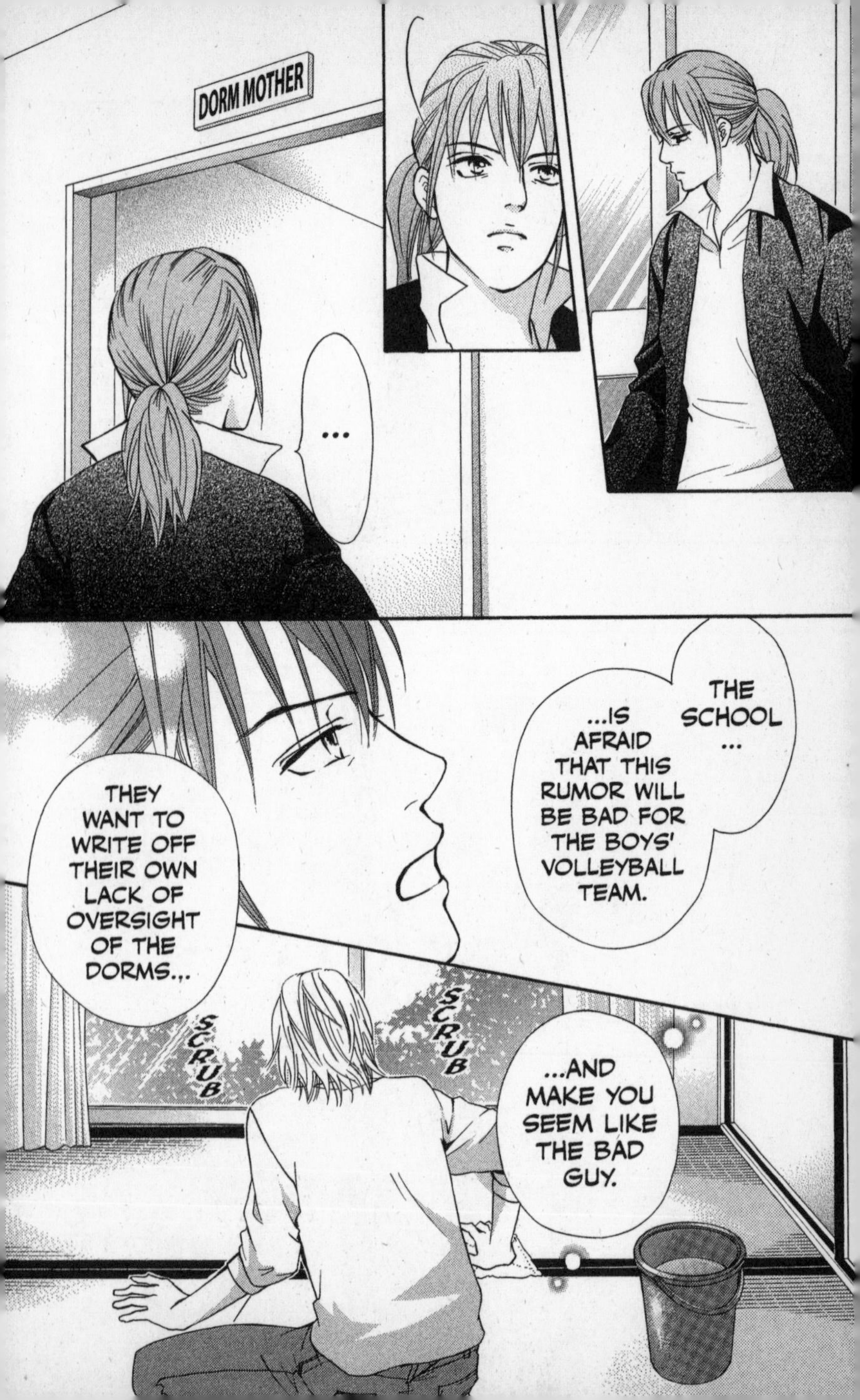
DORM MOTHER
...
THE SCHOOL... ...IS AFRAID THAT THIS RUMOR WILL BE BAD FOR THE BOYS' VOLLEYBALL TEAM.
THEY WANT TO WRITE OFF THEIR OWN LACK OF OVERSIGHT OF THE DORMS...
SCRUB
SCRUB
...AND MAKE YOU SEEM LIKE THE BAD GUY.

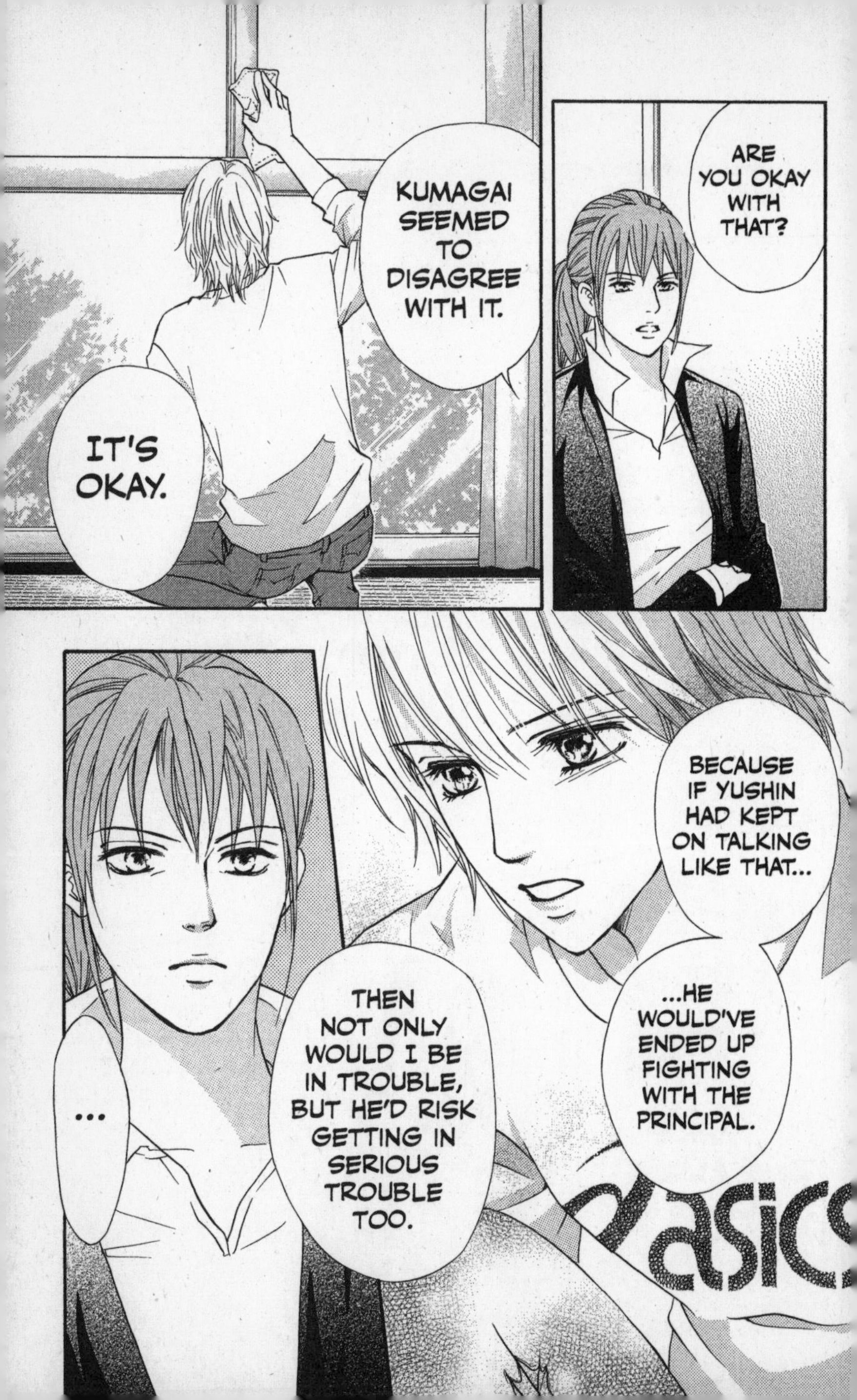
ARE YOU OKAY WITH THAT?
KUMAGAI SEEMED TO DISAGREE WITH IT.
IT'S OKAY.
BECAUSE IF YUSHIN HAD KEPT ON TALKING LIKE THAT...
...HE WOULD'VE ENDED UP FIGHTING WITH THE PRINCIPAL.
THEN NOT ONLY WOULD I BE IN TROUBLE, BUT HE'D RISK GETTING IN SERIOUS TROUBLE TOO.
...

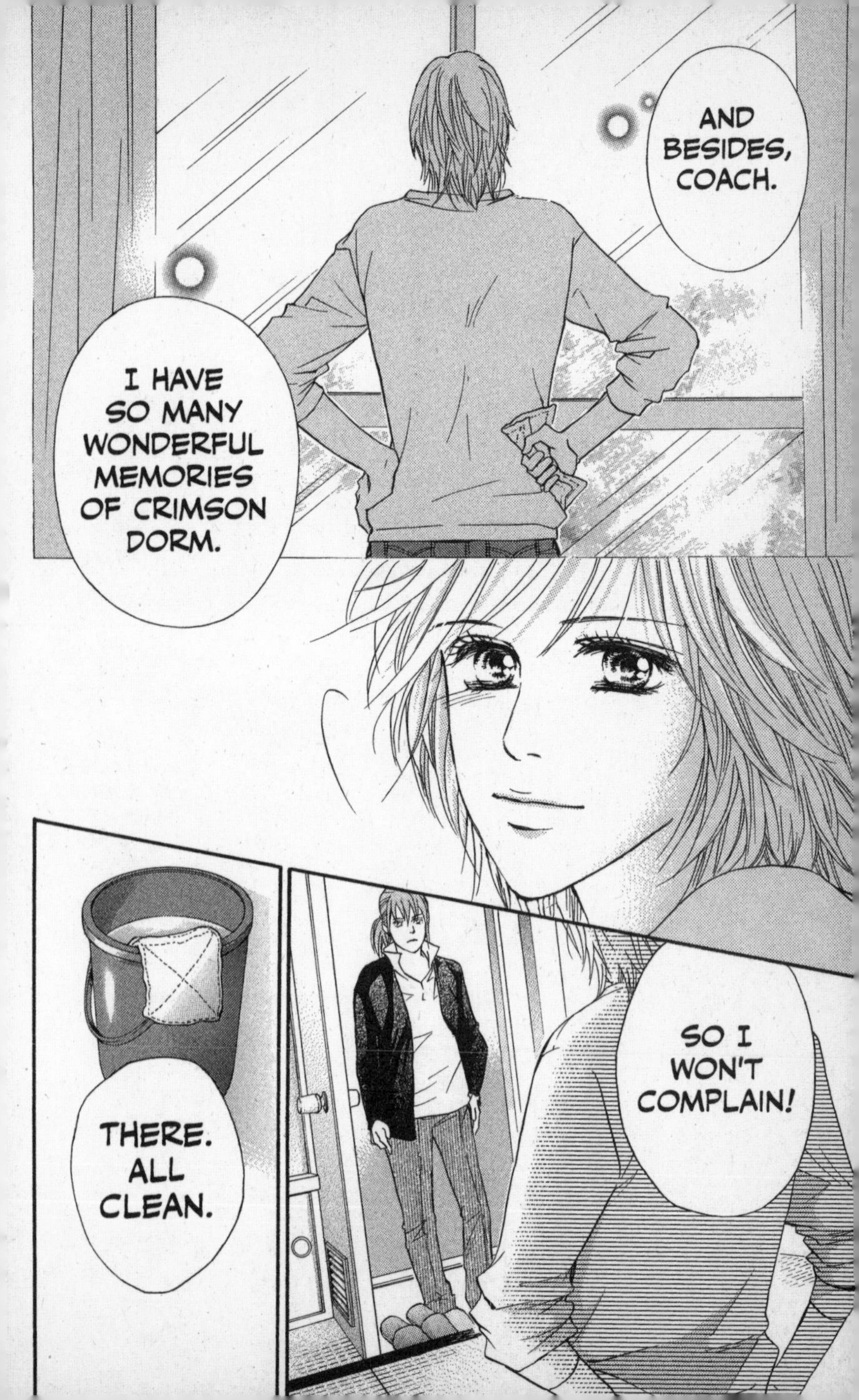
AND BESIDES, COACH.
I HAVE SO MANY WONDERFUL MEMORIES OF CRIMSON DORM.
SO I WON'T COMPLAIN!
THERE. ALL CLEAN.

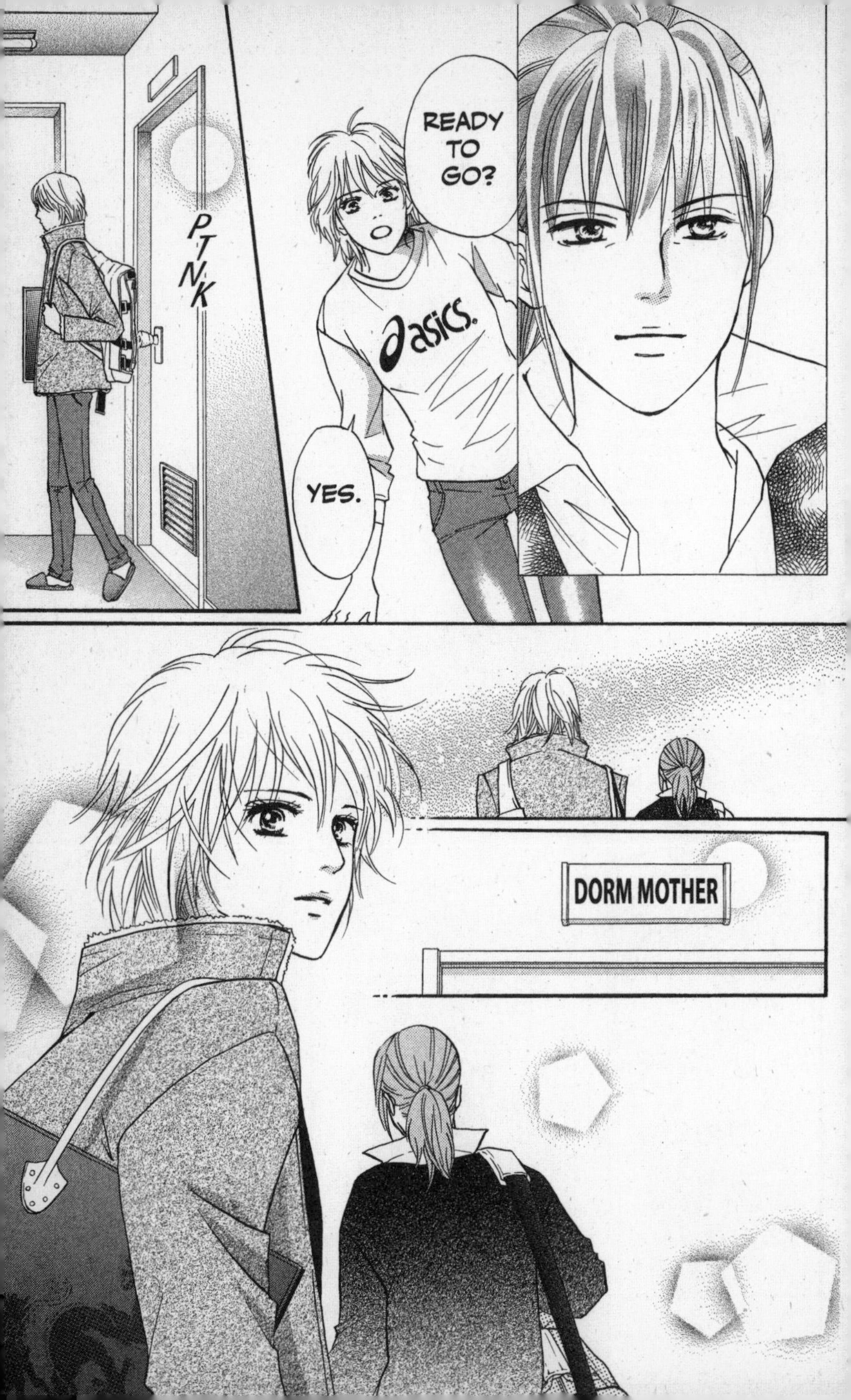
READY TO GO?
YES.
PTNK
DORM MOTHER

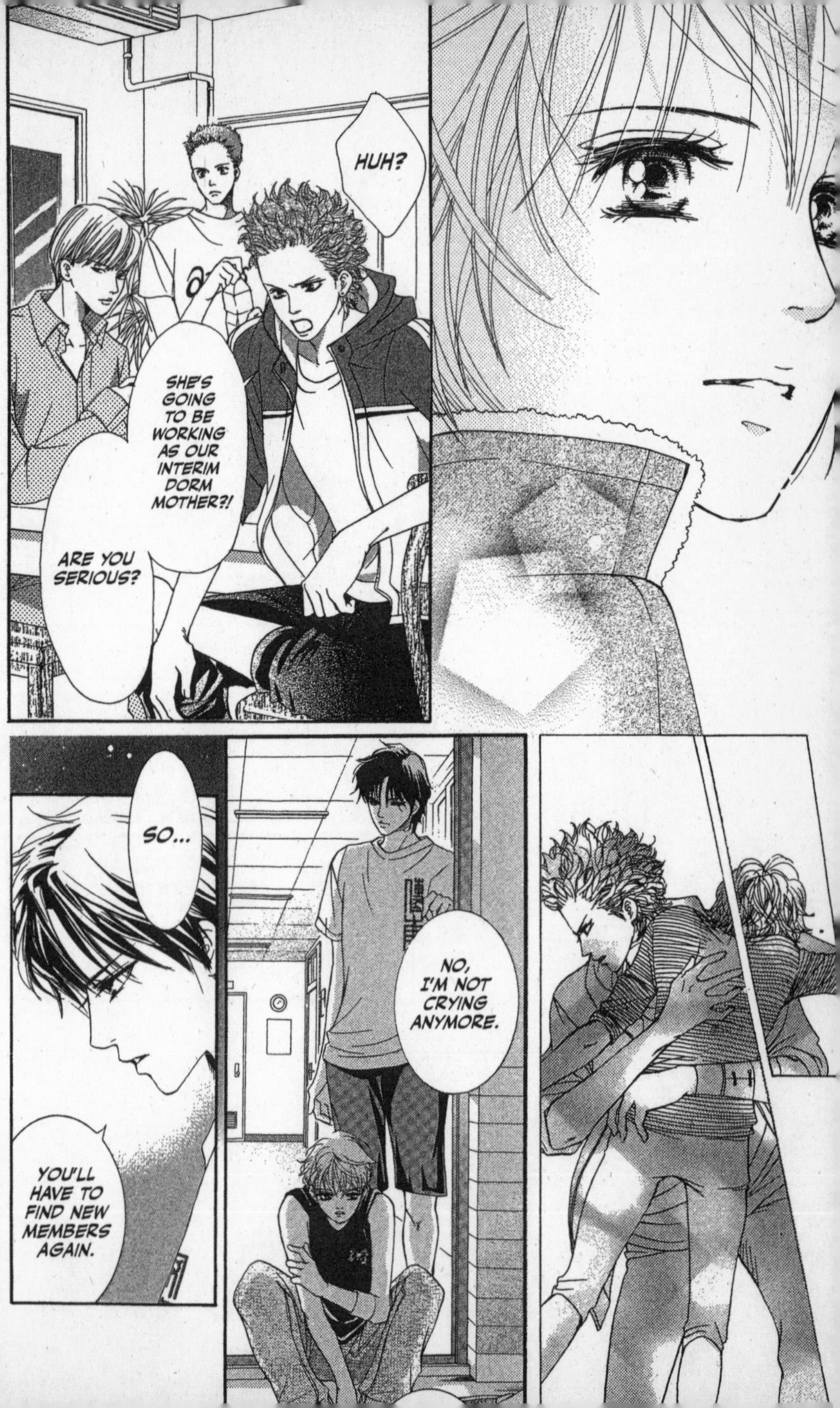
HUH?
SHE'S GOING TO BE WORKING AS OUR INTERIM DORM MOTHER?!
ARE YOU SERIOUS?
NO, I'M NOT CRYING ANYMORE.
SO...
YOU'LL HAVE TO FIND NEW MEMBERS AGAIN.

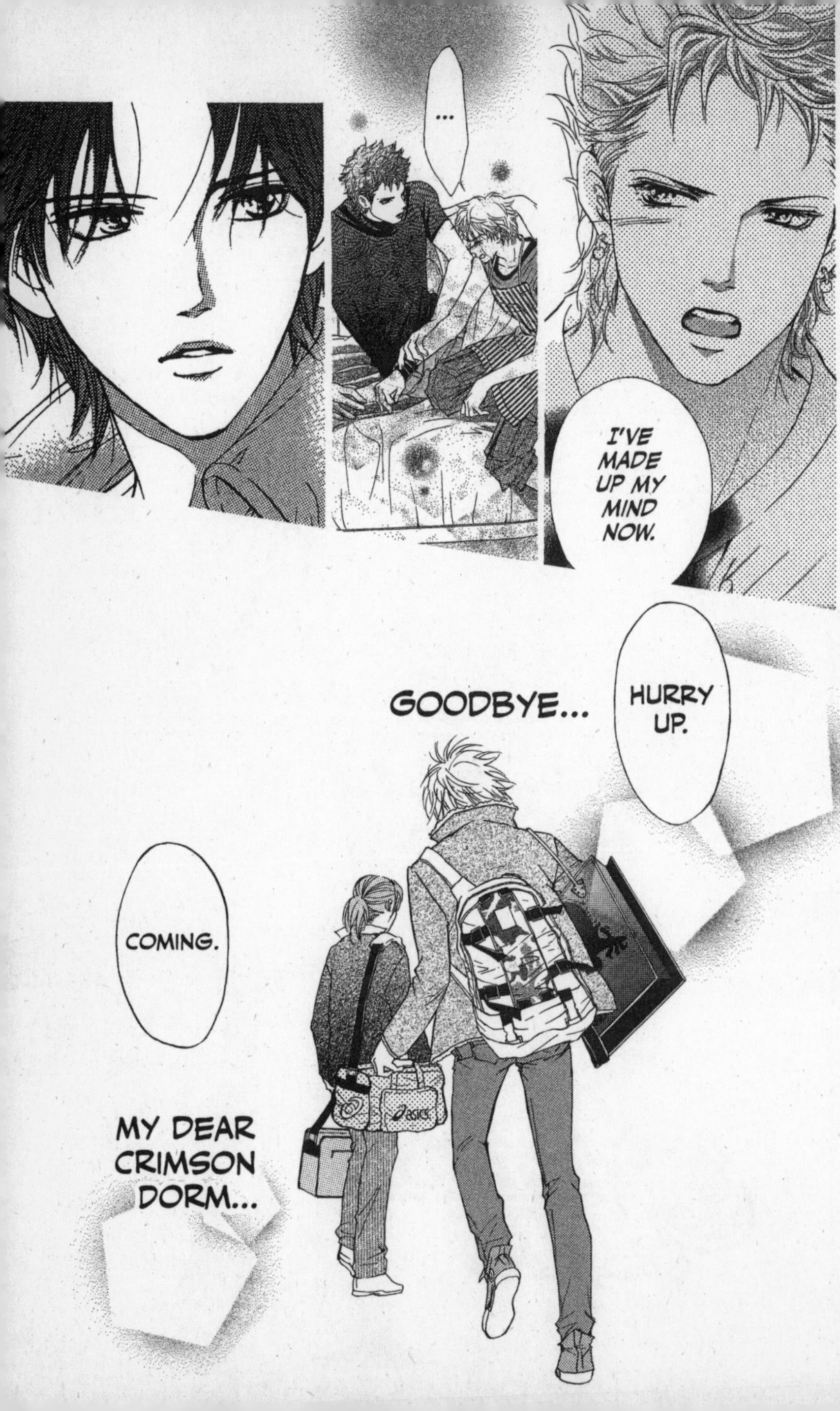
I'VE MADE UP MY MIND NOW.
...
HURRY UP.
GOODBYE...
COMING.
MY DEAR CRIMSON DORM...

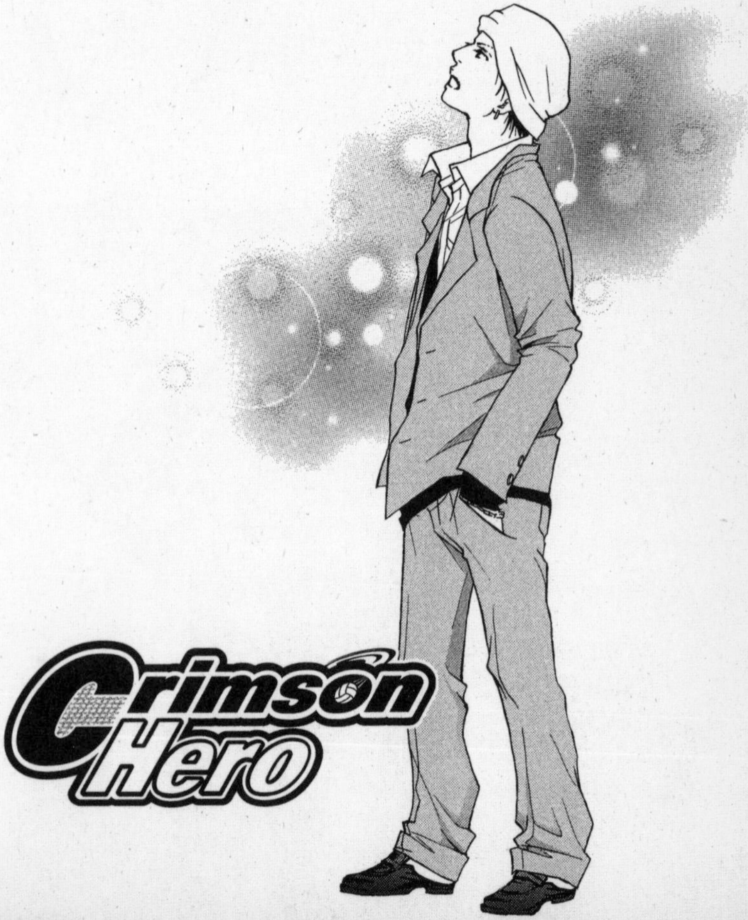
Crimson
Hero

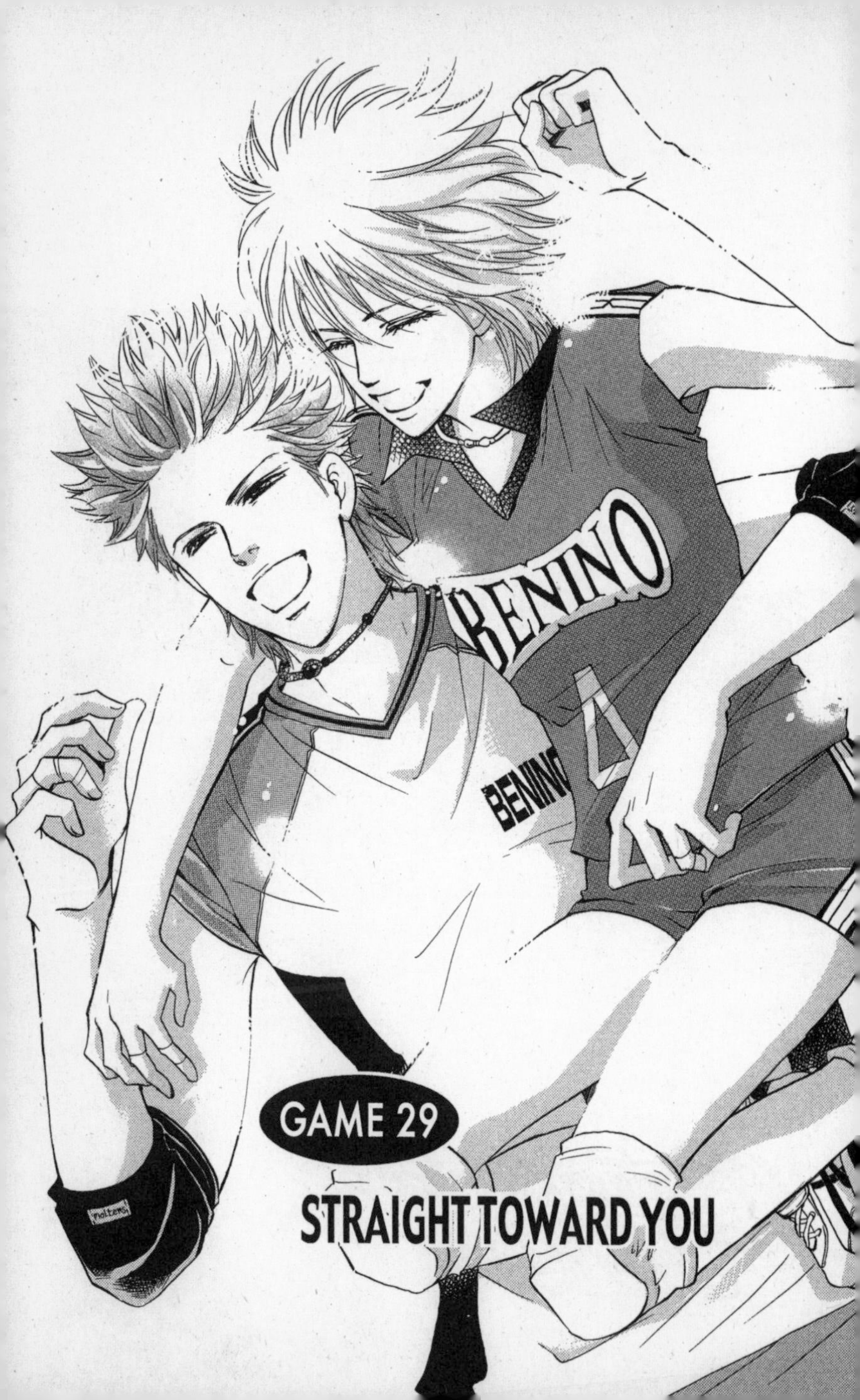
BENINO
GAME 29
STRAIGHT TOWARD YOU

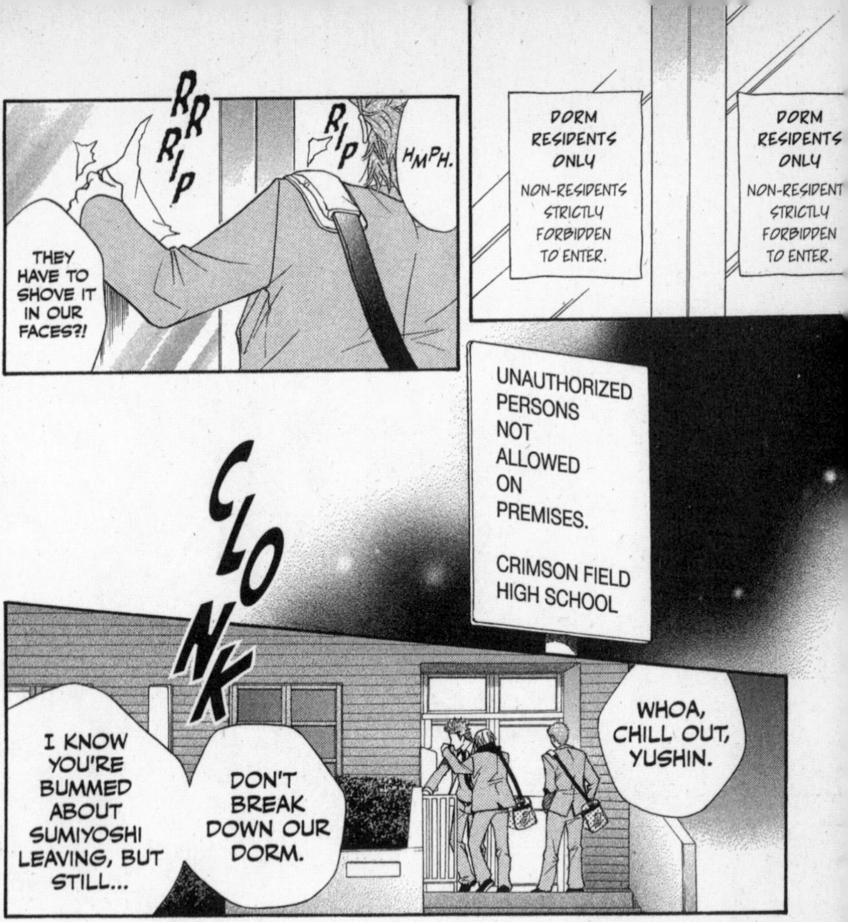
DORM RESIDENTS ONLY
NON-RESIDENTS STRICTLY FORBIDDEN TO ENTER.
DORM RESIDENTS ONLY
NON-RESIDENT STRICTLY FORBIDDEN TO ENTER.
HMPH.
RIP
RRRIP
THEY HAVE TO SHOVE IT IN OUR FACES?!
UNAUTHORIZED PERSONS NOT ALLOWED ON PREMISES.
CRIMSON FIELD HIGH SCHOOL
CLONK
WHOA, CHILL OUT, YUSHIN.
DON'T BREAK DOWN OUR DORM.
I KNOW YOU'RE BUMMED ABOUT SUMIYOSHI LEAVING, BUT STILL...

Crimson Hero

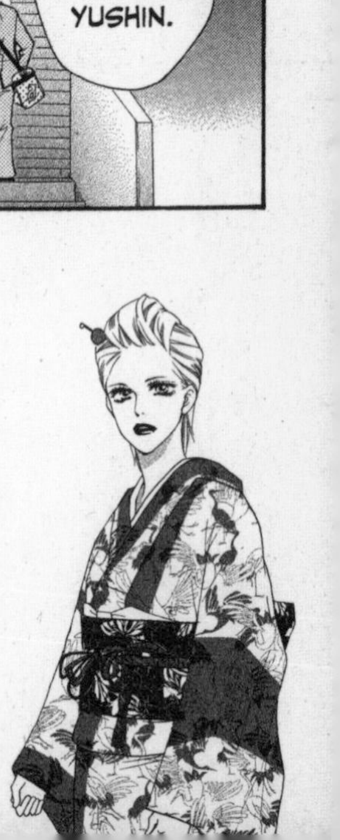

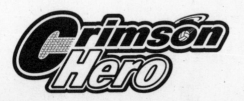

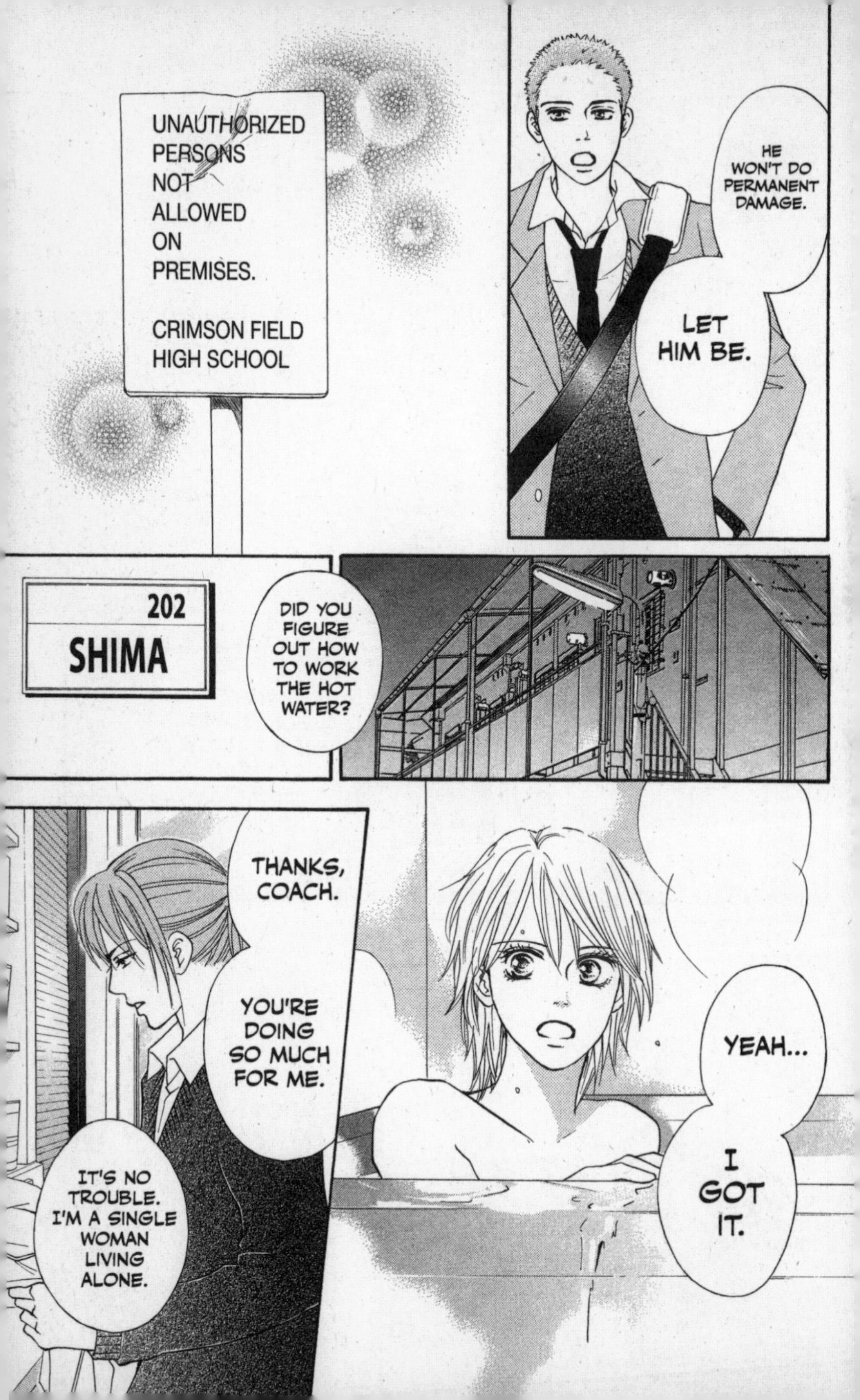
HE WON'T DO PERMANENT DAMAGE.
LET HIM BE.
UNAUTHORIZED PERSONS NOT ALLOWED ON PREMISES.
CRIMSON FIELD HIGH SCHOOL
202
SHIMA
DID YOU FIGURE OUT HOW TO WORK THE HOT WATER?
YEAH...
I GOT IT.
THANKS, COACH.
YOU'RE DOING SO MUCH FOR ME.
IT'S NO TROUBLE. I'M A SINGLE WOMAN LIVING ALONE.

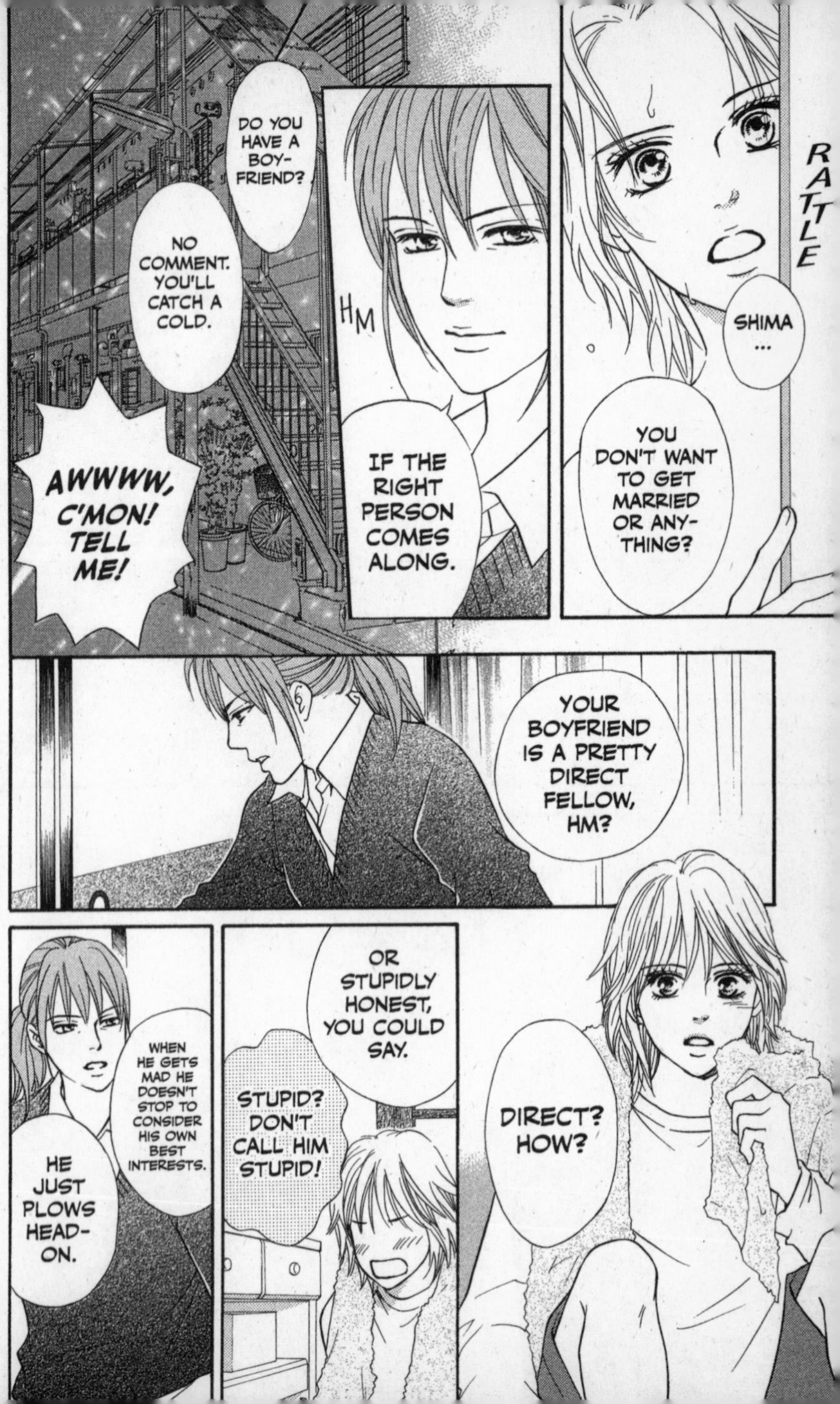
RATTLE
SHIMA ...
YOU DON'T WANT TO GET MARRIED OR ANYTHING?
HM
IF THE RIGHT PERSON COMES ALONG.
DO YOU HAVE A BOY-FRIEND?
NO COMMENT. YOU'LL CATCH A COLD.
AWWWW, C'MON! TELL ME!
YOUR BOYFRIEND IS A PRETTY DIRECT FELLOW, HM?
DIRECT? HOW?
OR STUPIDLY HONEST, YOU COULD SAY.
STUPID? DON'T CALL HIM STUPID!
WHEN HE GETS MAD HE DOESN'T STOP TO CONSIDER HIS OWN BEST INTERESTS.
HE JUST PLOWS HEAD-ON.

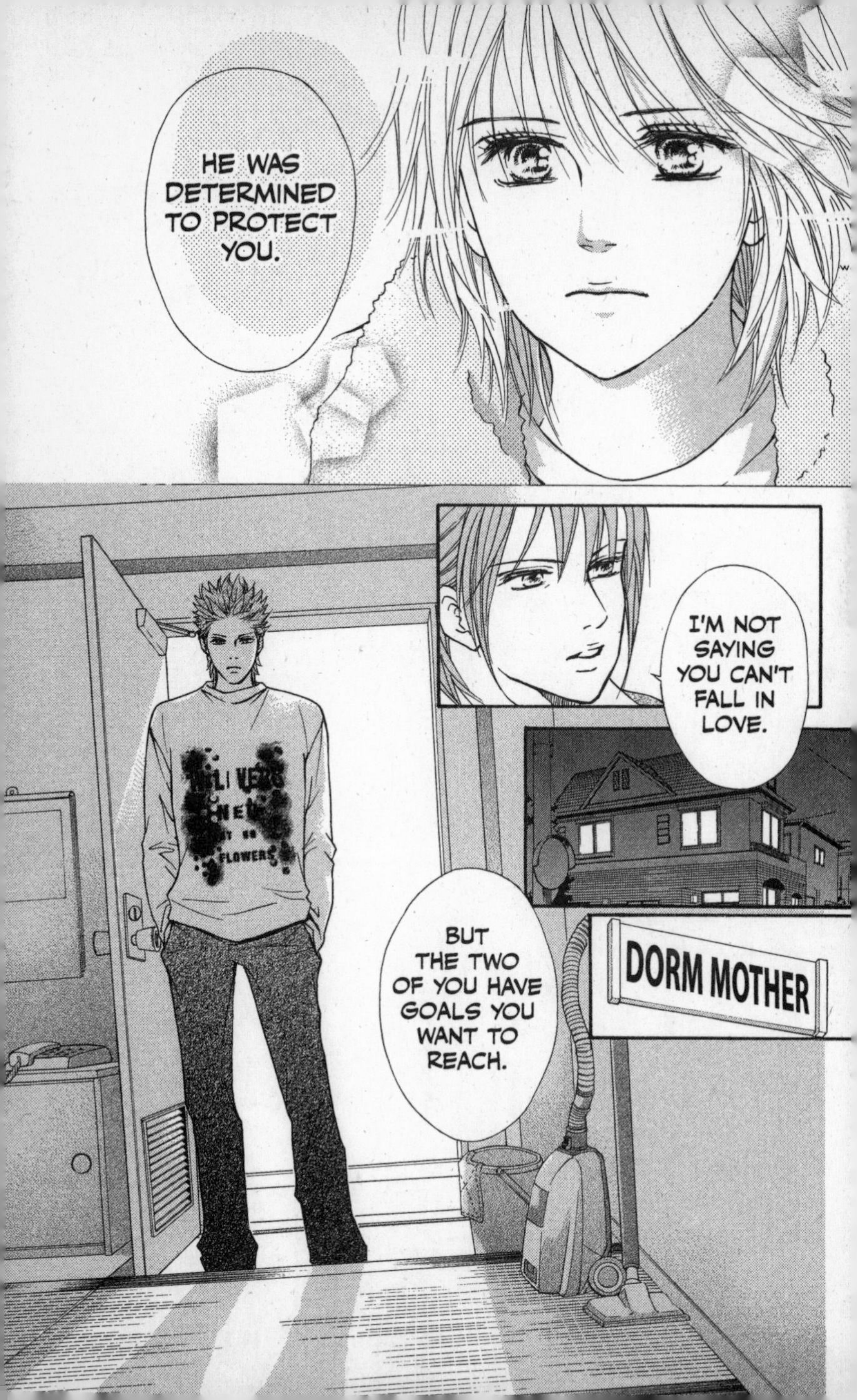
HE WAS DETERMINED TO PROTECT YOU.
I'M NOT SAYING YOU CAN'T FALL IN LOVE.
DORM MOTHER
BUT THE TWO OF YOU HAVE GOALS YOU WANT TO REACH.

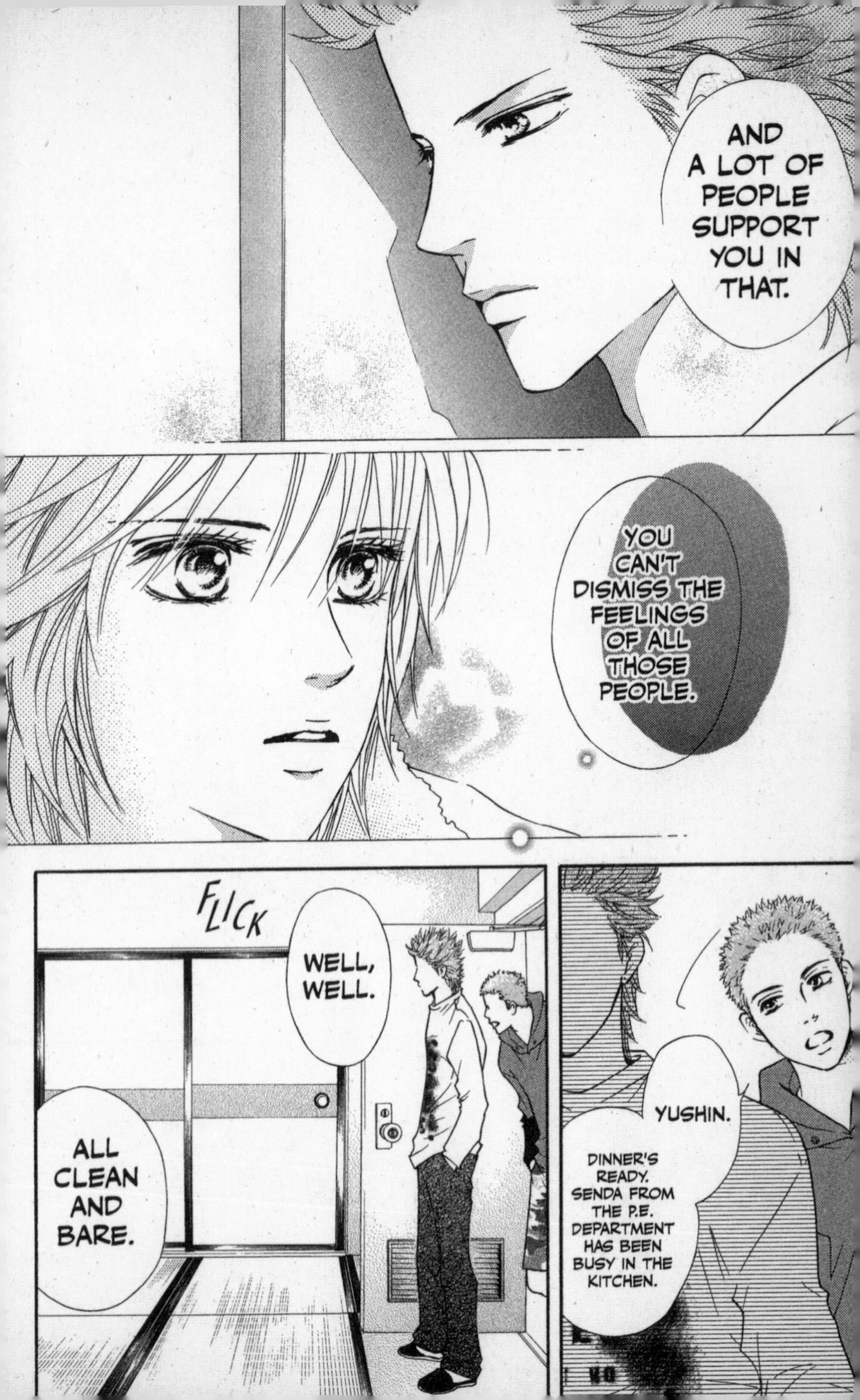
AND A LOT OF PEOPLE SUPPORT YOU IN THAT.
YOU CAN'T DISMISS THE FEELINGS OF ALL THOSE PEOPLE.
YUSHIN.
DINNER'S READY. SENDA FROM THE P.E. DEPARTMENT HAS BEEN BUSY IN THE KITCHEN.
WELL, WELL.
FLICK
ALL CLEAN AND BARE.

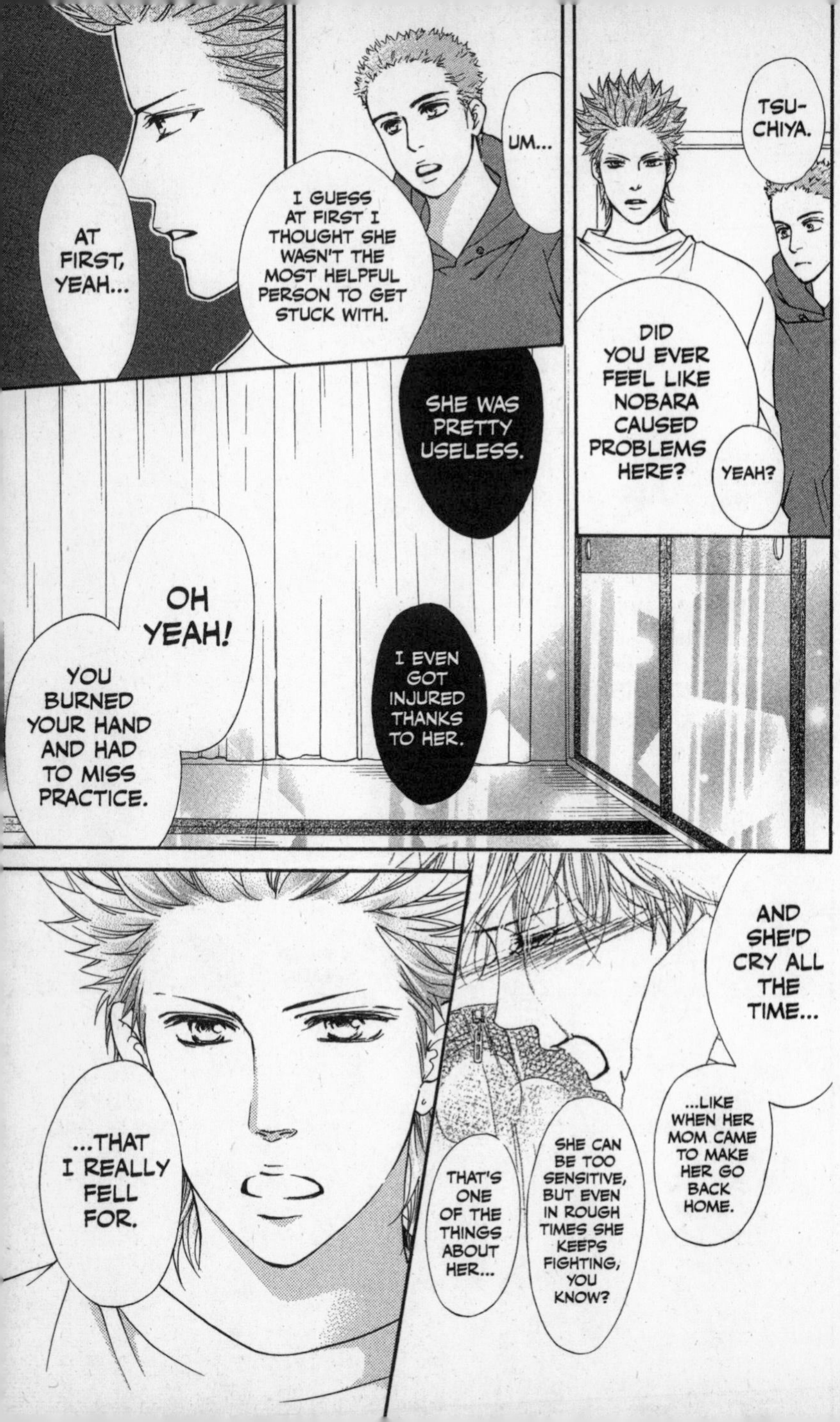

TSU-CHIYA.
DID YOU EVER FEEL LIKE NOBARA CAUSED PROBLEMS HERE?
YEAH?
UM...
I GUESS AT FIRST I THOUGHT SHE WASN'T THE MOST HELPFUL PERSON TO GET STUCK WITH.
AT FIRST, YEAH...
SHE WAS PRETTY USELESS.
I EVEN GOT INJURED THANKS TO HER.
OH YEAH!
YOU BURNED YOUR HAND AND HAD TO MISS PRACTICE.
AND SHE'D CRY ALL THE TIME...
...LIKE WHEN HER MOM CAME TO MAKE HER GO BACK HOME.
SHE CAN BE TOO SENSITIVE, BUT EVEN IN ROUGH TIMES SHE KEEPS FIGHTING, YOU KNOW?
THAT'S ONE OF THE THINGS ABOUT HER...
...THAT I REALLY FELL FOR.

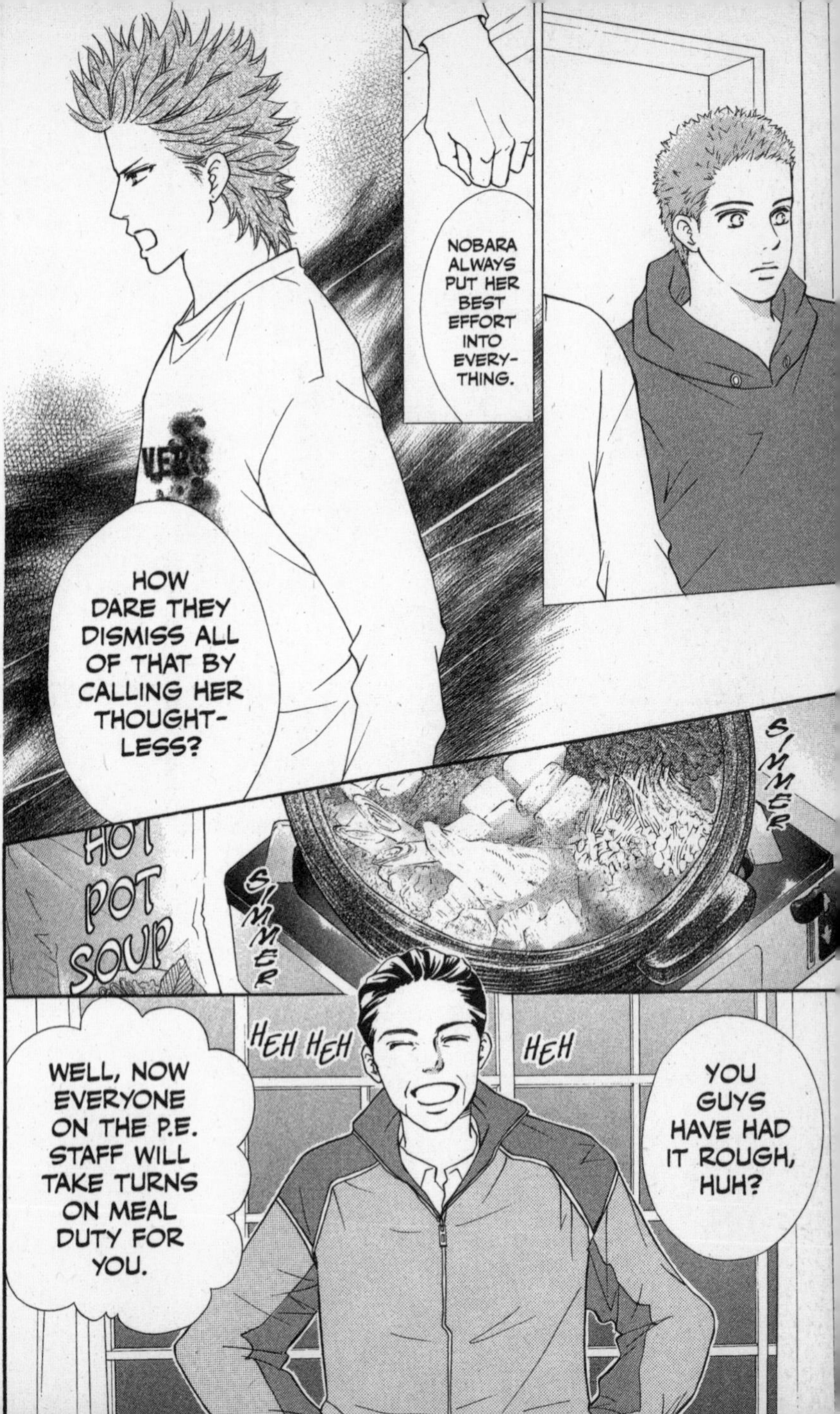
NOBARA ALWAYS PUT HER BEST EFFORT INTO EVERY-THING.
HOW DARE THEY DISMISS ALL OF THAT BY CALLING HER THOUGHT-LESS?
SIMMER
SIMMER
HOT POT SOUP
HEH
HEH HEH
YOU GUYS HAVE HAD IT ROUGH, HUH?
WELL, NOW EVERYONE ON THE P.E. STAFF WILL TAKE TURNS ON MEAL DUTY FOR YOU.

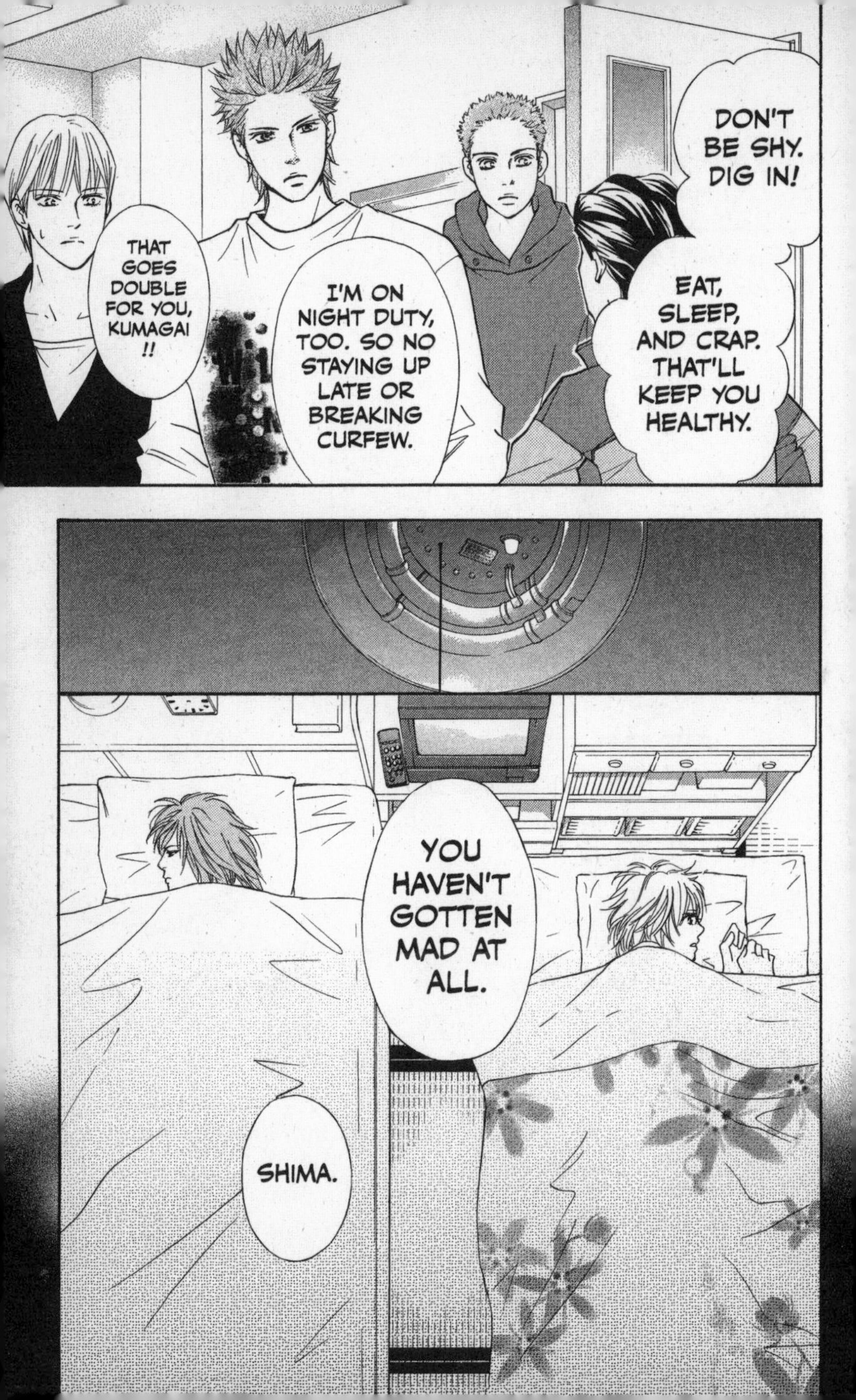
DON'T BE SHY. DIG IN!
EAT, SLEEP, AND CRAP. THAT'LL KEEP YOU HEALTHY.
I'M ON NIGHT DUTY, TOO. SO NO STAYING UP LATE OR BREAKING CURFEW.
THAT GOES DOUBLE FOR YOU, KUMAGAI !!
YOU HAVEN'T GOTTEN MAD AT ALL.
SHIMA.

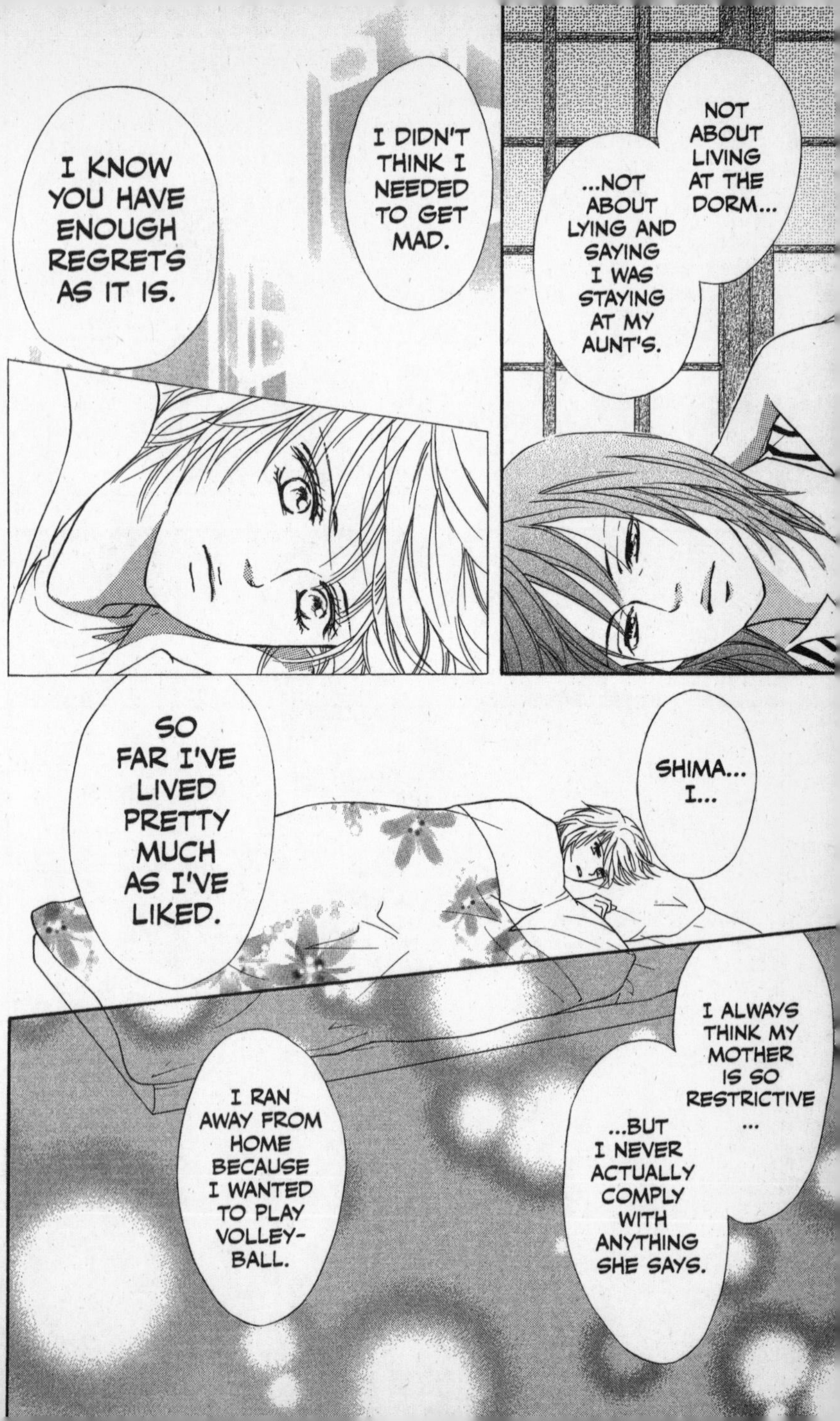
NOT ABOUT LIVING AT THE DORM...
...NOT ABOUT LYING AND SAYING I WAS STAYING AT MY AUNT'S.
I DIDN'T THINK I NEEDED TO GET MAD.
I KNOW YOU HAVE ENOUGH REGRETS AS IT IS.
SHIMA... I...
SO FAR I'VE LIVED PRETTY MUCH AS I'VE LIKED.
I ALWAYS THINK MY MOTHER IS SO RESTRICTIVE ...
...BUT I NEVER ACTUALLY COMPLY WITH ANYTHING SHE SAYS.
I RAN AWAY FROM HOME BECAUSE I WANTED TO PLAY VOLLEY-BALL.

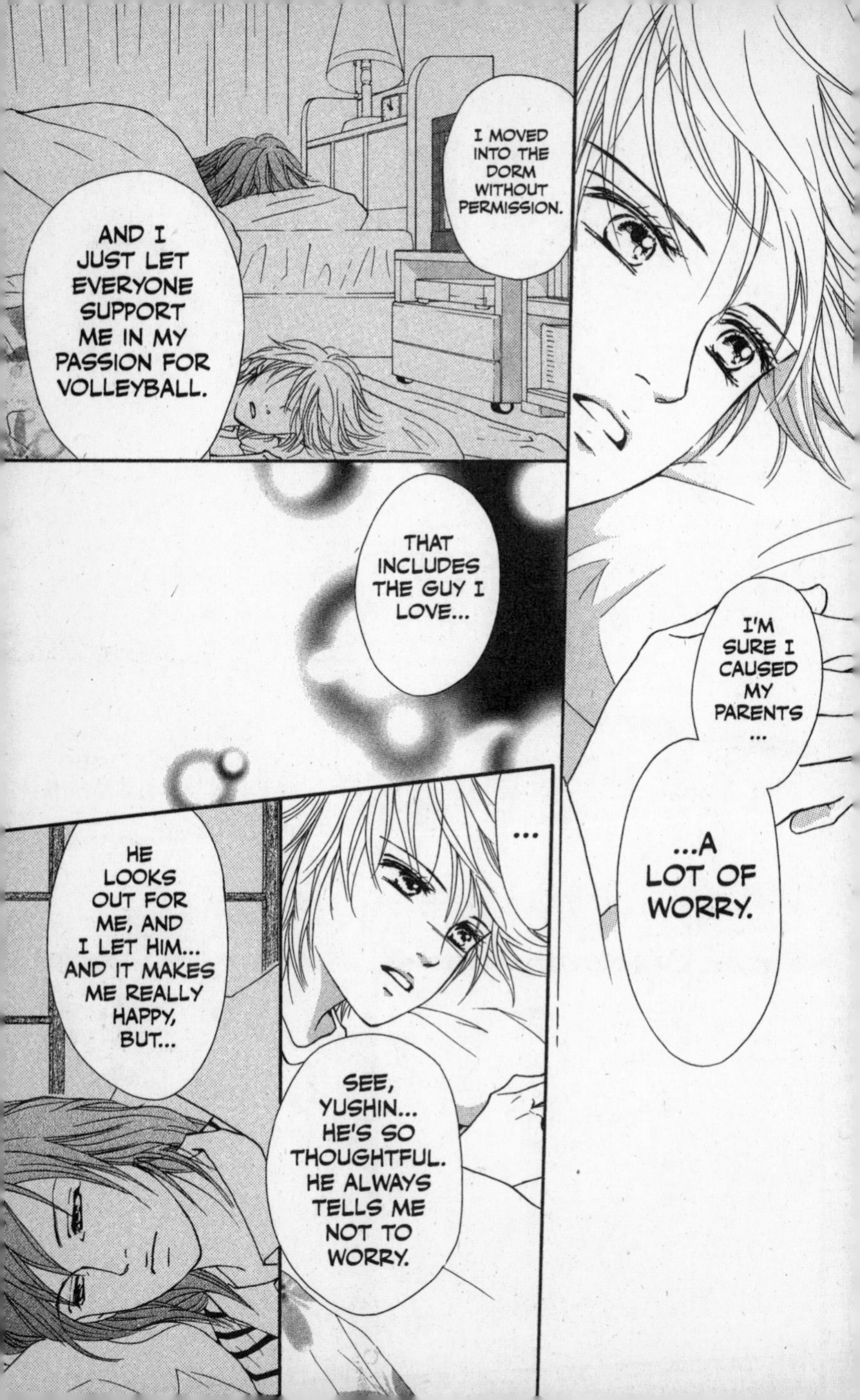
I'M SURE I CAUSED MY PARENTS ...
...A LOT OF WORRY.
I MOVED INTO THE DORM WITHOUT PERMISSION.
AND I JUST LET EVERYONE SUPPORT ME IN MY PASSION FOR VOLLEYBALL.
THAT INCLUDES THE GUY I LOVE...
...
SEE, YUSHIN... HE'S SO THOUGHTFUL. HE ALWAYS TELLS ME NOT TO WORRY.
HE LOOKS OUT FOR ME, AND I LET HIM... AND IT MAKES ME REALLY HAPPY, BUT...

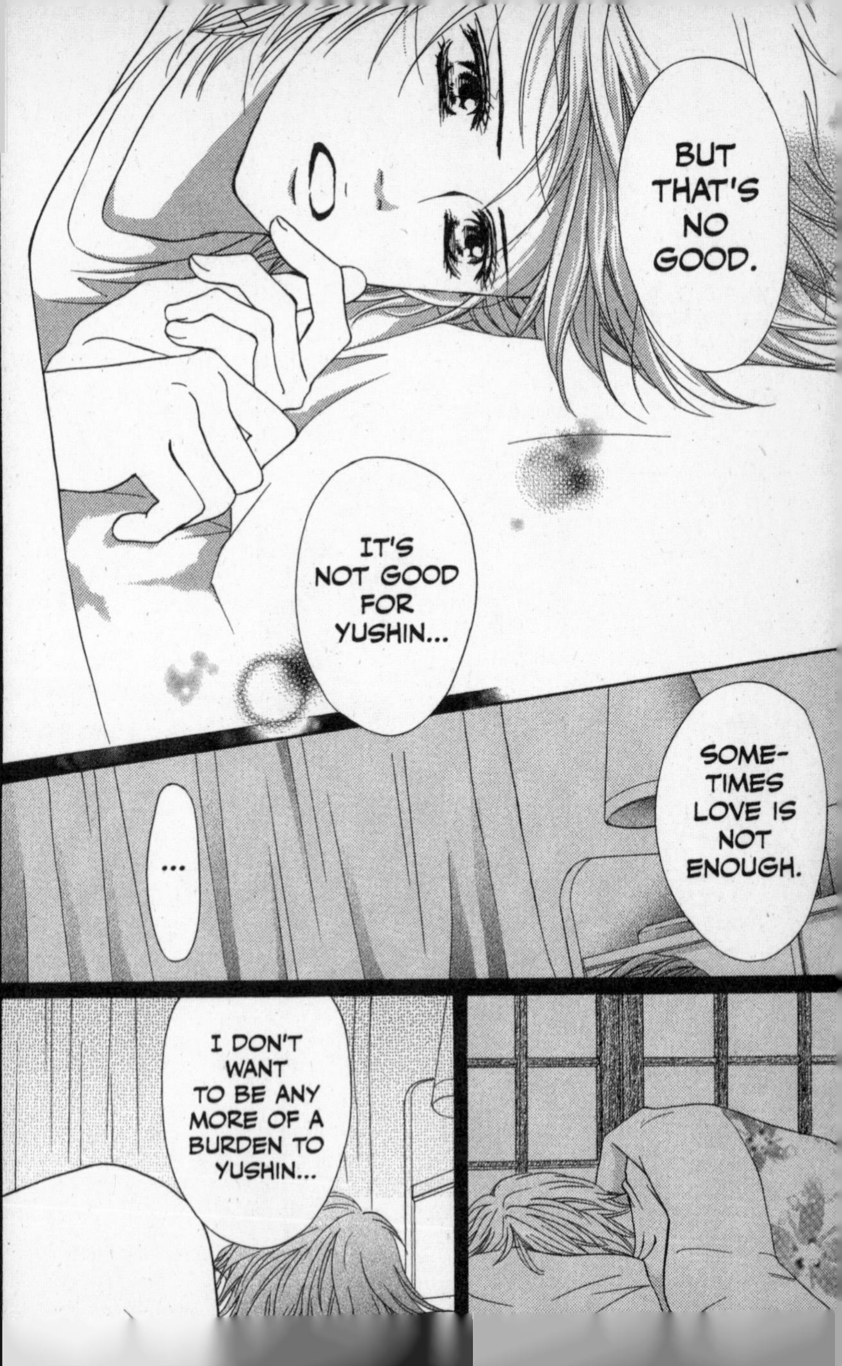
BUT THAT'S NO GOOD.
IT'S NOT GOOD FOR YUSHIN...
SOME-TIMES LOVE IS NOT ENOUGH.
...
I DON'T WANT TO BE ANY MORE OF A BURDEN TO YUSHIN...

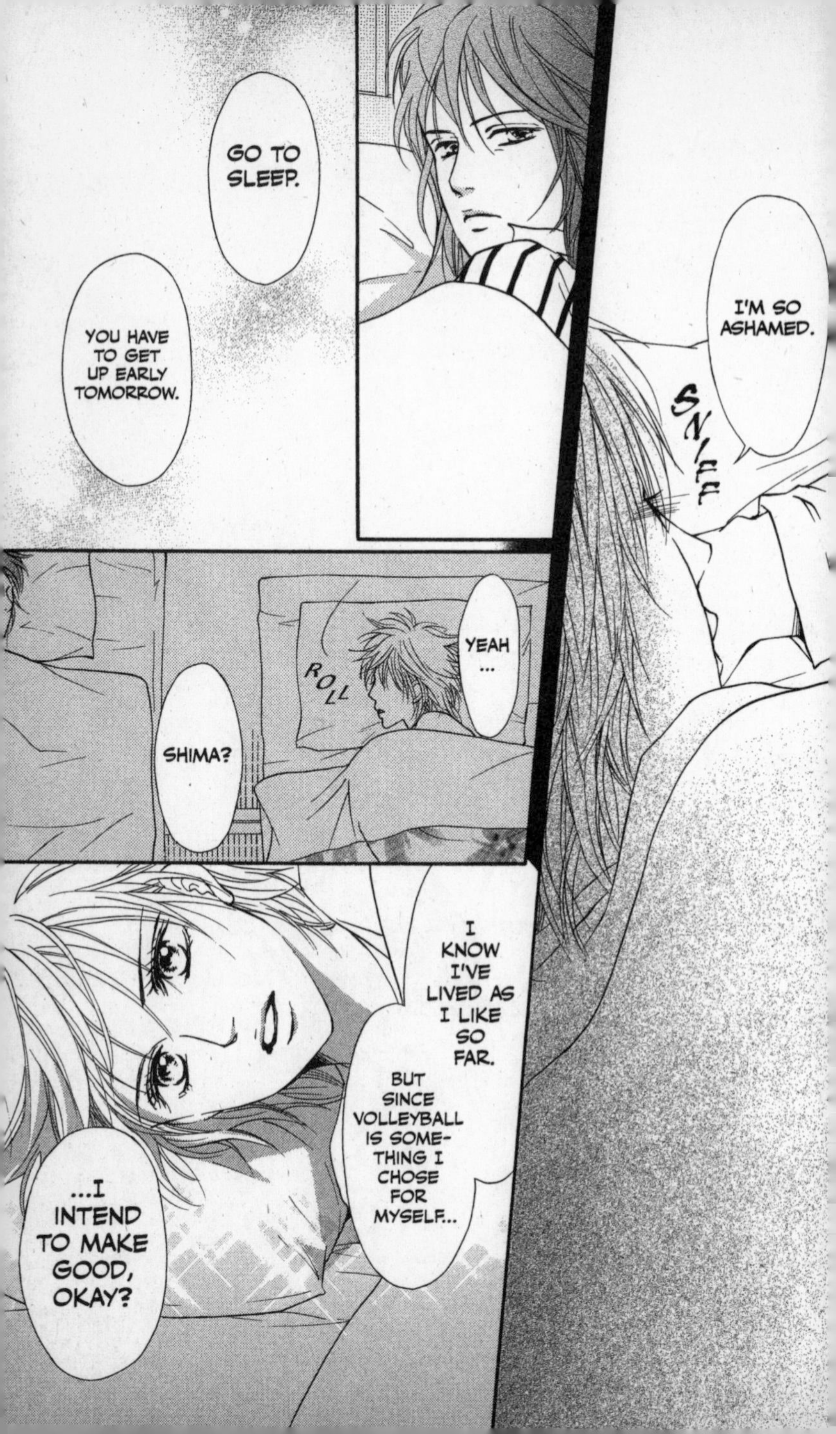
I'M SO ASHAMED.
SNIFF
GO TO SLEEP.
YOU HAVE TO GET UP EARLY TOMORROW.
YEAH ...
ROLL
SHIMA?
I KNOW I'VE LIVED AS I LIKE SO FAR.
BUT SINCE VOLLEYBALL IS SOME-THING I CHOSE FOR MYSELF...
...I INTEND TO MAKE GOOD, OKAY?

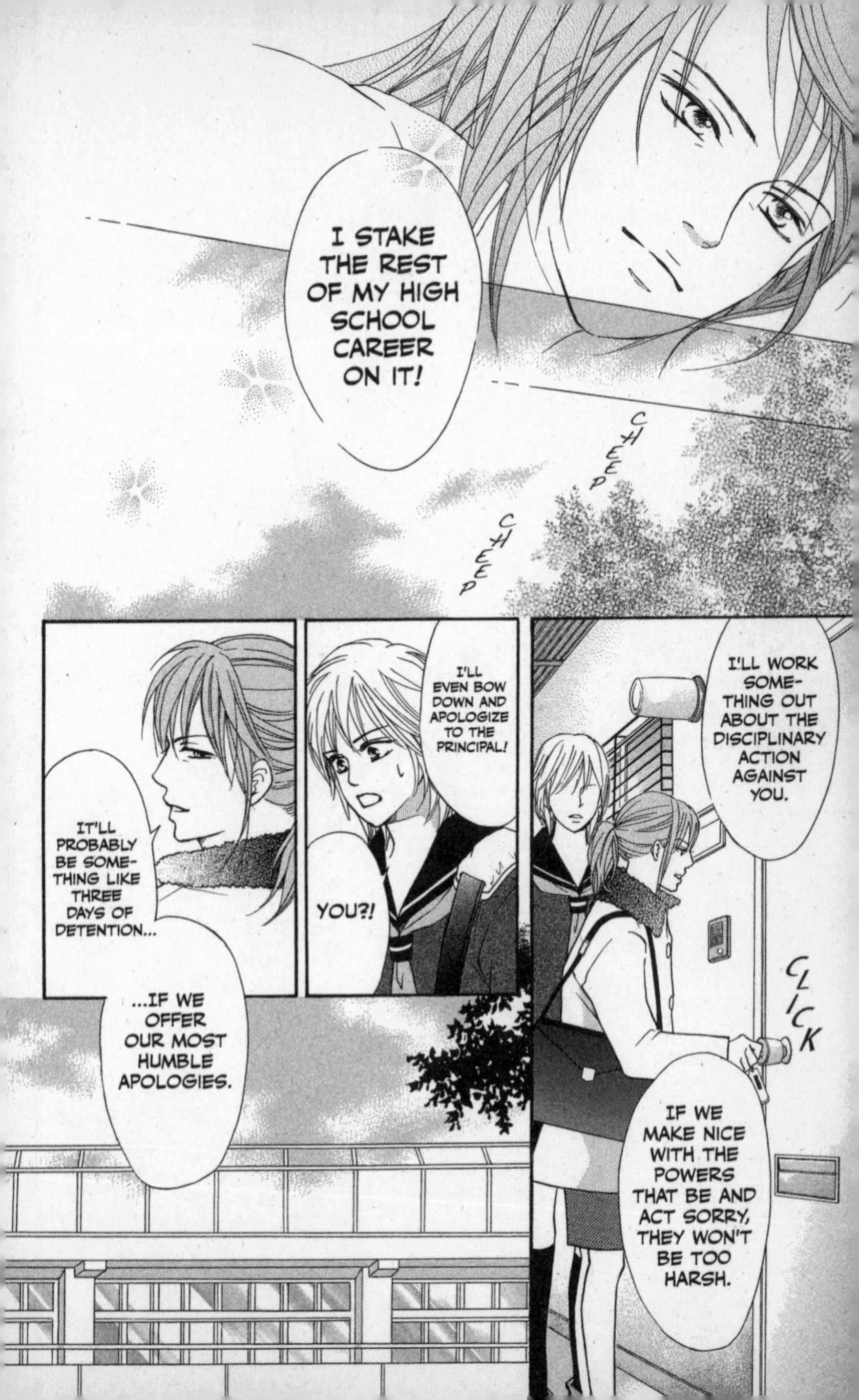
I STAKE THE REST OF MY HIGH SCHOOL CAREER ON IT!
CHEEP
CHEEP
I'LL WORK SOME-THING OUT ABOUT THE DISCIPLINARY ACTION AGAINST YOU.
CLICK
IF WE MAKE NICE WITH THE POWERS THAT BE AND ACT SORRY, THEY WON'T BE TOO HARSH.
I'LL EVEN BOW DOWN AND APOLOGIZE TO THE PRINCIPAL!
YOU?!
IT'LL PROBABLY BE SOME-THING LIKE THREE DAYS OF DETENTION...
...IF WE OFFER OUR MOST HUMBLE APOLOGIES.

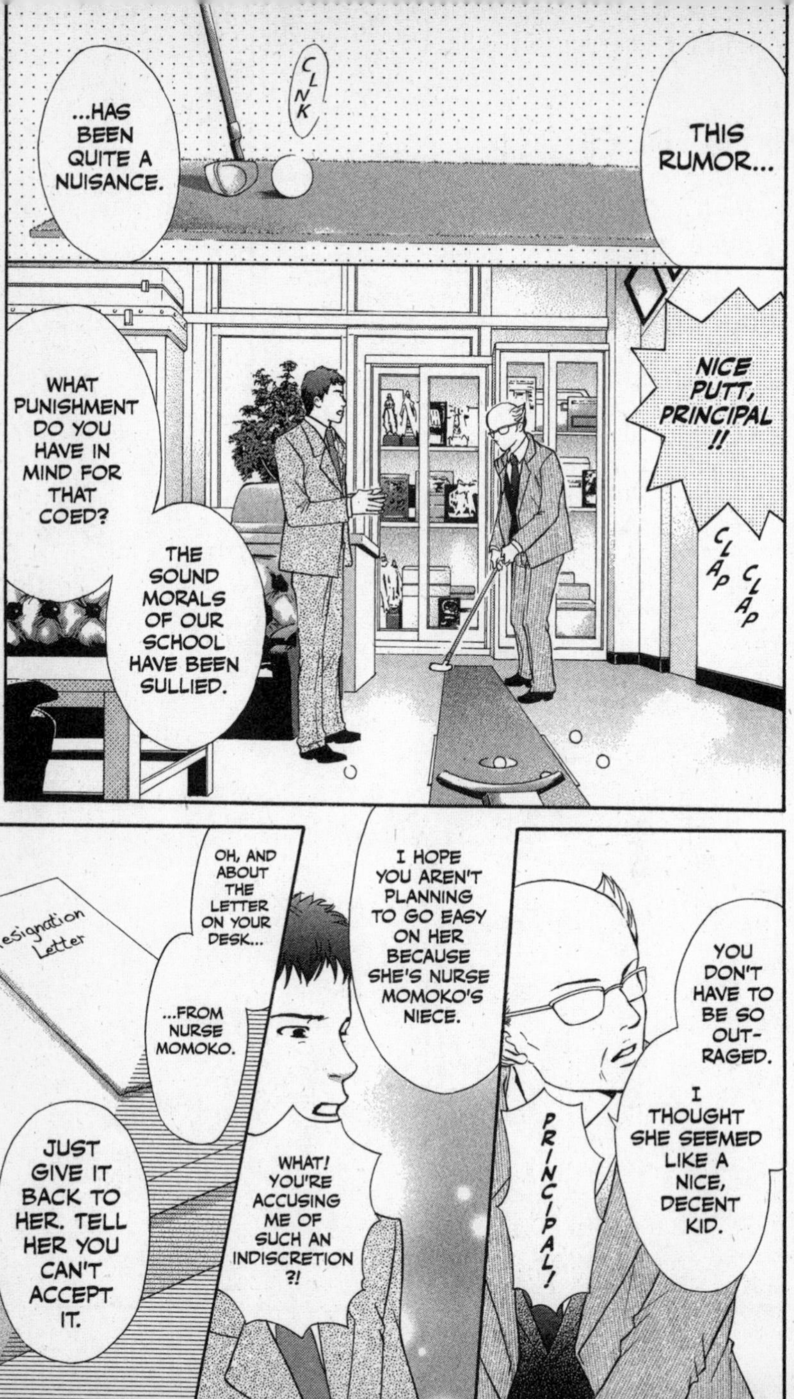
THIS RUMOR...
CLINK
...HAS BEEN QUITE A NUISANCE.
NICE PUTT, PRINCIPAL!!
CLAP CLAP
WHAT PUNISHMENT DO YOU HAVE IN MIND FOR THAT COED?
THE SOUND MORALS OF OUR SCHOOL HAVE BEEN SULLIED.
YOU DON'T HAVE TO BE SO OUT-RAGED.
I THOUGHT SHE SEEMED LIKE A NICE, DECENT KID.
PRINCIPAL!
I HOPE YOU AREN'T PLANNING TO GO EASY ON HER BECAUSE SHE'S NURSE MOMOKO'S NIECE.
WHAT! YOU'RE ACCUSING ME OF SUCH AN INDISCRETION?!
OH, AND ABOUT THE LETTER ON YOUR DESK...
...FROM NURSE MOMOKO.
Resignation Letter
JUST GIVE IT BACK TO HER. TELL HER YOU CAN'T ACCEPT IT.

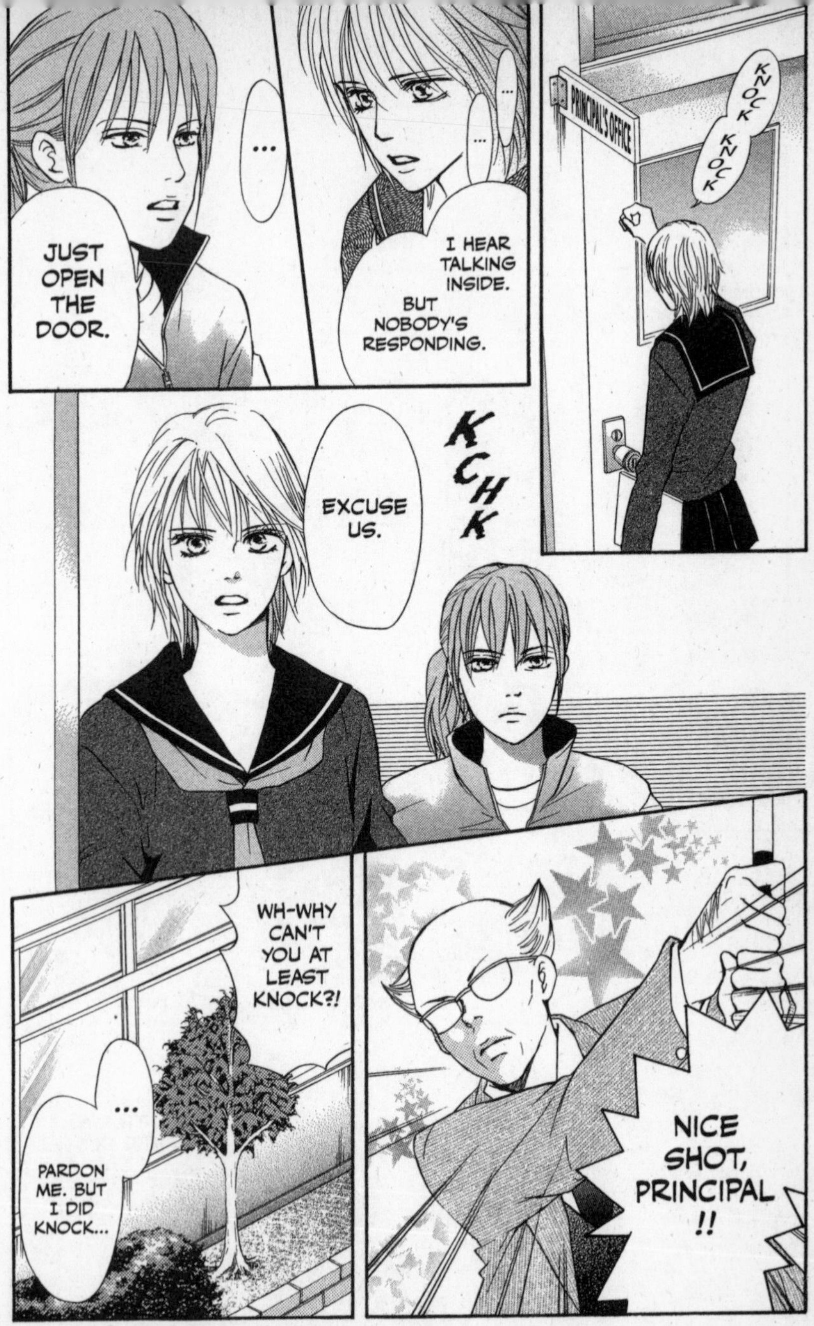
PRINCIPAL'S OFFICE
KNOCK KNOCK
...
...
I HEAR TALKING INSIDE.
BUT NOBODY'S RESPONDING.
...
JUST OPEN THE DOOR.
KCHK
EXCUSE US.
NICE SHOT, PRINCIPAL !!
WH-WHY CAN'T YOU AT LEAST KNOCK?!
...
PARDON ME. BUT I DID KNOCK...

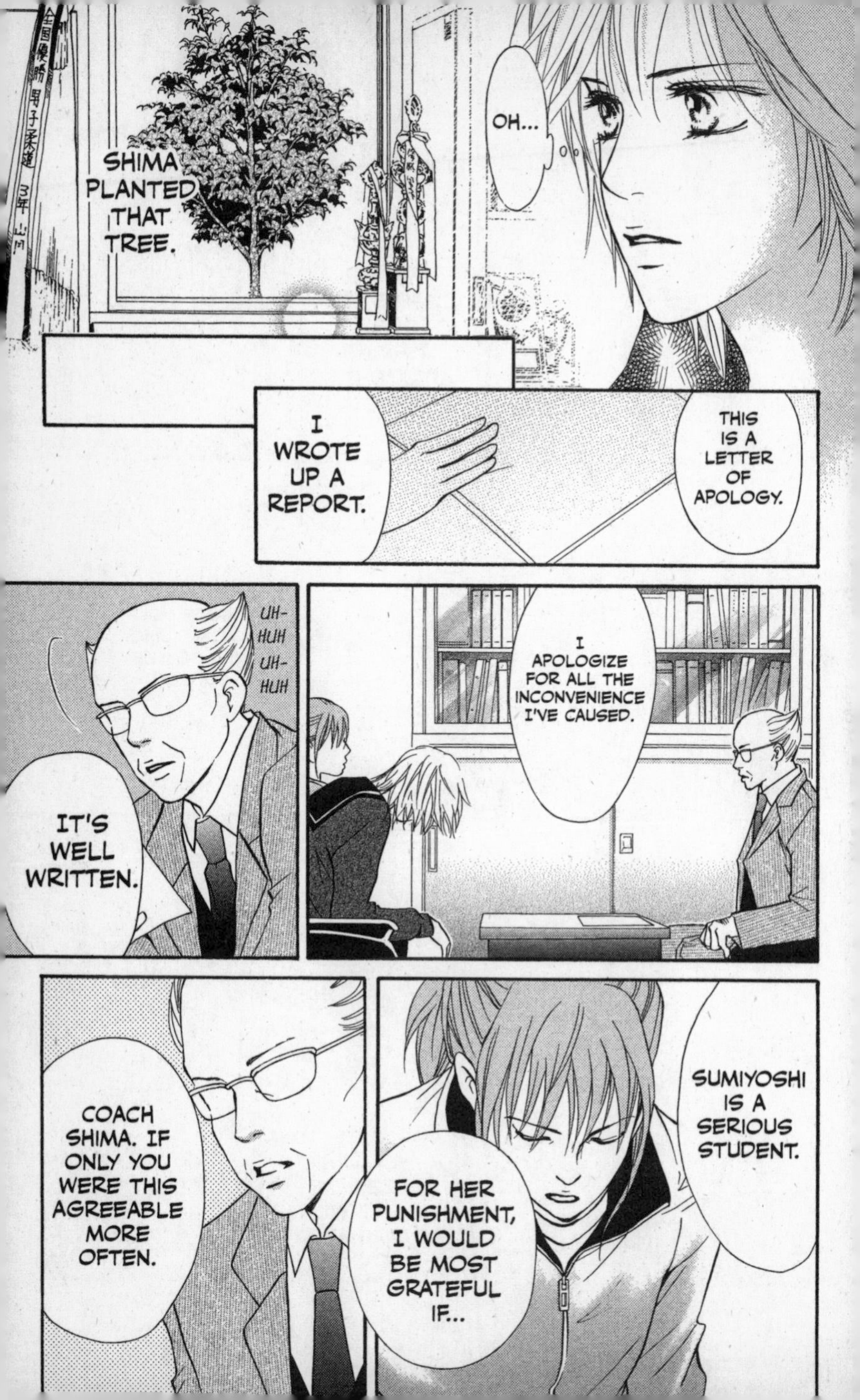
OH...
SHIMA PLANTED THAT TREE.
THIS IS A LETTER OF APOLOGY.
I WROTE UP A REPORT.
I APOLOGIZE FOR ALL THE INCONVENIENCE I'VE CAUSED.
UH-HUH UH-HUH
IT'S WELL WRITTEN.
SUMIYOSHI IS A SERIOUS STUDENT.
FOR HER PUNISHMENT, I WOULD BE MOST GRATEFUL IF...
COACH SHIMA. IF ONLY YOU WERE THIS AGREEABLE MORE OFTEN.

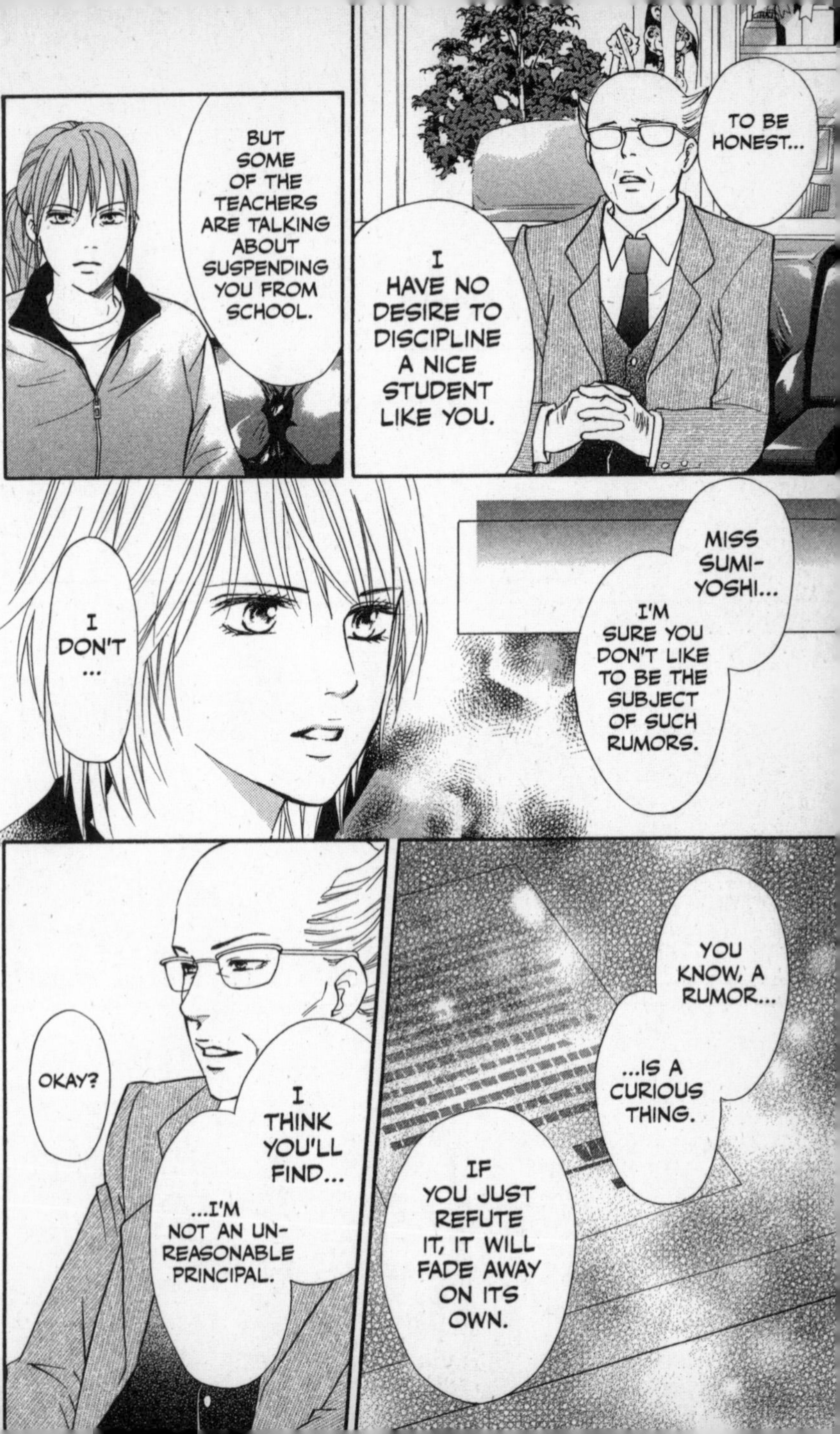
TO BE HONEST...
I HAVE NO DESIRE TO DISCIPLINE A NICE STUDENT LIKE YOU.
BUT SOME OF THE TEACHERS ARE TALKING ABOUT SUSPENDING YOU FROM SCHOOL.
MISS SUMI-YOSHI...
I'M SURE YOU DON'T LIKE TO BE THE SUBJECT OF SUCH RUMORS.
I DON'T ...
YOU KNOW, A RUMOR...
...IS A CURIOUS THING.
IF YOU JUST REFUTE IT, IT WILL FADE AWAY ON ITS OWN.
I THINK YOU'LL FIND...
...I'M NOT AN UN-REASONABLE PRINCIPAL.
OKAY?

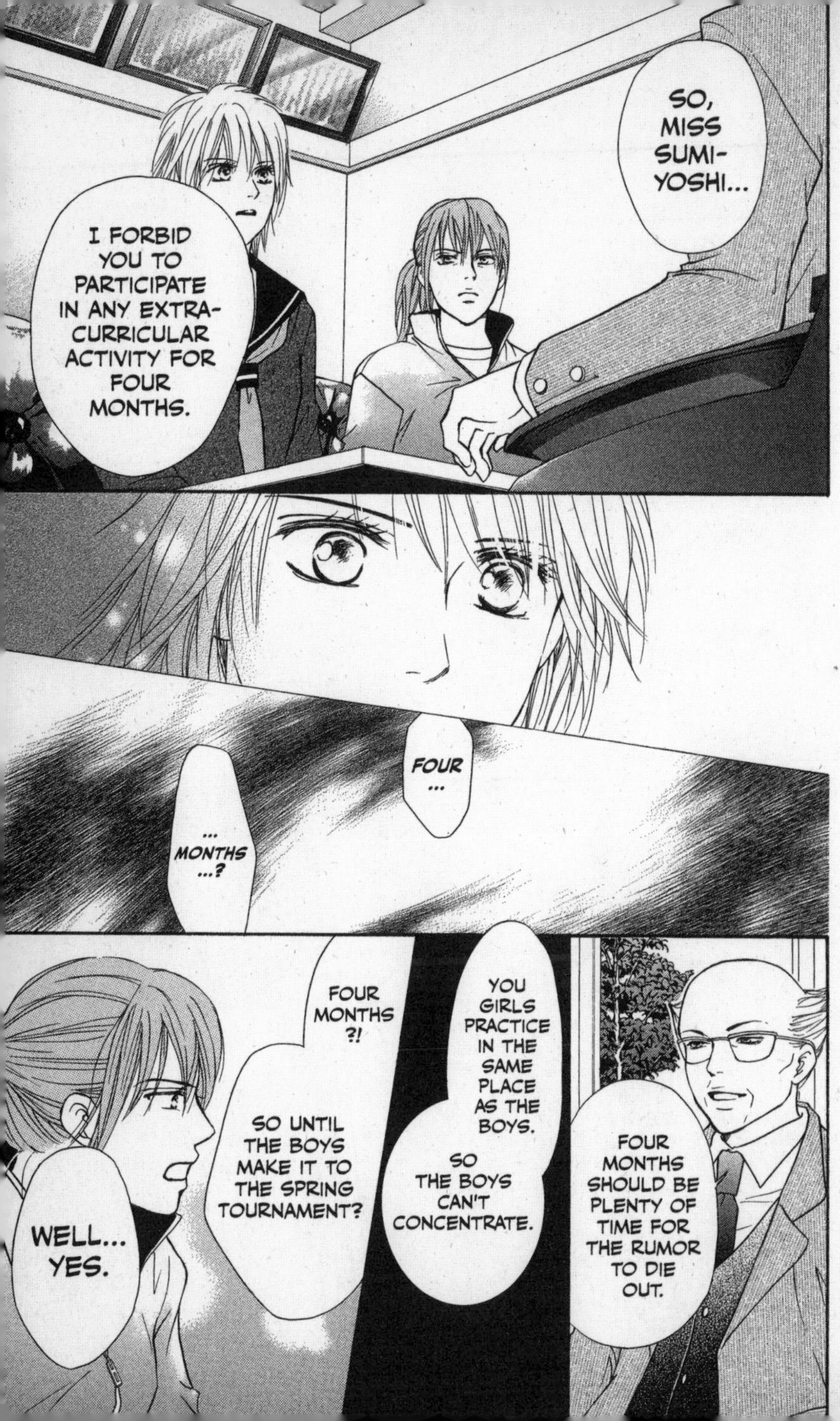
SO, MISS SUMI-YOSHI...
I FORBID YOU TO PARTICIPATE IN ANY EXTRA-CURRICULAR ACTIVITY FOR FOUR MONTHS.
FOUR...
...MONTHS...?
FOUR MONTHS?!
YOU GIRLS PRACTICE IN THE SAME PLACE AS THE BOYS.
SO THE BOYS CAN'T CONCENTRATE.
FOUR MONTHS SHOULD BE PLENTY OF TIME FOR THE RUMOR TO DIE OUT.
SO UNTIL THE BOYS MAKE IT TO THE SPRING TOURNAMENT?
WELL... YES.

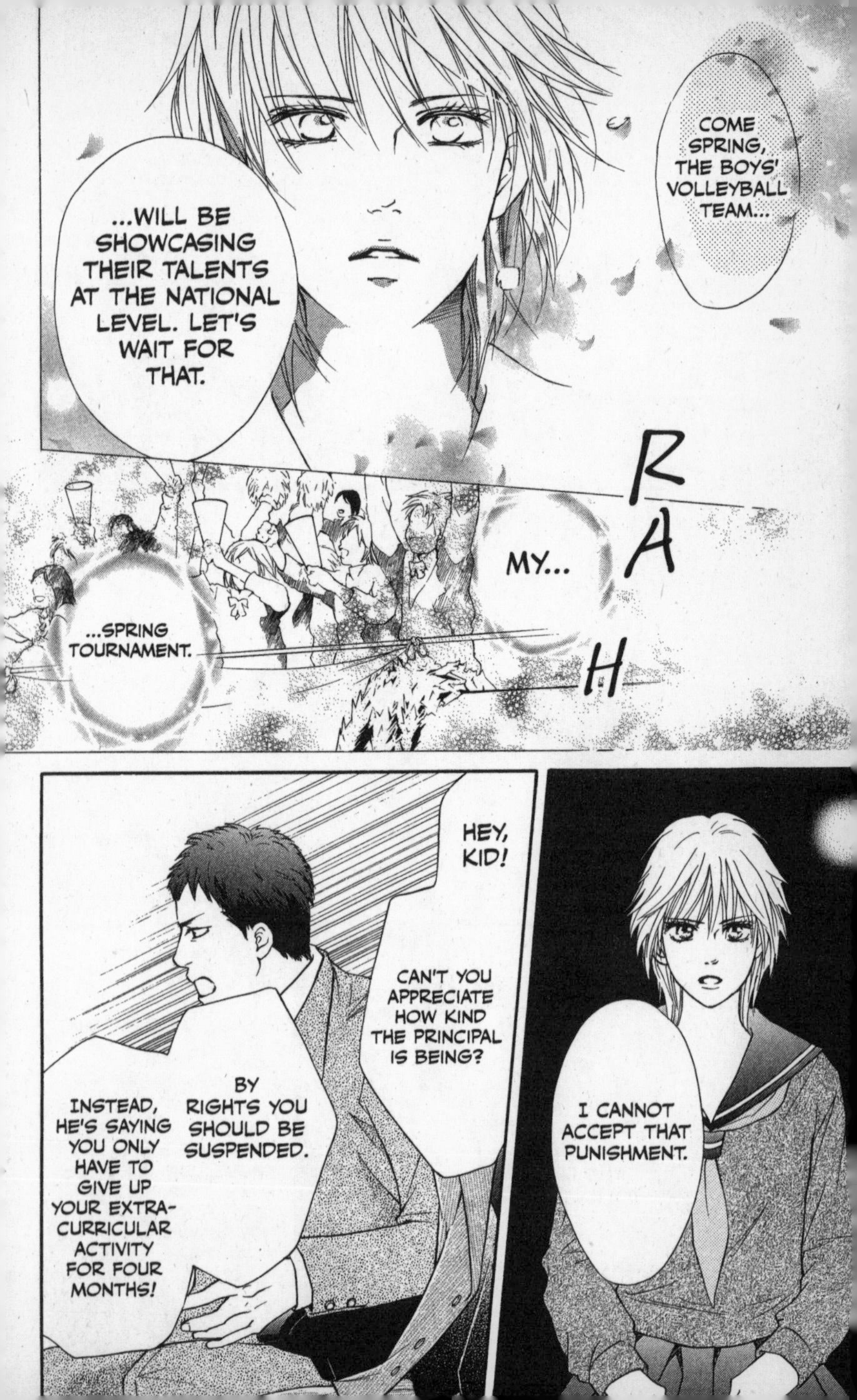
COME SPRING, THE BOYS' VOLLEYBALL TEAM...
...WILL BE SHOWCASING THEIR TALENTS AT THE NATIONAL LEVEL. LET'S WAIT FOR THAT.
RAH
MY...
...SPRING TOURNAMENT.
I CANNOT ACCEPT THAT PUNISHMENT.
HEY, KID!
CAN'T YOU APPRECIATE HOW KIND THE PRINCIPAL IS BEING?
BY RIGHTS YOU SHOULD BE SUSPENDED.
INSTEAD, HE'S SAYING YOU ONLY HAVE TO GIVE UP YOUR EXTRA-CURRICULAR ACTIVITY FOR FOUR MONTHS!

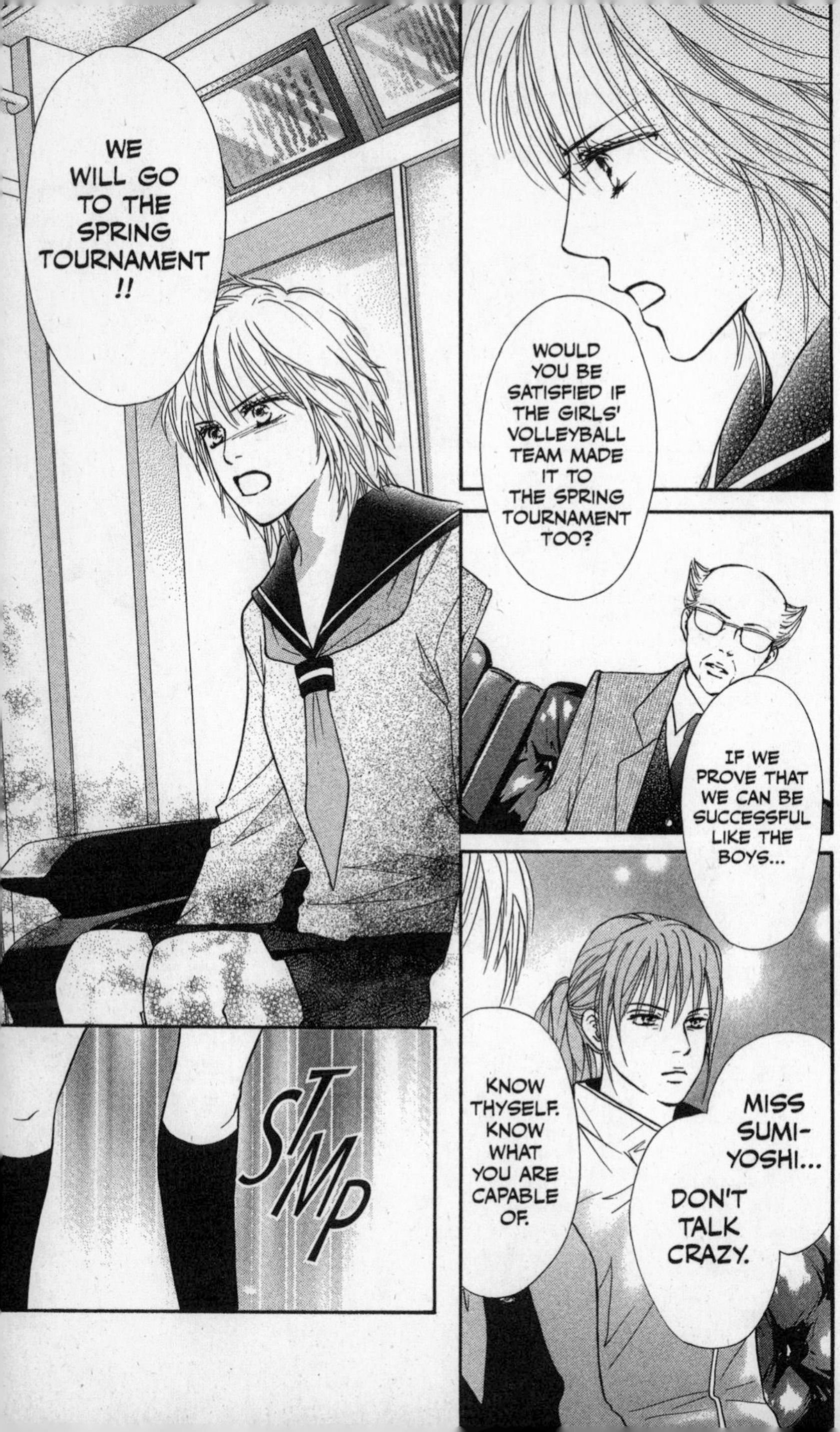
WOULD YOU BE SATISFIED IF THE GIRLS' VOLLEYBALL TEAM MADE IT TO THE SPRING TOURNAMENT TOO?
IF WE PROVE THAT WE CAN BE SUCCESSFUL LIKE THE BOYS...
MISS SUMI-YOSHI...
DON'T TALK CRAZY.
KNOW THYSELF. KNOW WHAT YOU ARE CAPABLE OF.
WE WILL GO TO THE SPRING TOURNAMENT !!
STMP

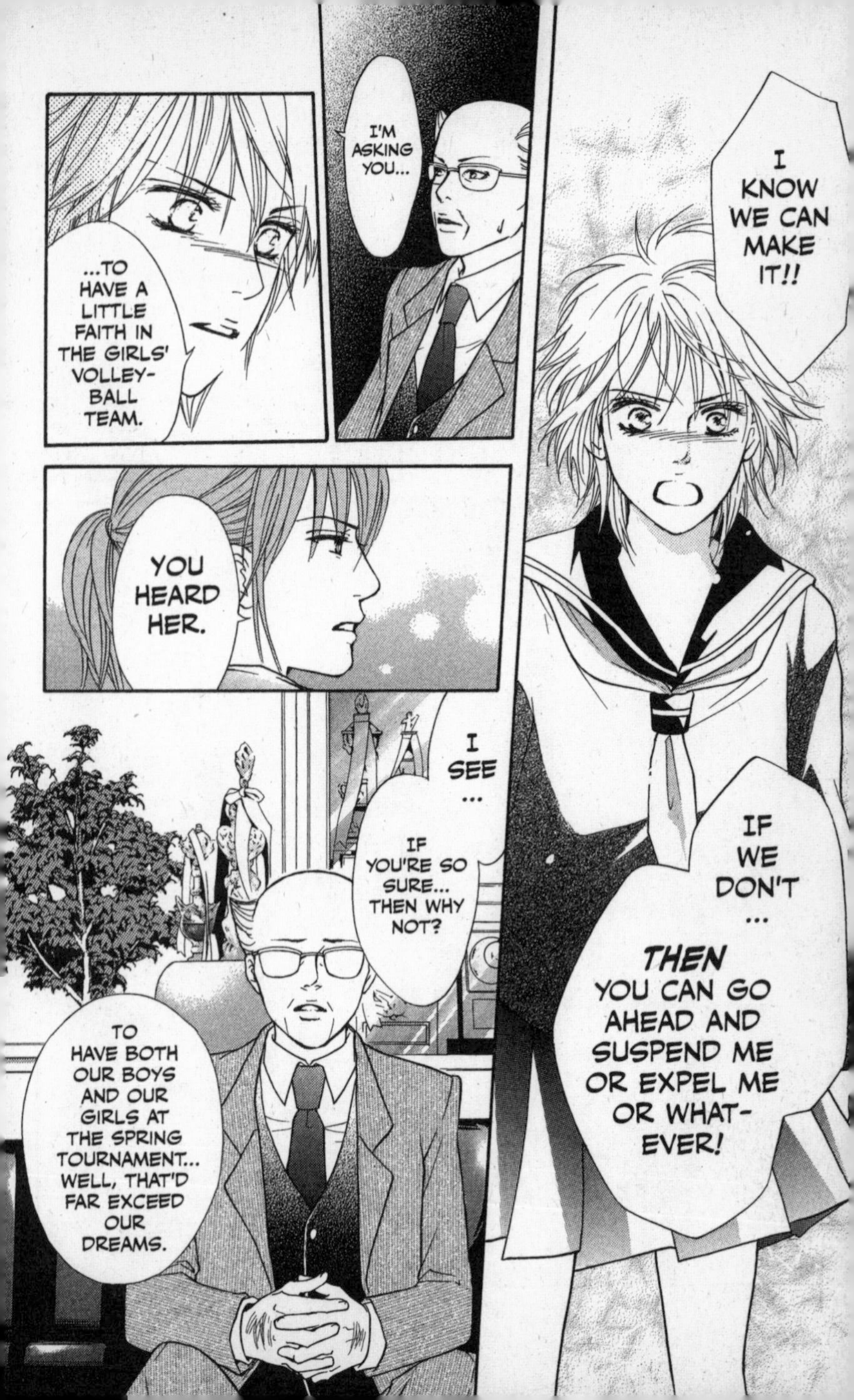
I KNOW WE CAN MAKE IT!!
IF WE DON'T...
THEN YOU CAN GO AHEAD AND SUSPEND ME OR EXPEL ME OR WHAT-EVER!
I'M ASKING YOU...
...TO HAVE A LITTLE FAITH IN THE GIRLS' VOLLEY-BALL TEAM.
YOU HEARD HER.
I SEE...
IF YOU'RE SO SURE... THEN WHY NOT?
TO HAVE BOTH OUR BOYS AND OUR GIRLS AT THE SPRING TOURNAMENT... WELL, THAT'D FAR EXCEED OUR DREAMS.

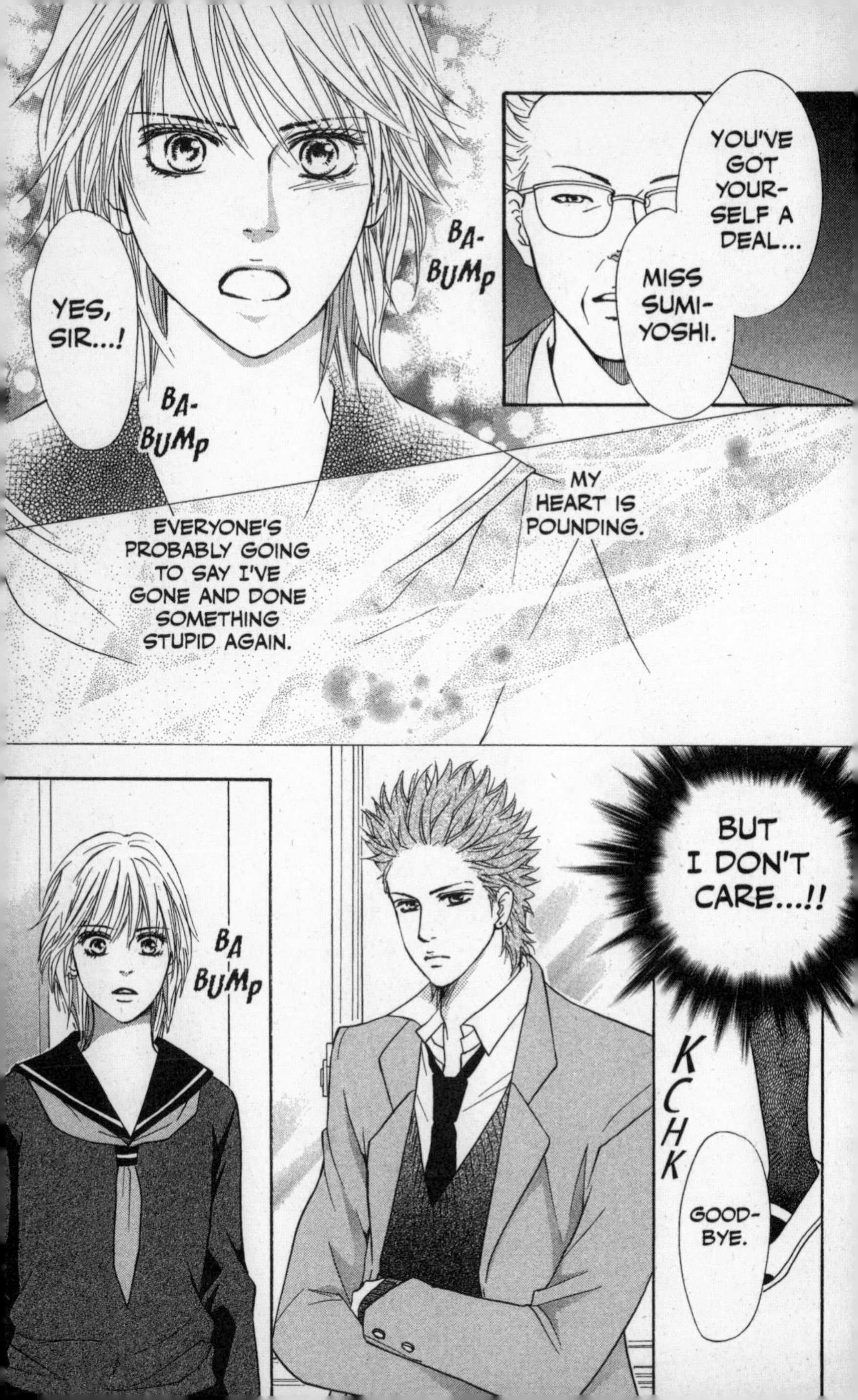

YOU'VE GOT YOURSELF A DEAL...
MISS SUMIYOSHI.
BA-BUMP
YES, SIR...!
BA-BUMP
MY HEART IS POUNDING.
EVERYONE'S PROBABLY GOING TO SAY I'VE GONE AND DONE SOMETHING STUPID AGAIN.
BUT I DON'T CARE...!!
KCHK
GOOD-BYE.
BA BUMP

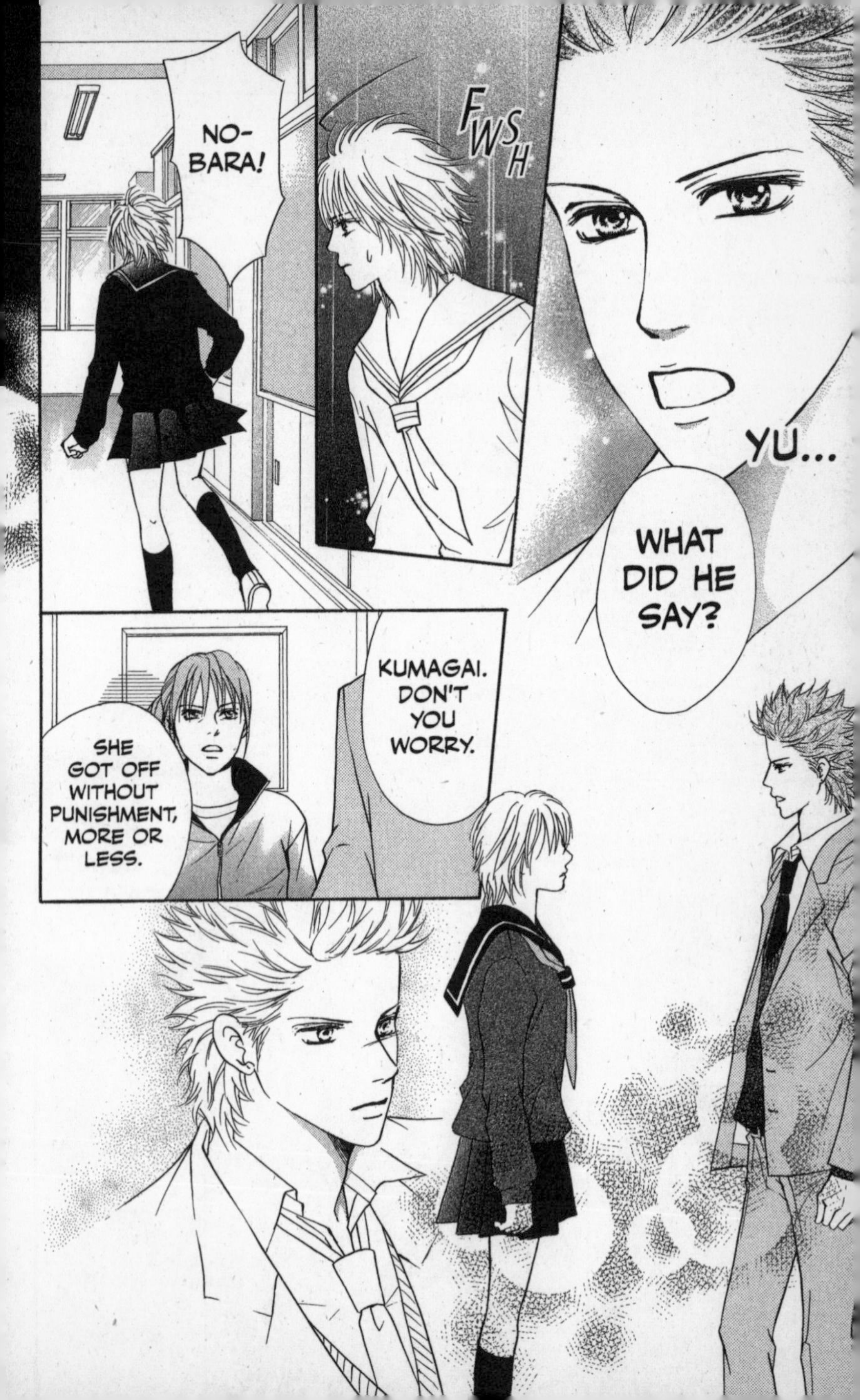
YU...
WHAT DID HE SAY?
FWSH
NO-BARA!
KUMAGAI. DON'T YOU WORRY.
SHE GOT OFF WITHOUT PUNISHMENT, MORE OR LESS.

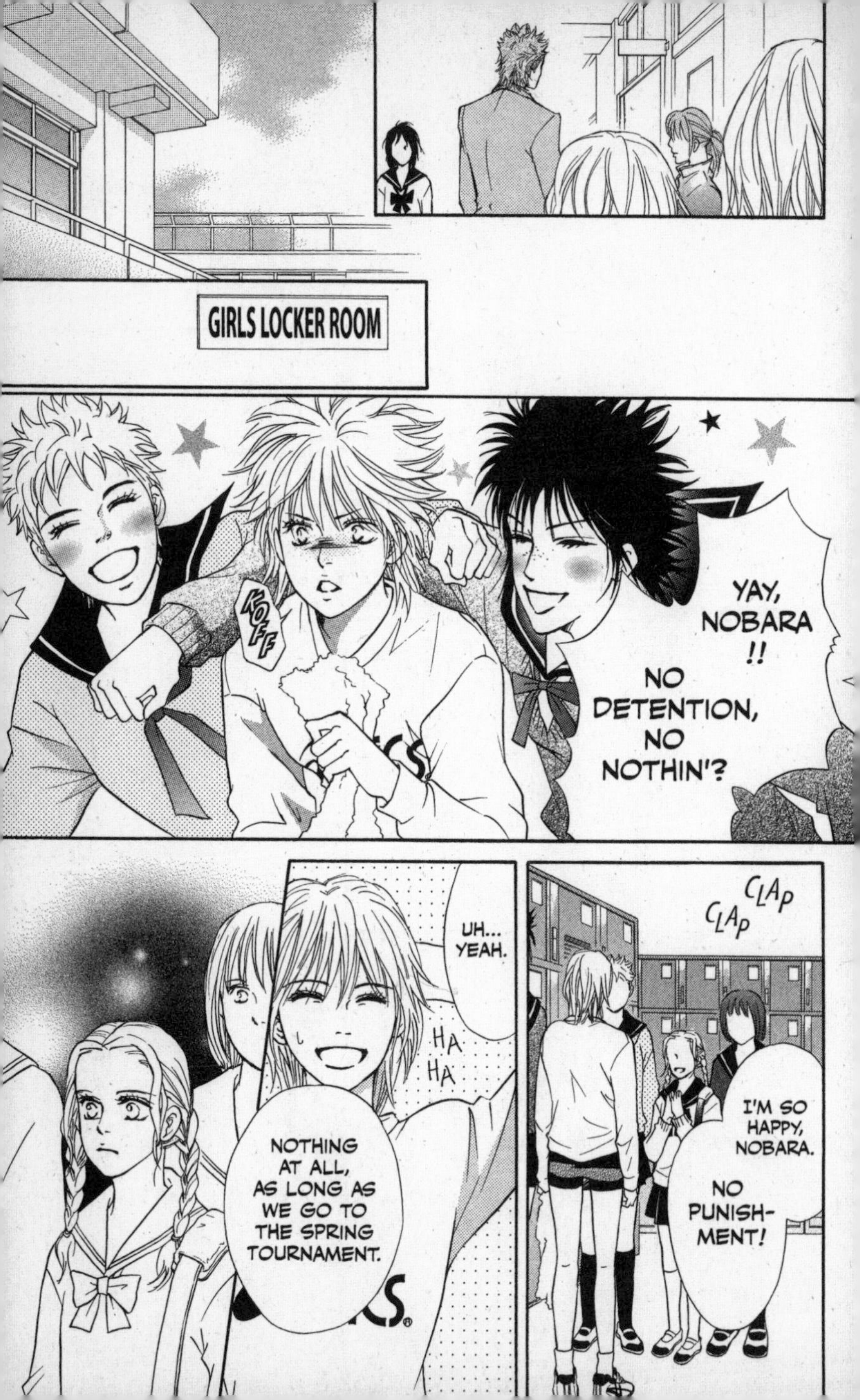
GIRLS LOCKER ROOM
YAY, NOBARA!!
NO DETENTION, NO NOTHIN'?
KOFF
CLAP CLAP
I'M SO HAPPY, NOBARA.
NO PUNISHMENT!
UH... YEAH.
HA HA
NOTHING AT ALL, AS LONG AS WE GO TO THE SPRING TOURNAMENT.

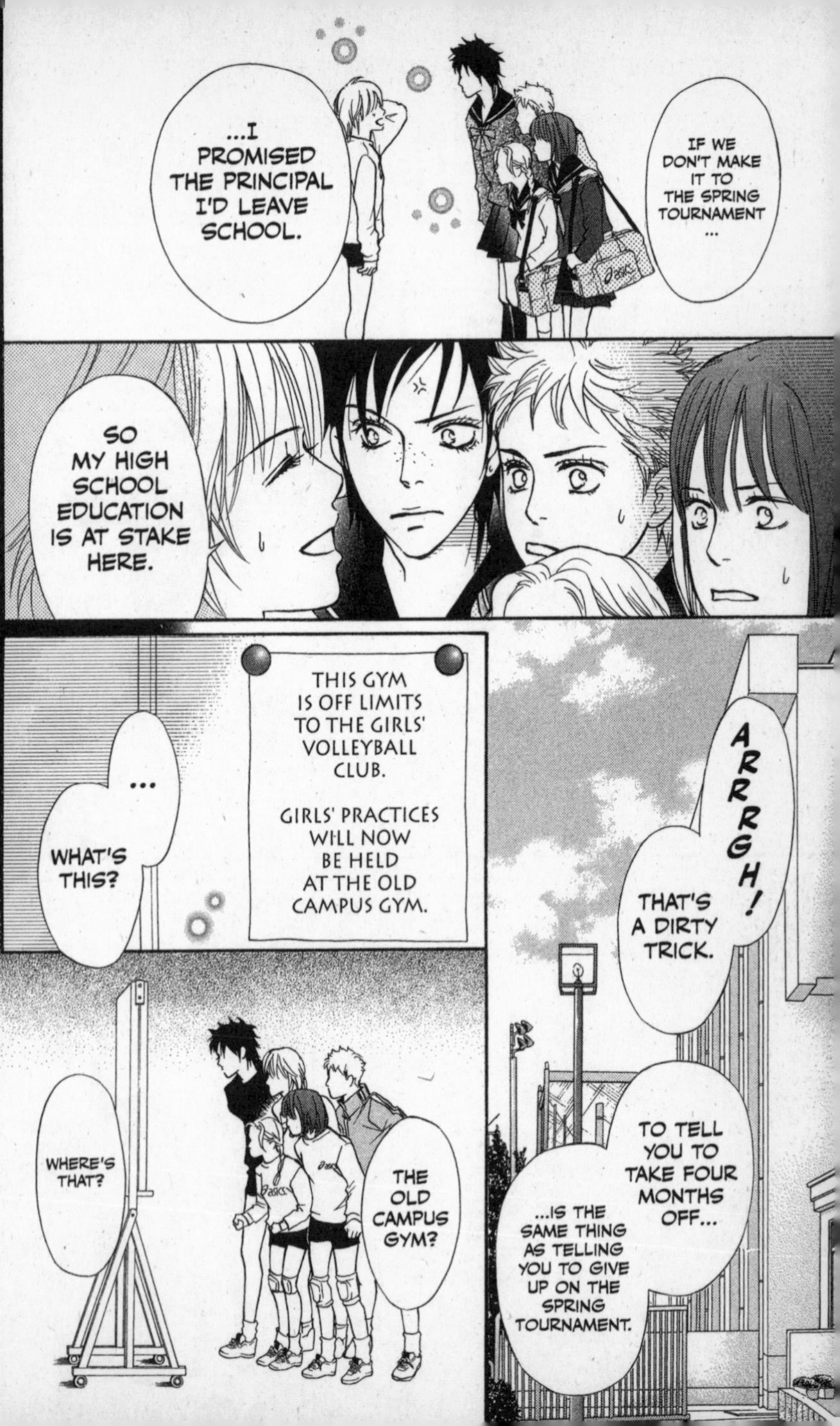
IF WE DON'T MAKE IT TO THE SPRING TOURNAMENT ...
...I PROMISED THE PRINCIPAL I'D LEAVE SCHOOL.
SO MY HIGH SCHOOL EDUCATION IS AT STAKE HERE.
ARRRGH!
THAT'S A DIRTY TRICK.
TO TELL YOU TO TAKE FOUR MONTHS OFF...
...IS THE SAME THING AS TELLING YOU TO GIVE UP ON THE SPRING TOURNAMENT.
THIS GYM IS OFF LIMITS TO THE GIRLS' VOLLEYBALL CLUB.
GIRLS' PRACTICES WILL NOW BE HELD AT THE OLD CAMPUS GYM.
...
WHAT'S THIS?
THE OLD CAMPUS GYM?
WHERE'S THAT?

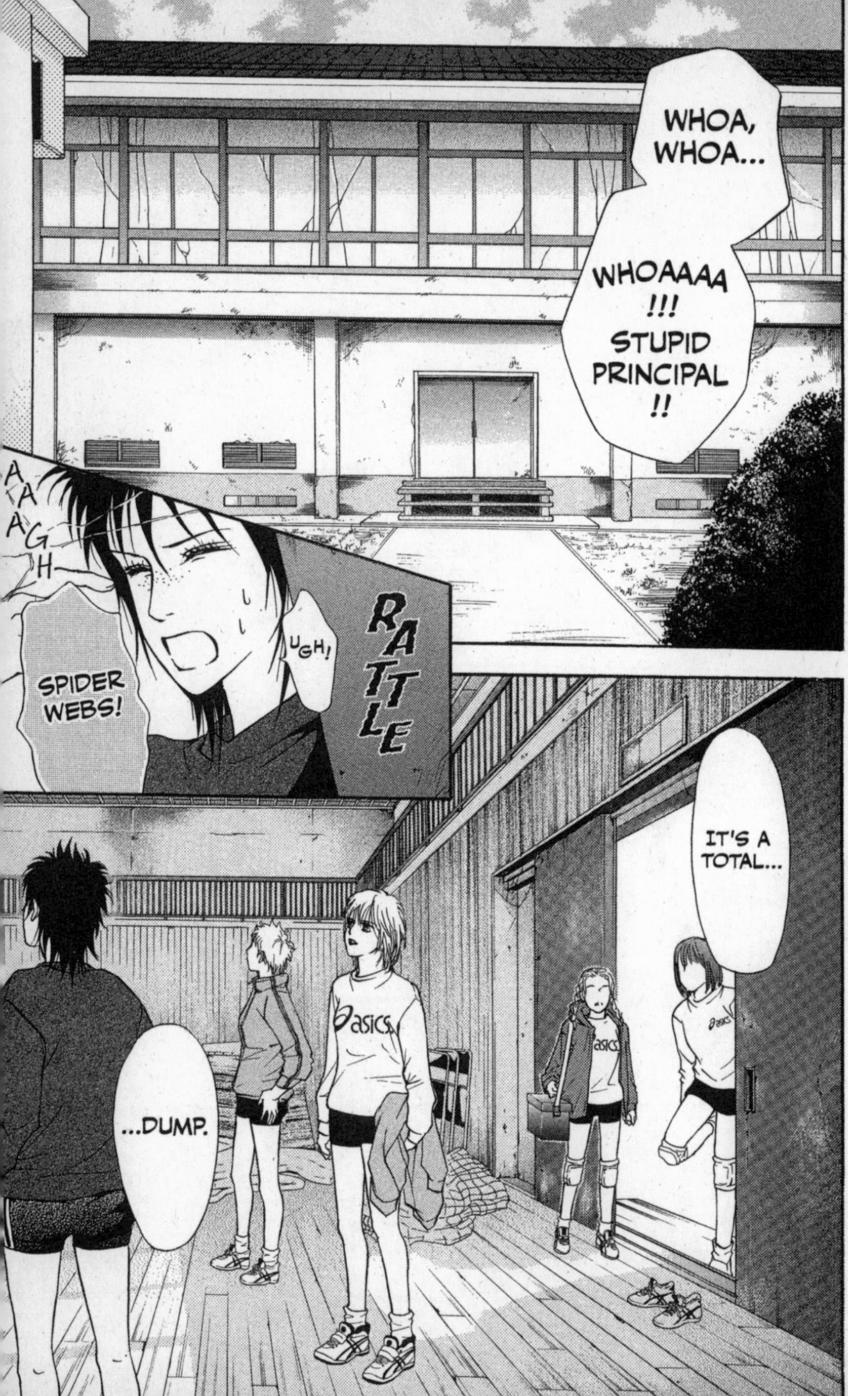
WHOA, WHOA...
WHOAAAA!!! STUPID PRINCIPAL!!
RATTLE
UGH!
AAAGH
SPIDER WEBS!
IT'S A TOTAL...
...DUMP.

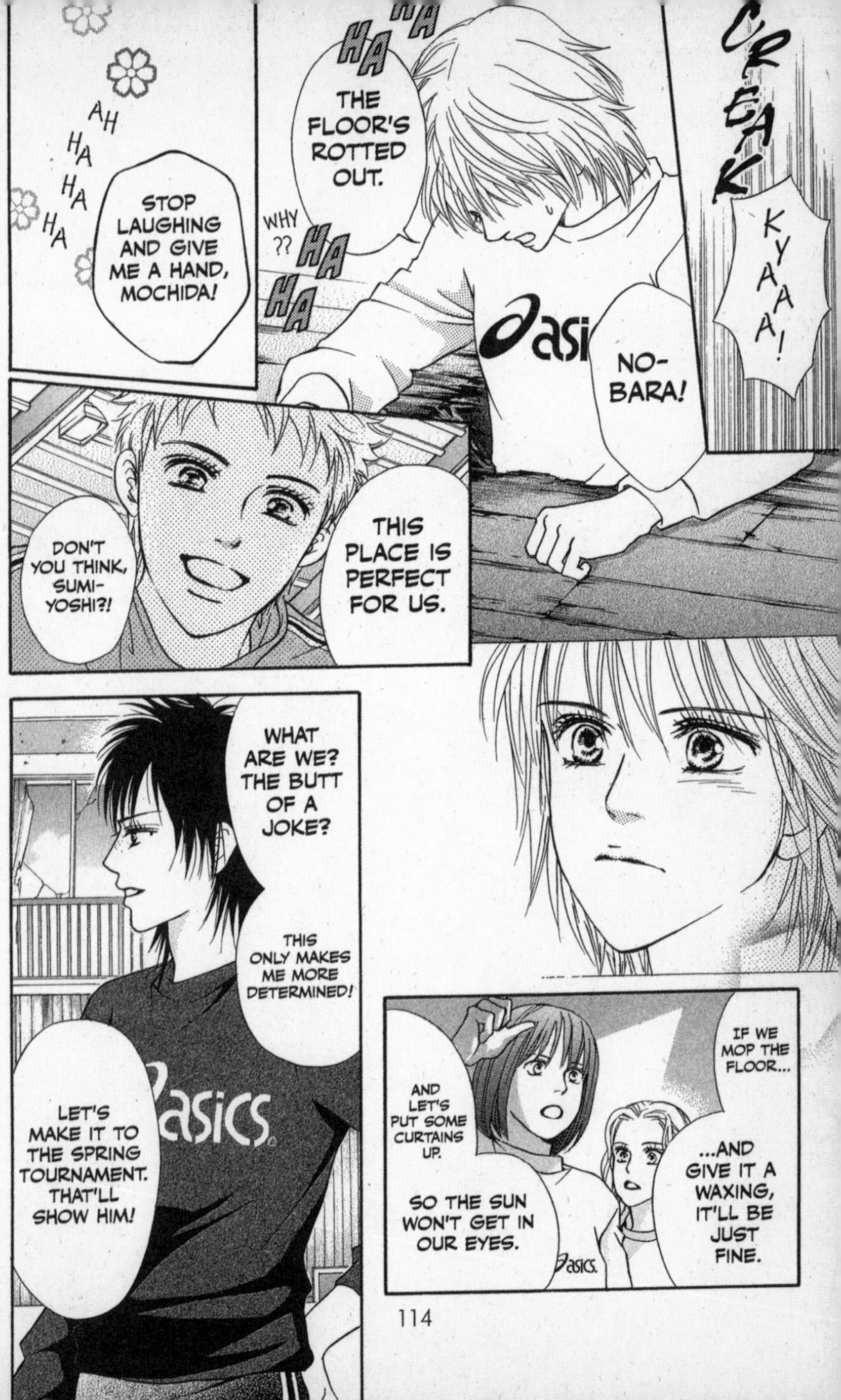
CREAK
KYAAA!
NO-BARA!
HA HA
THE FLOOR'S ROTTED OUT.
WHY ??
HA HA
AH HA HA HA HA
STOP LAUGHING AND GIVE ME A HAND, MOCHIDA!
THIS PLACE IS PERFECT FOR US.
DON'T YOU THINK, SUMI-YOSHI?!
IF WE MOP THE FLOOR...
...AND GIVE IT A WAXING, IT'LL BE JUST FINE.
AND LET'S PUT SOME CURTAINS UP.
SO THE SUN WON'T GET IN OUR EYES.
WHAT ARE WE? THE BUTT OF A JOKE?
THIS ONLY MAKES ME MORE DETERMINED!
LET'S MAKE IT TO THE SPRING TOURNAMENT. THAT'LL SHOW HIM!

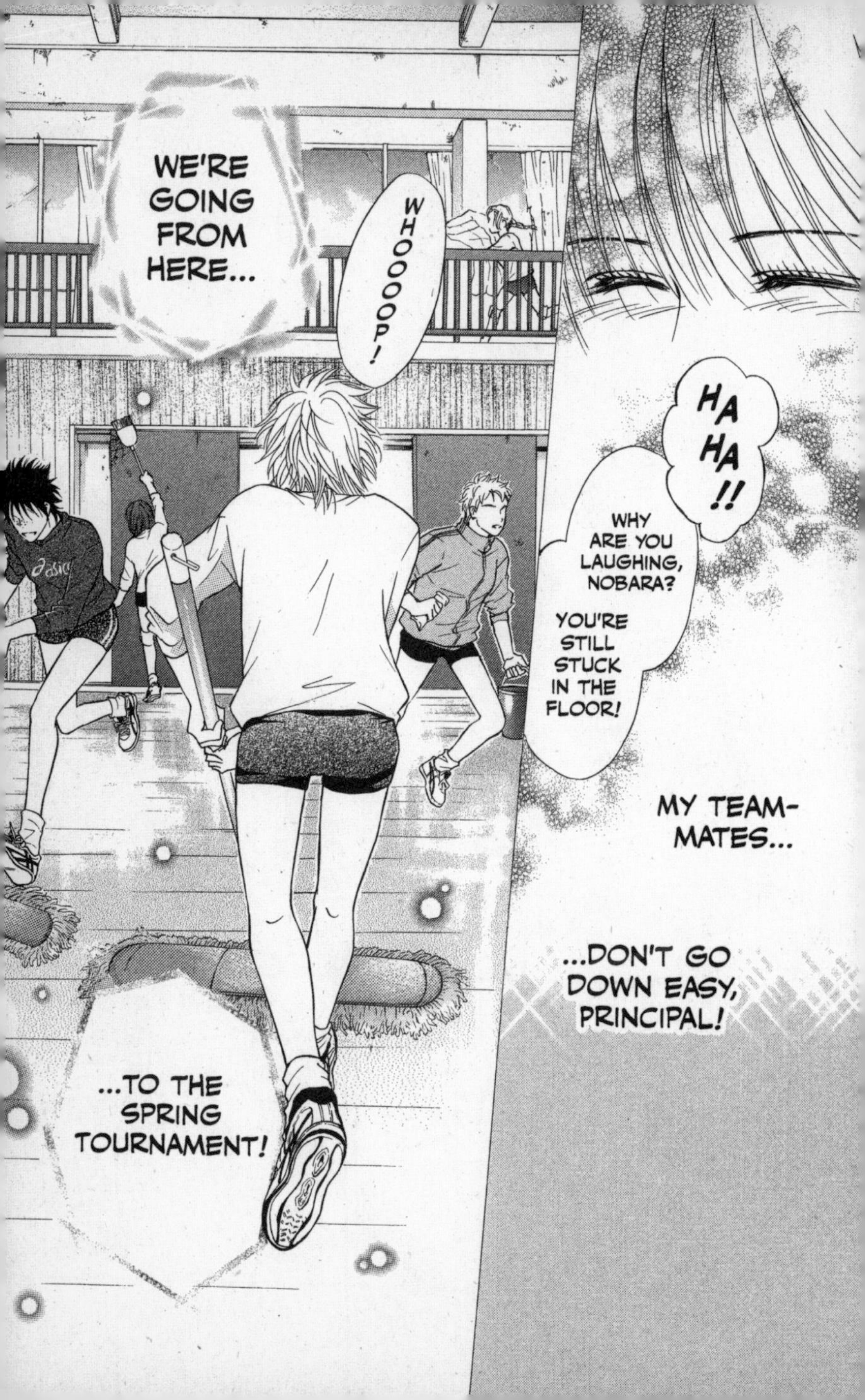
HA HA!!
WHY ARE YOU LAUGHING, NOBARA?
YOU'RE STILL STUCK IN THE FLOOR!
MY TEAM-MATES...
...DON'T GO DOWN EASY, PRINCIPAL!
WE'RE GOING FROM HERE...
WHOOOOOP!
...TO THE SPRING TOURNAMENT!

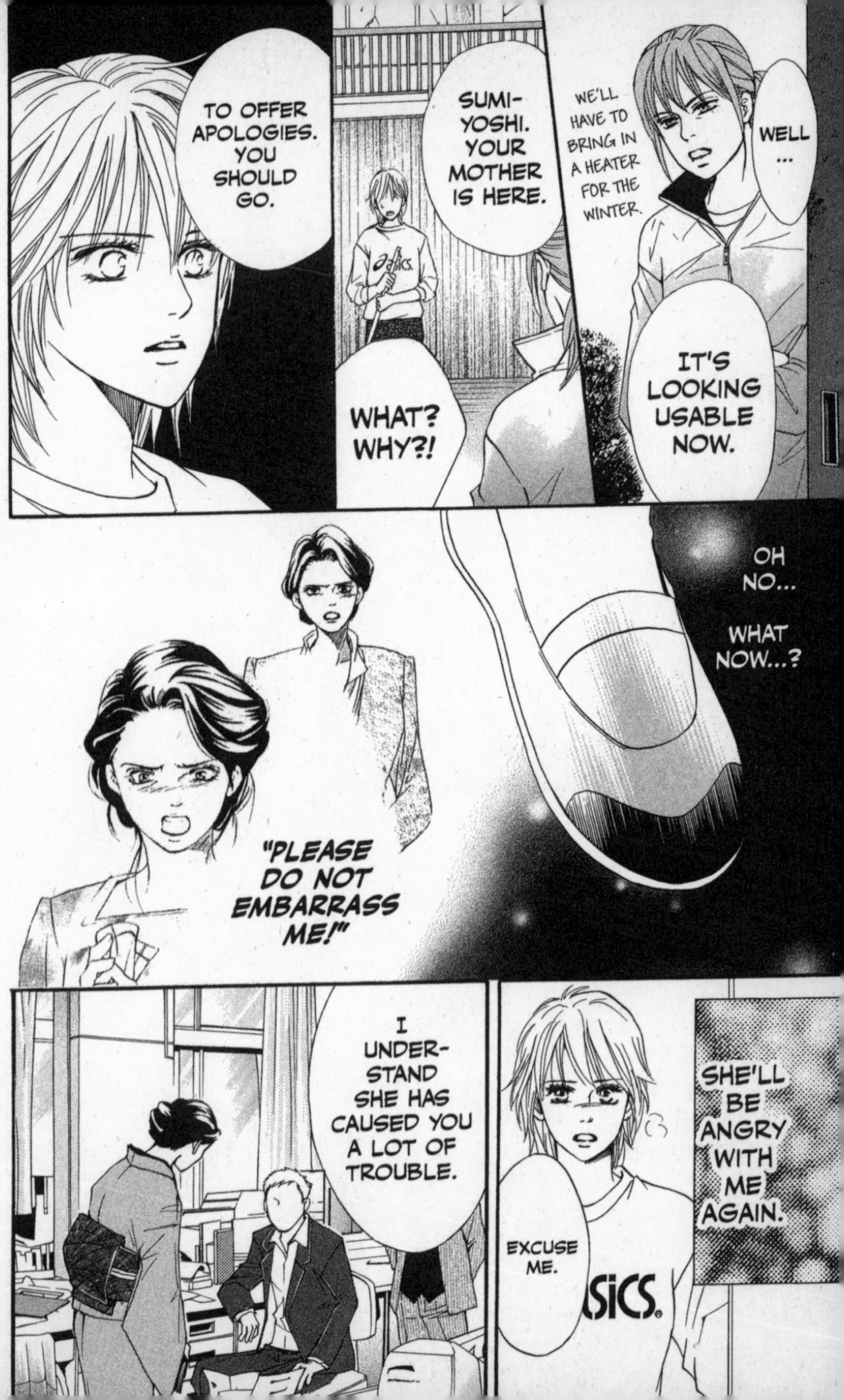
WELL ...
WE'LL HAVE TO BRING IN A HEATER FOR THE WINTER.
IT'S LOOKING USABLE NOW.
SUMI-YOSHI. YOUR MOTHER IS HERE.
WHAT? WHY?!
TO OFFER APOLOGIES. YOU SHOULD GO.
OH NO...
WHAT NOW...?
"PLEASE DO NOT EMBARRASS ME!"
SHE'LL BE ANGRY WITH ME AGAIN.
EXCUSE ME.
I UNDER-STAND SHE HAS CAUSED YOU A LOT OF TROUBLE.

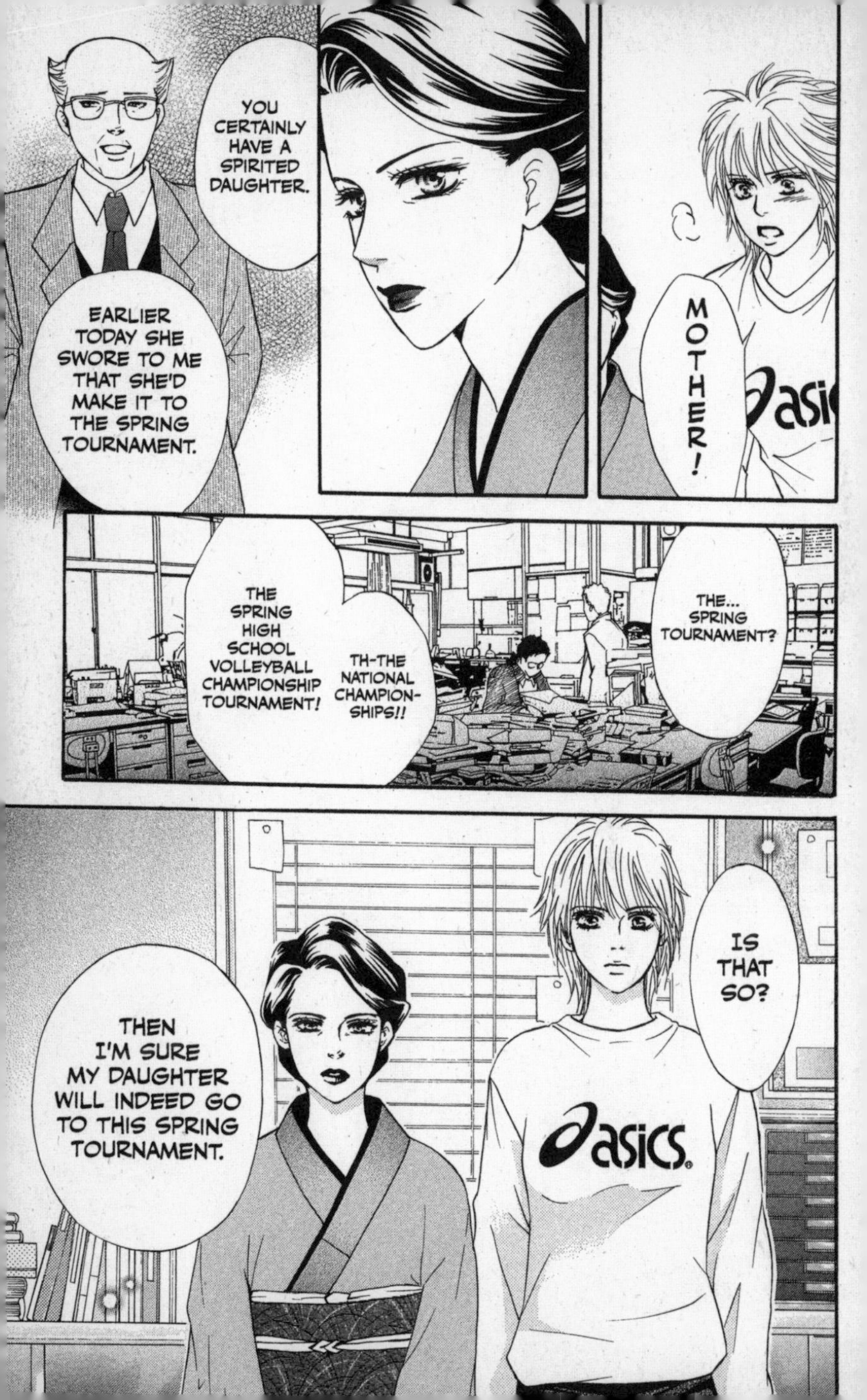
MOTHER!
YOU CERTAINLY HAVE A SPIRITED DAUGHTER.
EARLIER TODAY SHE SWORE TO ME THAT SHE'D MAKE IT TO THE SPRING TOURNAMENT.
THE... SPRING TOURNAMENT?
THE SPRING HIGH SCHOOL VOLLEYBALL CHAMPIONSHIP TOURNAMENT!
TH-THE NATIONAL CHAMPION-SHIPS!!
IS THAT SO?
THEN I'M SURE MY DAUGHTER WILL INDEED GO TO THIS SPRING TOURNAMENT.
asics

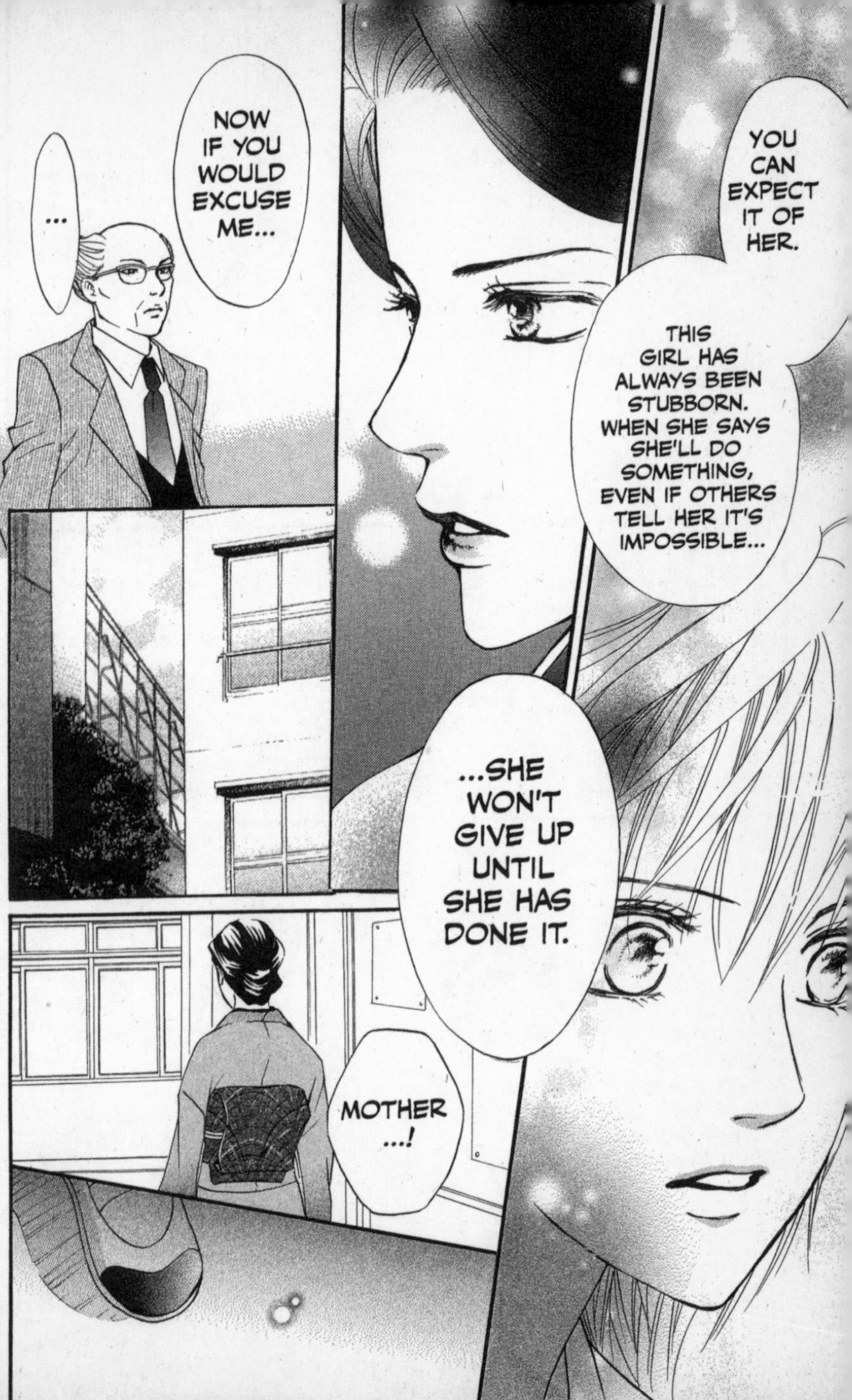

YOU CAN EXPECT IT OF HER.
THIS GIRL HAS ALWAYS BEEN STUBBORN. WHEN SHE SAYS SHE'LL DO SOMETHING, EVEN IF OTHERS TELL HER IT'S IMPOSSIBLE...
...SHE WON'T GIVE UP UNTIL SHE HAS DONE IT.
MOTHER ...!
NOW IF YOU WOULD EXCUSE ME...
...

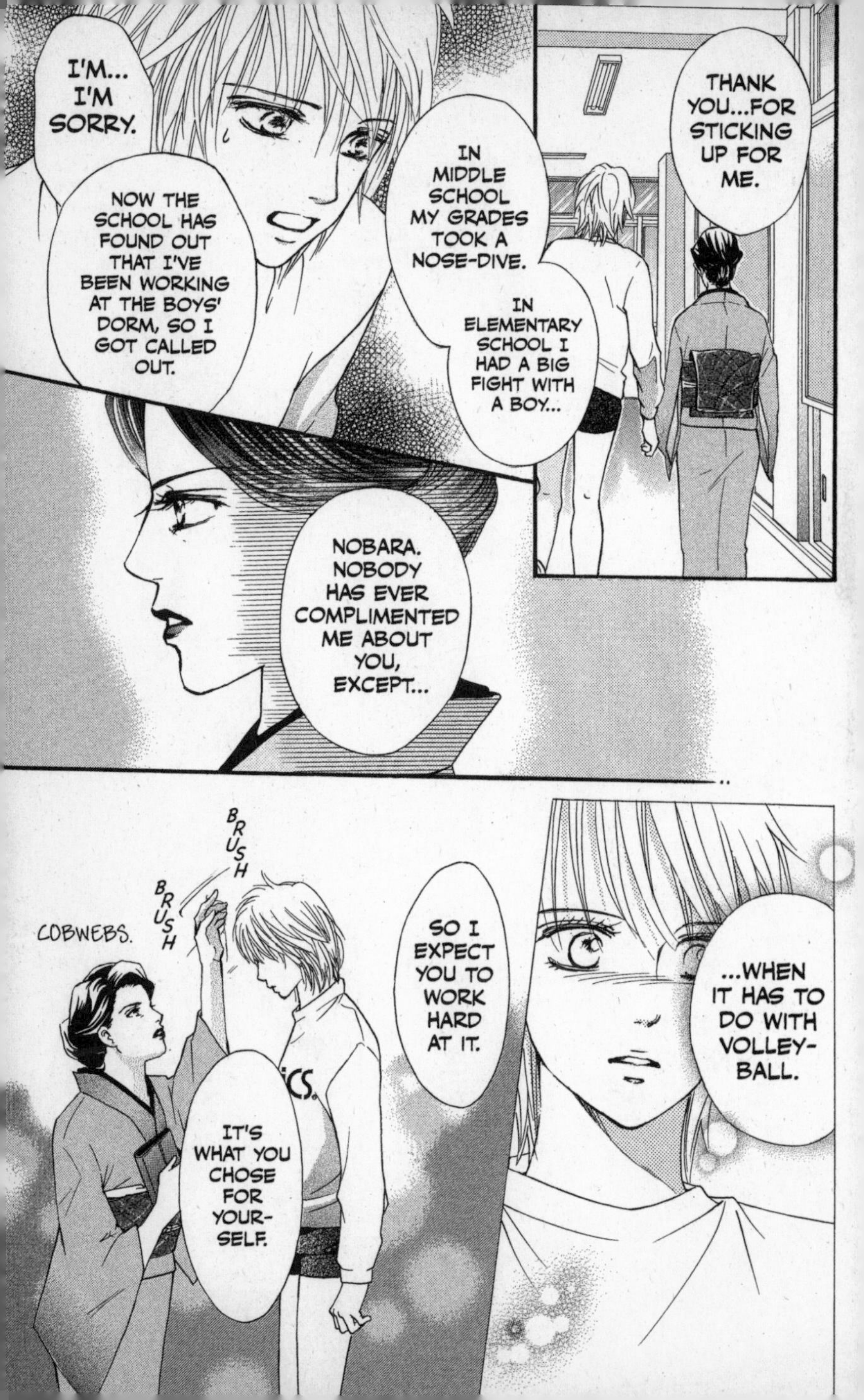
THANK YOU...FOR STICKING UP FOR ME.
I'M... I'M SORRY.
NOW THE SCHOOL HAS FOUND OUT THAT I'VE BEEN WORKING AT THE BOYS' DORM, SO I GOT CALLED OUT.
IN MIDDLE SCHOOL MY GRADES TOOK A NOSE-DIVE.
IN ELEMENTARY SCHOOL I HAD A BIG FIGHT WITH A BOY...
NOBARA. NOBODY HAS EVER COMPLIMENTED ME ABOUT YOU, EXCEPT...
...WHEN IT HAS TO DO WITH VOLLEY-BALL.
SO I EXPECT YOU TO WORK HARD AT IT.
BRUSH
BRUSH
COBWEBS.
IT'S WHAT YOU CHOSE FOR YOUR-SELF.

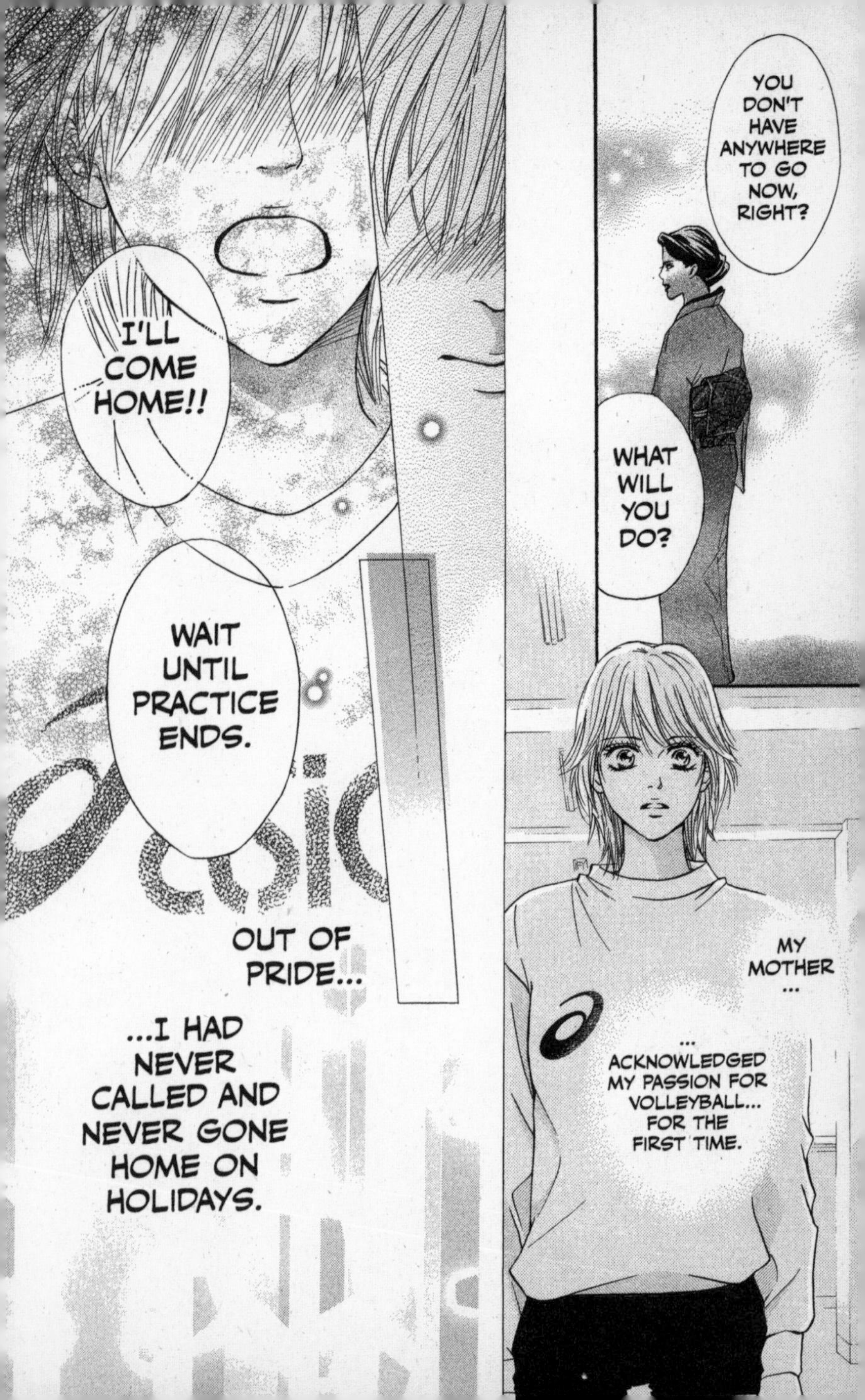
YOU DON'T HAVE ANYWHERE TO GO NOW, RIGHT?
WHAT WILL YOU DO?
MY MOTHER ...
... ACKNOWLEDGED MY PASSION FOR VOLLEYBALL... FOR THE FIRST TIME.
I'LL COME HOME!!
WAIT UNTIL PRACTICE ENDS.
OUT OF PRIDE...
...I HAD NEVER CALLED AND NEVER GONE HOME ON HOLIDAYS.

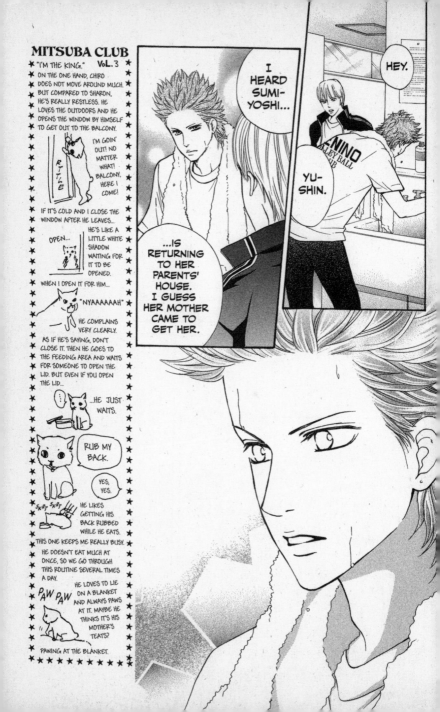

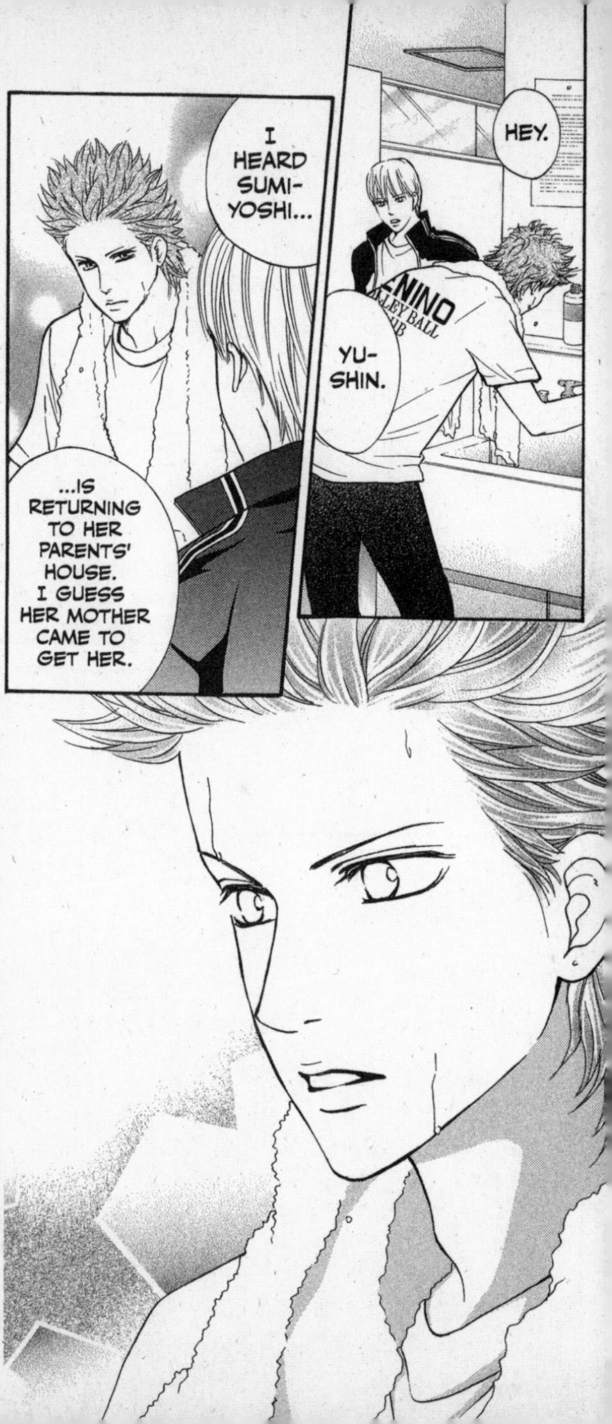
HEY.
YU-SHIN.
I HEARD SUMI-YOSHI...
...IS RETURNING TO HER PARENTS' HOUSE. I GUESS HER MOTHER CAME TO GET HER.

MITSUBA CLUB

"I'M THE KING." VoL. 3

ON THE ONE HAND, CHIRO DOES NOT MOVE AROUND MUCH. BUT COMPARED TO SHARON, HE'S REALLY RESTLESS. HE LOVES THE OUTDOORS AND HE OPENS THE WINDOW BY HIMSELF TO GET OUT TO THE BALCONY.

RTTLE

I'M GOIN' OUT! NO MATTER WHAT! BALCONY, HERE I COME!

IF IT'S COLD AND I CLOSE THE WINDOW AFTER HE LEAVES...

OPEN...

HE'S LIKE A LITTLE WHITE SHADOW WAITING FOR IT TO BE OPENED.

WHEN I OPEN IT FOR HIM...

"NYAAAAAAH"

HE COMPLAINS VERY CLEARLY.

AS IF HE'S SAYING, DON'T CLOSE IT. THEN HE GOES TO THE FEEDING AREA AND WAITS FOR SOMEONE TO OPEN THE LID. BUT EVEN IF YOU OPEN THE LID...

...

...HE JUST WAITS.

RUB MY BACK.

YES, YES.

SKRT SKRT

HE LIKES GETTING HIS BACK RUBBED WHILE HE EATS.

THIS ONE KEEPS ME REALLY BUSY. HE DOESN'T EAT MUCH AT ONCE, SO WE GO THROUGH THIS ROUTINE SEVERAL TIMES A DAY.

PAW PAW

HE LOVES TO LIE ON A BLANKET AND ALWAYS PAWS AT IT. MAYBE HE THINKS IT'S HIS MOTHER'S TEATS?

PAWING AT THE BLANKET.

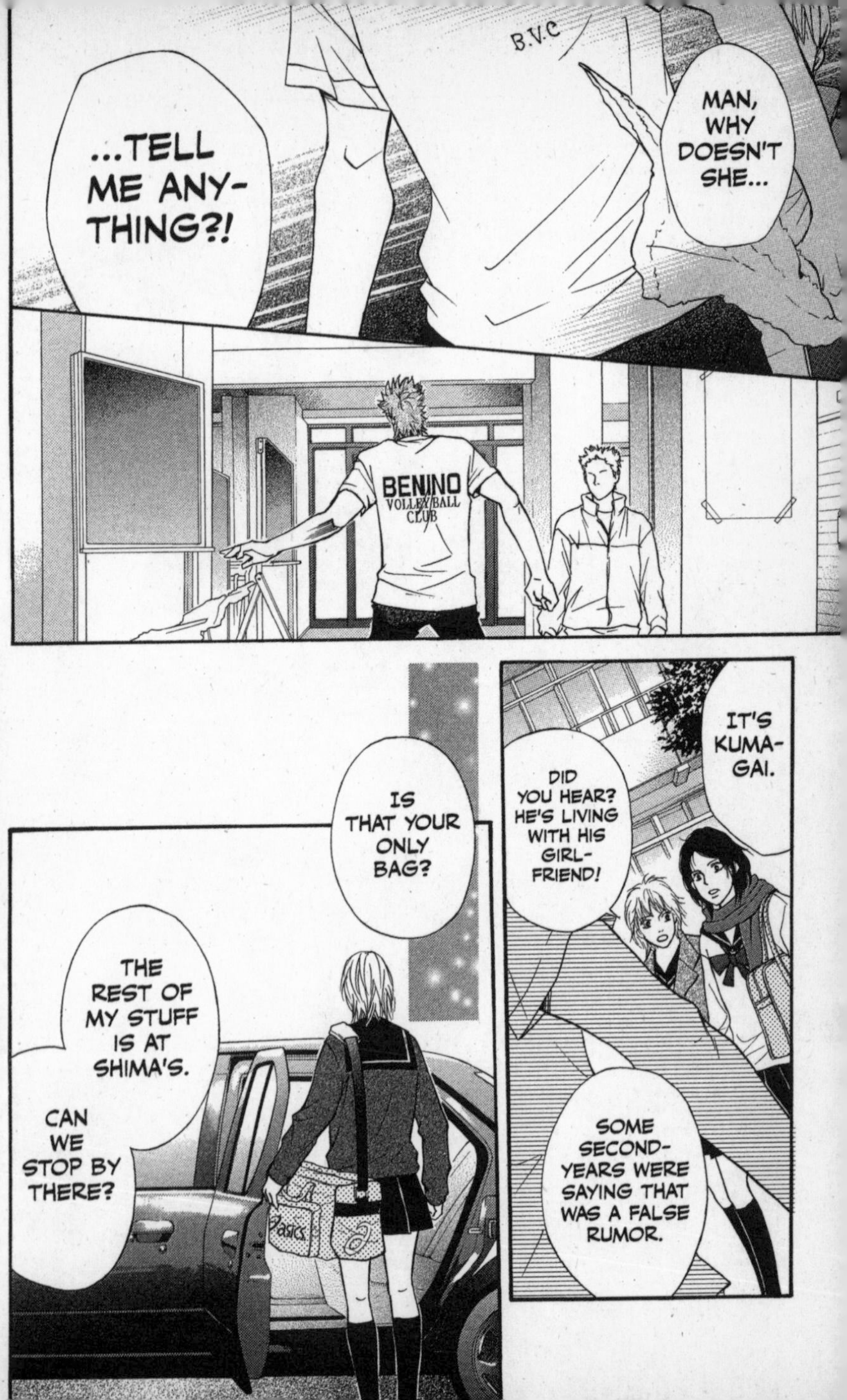
B.V.C
MAN, WHY DOESN'T SHE...
...TELL ME ANY-THING?!
BENINO VOLLEYBALL CLUB
IT'S KUMA-GAI.
DID YOU HEAR? HE'S LIVING WITH HIS GIRL-FRIEND!
SOME SECOND-YEARS WERE SAYING THAT WAS A FALSE RUMOR.
IS THAT YOUR ONLY BAG?
THE REST OF MY STUFF IS AT SHIMA'S.
CAN WE STOP BY THERE?
asics

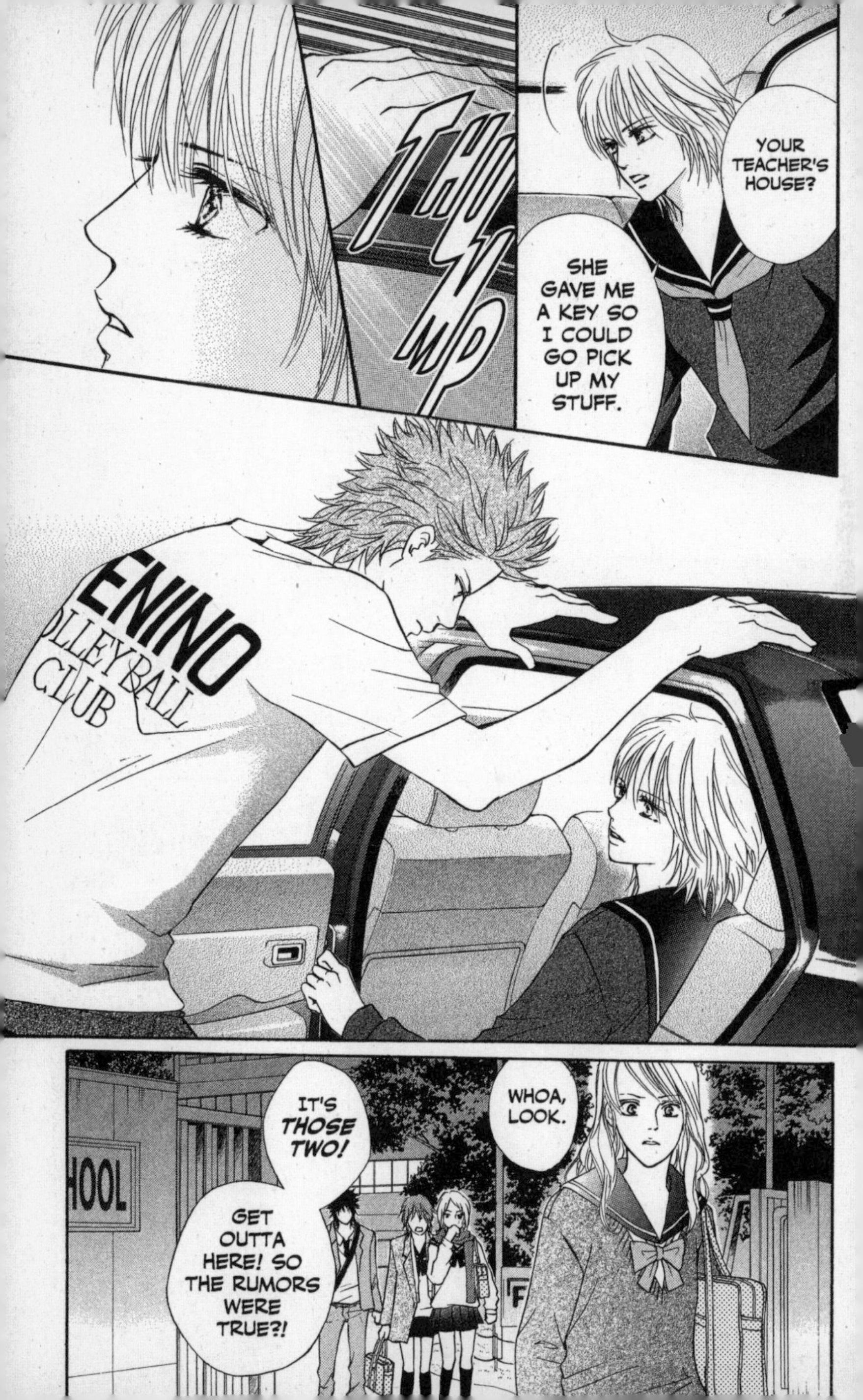
YOUR TEACHER'S HOUSE?
SHE GAVE ME A KEY SO I COULD GO PICK UP MY STUFF.
THUMP
ENINO
OLLEYBALL
CLUB
WHOA, LOOK.
IT'S *THOSE TWO!*
GET OUTTA HERE! SO THE RUMORS WERE TRUE?!
HOOL

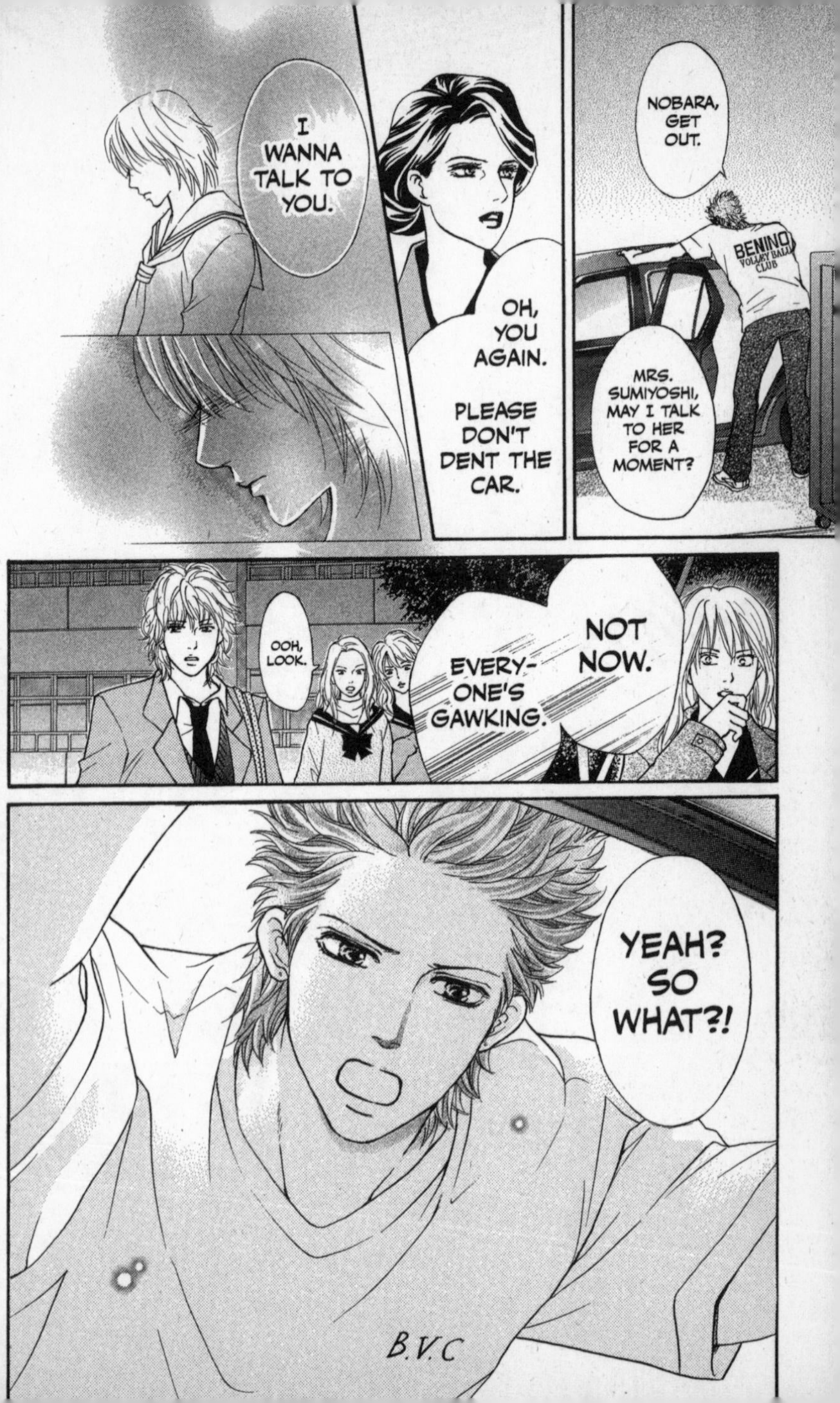
NOBARA, GET OUT.
BENINO VOLLEY BALL CLUB
MRS. SUMIYOSHI, MAY I TALK TO HER FOR A MOMENT?
OH, YOU AGAIN.
PLEASE DON'T DENT THE CAR.
I WANNA TALK TO YOU.
NOT NOW.
EVERY-ONE'S GAWKING.
OOH, LOOK.
YEAH? SO WHAT?!
B.V.C

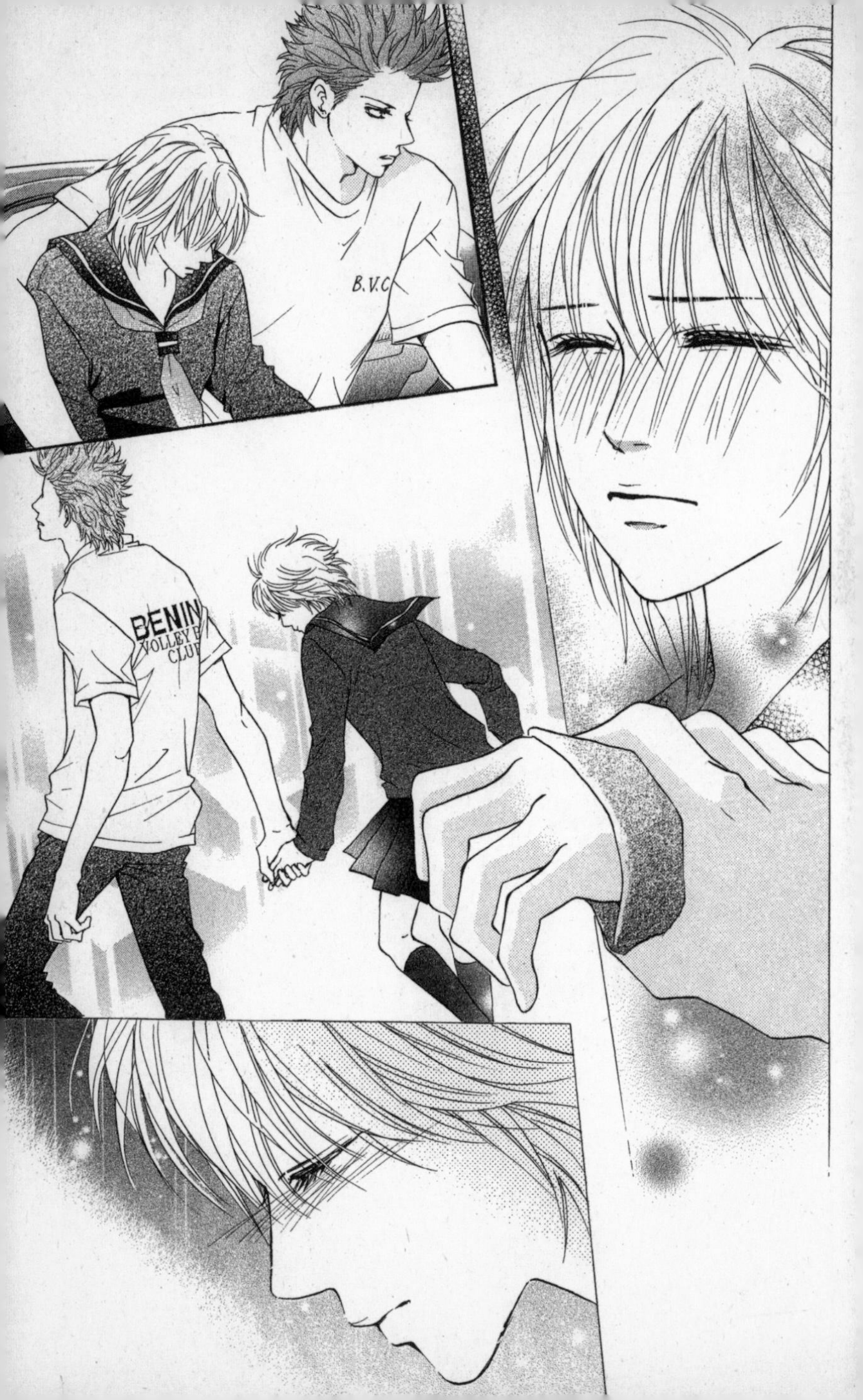
B.V.C
BENIN
VOLLEY

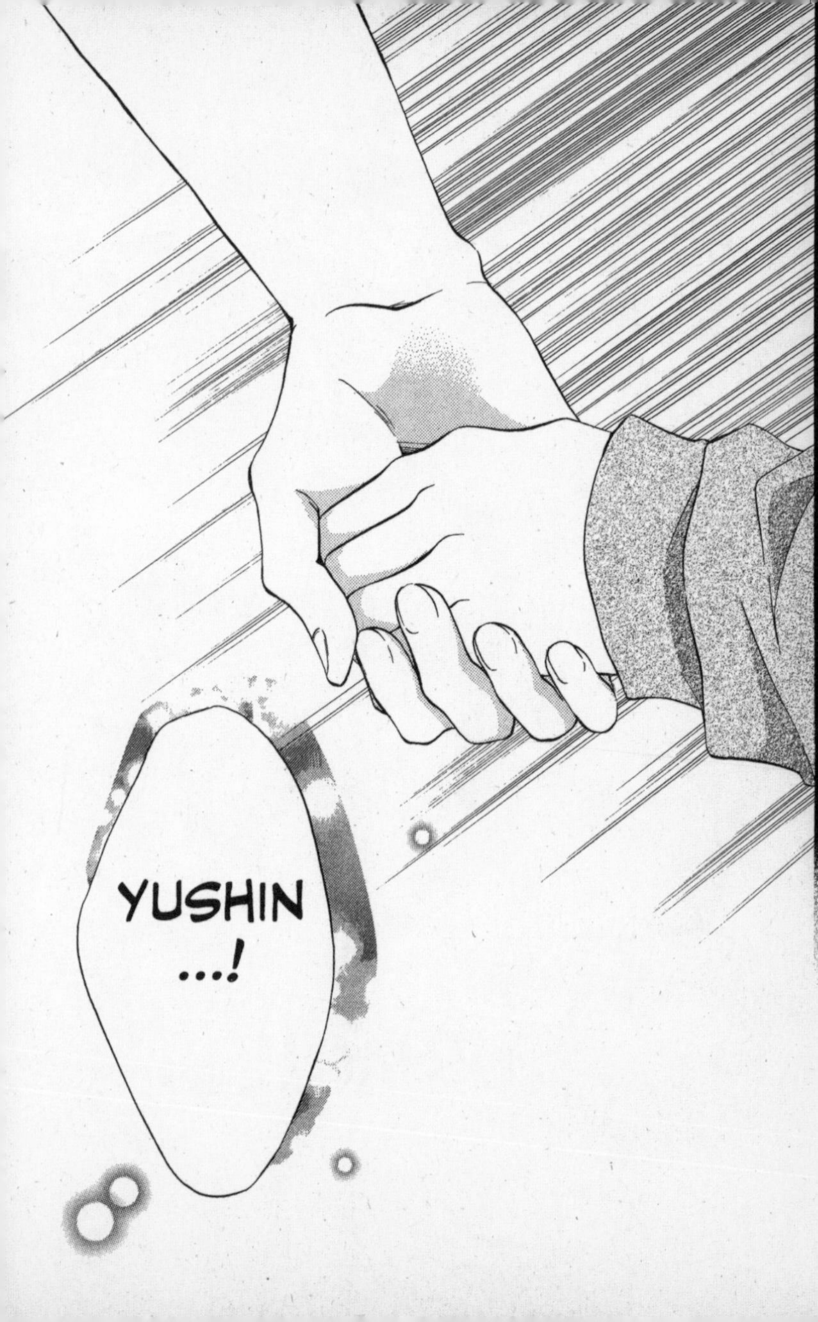
YUSHIN ...!

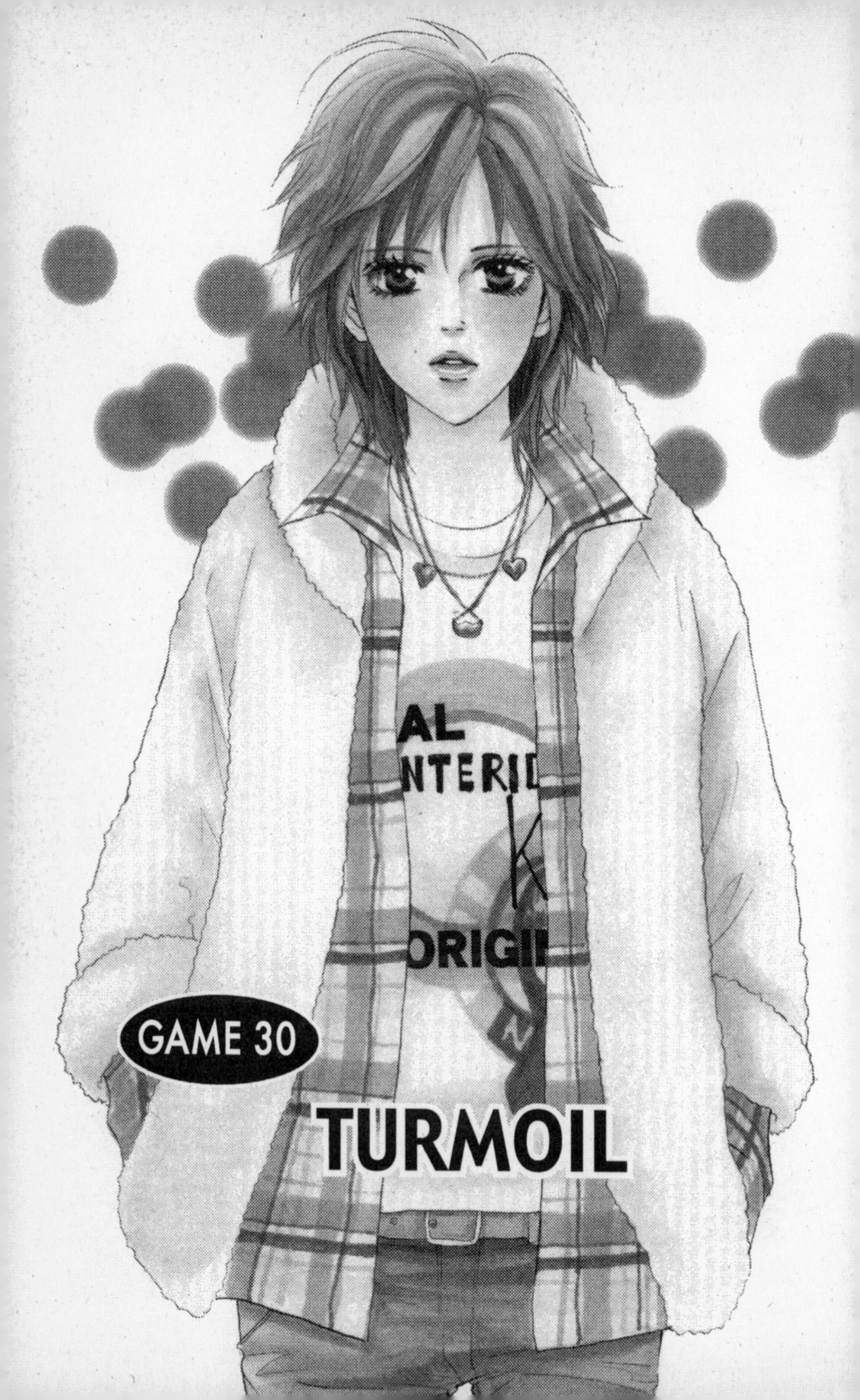
AL
NTERID
ORIGI

GAME 30

TURMOIL

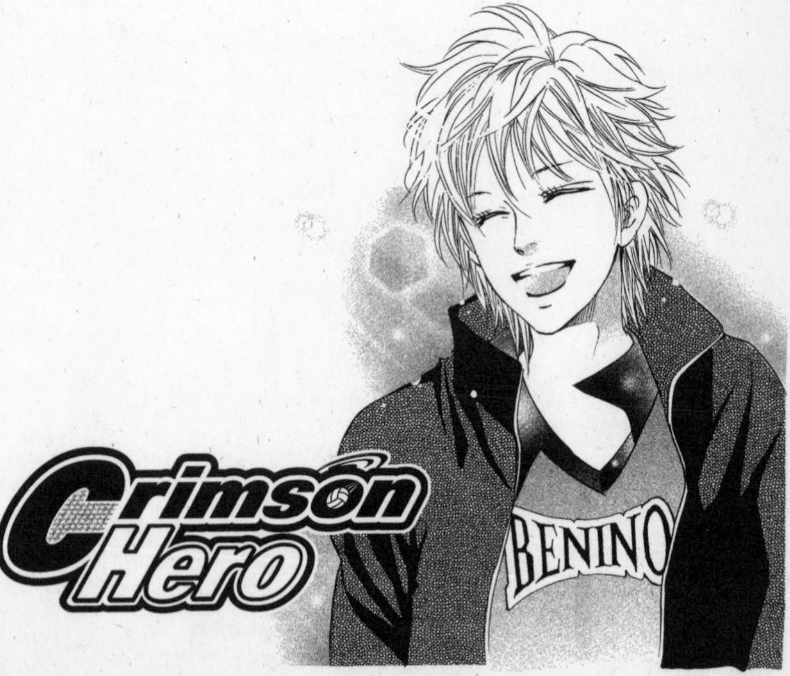
Crimson Hero
BENINO

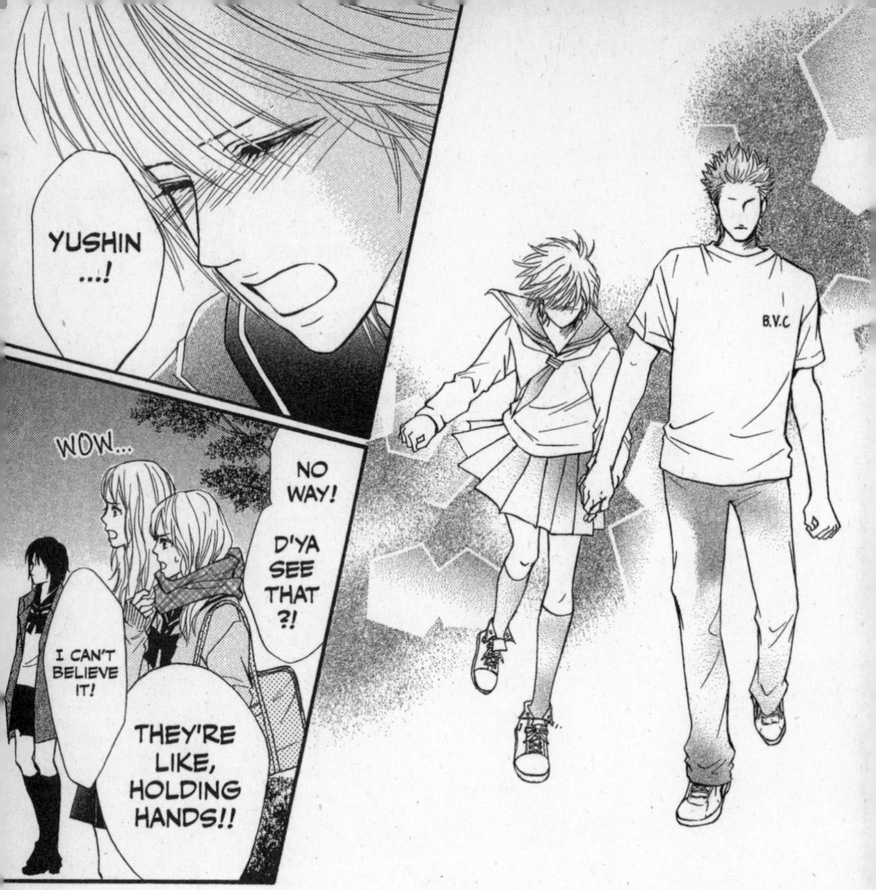
B.V.C
YUSHIN ...!
NO WAY! D'YA SEE THAT?!
WOW...
THEY'RE LIKE, HOLDING HANDS!!
I CAN'T BELIEVE IT!

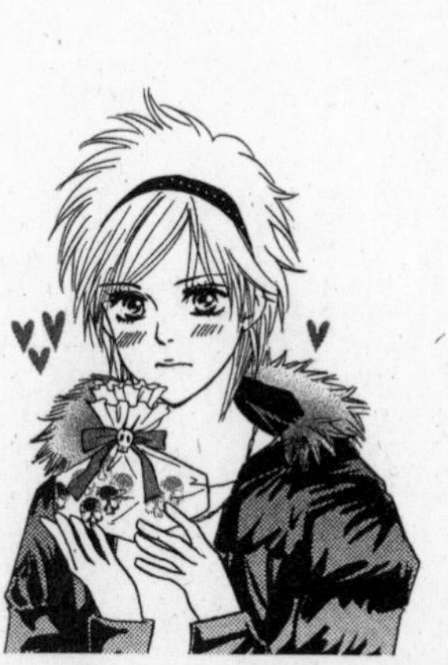

Crimson Hero

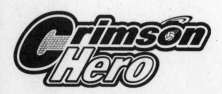

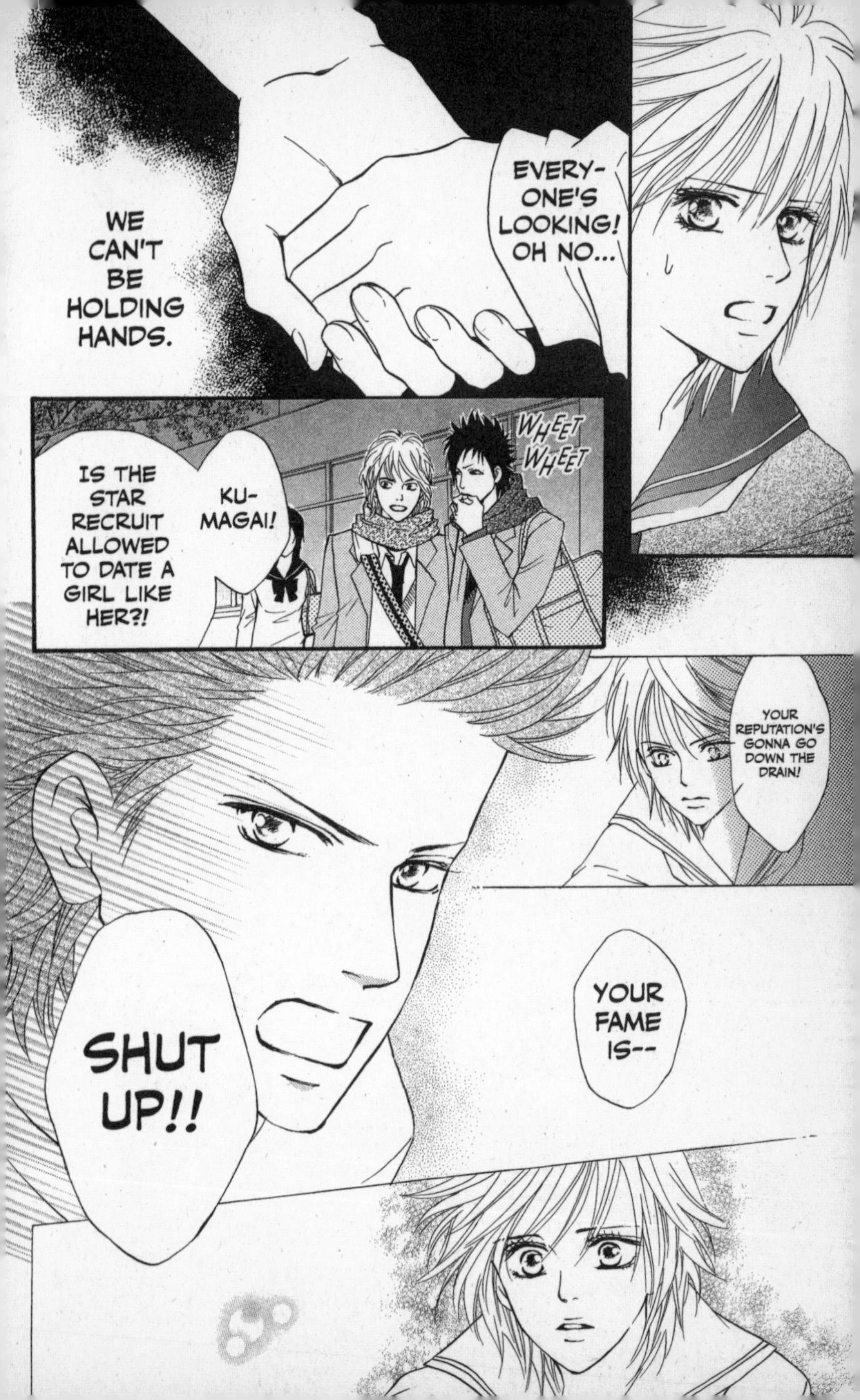
EVERY-ONE'S LOOKING! OH NO...
WE CAN'T BE HOLDING HANDS.
WHEET WHEET
KU-MAGAI!
IS THE STAR RECRUIT ALLOWED TO DATE A GIRL LIKE HER?!
YOUR REPUTATION'S GONNA GO DOWN THE DRAIN!
YOUR FAME IS--
SHUT UP!!

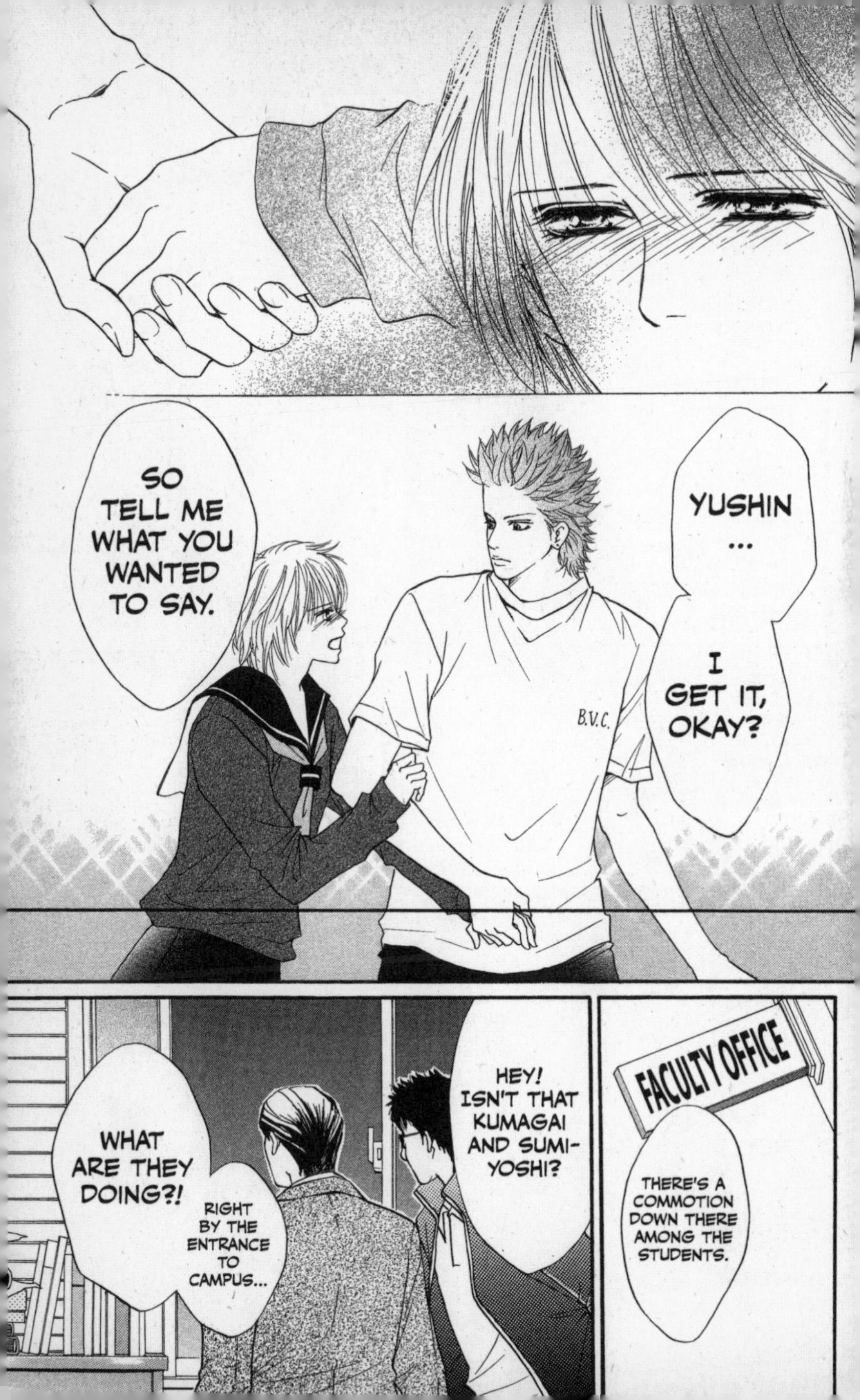
YUSHIN ...
I GET IT, OKAY?
SO TELL ME WHAT YOU WANTED TO SAY.
B.V.C.
FACULTY OFFICE
THERE'S A COMMOTION DOWN THERE AMONG THE STUDENTS.
HEY! ISN'T THAT KUMAGAI AND SUMI-YOSHI?
WHAT ARE THEY DOING?!
RIGHT BY THE ENTRANCE TO CAMPUS...

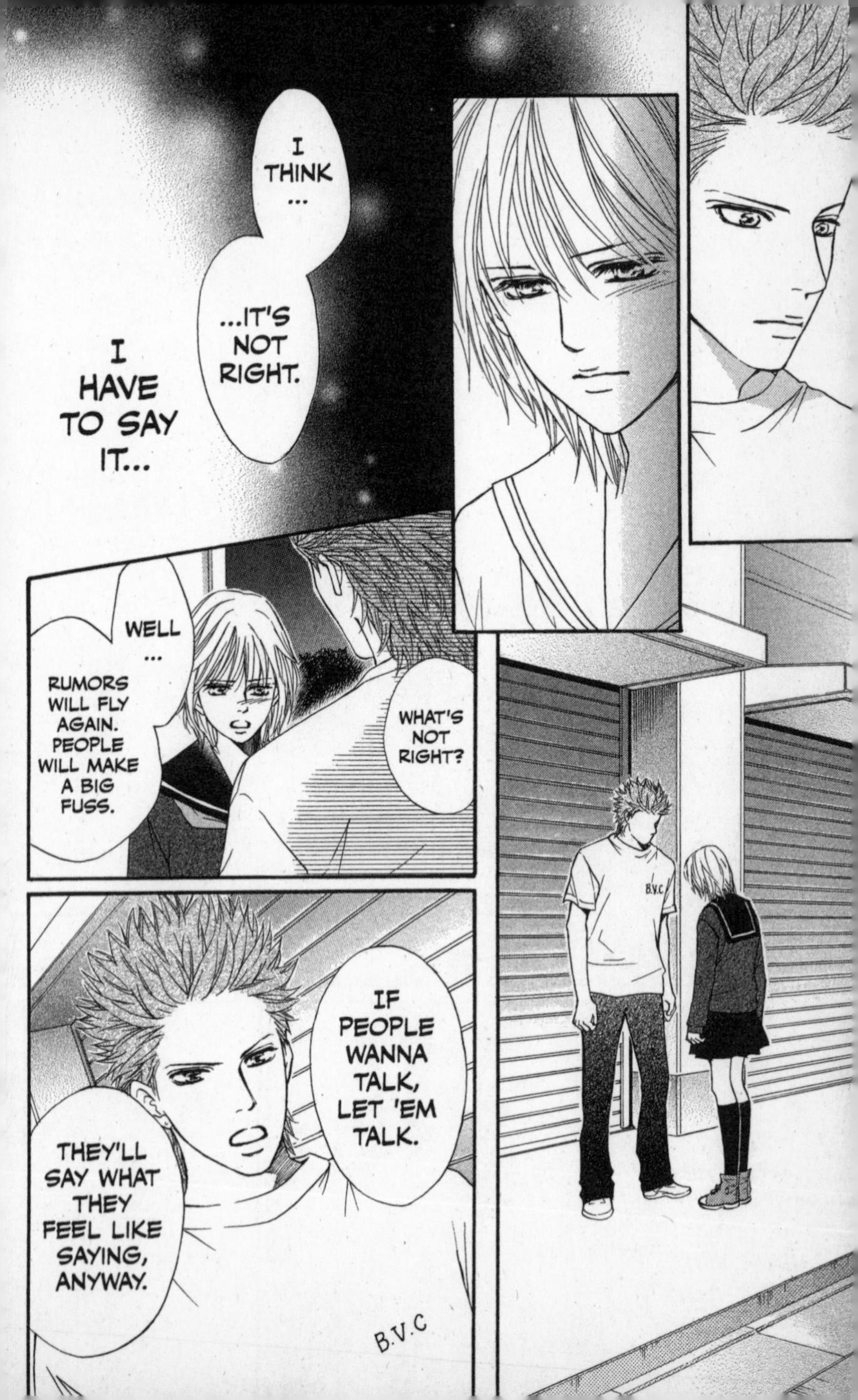
I THINK...
...IT'S NOT RIGHT.
I HAVE TO SAY IT...
WHAT'S NOT RIGHT?
WELL...
RUMORS WILL FLY AGAIN. PEOPLE WILL MAKE A BIG FUSS.
IF PEOPLE WANNA TALK, LET 'EM TALK.
THEY'LL SAY WHAT THEY FEEL LIKE SAYING, ANYWAY.
B.V.C

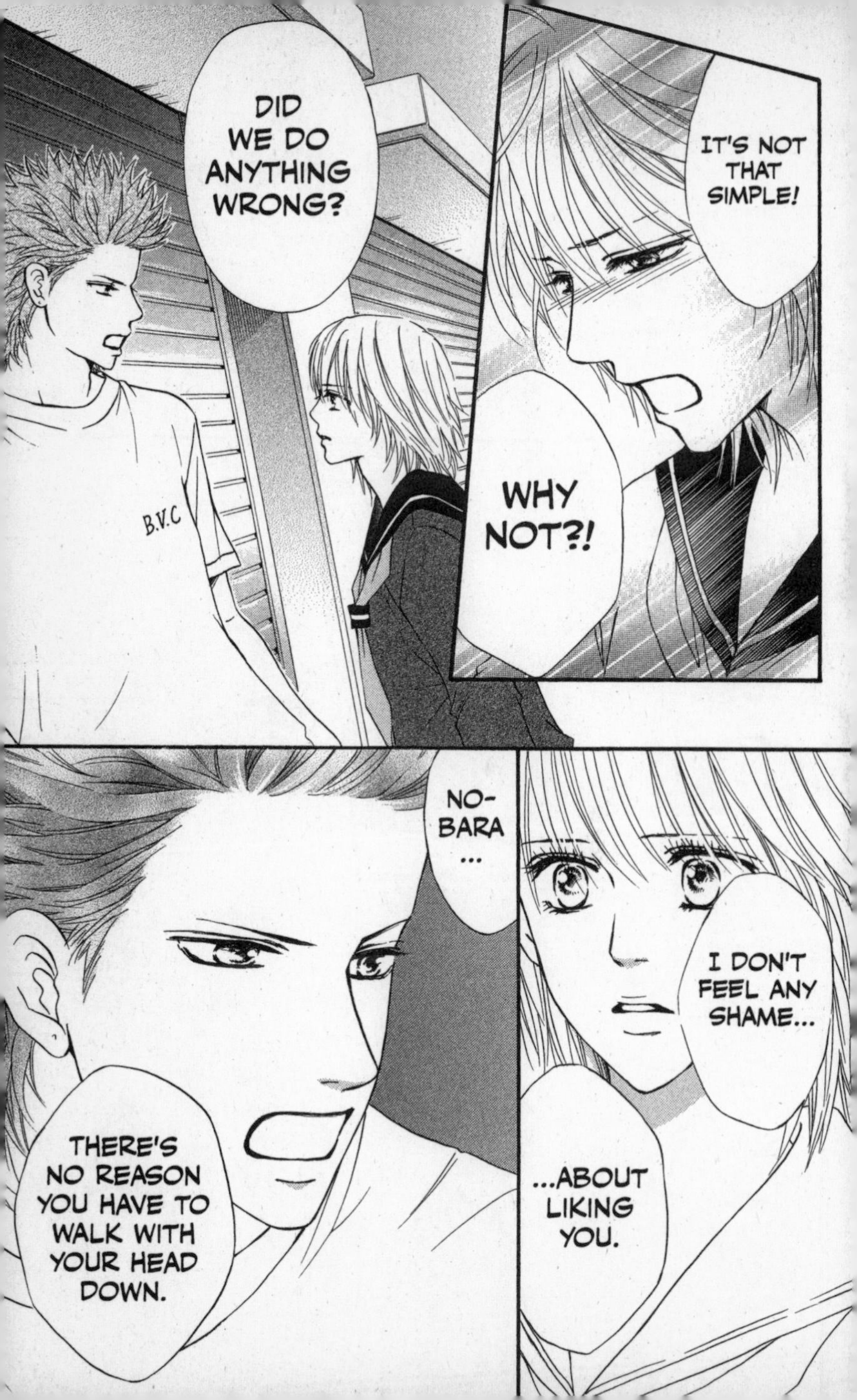
IT'S NOT THAT SIMPLE!
WHY NOT?!
DID WE DO ANYTHING WRONG?
B.V.C
I DON'T FEEL ANY SHAME...
...ABOUT LIKING YOU.
NO-BARA...
THERE'S NO REASON YOU HAVE TO WALK WITH YOUR HEAD DOWN.

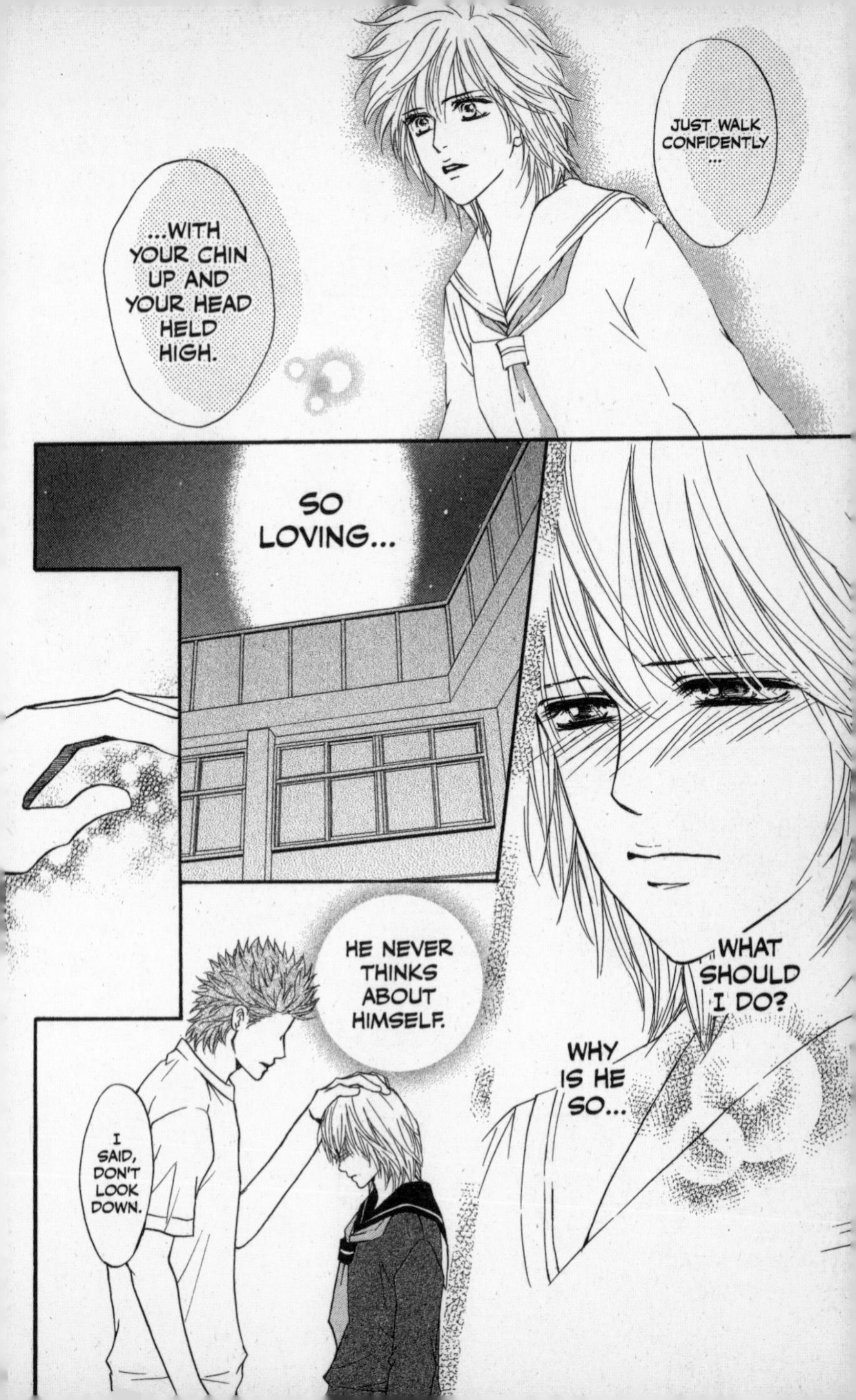
JUST WALK CONFIDENTLY...
...WITH YOUR CHIN UP AND YOUR HEAD HELD HIGH.
WHAT SHOULD I DO?
WHY IS HE SO...
SO LOVING...
HE NEVER THINKS ABOUT HIMSELF.
I SAID, DON'T LOOK DOWN.

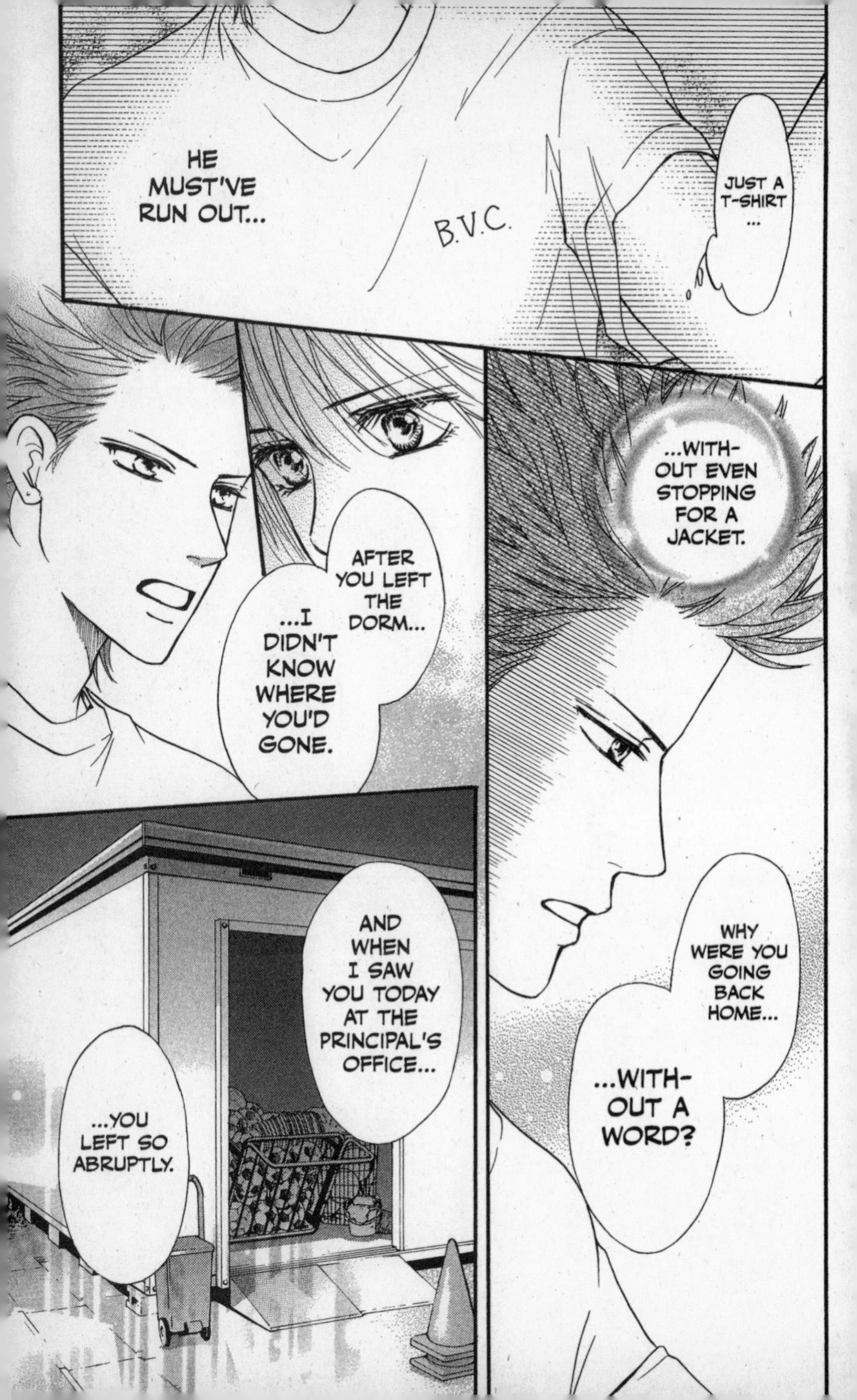
JUST A T-SHIRT ...
B.V.C.
HE MUST'VE RUN OUT...
...WITH-OUT EVEN STOPPING FOR A JACKET.
WHY WERE YOU GOING BACK HOME...
...WITH-OUT A WORD?
AFTER YOU LEFT THE DORM...
...I DIDN'T KNOW WHERE YOU'D GONE.
AND WHEN I SAW YOU TODAY AT THE PRINCIPAL'S OFFICE...
...YOU LEFT SO ABRUPTLY.

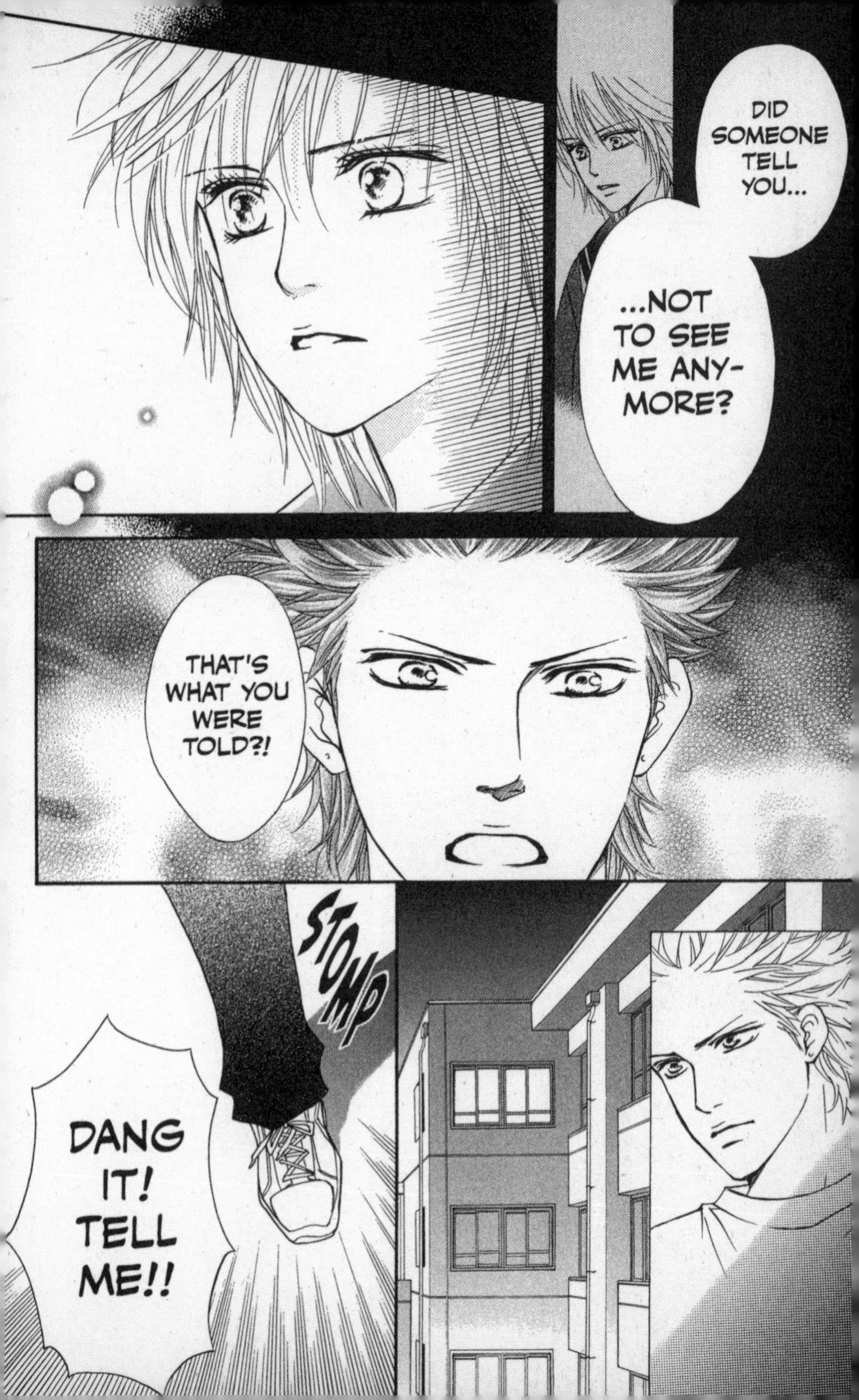
DID SOMEONE TELL YOU...
...NOT TO SEE ME ANY-MORE?
THAT'S WHAT YOU WERE TOLD?!
STOMP
DANG IT! TELL ME!!

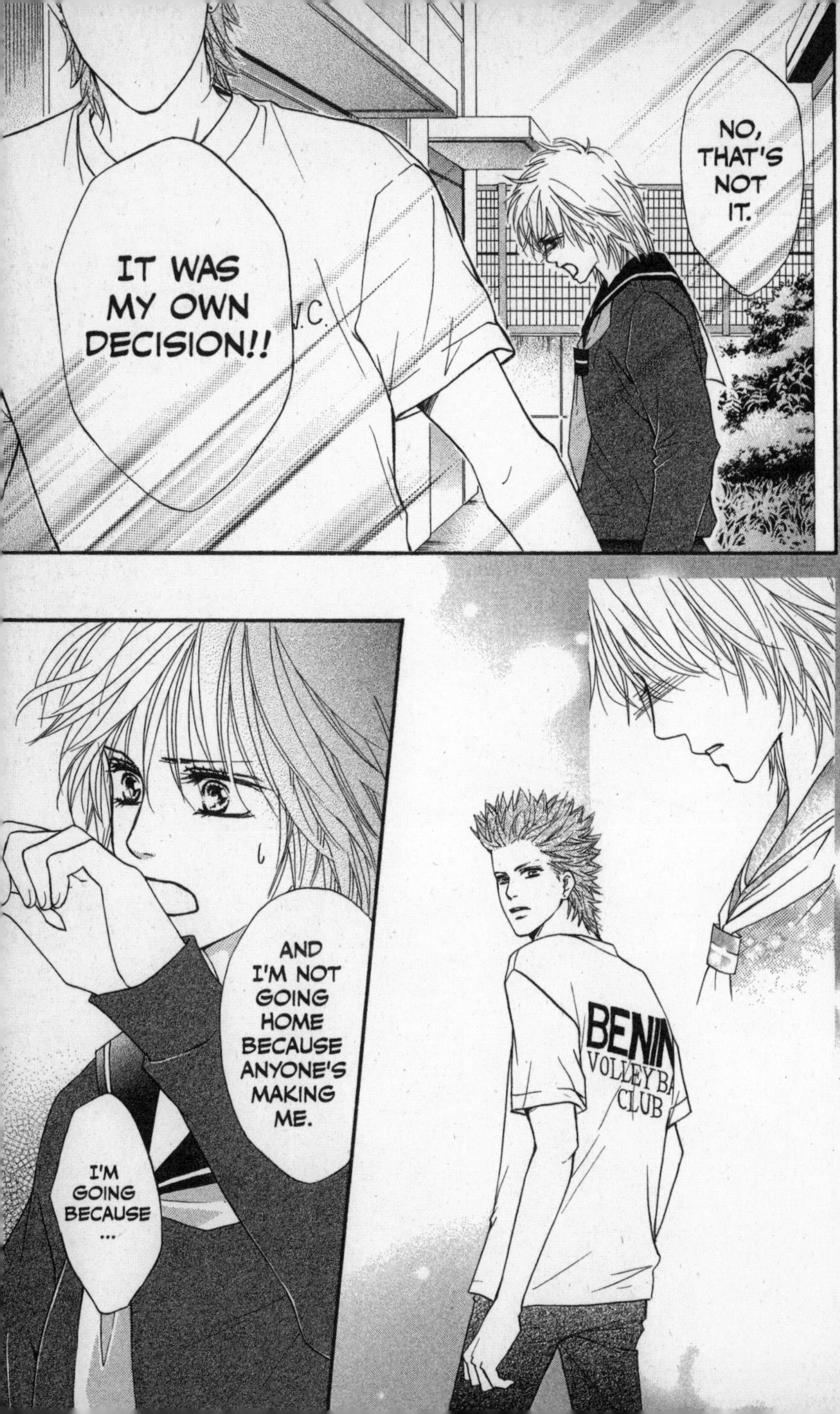
NO, THAT'S NOT IT.
IT WAS MY OWN DECISION!!
V.C.
BENIN
VOLLEYBA
CLUB
AND I'M NOT GOING HOME BECAUSE ANYONE'S MAKING ME.
I'M GOING BECAUSE ...

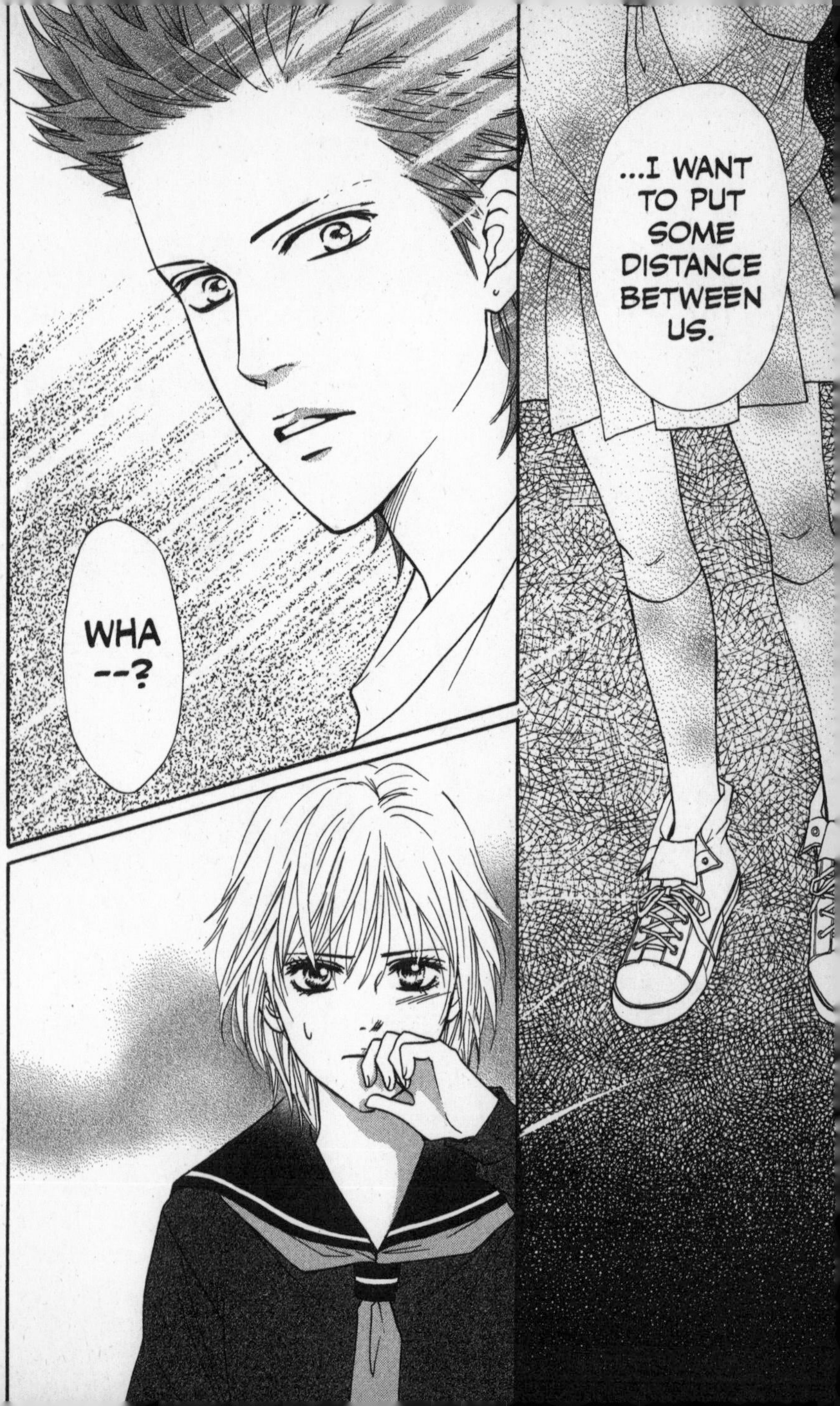
...I WANT TO PUT SOME DISTANCE BETWEEN US.
WHA --?

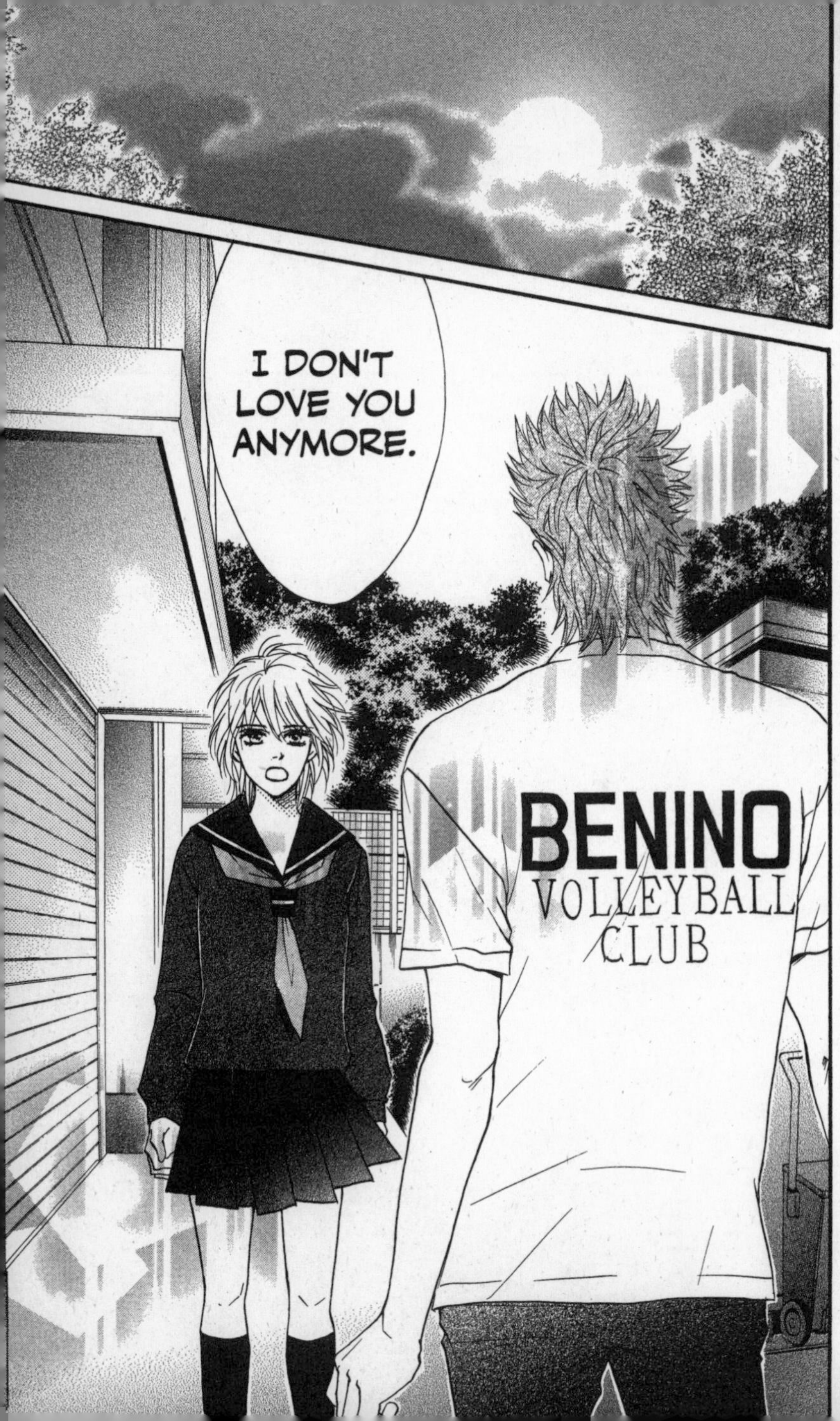
I DON'T LOVE YOU ANYMORE.
BENINO VOLLEYBALL CLUB

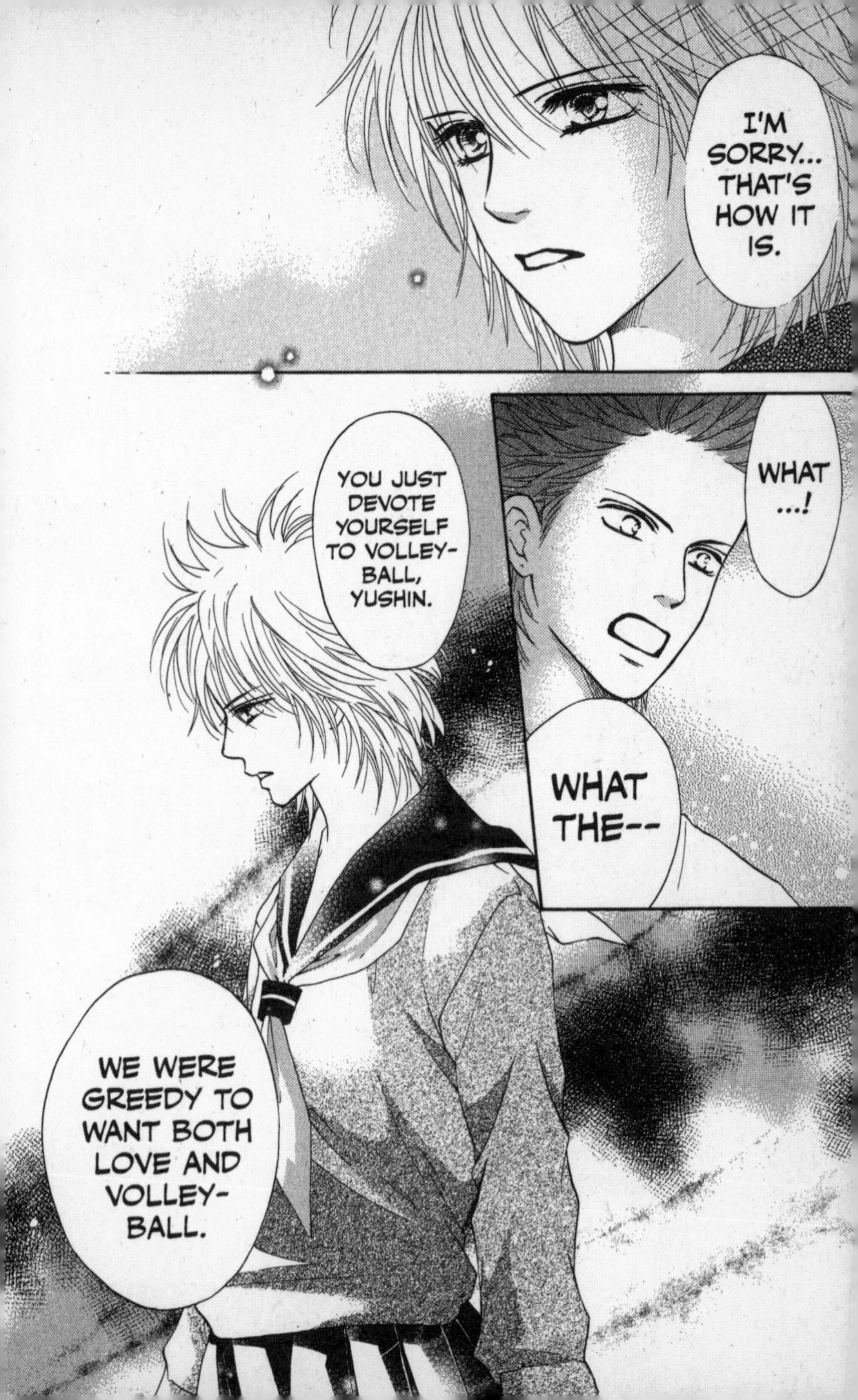
I'M SORRY... THAT'S HOW IT IS.
WHAT ...!
WHAT THE--
YOU JUST DEVOTE YOURSELF TO VOLLEY-BALL, YUSHIN.
WE WERE GREEDY TO WANT BOTH LOVE AND VOLLEY-BALL.

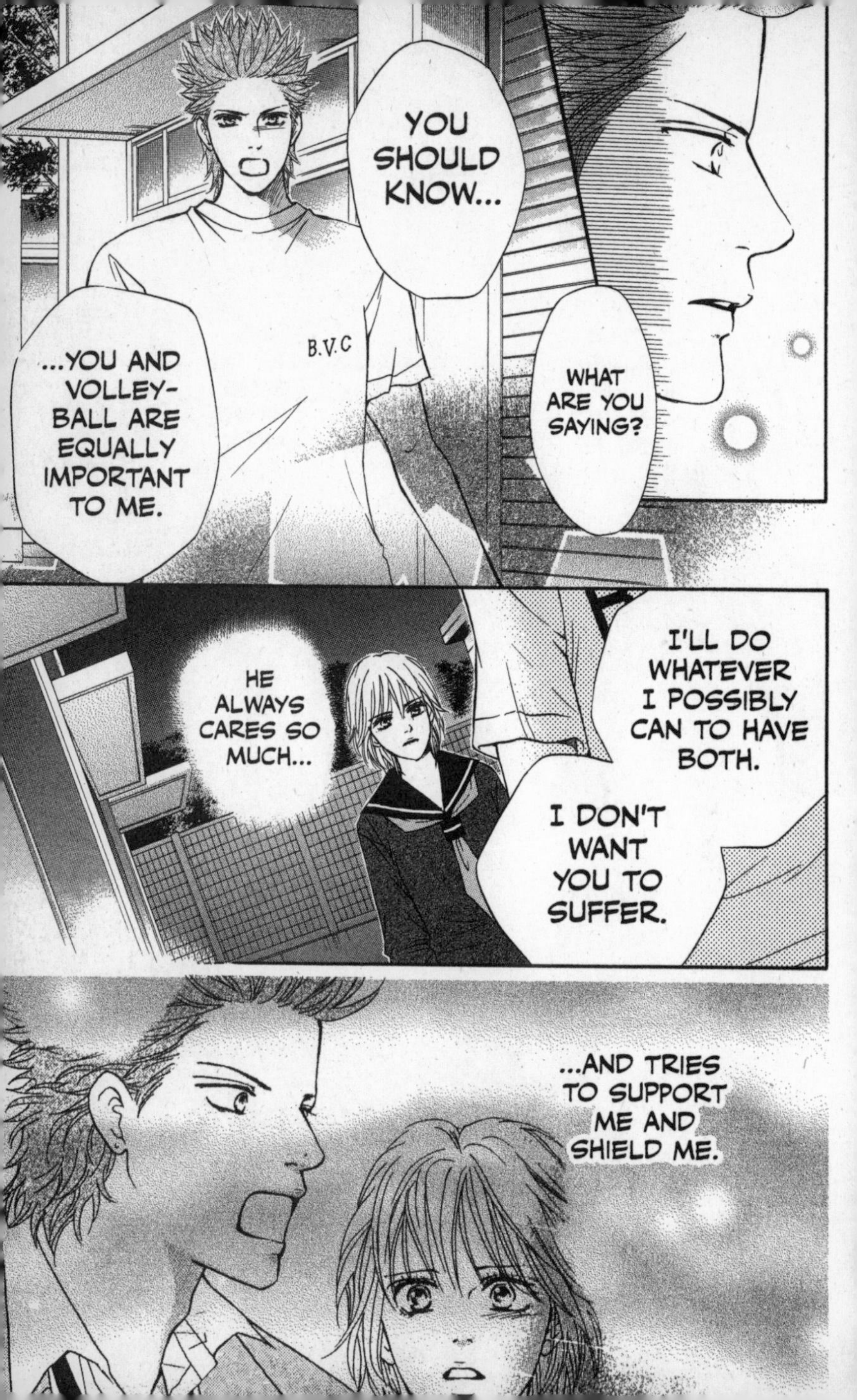
WHAT ARE YOU SAYING?
YOU SHOULD KNOW...
...YOU AND VOLLEY-BALL ARE EQUALLY IMPORTANT TO ME.
I'LL DO WHATEVER I POSSIBLY CAN TO HAVE BOTH.
I DON'T WANT YOU TO SUFFER.
HE ALWAYS CARES SO MUCH...
...AND TRIES TO SUPPORT ME AND SHIELD ME.

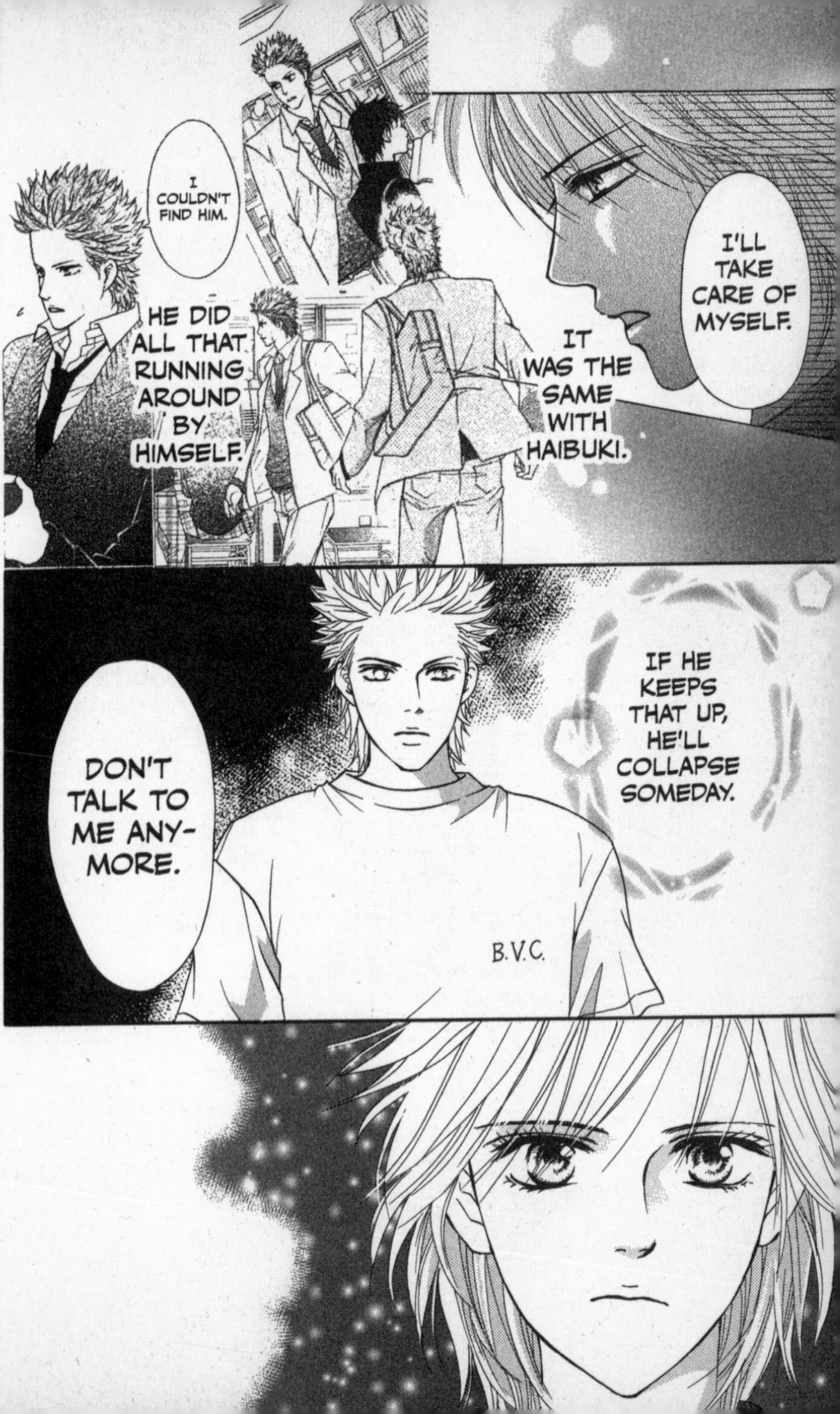
I'LL TAKE CARE OF MYSELF.
IT WAS THE SAME WITH HAIBUKI.
I COULDN'T FIND HIM.
HE DID ALL THAT RUNNING AROUND BY HIMSELF.
IF HE KEEPS THAT UP, HE'LL COLLAPSE SOMEDAY.
B.V.C.
DON'T TALK TO ME ANY-MORE.

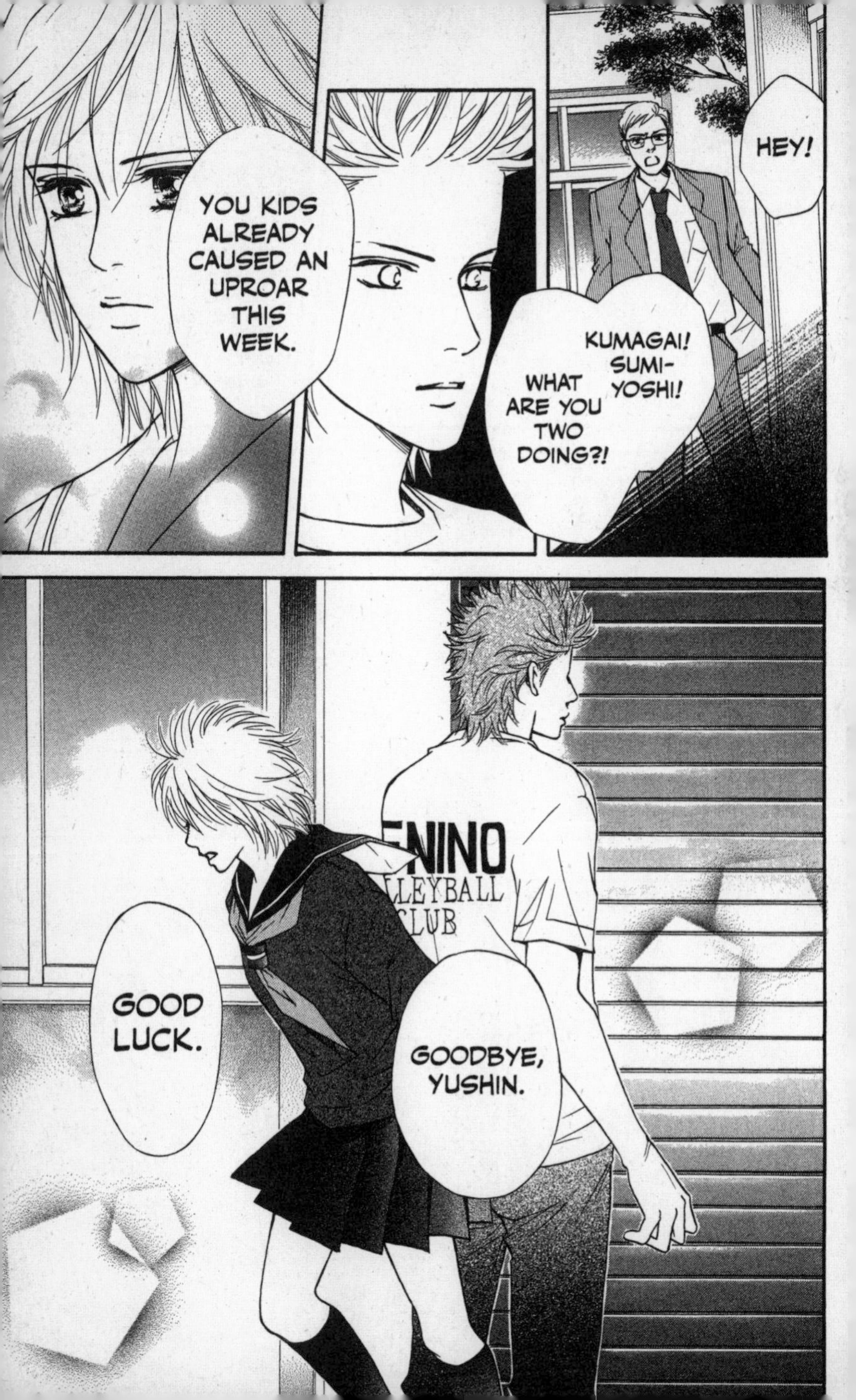
HEY!
KUMAGAI! SUMI-YOSHI!
WHAT ARE YOU TWO DOING?!
YOU KIDS ALREADY CAUSED AN UPROAR THIS WEEK.
NINO
LLEYBALL
CLUB
GOODBYE, YUSHIN.
GOOD LUCK.

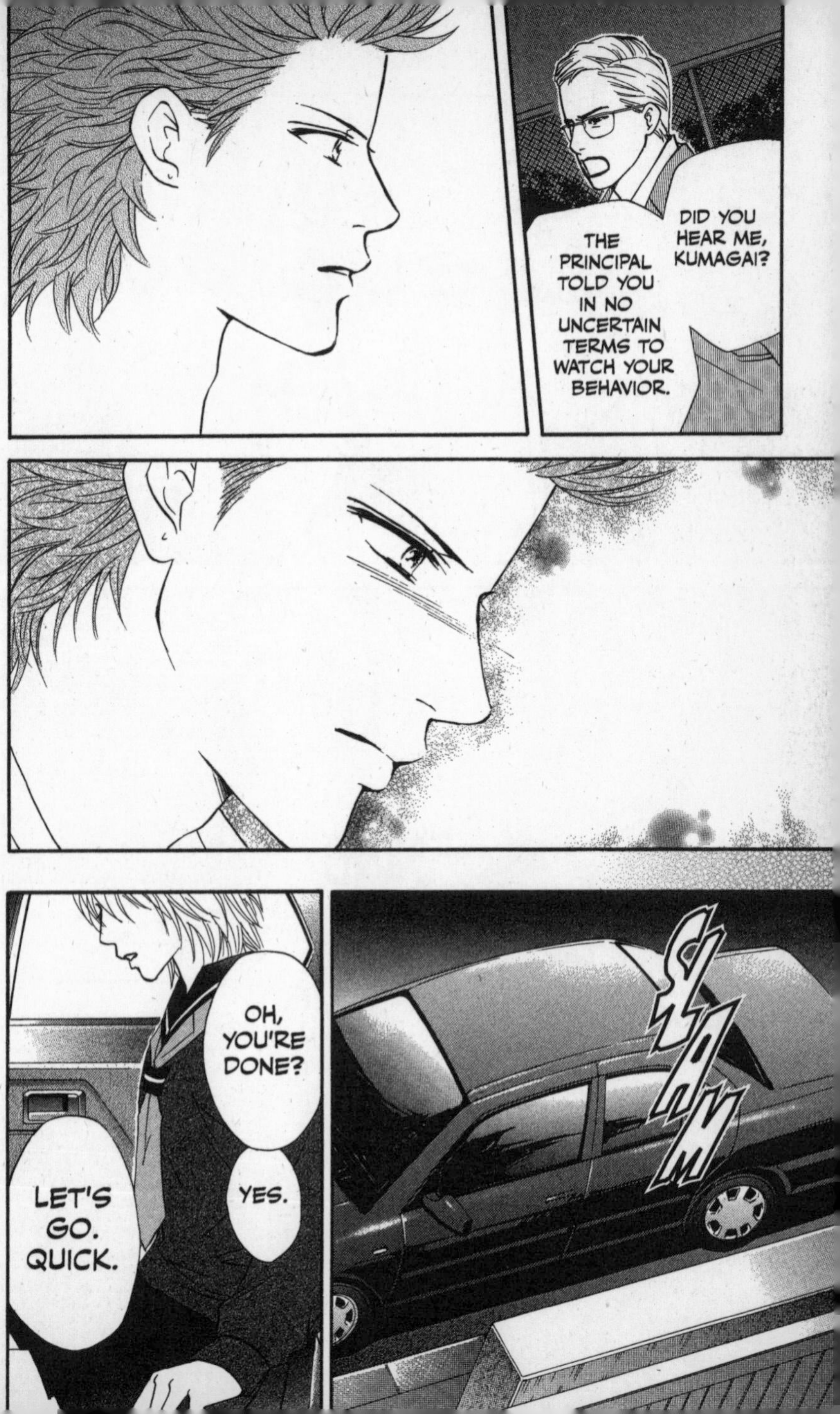
DID YOU HEAR ME, KUMAGAI?
THE PRINCIPAL TOLD YOU IN NO UNCERTAIN TERMS TO WATCH YOUR BEHAVIOR.
OH, YOU'RE DONE?
YES.
LET'S GO. QUICK.

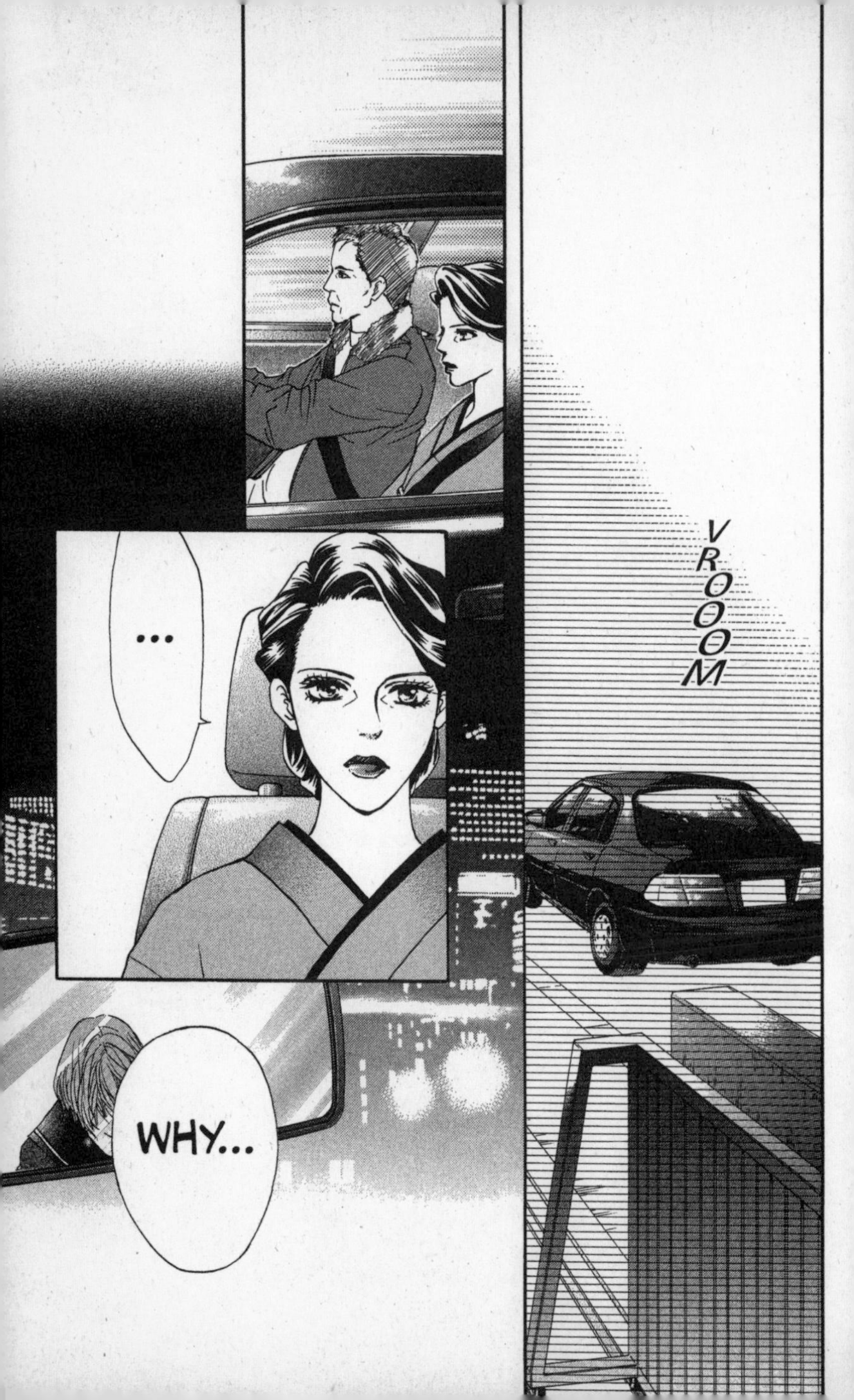
VROOOM
...
WHY...

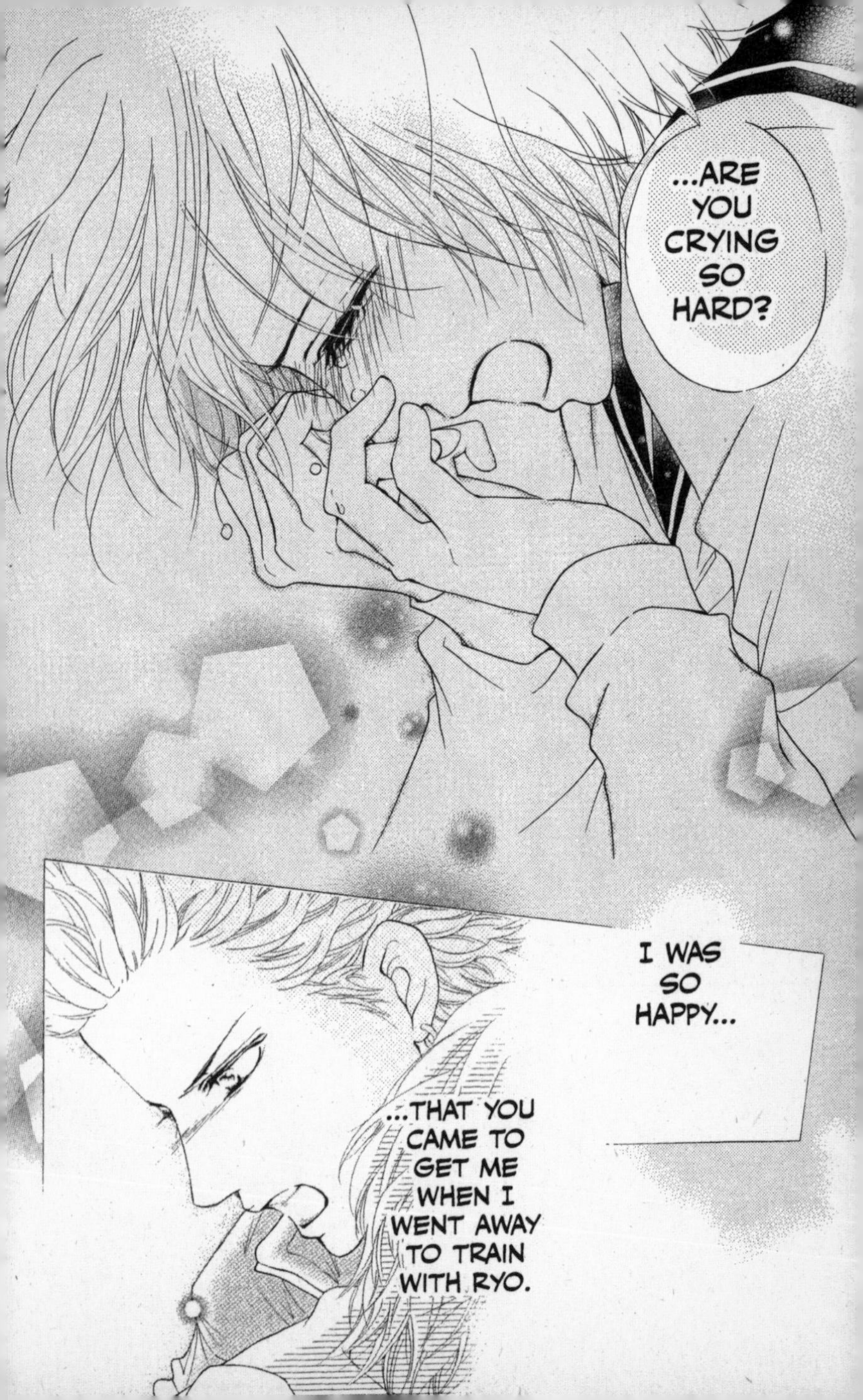
...ARE YOU CRYING SO HARD?
I WAS SO HAPPY...
...THAT YOU CAME TO GET ME WHEN I WENT AWAY TO TRAIN WITH RYO.

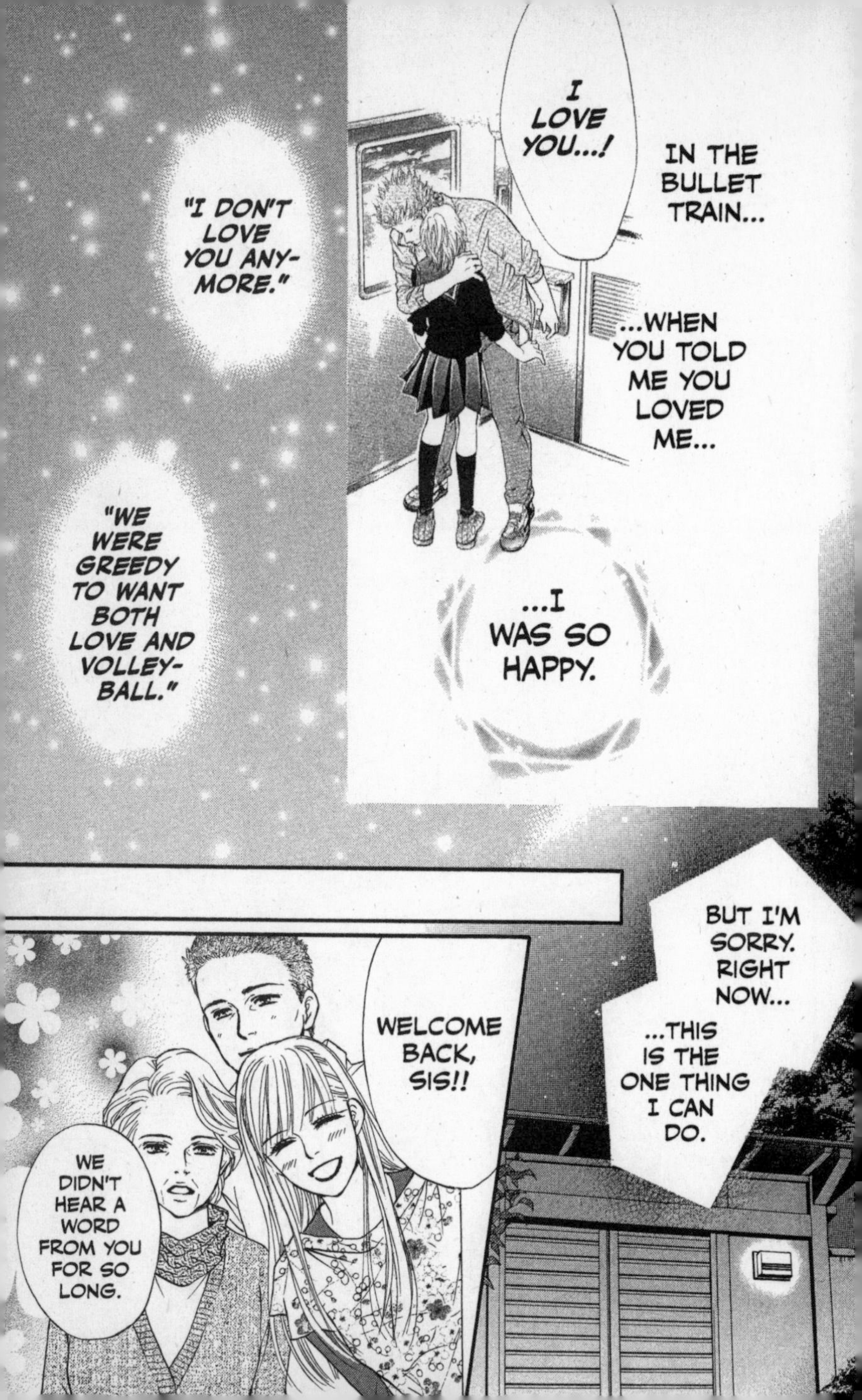
I LOVE YOU...!
IN THE BULLET TRAIN...
...WHEN YOU TOLD ME YOU LOVED ME...
...I WAS SO HAPPY.
"I DON'T LOVE YOU ANY-MORE."
"WE WERE GREEDY TO WANT BOTH LOVE AND VOLLEY-BALL."
BUT I'M SORRY. RIGHT NOW...
...THIS IS THE ONE THING I CAN DO.
WELCOME BACK, SIS!!
WE DIDN'T HEAR A WORD FROM YOU FOR SO LONG.

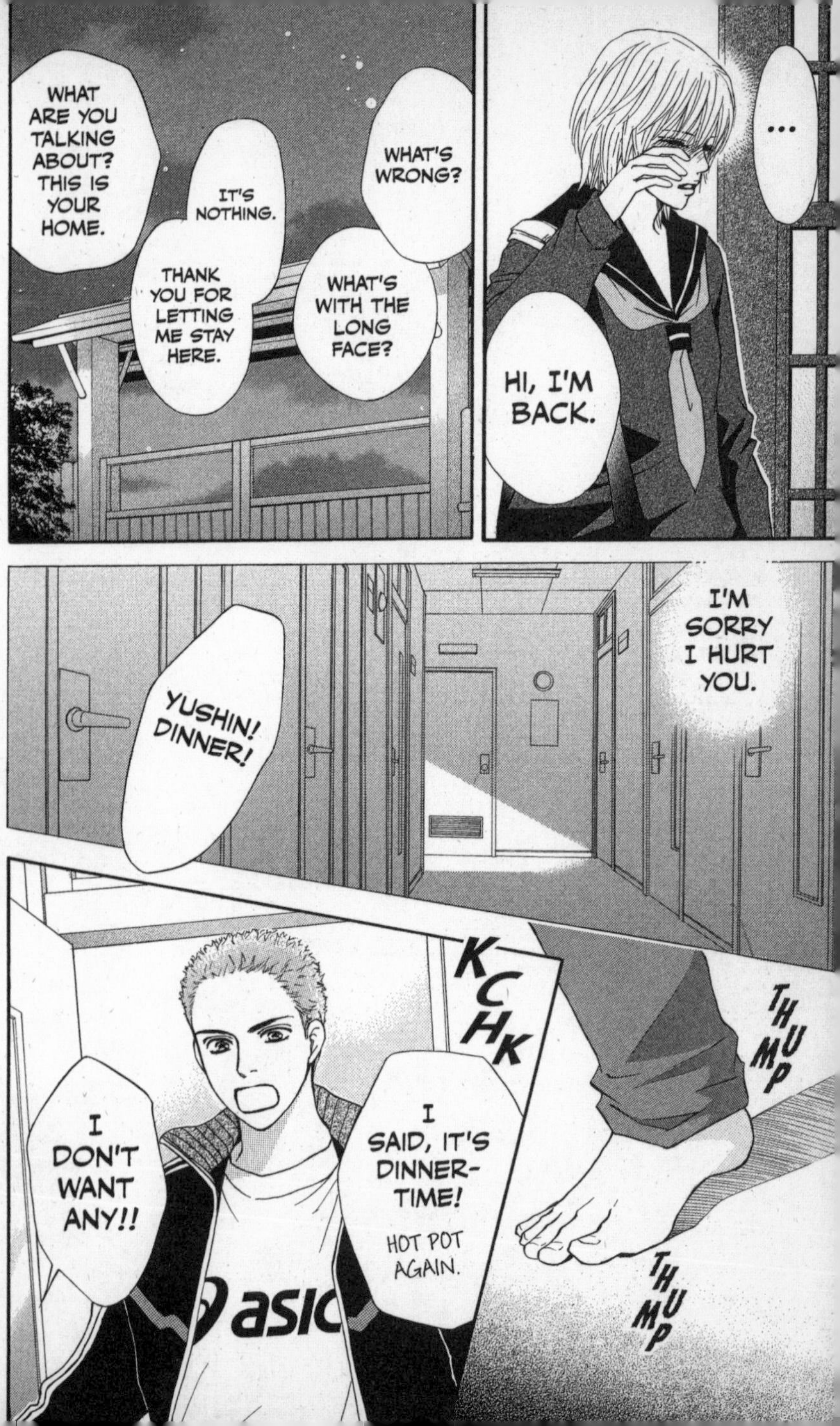
...
HI, I'M BACK.
WHAT'S WRONG?
WHAT'S WITH THE LONG FACE?
IT'S NOTHING.
THANK YOU FOR LETTING ME STAY HERE.
WHAT ARE YOU TALKING ABOUT? THIS IS YOUR HOME.
I'M SORRY I HURT YOU.
YUSHIN! DINNER!
THUMP
THUMP
KCHK
I SAID, IT'S DINNER-TIME!
HOT POT AGAIN.
I DON'T WANT ANY!!

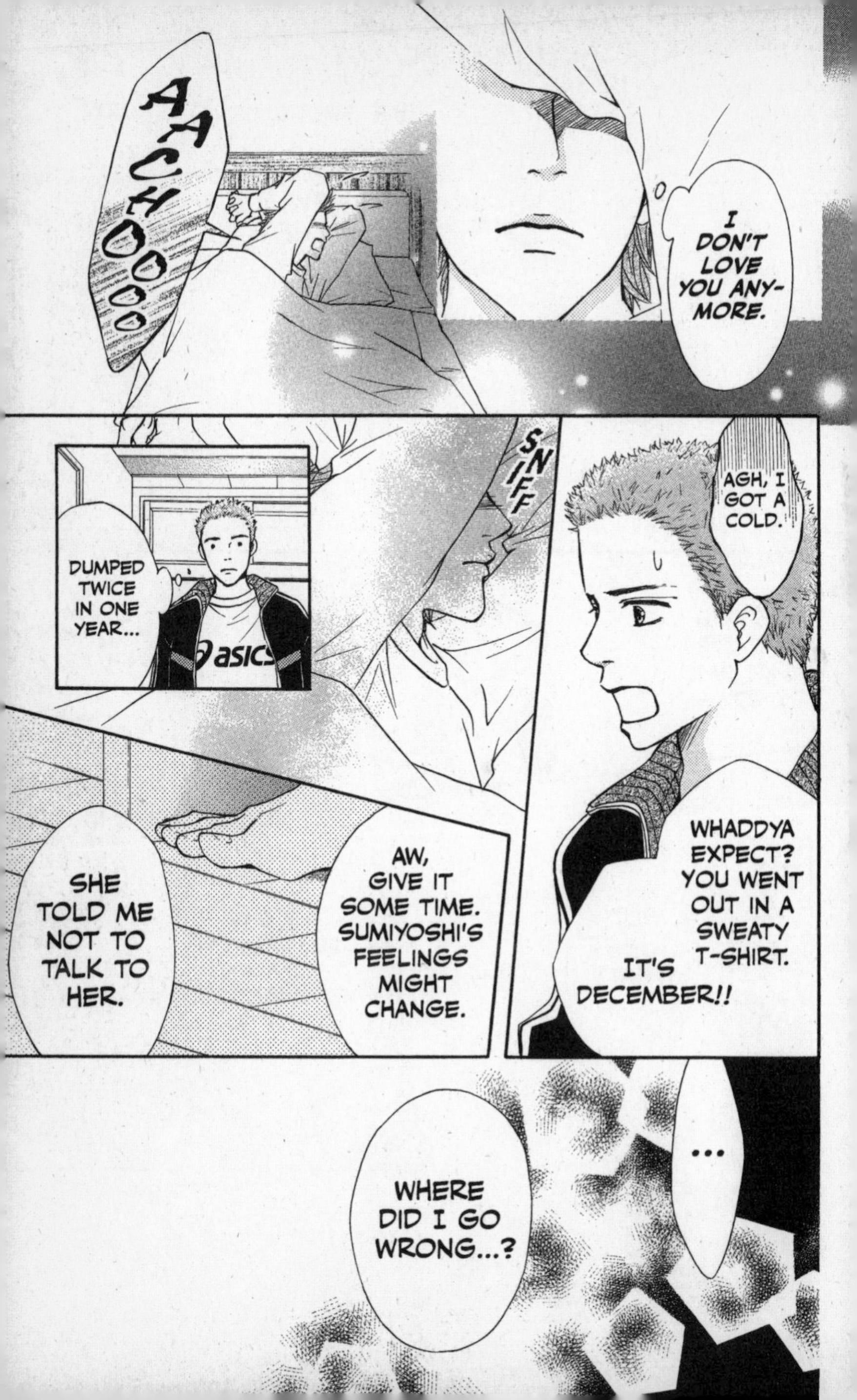
I DON'T LOVE YOU ANYMORE.
AACHOOOOO
AGH, I GOT A COLD.
WHADDYA EXPECT? YOU WENT OUT IN A SWEATY T-SHIRT.
IT'S DECEMBER!!
SNIFF
DUMPED TWICE IN ONE YEAR...
AW, GIVE IT SOME TIME. SUMIYOSHI'S FEELINGS MIGHT CHANGE.
SHE TOLD ME NOT TO TALK TO HER.
...
WHERE DID I GO WRONG...?
asics

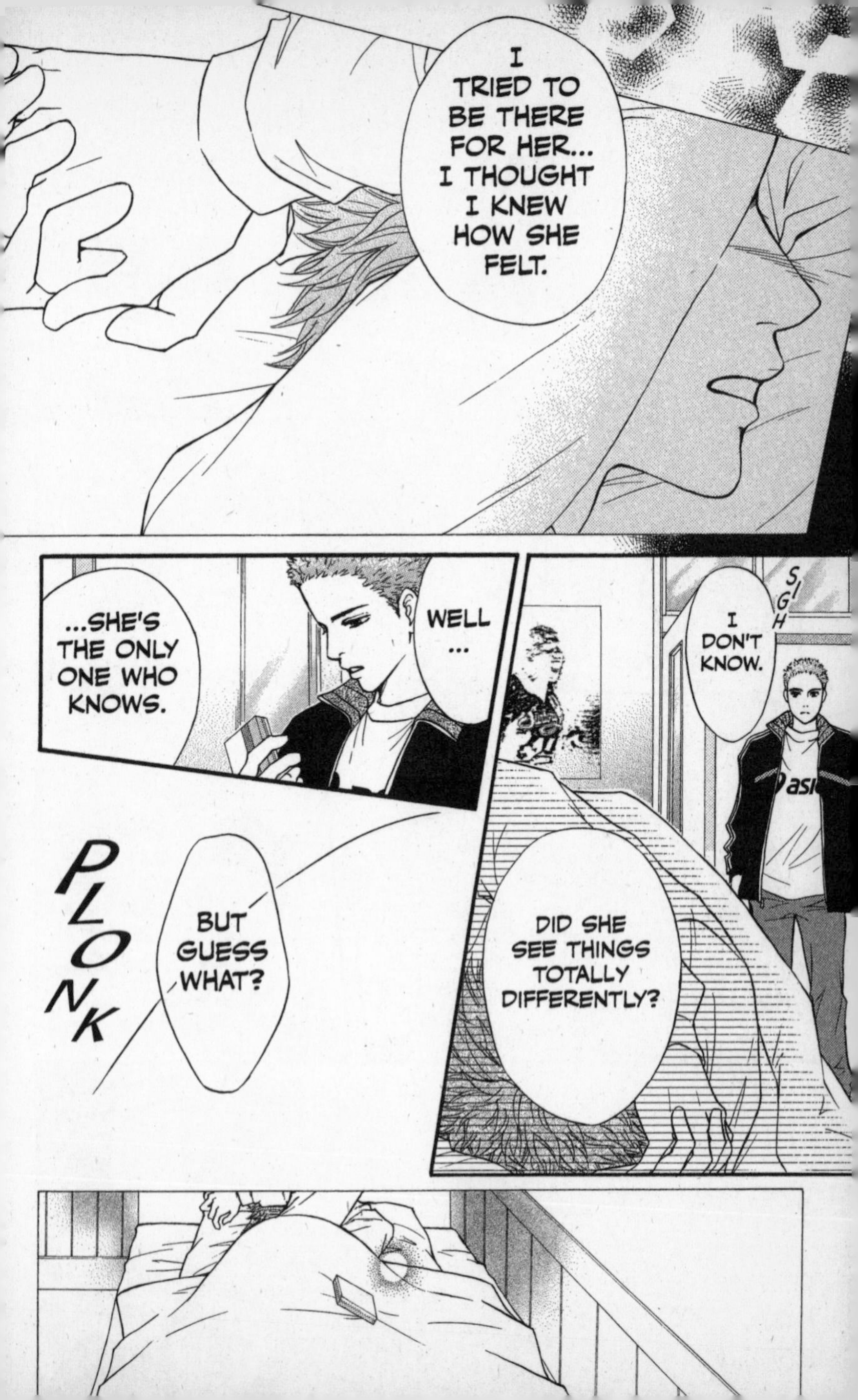
I TRIED TO BE THERE FOR HER... I THOUGHT I KNEW HOW SHE FELT.
SIGH
I DON'T KNOW.
DID SHE SEE THINGS TOTALLY DIFFERENTLY?
WELL ...
...SHE'S THE ONLY ONE WHO KNOWS.
BUT GUESS WHAT?
PLONK

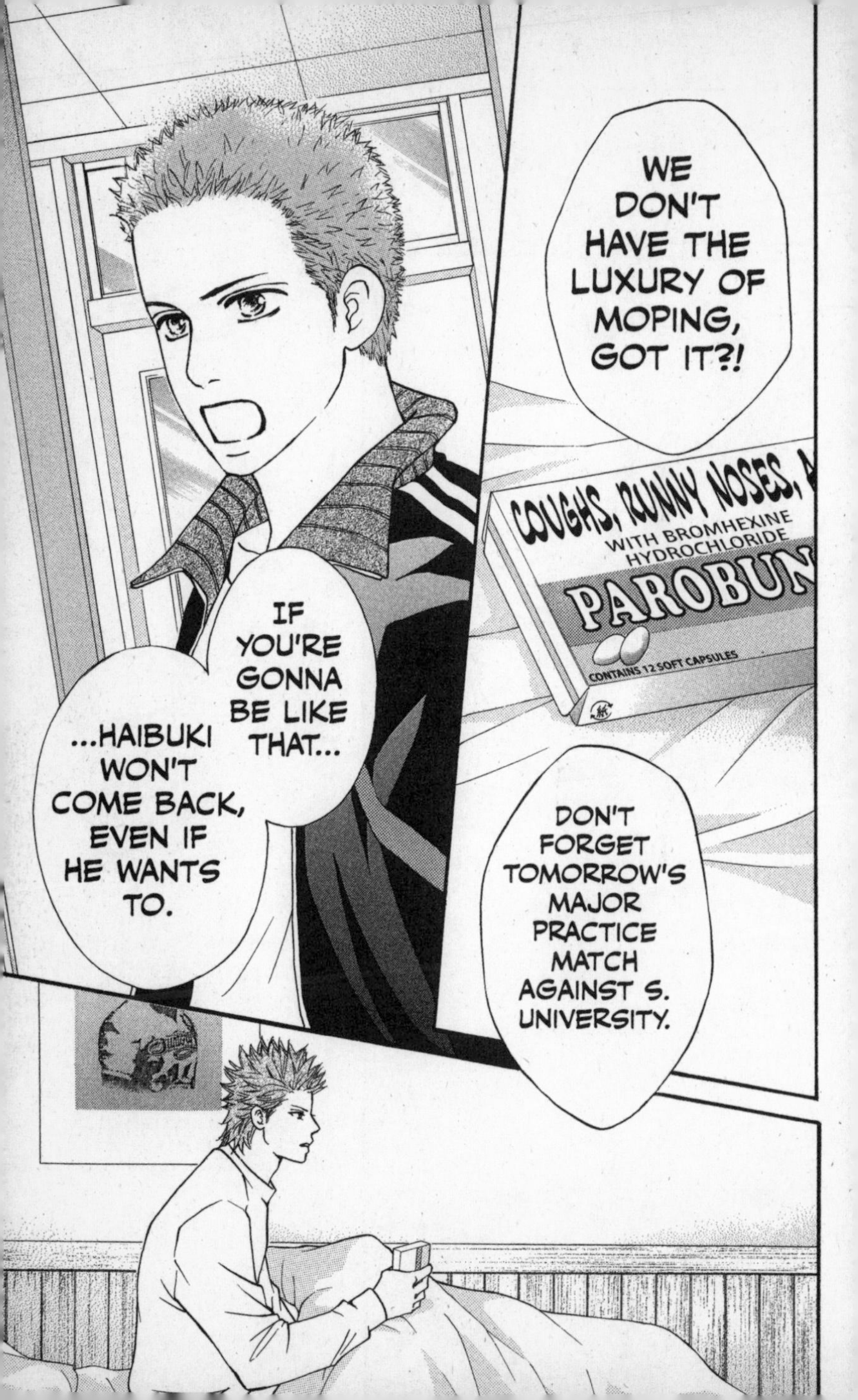

WE DON'T HAVE THE LUXURY OF MOPING, GOT IT?!
COUGHS, RUNNY NOSES,
WITH BROMHEXINE HYDROCHLORIDE
PAROBUN
CONTAINS 12 SOFT CAPSULES
IF YOU'RE GONNA BE LIKE THAT...
...HAIBUKI WON'T COME BACK, EVEN IF HE WANTS TO.
DON'T FORGET TOMORROW'S MAJOR PRACTICE MATCH AGAINST S. UNIVERSITY.

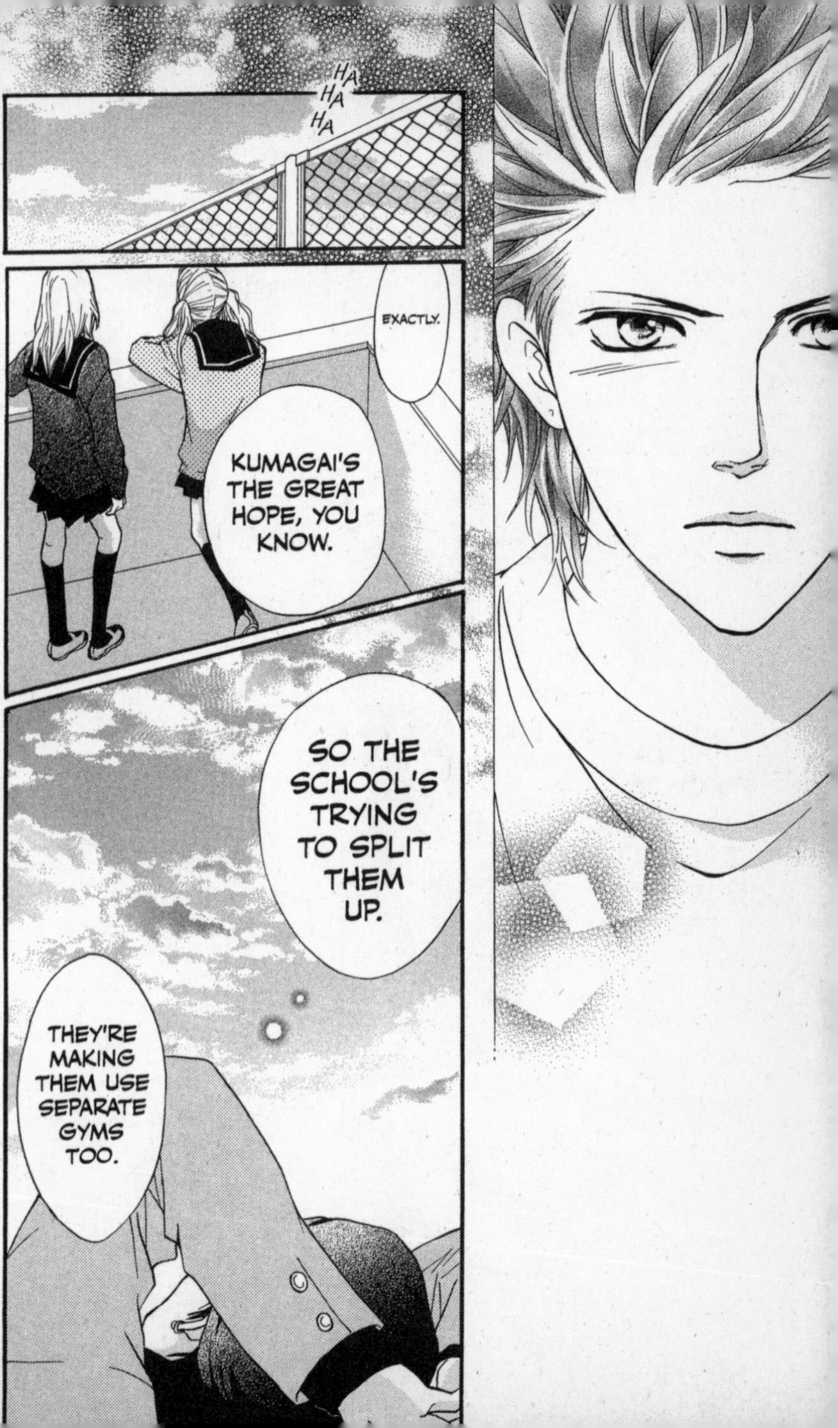
HA HA HA
EXACTLY.
KUMAGAI'S THE GREAT HOPE, YOU KNOW.
SO THE SCHOOL'S TRYING TO SPLIT THEM UP.
THEY'RE MAKING THEM USE SEPARATE GYMS TOO.

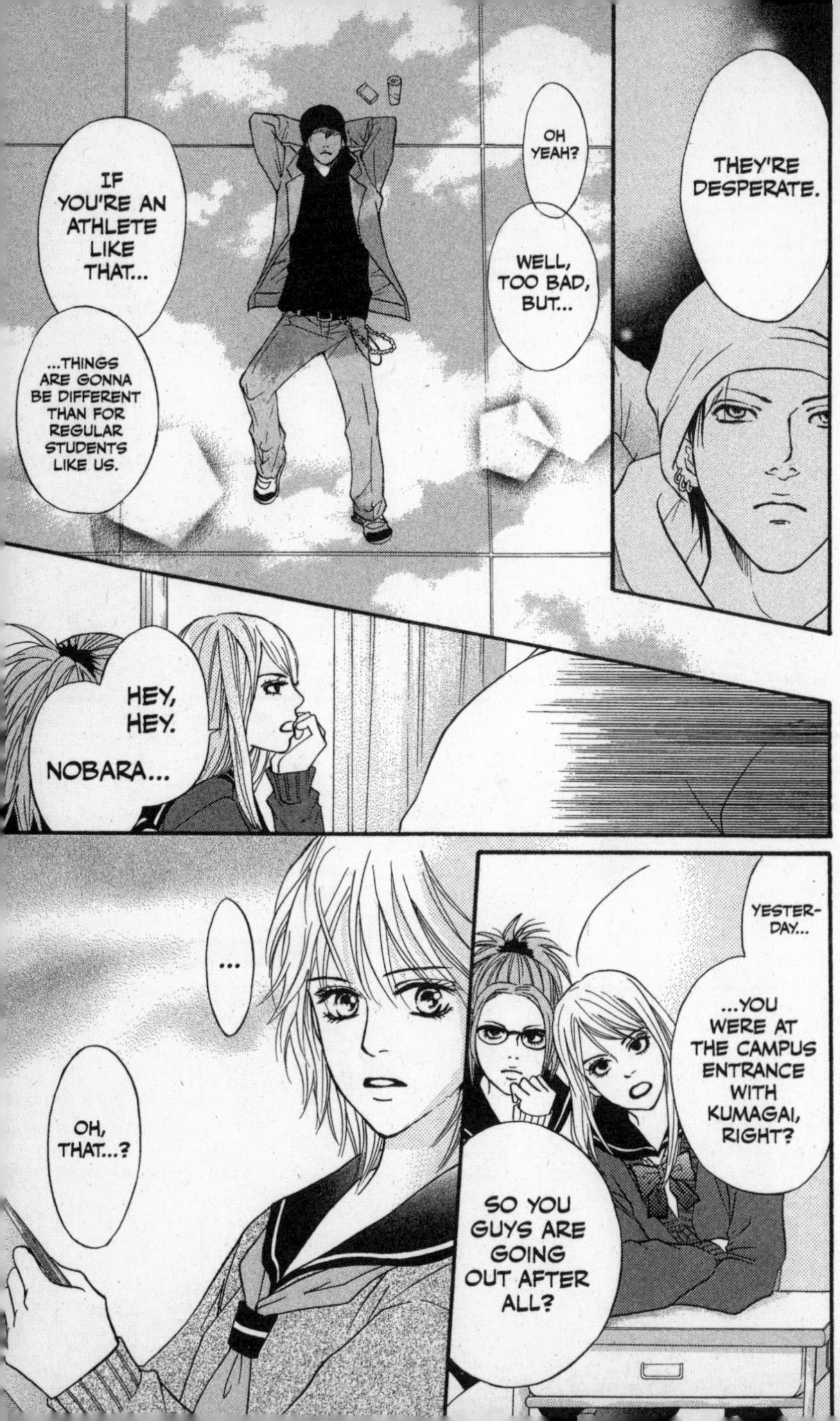
THEY'RE DESPERATE.
OH YEAH?
WELL, TOO BAD, BUT...
IF YOU'RE AN ATHLETE LIKE THAT...
...THINGS ARE GONNA BE DIFFERENT THAN FOR REGULAR STUDENTS LIKE US.
HEY, HEY.
NOBARA...
YESTER-DAY...
...YOU WERE AT THE CAMPUS ENTRANCE WITH KUMAGAI, RIGHT?
SO YOU GUYS ARE GOING OUT AFTER ALL?
...
OH, THAT...?

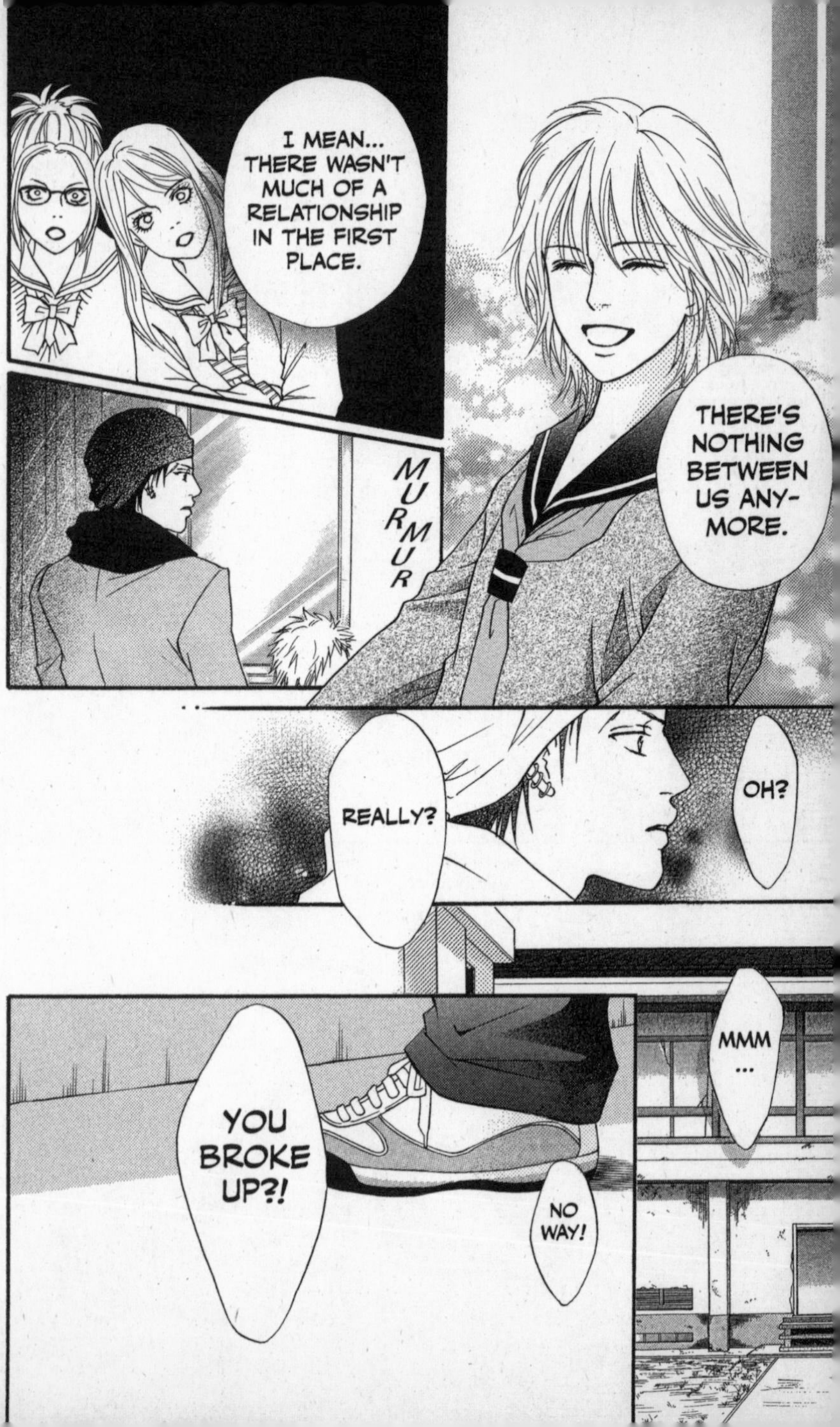
THERE'S NOTHING BETWEEN US ANY-MORE.
I MEAN... THERE WASN'T MUCH OF A RELATIONSHIP IN THE FIRST PLACE.
MURMUR MURMUR
OH?
REALLY?
MMM ...
NO WAY!
YOU BROKE UP?!

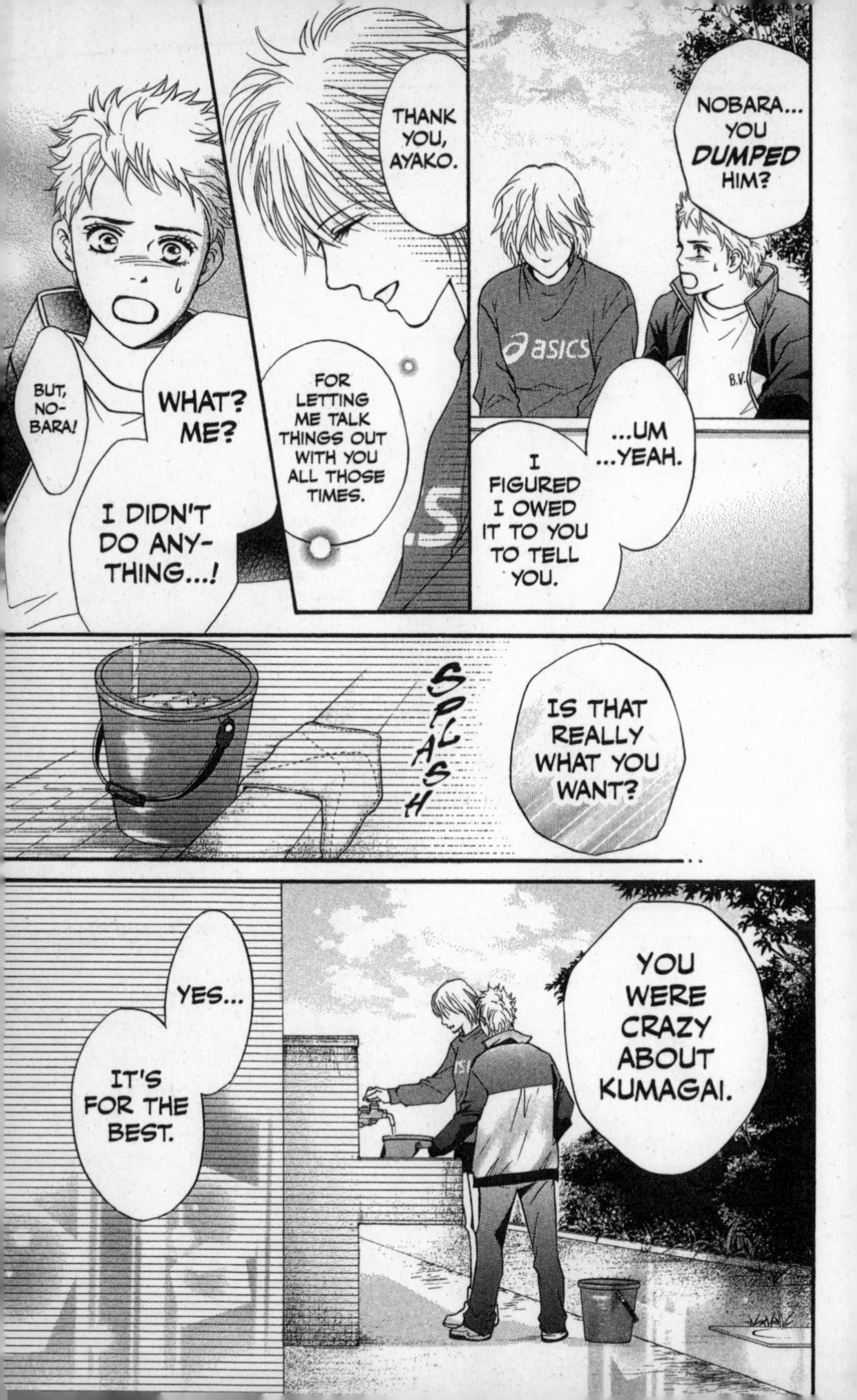
NOBARA... YOU DUMPED HIM?
...UM ...YEAH.
I FIGURED I OWED IT TO YOU TO TELL YOU.
THANK YOU, AYAKO.
FOR LETTING ME TALK THINGS OUT WITH YOU ALL THOSE TIMES.
WHAT? ME?
I DIDN'T DO ANY-THING...!
BUT, NO-BARA!
IS THAT REALLY WHAT YOU WANT?
SPLASH
YOU WERE CRAZY ABOUT KUMAGAI.
YES...
IT'S FOR THE BEST.

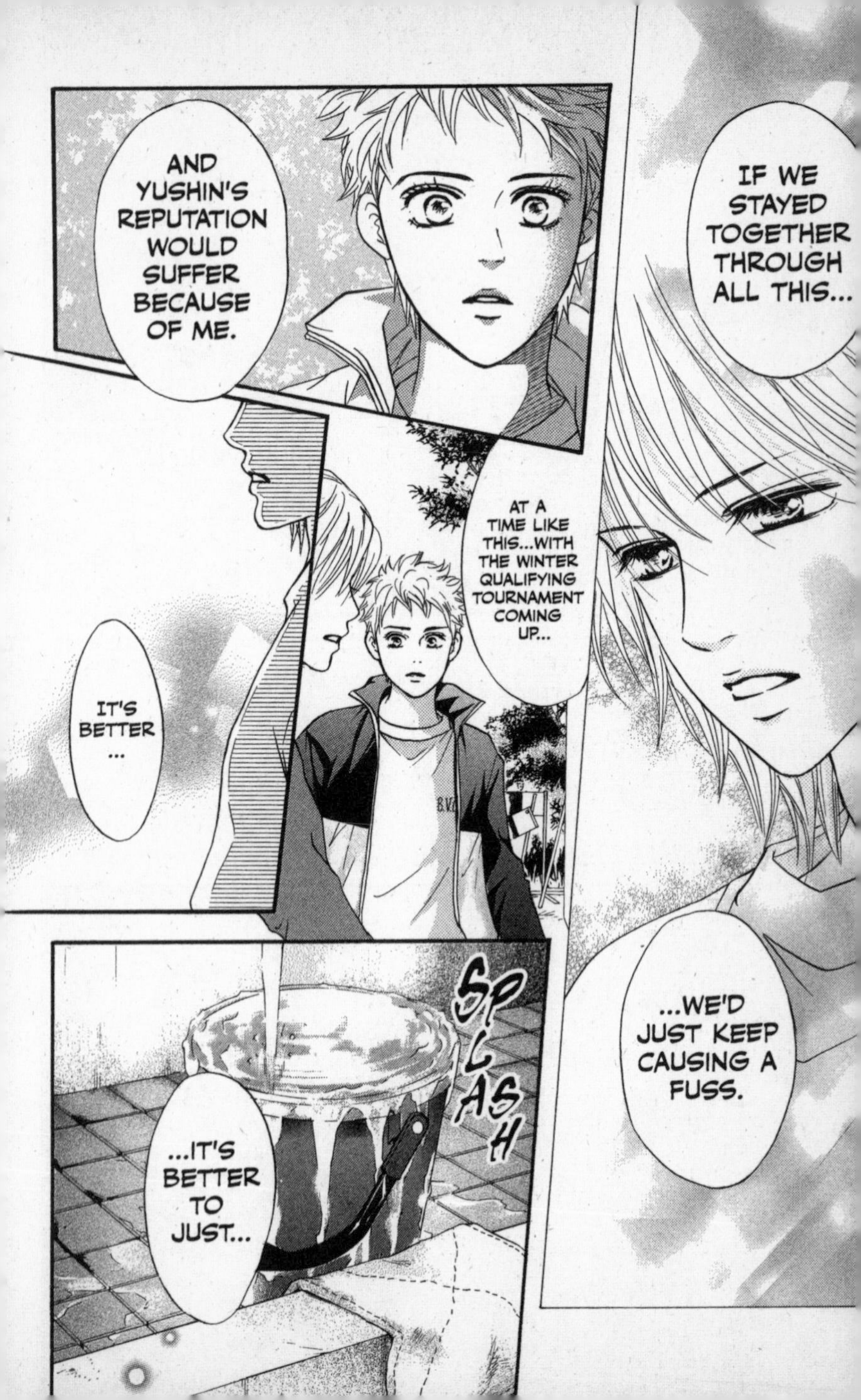
IF WE STAYED TOGETHER THROUGH ALL THIS...
...WE'D JUST KEEP CAUSING A FUSS.
AND YUSHIN'S REPUTATION WOULD SUFFER BECAUSE OF ME.
AT A TIME LIKE THIS...WITH THE WINTER QUALIFYING TOURNAMENT COMING UP...
IT'S BETTER ...
SPLASH
...IT'S BETTER TO JUST...

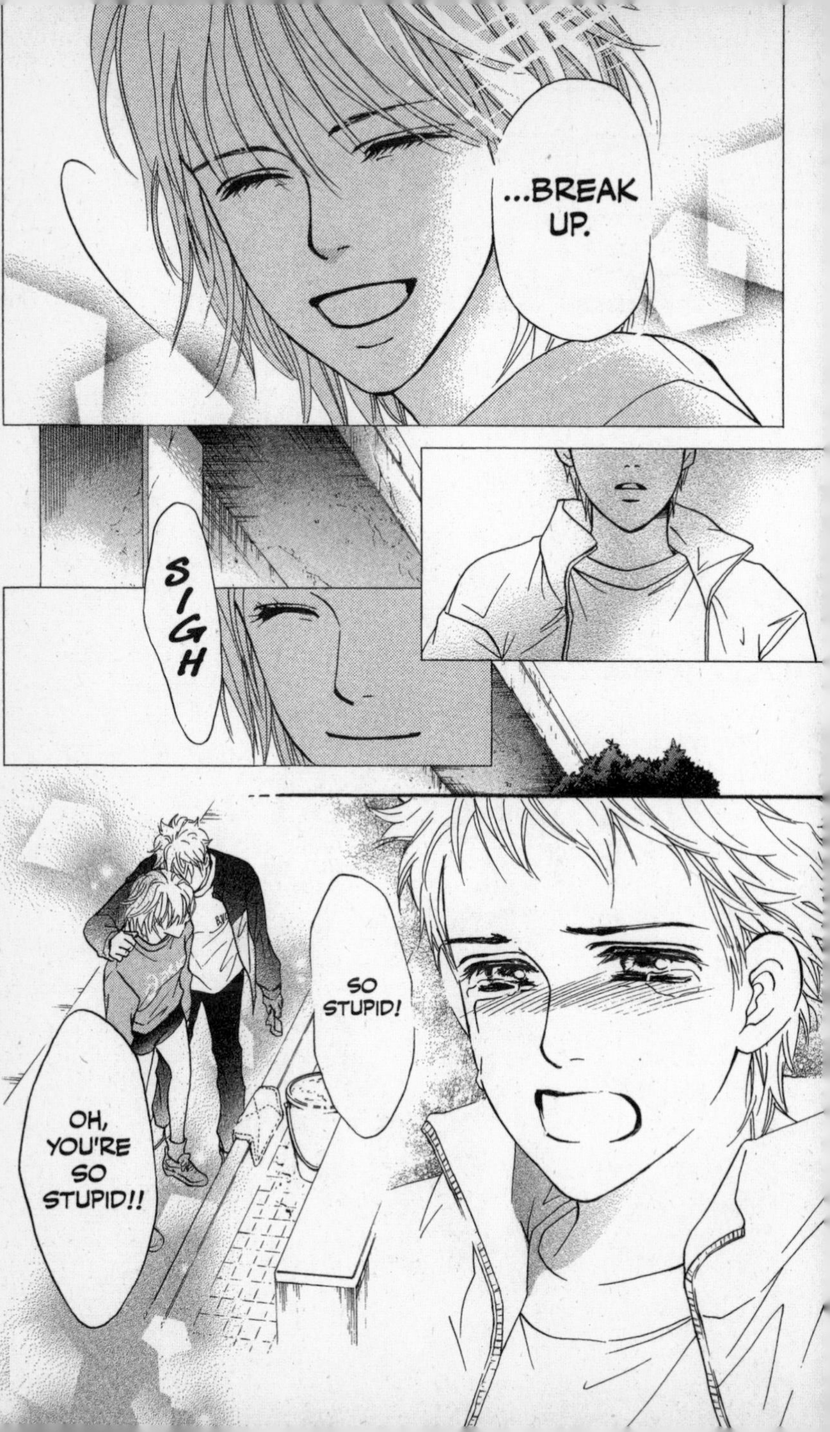
...BREAK UP.
SIGH
SO STUPID!
OH, YOU'RE SO STUPID!!

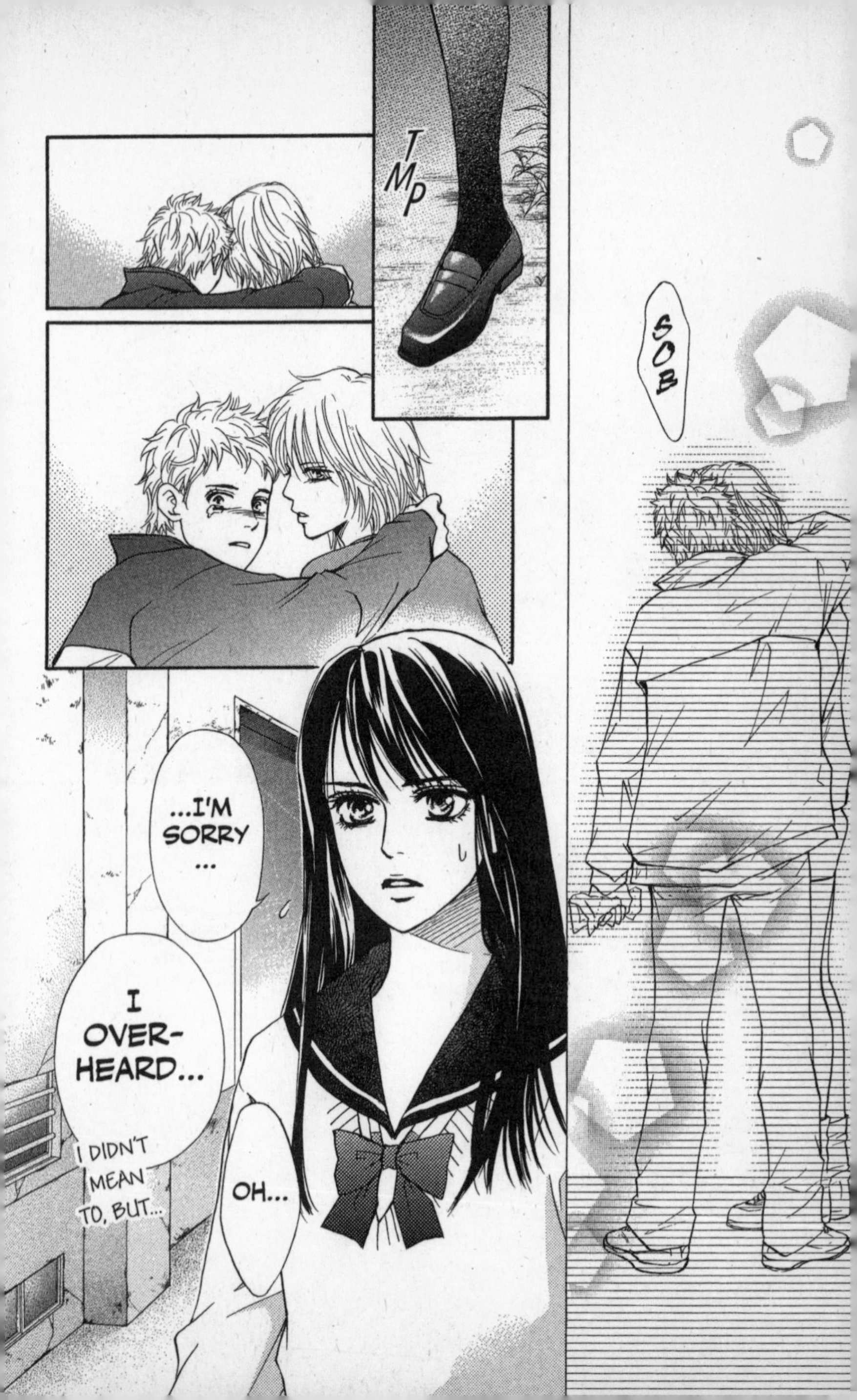

SOB
TMP
...I'M SORRY ...
I OVERHEARD...
I DIDN'T MEAN TO, BUT...
OH...

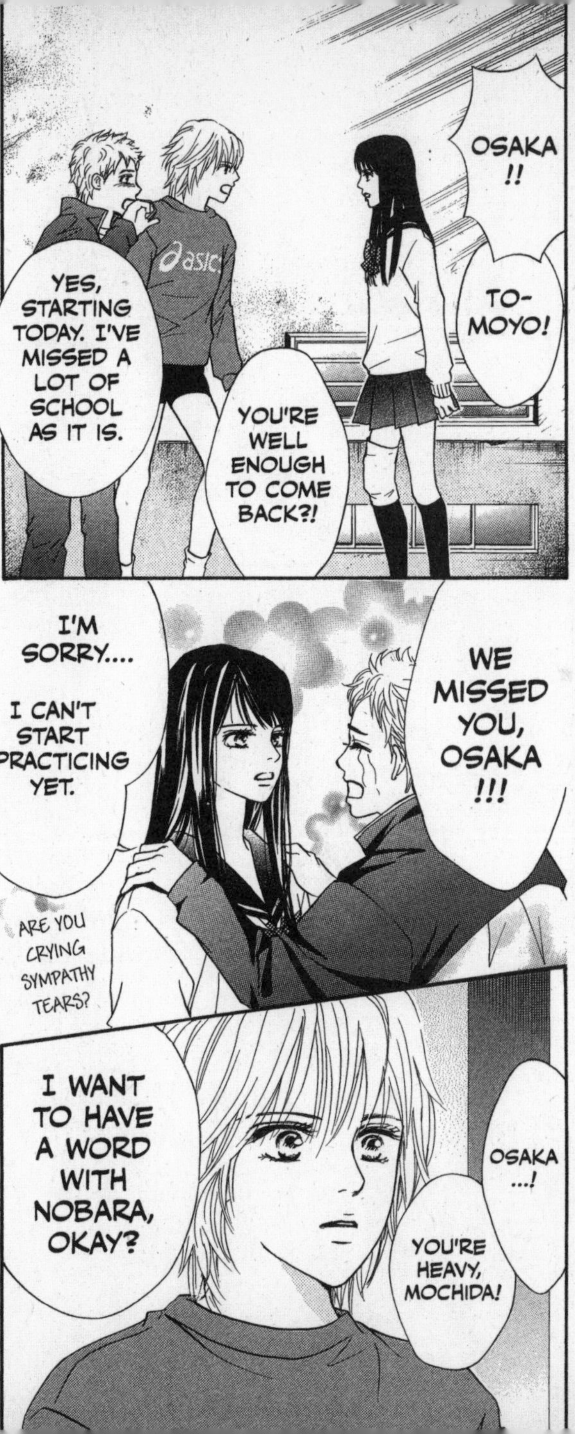
OSAKA !!
TO-MOYO!
YOU'RE WELL ENOUGH TO COME BACK?!
YES, STARTING TODAY. I'VE MISSED A LOT OF SCHOOL AS IT IS.
WE MISSED YOU, OSAKA !!!
I'M SORRY....
I CAN'T START PRACTICING YET.
ARE YOU CRYING SYMPATHY TEARS?
OSAKA ...!
YOU'RE HEAVY, MOCHIDA!
I WANT TO HAVE A WORD WITH NOBARA, OKAY?

MITSUBA CLUB

VoL.4

WELL, IT'S ALMOST TIME FOR US TO PART. I'VE MOSTLY WORKED OUT THE ENDING TO THE **CRIMSON HERO** SERIES, BUT NOW MY TASK IS TO FIGURE OUT HOW TO BUILD UP THE DRAMA THAT LEADS THERE. THIS IS A LONG STORY, BUT I STILL SOMETIMES FEEL LIKE MY PACING IS OFF. I'LL WORK REALLY HARD TO MAKE SURE I DON'T MISS ANYTHING. THANK YOU FOR ALL YOUR LETTERS. THEY REALLY KEEP ME GOING. I AWAIT YOUR COMMENTS.

SEND YOUR LETTERS TO:

MITSUBA TAKANASHI
SHOJO BEAT MANGA/
CRIMSON HERO
C/O VIZ MEDIA, LLC
P.O. BOX 77010
SAN FRANCISCO, CA 94107

I'LL BE WAITING!
THANK YOU!

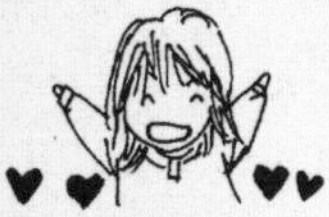

GOOD LUCK TO ALL THE VOLLEYBALL TEAMS HOPING TO MAKE IT TO THE SPRING TOURNAMENT. NOBARA AND HER FRIENDS WILL WORK HARD TO MAKE IT TOO!!

I'D LIKE TO DRAW RYO AND THE MEMBERS OF THE EAGLES AGAIN.
AND DO A STORY ABOUT YATCHAN AND MIKKO TOO.

SEE YOU LATER!
LET'S MEET IN VOLUME 14!

MITSUBA

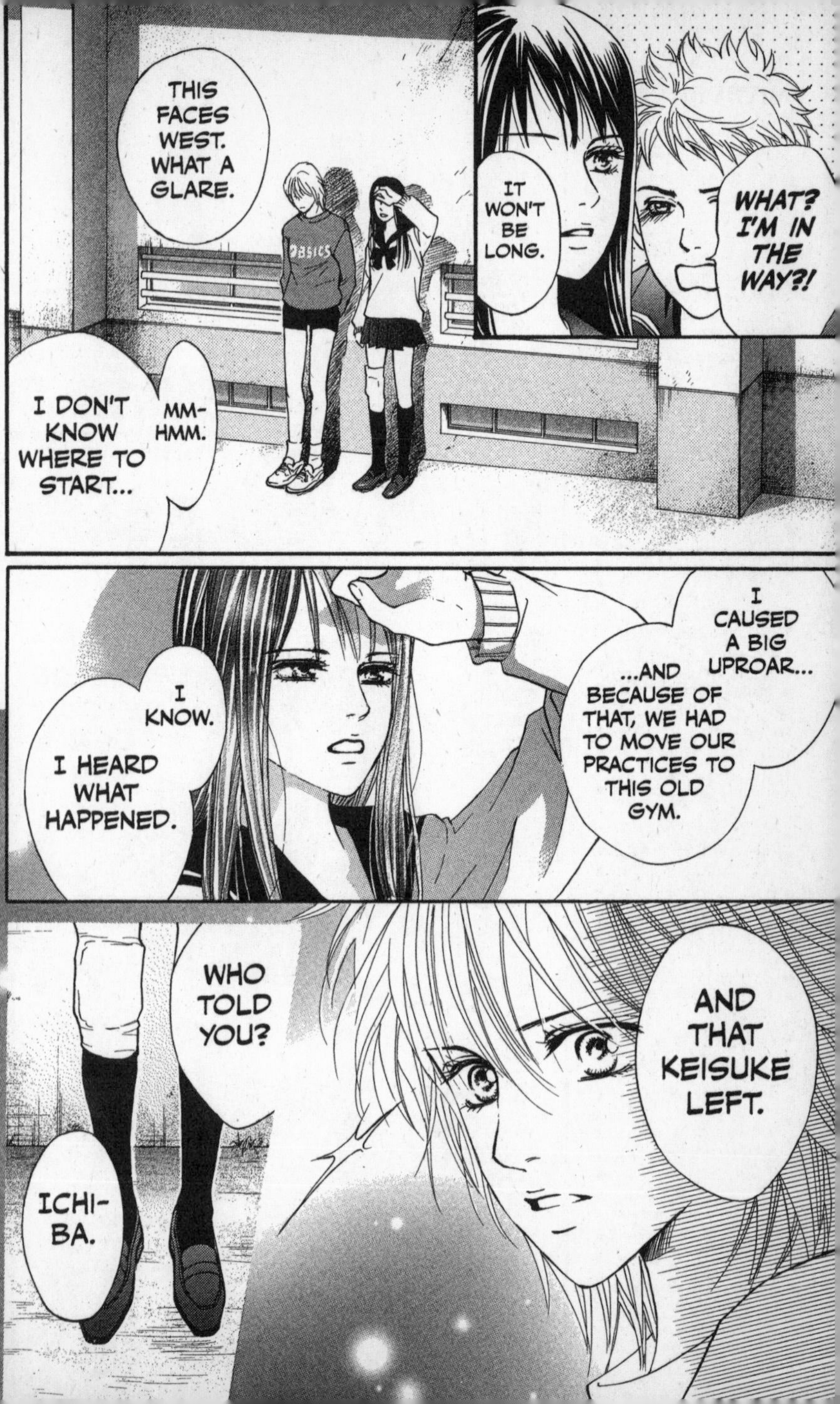
WHAT? I'M IN THE WAY?!
IT WON'T BE LONG.
THIS FACES WEST. WHAT A GLARE.
MM-HMM.
I DON'T KNOW WHERE TO START...
I CAUSED A BIG UPROAR...
...AND BECAUSE OF THAT, WE HAD TO MOVE OUR PRACTICES TO THIS OLD GYM.
I KNOW.
I HEARD WHAT HAPPENED.
AND THAT KEISUKE LEFT.
WHO TOLD YOU?
ICHIBA.

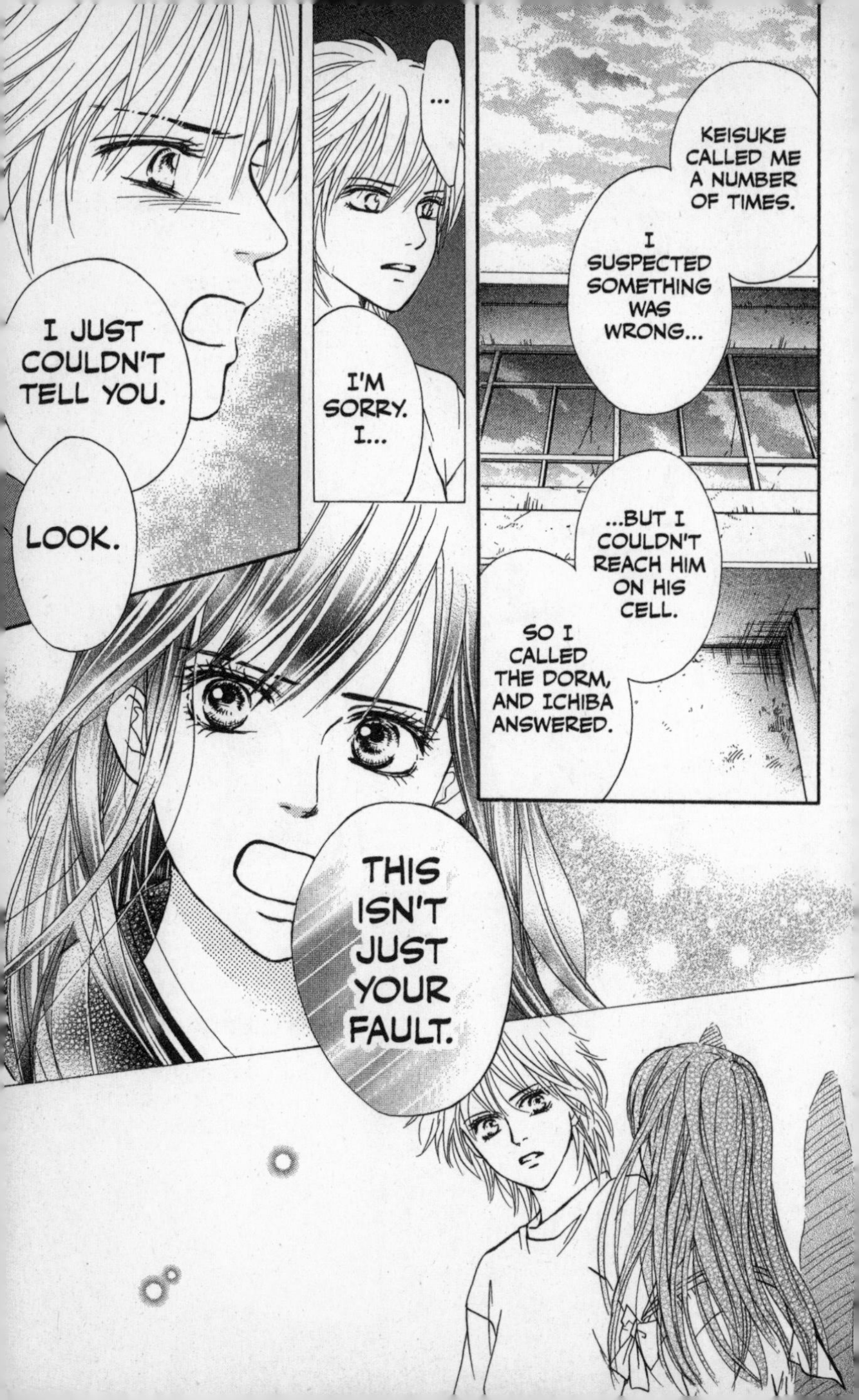
KEISUKE CALLED ME A NUMBER OF TIMES.
I SUSPECTED SOMETHING WAS WRONG...
...BUT I COULDN'T REACH HIM ON HIS CELL.
SO I CALLED THE DORM, AND ICHIBA ANSWERED.
...
I'M SORRY. I...
I JUST COULDN'T TELL YOU.
LOOK.
THIS ISN'T JUST YOUR FAULT.

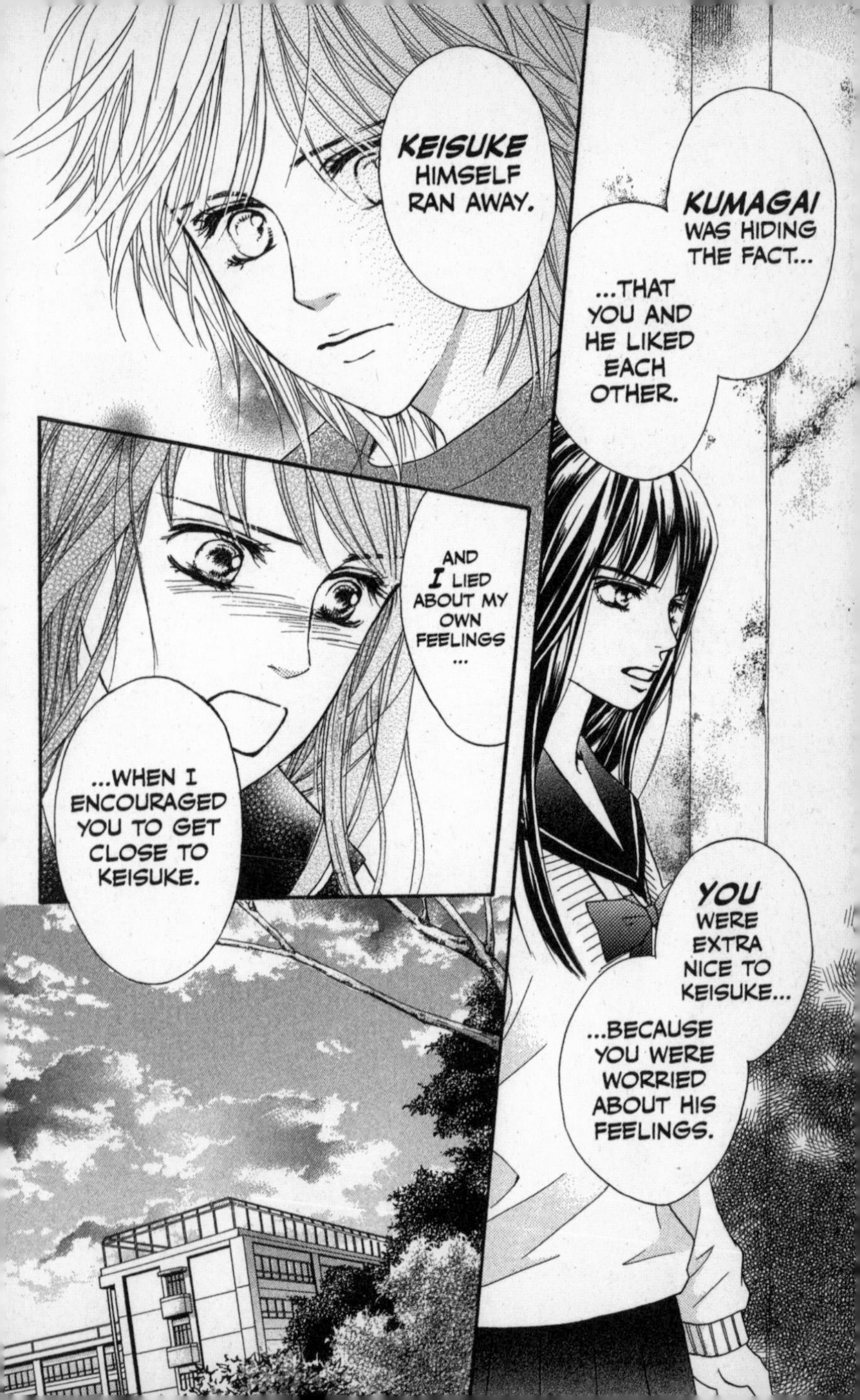
KUMAGAI WAS HIDING THE FACT...
...THAT YOU AND HE LIKED EACH OTHER.
YOU WERE EXTRA NICE TO KEISUKE...
...BECAUSE YOU WERE WORRIED ABOUT HIS FEELINGS.
KEISUKE HIMSELF RAN AWAY.
AND I LIED ABOUT MY OWN FEELINGS ...
...WHEN I ENCOURAGED YOU TO GET CLOSE TO KEISUKE.

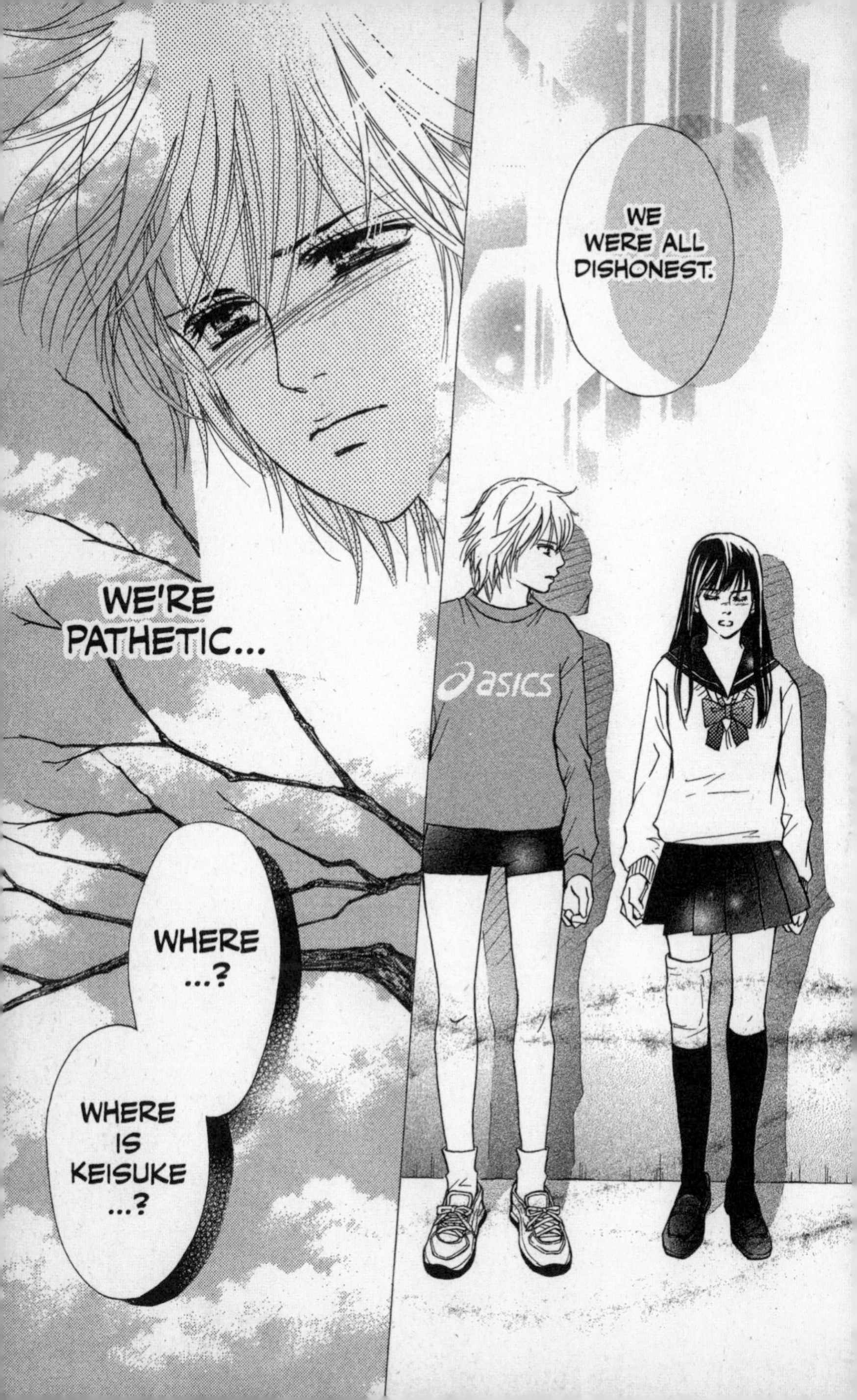
WE WERE ALL DISHONEST.
asics
WE'RE PATHETIC...
WHERE ...?
WHERE IS KEISUKE ...?

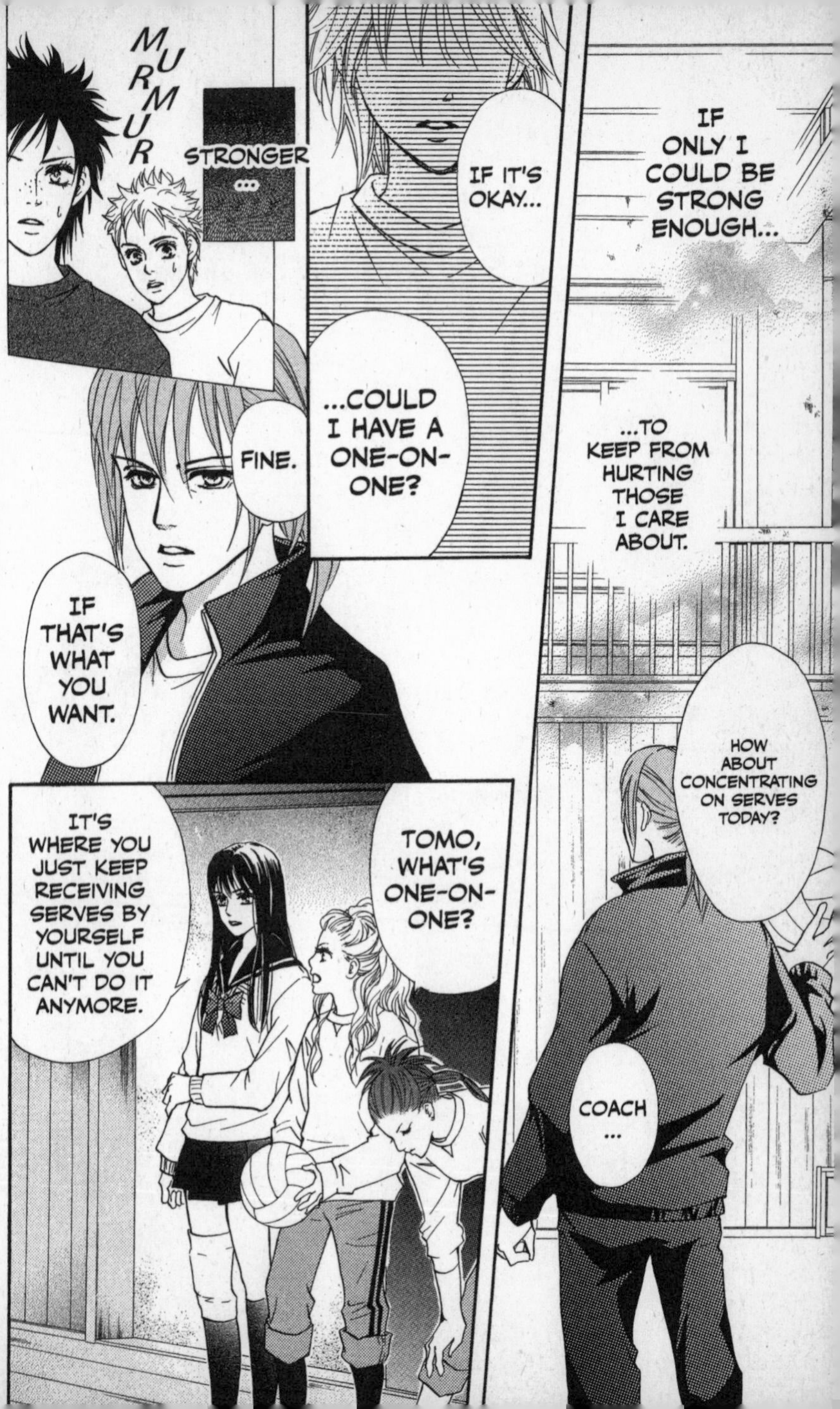
IF ONLY I COULD BE STRONG ENOUGH...
...TO KEEP FROM HURTING THOSE I CARE ABOUT.
HOW ABOUT CONCENTRATING ON SERVES TODAY?
COACH ...
IF IT'S OKAY...
STRONGER ...
MURMUR
...COULD I HAVE A ONE-ON-ONE?
FINE.
IF THAT'S WHAT YOU WANT.
TOMO, WHAT'S ONE-ON-ONE?
IT'S WHERE YOU JUST KEEP RECEIVING SERVES BY YOURSELF UNTIL YOU CAN'T DO IT ANYMORE.

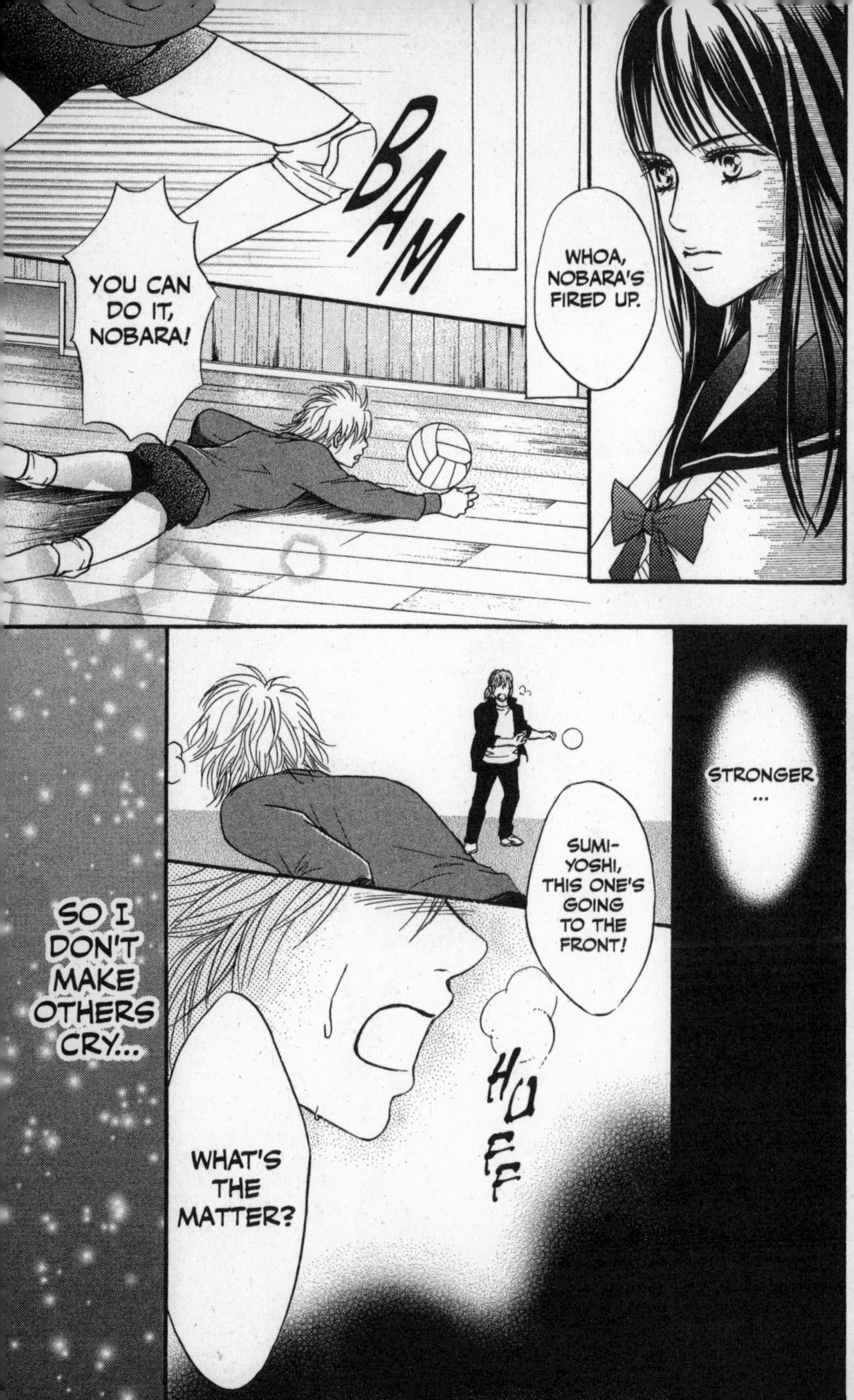
WHOA, NOBARA'S FIRED UP.
BAM
YOU CAN DO IT, NOBARA!
STRONGER ...
SUMI-YOSHI, THIS ONE'S GOING TO THE FRONT!
HUFF
WHAT'S THE MATTER?
SO I DON'T MAKE OTHERS CRY...

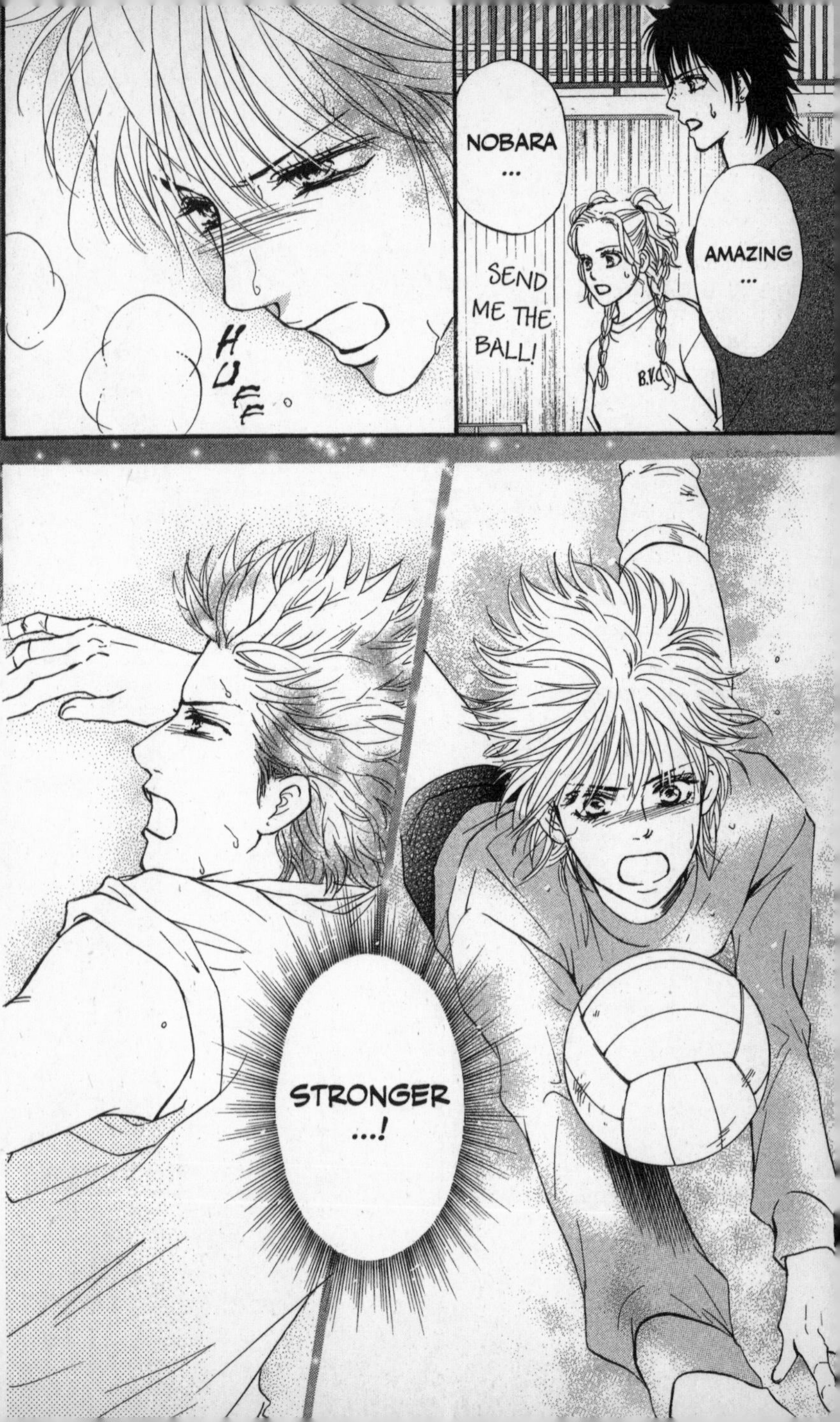
AMAZING ...
NOBARA ...
SEND ME THE BALL!
HUFF
STRONGER ...!

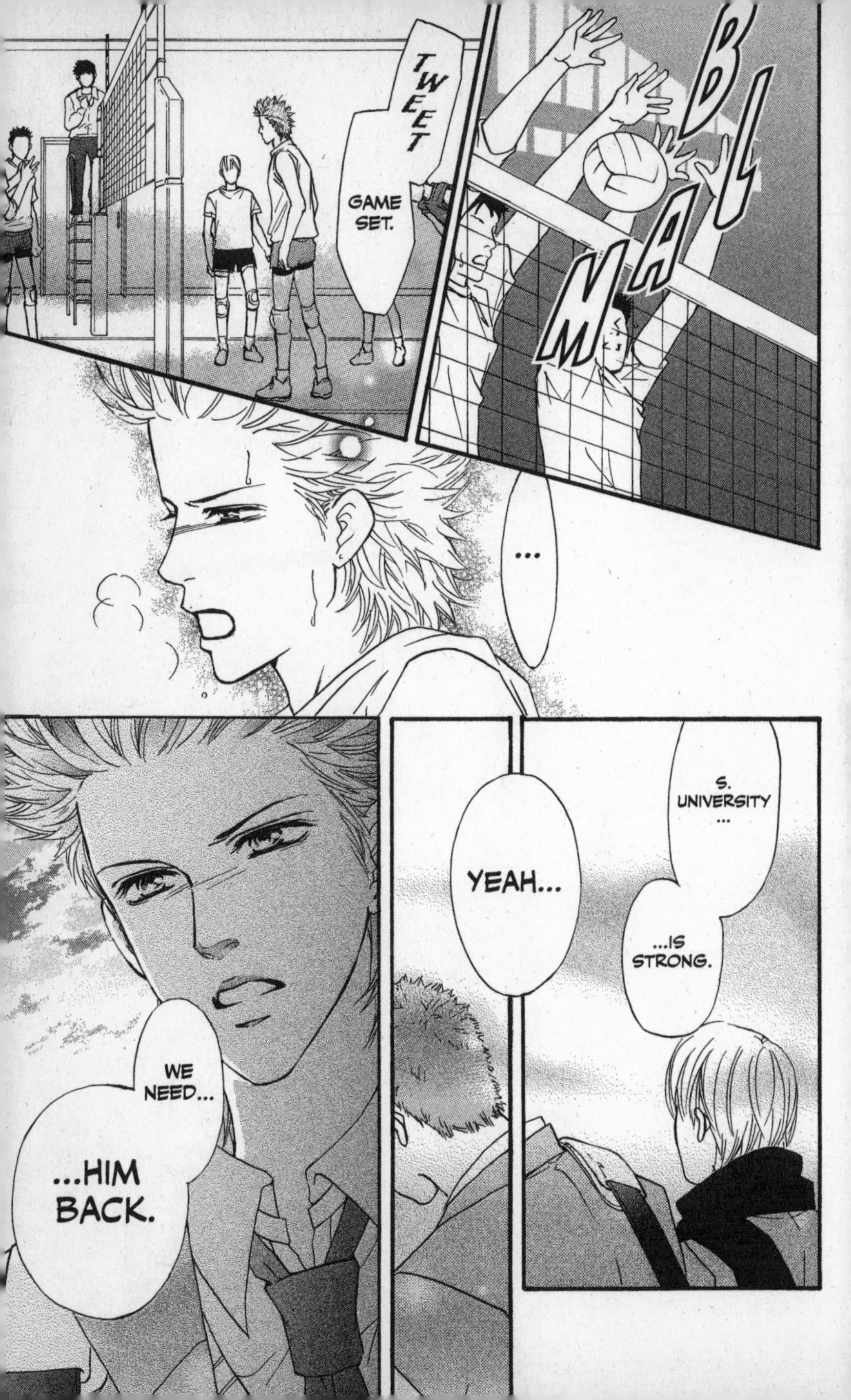
BLAM
TWEET
GAME SET.
...
S. UNIVERSITY ...
...IS STRONG.
YEAH...
WE NEED...
...HIM BACK.

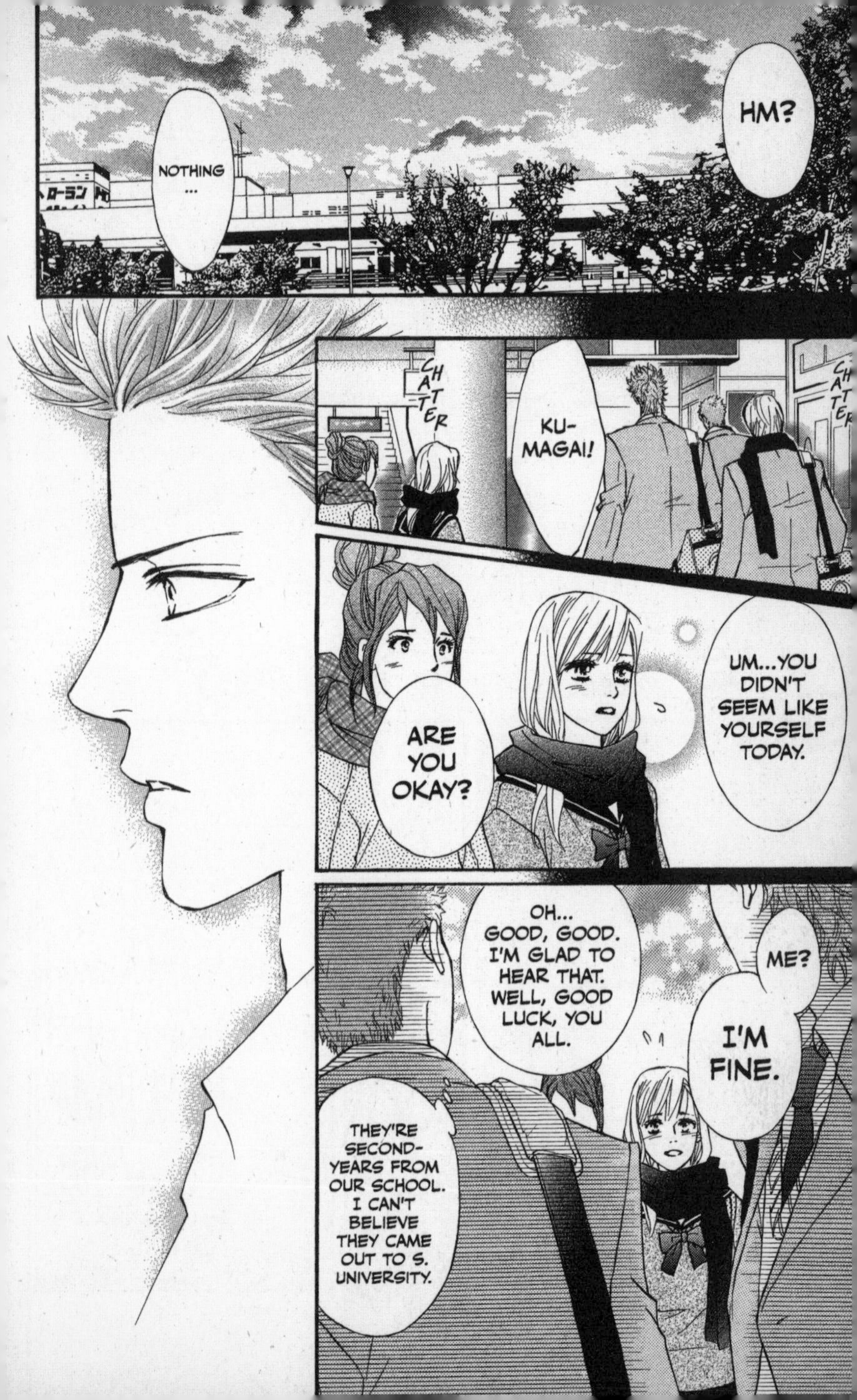
HM?
NOTHING ...
CHATTER
KU-MAGAI!
CHATTER
UM...YOU DIDN'T SEEM LIKE YOURSELF TODAY.
ARE YOU OKAY?
ME?
I'M FINE.
OH... GOOD, GOOD. I'M GLAD TO HEAR THAT. WELL, GOOD LUCK, YOU ALL.
THEY'RE SECOND-YEARS FROM OUR SCHOOL. I CAN'T BELIEVE THEY CAME OUT TO S. UNIVERSITY.

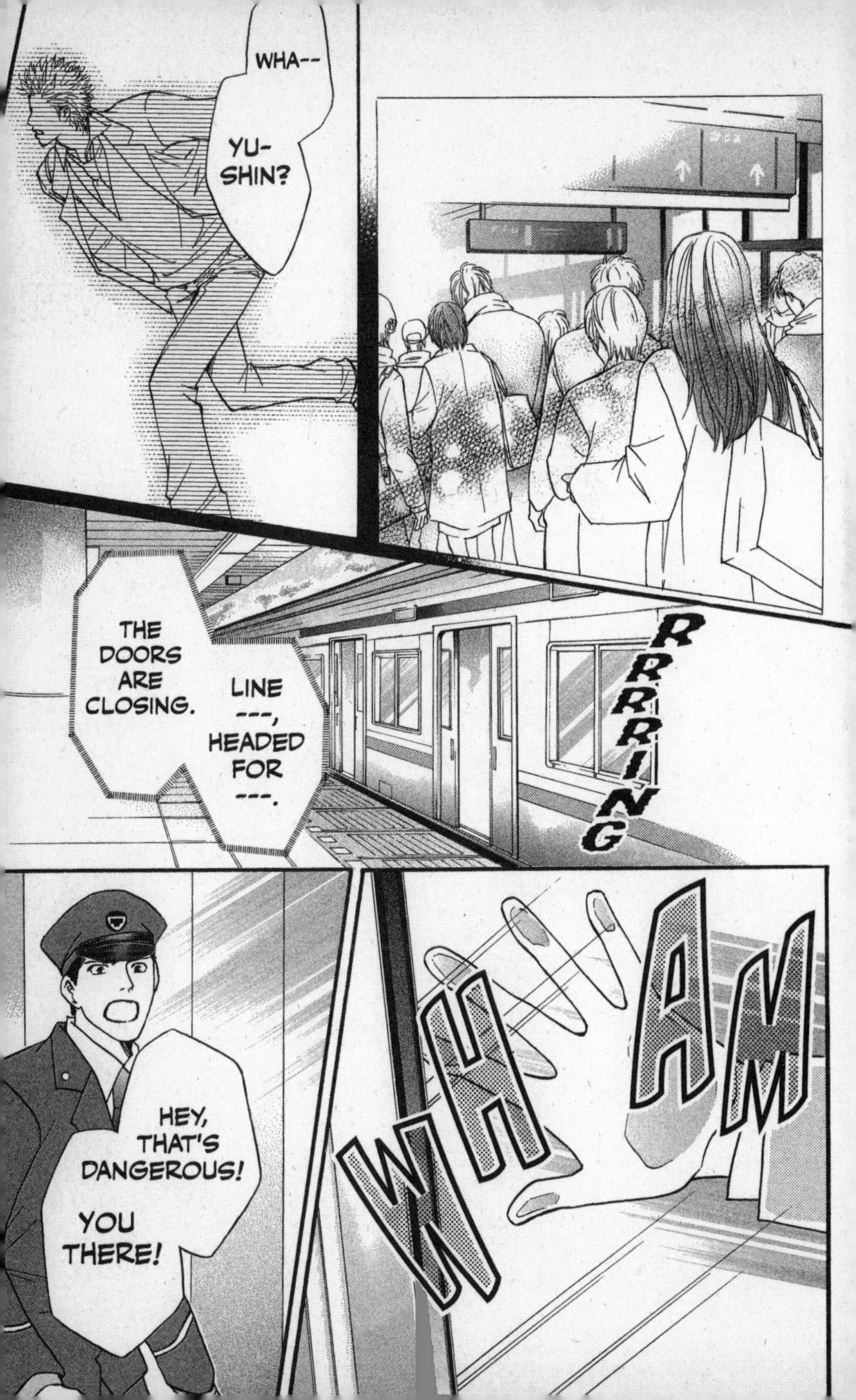
WHA--
YU-SHIN?
RRRRING
LINE ---, HEADED FOR ---.
THE DOORS ARE CLOSING.
WHAM
HEY, THAT'S DANGEROUS!
YOU THERE!

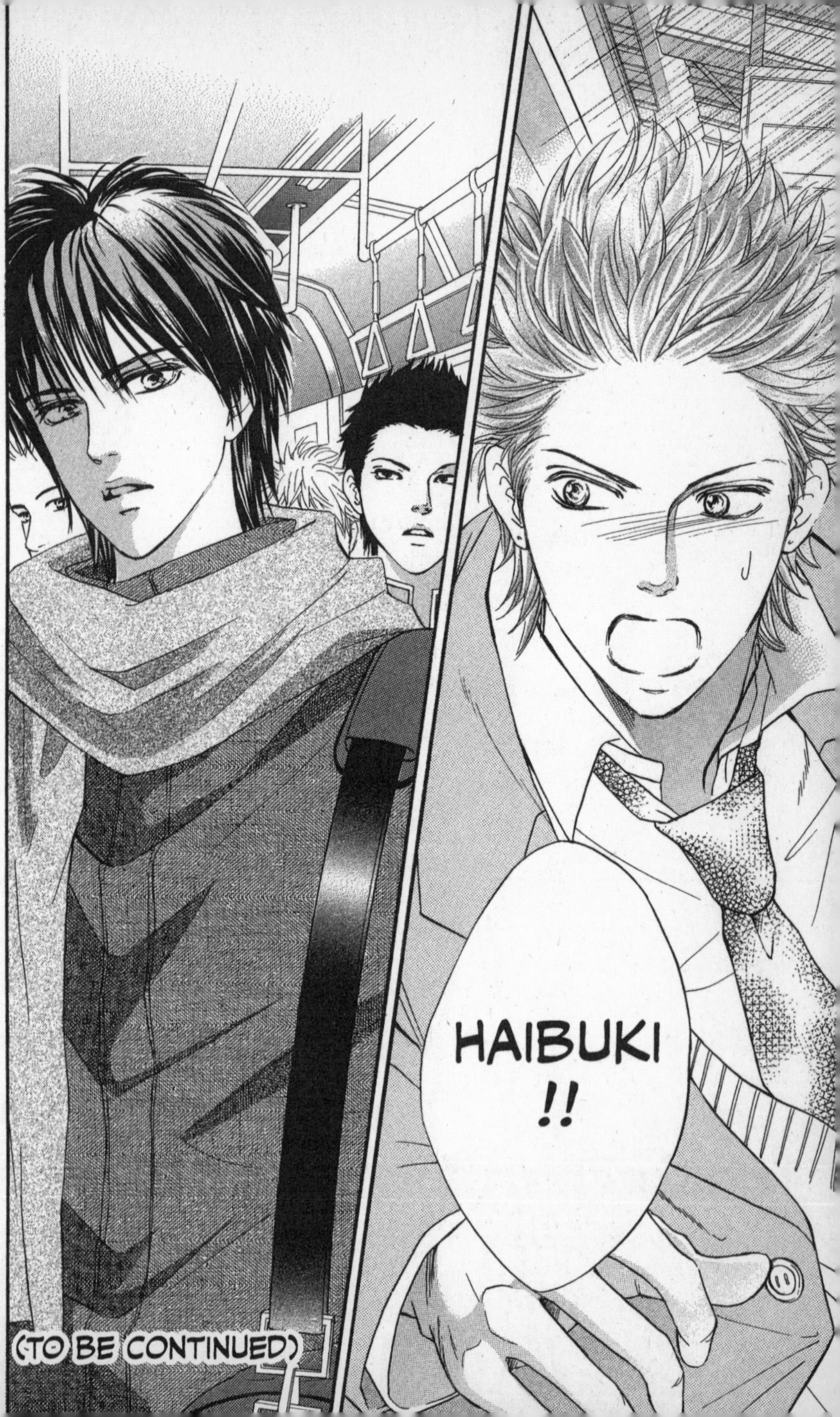
HAIBUKI !!
(TO BE CONTINUED)

Crimson
Hero

THESE ARE OUR ASSISTANTS, ABE-SAN AND YAMAZAKI-SAN. I KEPT THIS BECAUSE IT'S SO CUTE. THE TWO OF THEM DREW THIS.

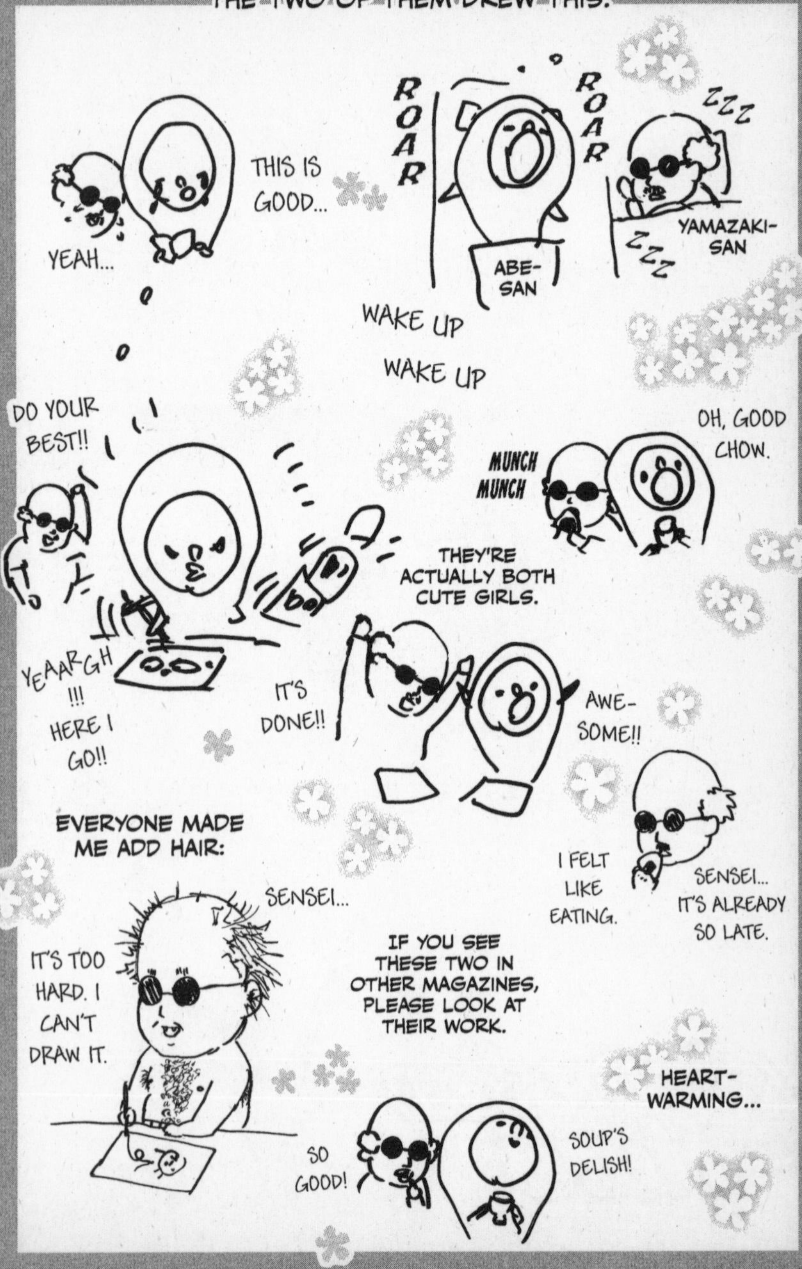
ZZZ
YAMAZAKI-SAN
ZZZ
ROAR
ROAR
ABE-SAN
WAKE UP
WAKE UP
THIS IS GOOD...
YEAH...
OH, GOOD CHOW.
MUNCH MUNCH
THEY'RE ACTUALLY BOTH CUTE GIRLS.
DO YOUR BEST!!
YEAARGH!!! HERE I GO!!
AWE-SOME!!
IT'S DONE!!
SENSEI... IT'S ALREADY SO LATE.
I FELT LIKE EATING.
EVERYONE MADE ME ADD HAIR:
SENSEI...
IT'S TOO HARD. I CAN'T DRAW IT.
IF YOU SEE THESE TWO IN OTHER MAGAZINES, PLEASE LOOK AT THEIR WORK.
HEART-WARMING...
SOUP'S DELISH!
SO GOOD!

HERE'S AN ILLUSTRATION KAZUNE KAWAHARA SENSEI DREW. THANK YOU VERY MUCH. WOW, WHAT A TREASURE! USUALLY I HAVE THIS UP IN MY WORKPLACE.

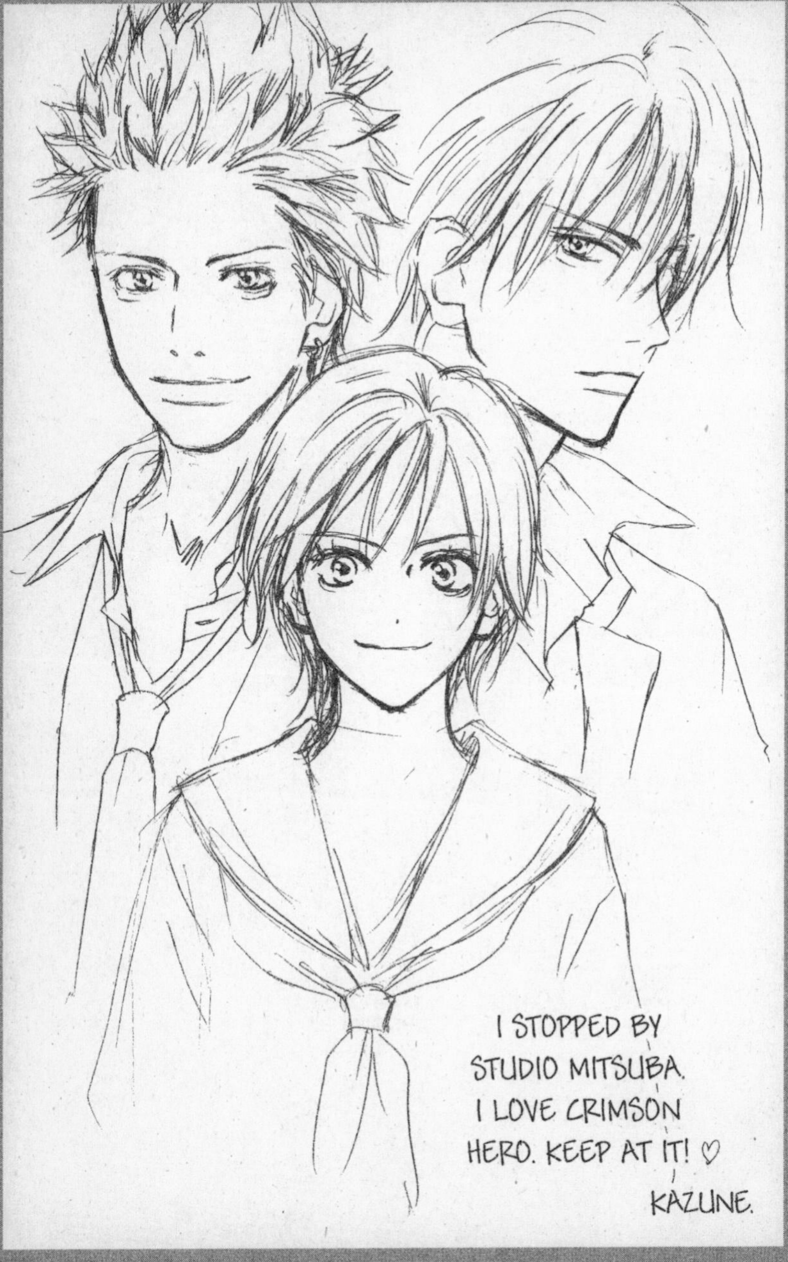
I STOPPED BY STUDIO MITSUBA. I LOVE CRIMSON HERO. KEEP AT IT! ♡
KAZUNE.

♥ I want a piano. The only songs I can play are "The Flea Waltz" and "Do-Re-Mi," but yesterday I spent half an hour in an electronics store wishfully playing on an electric piano. It wasn't that expensive, so I almost went ahead and bought it, but I could just hear people telling me it was my most useless purchase of the year, so I held off. Hmmm... I'm still thinking about it.

—Mitsuba Takanashi, 2008

At age 17, Mitsuba Takanashi debuted her first short story, *Mou Koi Nante Shinai* (Never Fall in Love Again), in 1992 in *Bessatsu Margaret* magazine and now has several major titles under her belt.

Born in the Shimane Prefecture of Japan, Takanashi now lives in Tokyo, where she enjoys taking walks, watching videos, shopping and going to the hair salon. Takanashi has a soft spot for the Japanese pop acts Yellow Monkey and Hide and is good at playing ping-pong.

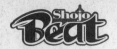

CRIMSON HERO

VOL. 13
Shojo Beat Edition

STORY AND ART BY
MITSUBA TAKANASHI

Translation & English Adaptation/Naoko Amemiya
Touch-up Art & Lettering/Jim Keefe
Graphics & Cover Design/Julie Behn
Editor/Megan Bates

VP, Production/Alvin Lu
VP, Sales & Product Marketing/Gonzalo Ferreyra
VP, Creative/Linda Espinosa
Publisher/Hyoe Narita

Printed in Canada

Published by VIZ Media, LLC
P.O. Box 77010
San Francisco, CA 94107

10 9 8 7 6 5 4 3 2 1
First printing, June 2010

www.viz.com www.shojobeat.com

RATED T FOR TEEN

PARENTAL ADVISORY
CRIMSON HERO is rated T for Teen and is recommended for ages 13 and up. This volume contains suggestive themes.

ratings.viz.com

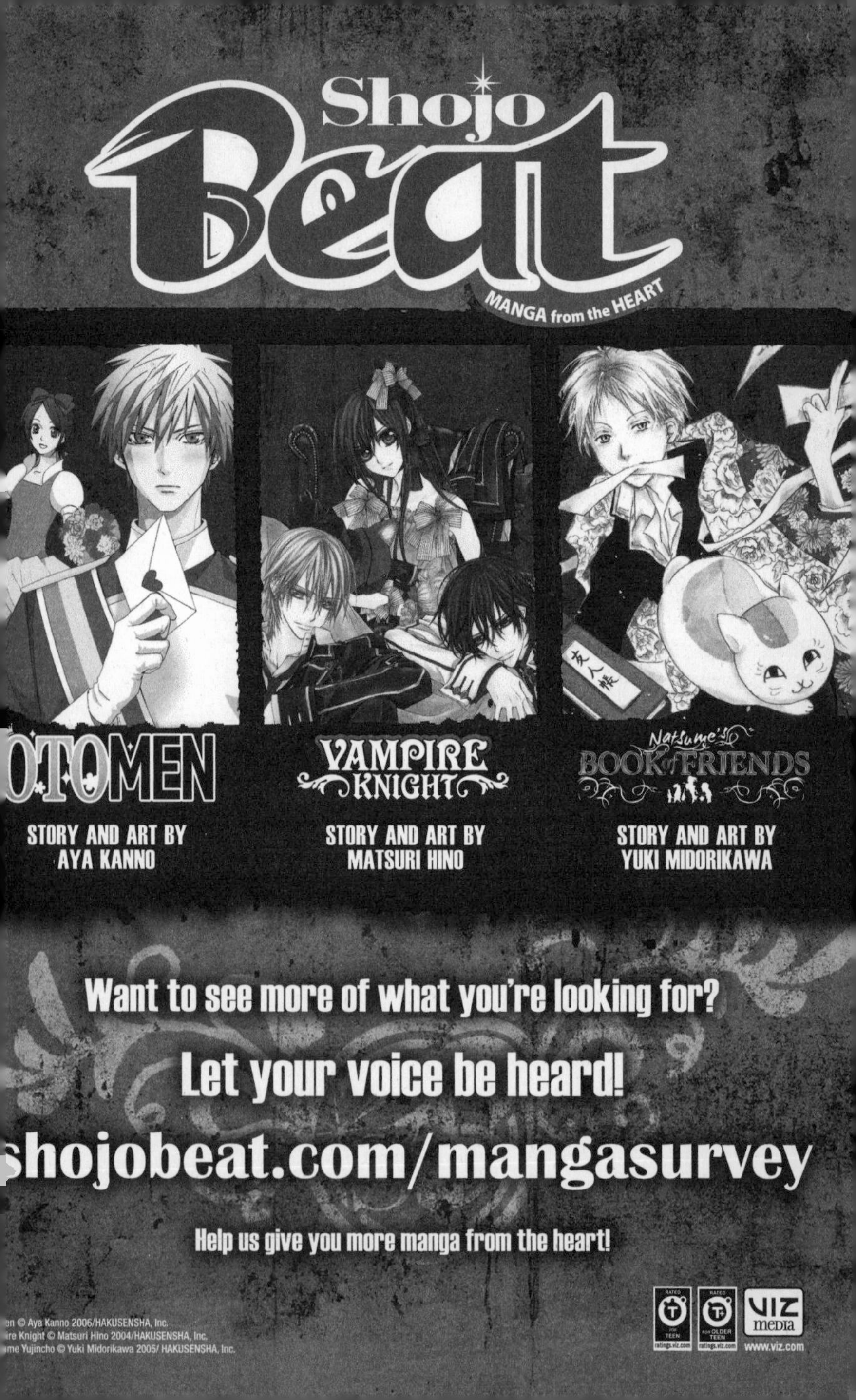
Shojo Beat
MANGA from the HEART
OTOMEN
STORY AND ART BY
AYA KANNO
VAMPIRE KNIGHT
STORY AND ART BY
MATSURI HINO
Natsume's BOOK of FRIENDS
STORY AND ART BY
YUKI MIDORIKAWA
Want to see more of what you're looking for?
Let your voice be heard!
shojobeat.com/mangasurvey
Help us give you more manga from the heart!
en © Aya Kanno 2006/HAKUSENSHA, Inc.
ire Knight © Matsuri Hino 2004/HAKUSENSHA, Inc.
ıme Yujincho © Yuki Midorikawa 2005/ HAKUSENSHA, Inc.
RATED T FOR TEEN ratings.viz.com
RATED T+ FOR OLDER TEEN ratings.viz.com
VIZ media
www.viz.com